A Dictionary of

Education

SECOND EDITION

Edited by SUSAN WALLACE

OXFORD
UNIVERSITY PRESS

OXFORD
UNIVERSITY PRESS

Great Clarendon Street, Oxford, OX2 6DP,
United Kingdom

Oxford University Press is a department of the University of Oxford.
It furthers the University's objective of excellence in research, scholarship,
and education by publishing worldwide. Oxford is a registered trade mark of
Oxford University Press in the UK and in certain other countries

© Oxford University Press 2008, 2009, 2015

The moral rights of the author have been asserted

First edition 2008
Published in the Oxford Paperback Reference series 2009
Second edition 2015

Impression: 1

Published in the United States of America by Oxford University Press
198 Madison Avenue, New York, NY 10016, United States of America

British Library Cataloguing in Publication Data
Data available

Library of Congress Control Number: 2014942244

ISBN 978-0-19-967939-3

Printed in Great Britain by
Clays Ltd, St Ives plc

Contents

Preface to the Second Edition

One of the pleasures of writing a Dictionary of Education is the knowledge that it focuses on a topic which is of relevance to everyone at some stage in their life, and of enduring interest to many in their personal or professional capacity. Moreover, such a dictionary is an additionally valuable and necessary resource today, when education policy in Great Britain remains in a state of development and change, and when new terminology is generated with a rapidity which can prove bewildering, even to those within the educational professions themselves.

However, that very factor of constant change creates enormous difficulties for anyone attempting to compile a dictionary in this field. There will always be the temptation to take the easiest approach, which would be a historical one, with an emphasis on educational legislation over the past two centuries, and on organizations and qualifications which have had their day and passed into recent history. These are 'safe' entries which can be described definitively, and are therefore a great comfort to a compiler of dictionaries. Unfortunately, however, it is unlikely that this sort of information is what users of the dictionary will be most frequently looking for. Indeed, it has been my assumption that parents, pupils, students, teachers, governors, social workers, and others for whom this Dictionary is intended will be most concerned with current terminology, qualifications, and legislation. So, although the reader who wishes it will find a historical perspective here, it will be in the form of entries on recognized landmark legislation, publications, and provision; and, in addition, a Time Line in Appendix 1, which sets out in sequence the major developments of the past century or so.

The approach taken, therefore, has been wherever possible to identify trends in educational policy and philosophy and, through the use of extensive cross-referencing, to allow the reader to explore key topics such as assessment, research, and the national curriculum, in all their complexity and across a range of contexts. Links to relevant and reliable Internet sources are provided wherever appropriate in order to ensure, as far as it is possible to do so, that readers are guided towards additional information which is both current and accurate. In terms of trends, some clear themes are emerging in the development of educational policy and provision in the first two decades of the 21st century. These include a growing emphasis on children's and young people's welfare and safety as central to ensuring their access to educational opportunity; and a trend in 14–19 policy towards the creation of closer links and equivalencies between academic or general qualifications and the acquisition of work-related skills. Both of these developments are reflected in the expansion of Ofsted's role and title to include children's services, and skills. Another theme to emerge is the increasing focus on personalized learning, and the ideal of a curriculum tailored to meet the needs of the individual learner. This has gone hand in hand with a gradual increase in the flexibility with which the national curriculum is applied, allowing for developments such as academies. Also emerging is a growing recognition that policies affecting schools' recruitment and admission of pupils, such as the emphasis on parental choice and on competition between schools, may have an impact on wider issues of concern, such as social cohesion. These themes—the welfare and safety of young learners, the tension between a national curriculum and personalized learning, and the contradictions between market forces and inclusion—emerge as common factors in many otherwise disparate entries.

In an era when 'lifelong learning' has become a buzzword in education, particularly at a policy level, it is important that the Dictionary reflects this concept by not restricting entries to matters relating only or mainly to schools, but giving due coverage also to vocational education and training, to adult education, and to the further and higher education sectors, and exploring the relationships and distinctions between these. Special education at all levels has not been treated as a separate or discrete topic, but has been addressed extensively through a comprehensive range of entries integrated into the order of the Dictionary as a whole.

The Dictionary also sets out to identify the points of comparison and contrast in education and training provision across England, Northern Ireland, Scotland, and Wales, in terms of structures, organizations, qualifications, and legislation. Each of these has a lengthy entry which provides an overview of educational policy, provision, and trends. Additional entries relating to each, and providing detailed and specific definitions, are cross-referenced, where appropriate, to the relevant main entry. For readers of the Dictionary who wish to refer to British education in the wider context of English-speaking countries worldwide, a comparative table is set out in Appendix 2.

In the current process of rapid development and change, education is notorious for its steady proliferation of acronyms and other forms of abbreviation which prove a bane to students, teachers, and parents alike. For convenience, a comprehensive list of these is provided below. Within the text of the Dictionary itself, definitions are listed in almost all cases according to the full-length form of words, which is followed by the abbreviation in parentheses, thus: *National College for Teaching and Leadership (NCTL)*.

The writing of this Dictionary has been a team effort, and my thanks go to the contributors, who include specialists from all sectors of education and from a range of professional backgrounds: academics, advisers, classroom practitioners, and educational managers. Their specialist entries are followed by their initials in the print edition or full names in the online edition, and a brief biographical note on each of them can be found in the Notes on the Contributors. Most of these contributor entries were written for the first (2008) edition of the Dictionary, and I have revised and updated them, where necessary, for this second edition. All other entries are written by me; but I would also like to acknowledge here the very helpful suggestions and advice I have received from a number of colleagues whose professional practice gives them a national perspective on developments in the field; these include Professor Gill Richards and Stevie Vanhegan. To them, and to all those others who gave generous advice on the compiling and writing of this Dictionary, very many thanks.

Finally, and appropriately for a dictionary, a word about language. Many of the entries relate to subjects which are not sector-specific but which may be applied to all phases of education from primary to higher. In such cases the word 'learner' has been used as a generic term for pupil, student, and trainee. The term 'trainee' itself is in some senses problematic, referring as it usually does to learners engaged in further education on programmes of vocational training, but also used in government discourse to describe student teachers. I have used both terms here, according to the context, in describing those undertaking a teaching qualification. Then again, some of the vocabulary we readily employ in relation to education repays closer critical consideration, too: words such as 'deliver' and 'choice' and 'standards'. These terms are subjected here to a certain amount of critical scrutiny as part of the process of exploring their meaning. Lastly, faced with a choice between the two synonymous terms 'educationalist' and 'educationist' I have chosen to use the former throughout.

SW

Editors and Contributors

First and second editions

Susan Wallace is Emeritus Professor of Education at Nottingham Trent University. She previously taught for ten years outside the higher education sector, and has also worked in a local authority advisory role for 14–19 education. She has published widely on the professional development of teachers, including books on educational research and on mentoring. Her current research interests focus on the motivation and behaviour of 14–19-year-old learners.

Isabella Wallace (IW) is an educational consultant working with the primary and secondary sectors in Great Britain and overseas. An experienced teacher, manager, and presenter, she is author of two books for teachers. She is active in school governance and is the founder of the international charity, *Reach Out to Schools*.

Annie Woods (AW) had many years' experience of teaching in early years education before becoming a university lecturer in initial teacher training for the primary sector. She recently took a year's secondment from her university post to act as assistant head teacher in an inner-city primary school which takes an innovative approach to early years education.

First edition only

Liz Atkins (LA) is a part-time lecturer and researcher in higher education. Her published work focuses on issues of class and identity in tertiary education.

Karl Aubrey (KA), formerly senior lecturer at Bishop Grosseteste University, Lincoln, and Academic Coordinator for the Foundation Degree in Educational Studies for teaching assistants and the BA (Hons) Professional Studies in Education, has research interests which include inclusive practice and access routes into the teaching profession.

Robert Bowen (RB), formerly Associate Dean in the School of Education at Nottingham Trent University with responsibility for leading the School's Initial Teacher Education provision for all sectors, has published widely in the field of primary design and technology.

Trisha Bowen (TB) has been involved in the field of special educational needs, and in particular physical disability, for over 20 years. She is an active SEN school governor; a steering group member of the National Network for Advisory Teachers of Physically Impaired Pupils; and has worked as an MA Education tutor at Northampton University.

Viv Channing (VC) was formerly a teacher educator at Lincoln College where she coordinated initial teacher training and was involved in the provision of continuing professional development for experienced teachers.

Liz Ellis (LE) is a Learning Director and local authority special educational needs coordinator, leading enhanced resource facilities for students on the autistic spectrum at the time of her contribution to the first edition. She has worked as an advisory teacher for SEN, written and delivered training programmes for educational professionals on SEN and inclusion, and is co-author of the guidance for teachers on differentiation in literacy.

Heather Graham (HG) was the Director of the Open University in Wales from 2003 to 2007. In that role she served as Chair of the Welsh Assembly's review into funding and support for part-time students at Welsh universities.

Morwenna Griffiths (MG) is Professor of Classroom Learning in the Moray House School of Education at Edinburgh University. She has taught in primary schools in Bristol, and at the University of Isfahan, Iran, at Christ Church College of Higher Education in Canterbury, and at Oxford Brookes, Nottingham, and Nottingham Trent universities. Her books include *Action for Social Justice in Education: Fairly Different* (2003), *Educational Research for Social Justice* (1998), and *Feminisms and the Self: The Web of Identity* (1995).

Julia Hardwick (JH) is an Advanced Practitioner for Creative Studies at Burton College. She has many years of teaching experience, both in the UK and overseas, and has a particular interest in lexicography.

Chris Hudson (CH) is a lecturer and researcher working in higher education.

Susan Meggett (SM) teaches in the secondary sector. She has worked on local authority initiatives for gifted and talented pupils and as a General Certificate of Secondary Education examiner. Her previous experience includes teaching and researching in higher education.

Lindsay Paterson (LP) is Professor of Educational Policy at Edinburgh University. His current research interests are in the 20th-century history of Scottish education, social mobility, and the relationship between education and civic values. His books include *Crisis in the Classroom: The Exam Debacle and the Way Ahead for Scottish Education* (2000), *A Diverse Assembly: The Debate on a Scottish Parliament* (1998), *Education and a Scottish Parliament* (1996), and *The Autonomy of Modern Scotland* (1994).

Abbreviations

AAC	augmentative and alternative communication	BELB	Belfast Education and Library Board
ACCAC	Qualifications, Curriculum, and Assessment Authority for Wales	BERA	British Educational Research Association
ACE	Advisory Centre for Education	BESd	behavioural, emotional, and social difficulties
ADHD	Attention Deficit Hyperactivity Disorder	BSA	Boarding Schools Association; British Science Association
AEA	Advanced Extension Award	B.Sc.	Bachelor of Science
AELP	Association of Employment and Learning Providers	BTEC	Business and Technology Education Council
AET	Award in Education and Training	BYOD	bring your own device
AFA	Achievement for All	CACHE	Council for Awards in Children's Care and Education
AfL	Assessment for Learning	CAF	Common Assessment Framework
A4e	Action for Employment		
AGQ	Applied General Qualifications	CAL	computer-assisted learning
AIUTA	International Association of Universities of the Third Age	CAMHS	Child and Adolescent Mental Health Services
A level	Advanced Level	CAT	credit accumulation and transfer; cognitive abilities test
AoC	Association of Colleges	CCEA	Council for the Curriculum, Examinations, and Assessment (Northern Ireland)
APEL	accreditation of prior experience and learning		
APL	accreditation of prior learning	CCMS	Council for Catholic Maintained Schools
APR	age participation rate		
AQA	Assessment and Qualifications Alliance	CCW	Curriculum Council for Wales
ASD	autistic spectrum disorder	CDT	craft, design, and technology
ASE	Association for Science Education	CEDP	Career Entry and Development Profile
AS level	Advanced Subsidiary Level; Advanced Supplementary Level	CEFRL	Common European Framework of Reference for Languages
AST	advanced skills teacher	CEL	Centre for Excellence in Leadership
ATL	Association of Teachers and Lecturers	CERI	Centre for Educational Research and Innovation
AUT	Association of University Teachers	Cert. Ed.	Certificate of Education
AV	audiovisual	CET	Certificate in Education and Training
BA	Bachelor of Arts		
Becta	British Educational Communications and Technology Agency	CETT	Centre for Excellence in Teacher Training
		CfE	Curriculum for Excellence
B.Ed.	Bachelor of Education	CIF	Common Inspection Framework
BEI	British Education Index		

CILT	National Centre for Languages	ELWa	Further Education Funding Council for Wales
CNAA	Council for National Academic Awards	EMA	Education Maintenance Allowance
CoP	Code of Practice		
COVE	Centre of Vocational Excellence	EOTAS	education otherwise than at school
CPD	continuing professional development	EQARF	European Quality Assurance Reference Framework
CPS	Centre for Policy Studies	ERA	Education Reform Act 1988
CPVE	Certificate of Pre-Vocational Education	ESOL	English for Speakers of Other Languages
CQFW	Credit and Qualifications Framework for Wales	ESRC	Economic and Social Research Council
CSE	Certificate of Secondary Education	ETS	Excellent Teacher Scheme
		EV	external verifier
CSIE	Centre for Studies in Inclusive Education	EWO	education welfare officer
		EWS	Education Welfare Service
CSYS	Certificate of Sixth Year Studies	EYFS	Early Years Foundation Stage
C2K	Curriculum 2000	FAS	Fetal Alcohol Syndrome
DBIS	Department for Business, Innovation, and Skills	FE	further education
		FLA	foreign language assistant
DEETI	Department for Education's Education and Training Inspectorate	FTE	full-time equivalent
		GCE	General Certificate of Education
		GCSE	General Certificate of Secondary Education
DEL	Department for Employment and Learning	GMS	grant-maintained school
DENI	Department of Education, Northern Ireland	GNVQ	General National Vocational Qualification
DES	Department of Education and Science	GTC	General Teaching Council
		GTCNI	General Teaching Council (Northern Ireland)
DET	Diploma in Education and Training	GTCS	General Teaching Council (Scotland)
DfE	Department for Education		
DfEE	Department for Education and Employment	GTCW	General Teaching Council (Wales)
DfES	Department for Education and Skills	GTP	Graduate Teacher Programme
		GTTR	Graduate Teacher Training Registry
D.Phil.	Doctor of Philosophy		
DtS	Determined to Succeed	HE	higher education
EAL	English as an Additional Language	HEFCE	Higher Education Funding Council for England
EAZ	Education Action Zone	HEFCNI	Higher Education Funding Council for Northern Ireland
EBacc	English Baccalaureat		
EBT	evidence-based teaching	HEFCW	Higher Education Funding Council for Wales
EFA	Education Funding Agency		
EFL	English as a Foreign Language	HEI	higher education institution
EHCP	Education, Health, and Care Plan	HEW	Higher Education Wales
		HMI	Her Majesty's Inspectorate
EiC	Excellence in Cities	HMIE	Her Majesty's Inspectorate of Education (Scotland)
EIS	Educational Institute of Scotland	HNC	Higher National Certificate

HND	Higher National Diploma
IAPC	Institute for the Advancement of Philosophy for Children, New Jersey
IB	International Baccalaureate
ICR	income-contingent repayment
ICS	integrated community school
ICT	information communication technology
IE	instrumental enrichment
IEP	individual education plan
IfL	Institute for Learning
ILA	Individual Learning Account
ILT	information learning technology
INSET	in-service education of teachers
IQ	intelligence quotient
ISI	Independent Schools Inspectorate
ISP	Intensifying Support Programme
IT	information technology
ITA	initial teaching alphabet
ITT	initial teacher training
IV	internal verifier
JCQ	Joint Council for Qualifications
JNCHES	Joint National Committee for Higher Education Staff
KAL	knowledge about language
KS	key stage
LA	local authority
LAC	looked-after children
LDA	learning difficulty assessment
LDSS	Learning Development and Support Services
LEA	local education authority
LEC	Local Enterprise Company
LGA	Local Government Association
LLM	Master of Laws
LLS	language-learning strategies
LMS	Local Management of Schools
LSU	Learning Support Unit
MA	Master of Arts
M.Ed.	Master of Education
mfl	modern foreign language
MLD	moderate learning difficulties
MLE	managed learning environment
M.Phil.	Master of Philosophy
M.Sc.	Master of Science
NAB	National Assessment Bank

NAgC	National Association for Gifted Children
NAHT	National Association of Head Teachers
NARE	National Association for Remedial Education
Nasen	National Association for Special Educational Needs
NASUWT	National Association of Schoolmasters Union of Women Teachers
NC	national curriculum
NCB	National Children's Bureau
NCSE	National Council for Special Education
NCTL	National College for Teaching and Leadership
NEC	National Extension College
NEELB	North Eastern Education and Library Board
NEET	not in employment, education, or training
NET	National Education Trust
NFER	National Foundation for Educational Research
NIACE	National Institute of Adult Continuing Education
NICIE	Northern Ireland Council for Integrated Education
NJF	National Joint Forum
NLS	National Literacy Strategy
NLSC	National Learning and Skills Council
NLT	National Literacy Trust
NOCN	National Open College Network
NPA	National Progression Award
NPQH	National Professional Qualification for Headship
NQs	National Qualifications
NQF	National Qualifications Framework
NQGA	National Qualification Group Award
NQT	newly qualified teacher
NRA	National Record of Achievement
NUS	National Union of Students
NUT	National Union of Teachers
NVQ	National Vocational Qualification
NYA	National Youth Agency

OCN	Open College Network	REF	Research Excellence Framework
Ofqual	Office of the Qualifications and Examinations Regulator	RLD	reference-level descriptor
Ofsted	Office for Standards in Education; from 2007 the Office for Standards in Education, Children's Services, and Skills	Rosla	raising of the school-leaving age
		RP	received pronunciation
		RSA	Royal Society of Arts
		RSG	revenue support grant
O grade	Ordinary Grade	SAAS	Student Awards Agency for Scotland
O level	Ordinary Level		
OU	Open University	SAR	self-assessment report
PAYP	Positive Activities for Young People	SATs	Standard (Assessment) Tasks
		SCE	Service Children's Education
PCAS	Polytechnics Central Admissions Systems	SCOTCAT	Scottish Credit Accumulation and Transfer
PCET	post-compulsory education and training	Scotvec	Scottish Vocational Education Council
PCFC	Polytechnics and Colleges Funding Council	SCQF	Scottish Credit and Qualifications Framework
PE	physical education	SCT	senior curriculum team
PECS	picture exchange communication system	SDP	school development plan
		SEAC	Schools Examinations and Assessment Council
PEP	personal education plan		
PGCE	Postgraduate Certificate of Education; Professional Graduate Certificate of Education	SEAL	social and emotional aspects of learning
		SEELB	South Eastern Education and Library Board
PGDE	Professional Graduate Diploma in Education	SEF	self-evaluation form
		SELB	Southern Education and Library Board
Ph.D.	Doctor of Philosophy		
PHE	Postgraduate Certificate in Higher Education	SENCO	special educational needs coordinator
PI	performance indicator	SEND	special educational needs and disabilities
PMLD	profound and multiple learning difficulties		
PoS	programme of study	SENDA	Special Educational Needs and Disability Act 2001
PRU	pupil referral unit	SENDIST	Special Educational Needs and Disability Tribunal
PSCL	primary strategy consultant leader		
		SFC	Scottish Funding Council
PSE	personal and social education	SFCC	school facing 'challenging circumstances'
PSHE	personal, social, and health education		
		SGA	Scottish Group Award
PTA	Parent–Teacher Association	SHA	Secondary Heads Association
QAA	Quality Assurance Agency for Higher Education	SLC	Student Loans Company
		SLD	severe learning difficulties; specific learning difficulties
QCF	Qualifications and Credit Framework		
		SLSU	Skills for Life Strategy Unit
QTLS	qualified teacher learning and skills	SLT	senior leadership team
		SMSCE	spiritual, moral, social, and cultural education
QTS	qualified teacher status		
RE	religious education	SMT	senior management team

SNCT	Scottish Negotiating Committee for Teachers	TVEI	Technical and Vocational Education Initiative
SPA	Scottish Progression Award	UCAS	Universities and Colleges Admissions Service
SQA	Scottish Qualifications Authority	UCEA	Universities and Colleges Employers' Association
SQC	Scottish Qualifications Certificate	UCU	University and College Union
SQH	Scottish Qualification for Headship	U3A	University of the Third Age
SRE	sex and relationship education	VET	vocational education and training
SSA	standard spending assessment	VLE	virtual learning environment
SSC	sector skills councils	VOCA	voice output communication aid
SSR	staff–student ratio		
STRB	School Teachers' Review Body	VSO	Voluntary Service Overseas
SVQ	Scottish Vocational Qualification	WBL	work-based learning
		WEA	Workers' Educational Association
TA	teaching assistant		
TAT	Third Age Trust	WELB	Western Education and Library Board
TESOL	Teachers of English to Speakers of Other Languages	YOP	Youth Opportunities Programme
TfW	Training for Work	YOT	youth offending team
TLR	teaching and learning responsibility	YT	Youth Training
TMA	tutor-marked assignment	YTS	Youth Training Scheme
TP	teaching practice	ZPD	zone of proximal development

A* A *grade originally awarded for exceptionally good performance in any subject at *General Certificate of Secondary Education. Previously, the highest grade awarded was an A grade. When the introduction of an A* grade also for *General Certificate of Education *Advanced Levels was proposed in 2002, it became part of the debate about *standards. Those who supported the introduction argued that the additional grade was necessary to reward and acknowledge the achievement of outstanding candidates, while opponents suggested that it represented an inflation of the grading system and was indicative of a general lowering of standards. Reforms to the grading system have resulted in A* being replaced by a grade 9 from 2017.

ability Used in education in the sense of 'potential for performance'. It is unclear, however, how ability might be accurately measured, if not in terms of performance. Nevertheless, it is synonymous neither with 'achievement' nor with 'attainment', and refers to what a student is capable of, rather than to what they have proved themselves able to do. This is best illustrated by the fact that a student may be described as having high ability but performing poorly; or as having low ability but performing well. The idea of ability as a potential is evident in such phrases as 'late developer', commonly used to describe someone whose innate ability does not become evident until late in their school career, or even after they have left formal education.

ability grouping Grouping pupils together in classes to be taught according to their *ability. In the United Kingdom this is not usually the case, as pupils are normally grouped according to age, and within a national framework of *key stages of development. However, *primary schools often use **target grouping** for *literacy and/or *numeracy, which is, in effect, grouping by ability for the purpose of teaching in these *curriculum areas. Similarly, in secondary schooling, pupils may be grouped according to ability within their age group cohort for specific subjects, so that there might be, for example, three Year 9 classes for English: one for high achievers, one for those pupils of average achievement, and one for those expected to do less well. *See also* SETS.

Abitur The German *examination equivalent to the *General Certificate of Education *Advanced Level. It is often held up by educators in the United Kingdom as a model to be emulated as it offers the *academic rigour necessary for a *university entrance qualification as well as the breadth required to prepare school-leavers for employment. In this sense it can be cited as an example of how the academic–*vocational divide may be successfully bridged. *See also* BACCALAURÉAT.

academic 1. An adjective used to describe learning and related activities which are largely of a *cognitive nature and involve the acquisition, exploration, or application of knowledge, often of an abstract kind or for its own sake. It is often applied to point up the distinction between this type of activity and the more practical or instrumental types of learning which fall into the category of *vocational. In this context it can be used in a derogatory sense, as in the phrase, 'too academic', meaning that the learning in question is too far removed from the practicalities of life. This understanding of the term emerges also in the phrase 'That's academic', applied to a question raised about a merely hypothetical or fictional issue, about which further discussion would be fruitless.
  2. A *teacher or researcher, usually in *higher education. This sector itself is sometimes referred to as Academe.

academic board A committee of staff and managers in a *university or *college which meets regularly for the purpose of regulating and monitoring the academic affairs of the institution. Staff members are usually nominated and elected by their peers, although such a board will normally include some co-opted members.

academic monitoring The process of observing students' academic progress in one or more subject over a period of time. It is used by teachers to compare the performance of a particular student to that of his/her classmates and to identify students who are struggling, excelling, or underachieving. Information for examining students' progress is usually collected in the form of *test marks and *teacher assessment levels or grades. These are often recorded on **tracking sheets**, or **progress reports**, which can then be issued to parents at intervals during the academic year. Usual practice is for these documents to be completed three times annually in order to illustrate a student's level of achievement at the beginning, middle, and end of the school year. The same documentation can also be used on a whole-school level by the *senior leadership team, in order to assess the success of intervention strategies, and also to monitor the effectiveness of teaching across all subjects. Academic monitoring is useful to pupils because it allows them to become aware of their *examination prospects and any disparity between their current and predicted performance.   IW

academic rigour The strict and consistent application of high academic standards. It is a term often used to point up the contrast between written *examinations carried out under strict invigilation and time constraints, and the production of *coursework for *continuous assessment to which comparable constraints do not apply. Rigour here implies not only that the standard of achievement required is high and that the work assessed is entirely the student's own, but also that the assessment is both *reliable and *valid. The term is increasingly found in the rhetoric surrounding government reforms to

educational provision and processes, and has become synonymous with the
principle of raising educational standards.

academy 1. A publicly funded independent school, set up as a trust and
supported by a sponsor such as a business, a university, a charity, a religious
body, or another successful school. The sponsor is accountable for the
continuing improvement of the school's performance. Academies receive
their funding from the *Education Funding Agency, rather than the *local
authority, and are granted some autonomy in how this budget is spent.
Unlike state schools, they are permitted to set the length of their school terms
and school day; they are able independently to set pay and conditions of service
for their teachers and other staff; and they are allowed some flexibility in the
delivery of the school *curriculum. Their *governing bodies are given more
autonomy than those of state schools, but must include two *parent governors.
Academies are a continuation of the city academies initiative which was aimed at
improving the standards of performance in inner-city schools in England,
particularly in areas of social deprivation. Those who supported that initiative,
which was introduced in 2002, argued that schools that are well resourced with
the latest learning technology would be more likely to succeed in motivating
disaffected and disengaged learners; and that the example of success provided by
the city academy sponsors themselves would encourage and inspire young
people to work hard at school and aspire to worthwhile goals in terms of career
and qualifications. It was also suggested that the existence of city academies and
the example they set of high pupil achievement would encourage other,
competing schools to raise their own standards. To become an academy,
a school was required to raise up to £2 million in private sponsorship. The
government then contributed a further sum—usually in the region of £25
million—towards the school's start-up costs. The establishment of an academy
sometimes involved the demolition and replacement of old school buildings on
existing sites; or the creation of an entirely new school. The influence, expertise,
and business acumen of external sponsors was, it was argued, vital to the
regeneration and improvement of inner-city schools. To this end, sponsors
occupied the majority of places on the governing body which controlled the
academy's trust.

One of the claims made for city academies was that they would create a
positive ethos, and that each would have the freedom to establish its own specific
ethos, which would be significantly influenced by the values and beliefs of its
sponsors. This led to some criticisms on the grounds that the curriculum could
be employed to reflect contentious beliefs, such as that of creationism. The
academies have also been criticized on the grounds of their performance, since,
in almost half of those established by 2007, pupils' results in the *General
Certificate of Secondary Education examinations had not improved under the
trust arrangement, and, in some, achievement was actually lower than under
the state-school system. The word 'city' was dropped in 2010 to allow the
setting up of academies in locations other than inner cities. Since then they

have proliferated in number, with 'chains' of academies being created under the same sponsor.

Although the government requires academies to take pupils of all abilities, the substantial government funding invested in the academies, and the publicity surrounding the implementation of the initiative, has created significant pressure on them to succeed, and this, according to many education commentators, may be why pupil *exclusion and expulsion figures for some academies have been relatively high, and why there were fears that the pressure to succeed could result in their seeking to recruit mainly pupils with good test results and with no learning difficulties. Educational opinion on the role and principle of academies remains divided.

2. A *specialist school or *college, usually providing training in the arts or in a specific profession; for example, a music academy or a military academy. The word 'academy' itself derives from the garden near Athens where Plato taught his students and from which his school of philosophy took its name. In this sense the term carries connotations of serious scholarship and learning suggestive of high status and academic respectability.

3. A generic term used to describe comprehensive schools in Scotland.

(⊕) SEE WEB LINKS
• Explains the nature and purpose of academies (1) and the means by which a state school can apply for academy status.

accelerated learning A range of techniques which are claimed to increase the learner's capacity to absorb and retain information by focusing on learning how to learn. Proponents suggest that we use only a small percentage of our potential mental capacity, and that we could increase this by, for example, identifying our preferred learning style and adopting strategies such as the use of memory maps. Training in accelerated learning often draws on the theory of *multiple intelligences.   IW

(⊕) SEE WEB LINKS
• Summarizes the claims made for accelerated learning and how it can be applied in various sectors of education and training.

access arrangements Adjustments which are made which enable students with particular needs to access *tests and *examinations. Such arrangements must not give students an unfair advantage. Students entitled to access arrangements are those who have a *statement of *special educational needs (SEN), who are at school action or school action plus of the SEN Code of Practice, and who receive special educational provision. Students whose access to the tests is significantly impaired by a *learning difficulty or a disability may also qualify. Students who have difficulty concentrating may also be entitled, as are those whose first language is not English or who lack fluency in English. Typical access arrangements include the use of readers, *amanuenses, scribes, and transcripts. Rest breaks can be given. Schools and colleges are required to give evidence of a history of special provision in support of a request for special access arrangements.   TB, LE

Access course Known in full as an 'Access to Higher Education course', this is a programme of study specifically designed for adults without formal entry qualifications such as *Advanced Levels (A levels) seeking to gain access to *higher education. Since their inception into education provision in the late 1970s, Access courses have been regarded as the 'third route' into higher education, differentiating them from A levels and diplomas. It is, though, worth noting the difference between 'access' and 'Access'. The former refers to any educational courses which provide entry into education, while the latter is specifically designed as a pathway for adults into higher education. Although the development of Access courses can be seen to be part of a long history of *adult educational programmes in tertiary education, dating back as far as the original *mechanics institutes of the mid-19th century, more recently they have been shaped by specific governmental education policies which emphasize the role played by education and a highly trained workforce in creating economic health and stability. To this end, *widening participation in higher education has been the focus of policy reports and research, such as the *Dearing Report, the *Kennedy Report, and of the subsequent *Green Paper *The Learning Age* (DfEE, 1998). In this context, Access courses represent one major route towards widening participation in higher education. They are subject-based and are taught mainly in *colleges of further education, offering subjects such as sociology, psychology, English, and philosophy. They are internally assessed by *continuous assessment; and academic references from tutors play a key role in securing students' progression to undergraduate study.   CH

accessibility plans Since 2003 it has been a requirement that all schools possess an accessibility plan. These must describe how the school intends to improve access for pupils with disabilities to the curriculum, environment, and information (which includes all written information including signage, handouts, and textbooks). Plans must be in writing and adequately resourced. They must be implemented, reviewed, and revised as necessary. Before drafting their plan, schools are required to consult widely. Plans are renewable every three years and must be published annually.   TB, LE

Access to Learning Fund Students suffering financial hardship may be eligible to apply to this fund to help them enter or remain in *higher education in England, once they have applied for a *student loan and any other relevant grant or bursary that might be available. The decision rests with the higher education institution itself about who should receive funding and in what amount. Unlike student loans, most awards from this fund do not have to be repaid. Priority is given to certain groups, including single parents, students with a disability, or those who are homeless.

(⊕) SEE WEB LINKS
• Explains the purpose of the fund and provides details of eligibility.

accountability Educational institutions, in the persons of their managers and governing bodies, are required to account publicly and, in the case of schools, particularly to parents for their performance through such means as

*performance indicators and *league tables. This is termed 'accountability'. It is an example of the trend for a vocabulary more usually associated with business and commerce being applied in the context of schools and other educational institutions following measures to create a *market in education since the 1980s.

accreditation **1.** The awarding of credit to an individual student for achievement of, or towards, a qualification. *See also* ACCREDITATION OF PRIOR LEARNING.

   2. A process by which an organization or institution, such as a college or university, wins approval for one or more of its awards, involving confirmation from a panel including representatives of peer institutions that the award or awards in question meet nationally accepted standards. *See also* VALIDATION.

accreditation of prior learning The process or practice of awarding *credits which can be counted towards a qualification, based on the candidate's previous experience, learning, or achievements. This practice has become widely used in the *further education sector since the introduction of *National Vocational Qualifications (NVQs), as the nature of these qualifications allows a candidate to be assessed on their current *competence, rather than requiring attendance on a *course or the successful completion of *examinations. Candidates for *accreditation are usually required to present a portfolio of evidence which may include observer or assessor reports, witness statements, previously gained certification, evidence of competence in the workplace, photographs, or recordings. The process of compilation is usually supported by a qualified adviser and the portfolio is assessed by a qualified assessor, both of whom are required to hold the NVQ units appropriate to their role. The process of compiling a portfolio can be time-consuming and, in terms of support and assessment, can prove as costly as the enrolment fee for a course of study. Accreditation of prior learning is also used outside the system of NVQ qualifications; for example, for some candidates applying for a qualification in teacher training for further education. In such a case, the assessment of portfolios does not require an NVQ-qualified assessor but is instead subject to the quality assurance system operating within that institution.

achievement The performance or *attainment of a *student or *pupil. It may be measured in a number of ways, such as the successful demonstration of a pre-specified *competence, the award of a pass mark, or the gaining of a satisfactory *grade for work accomplished. A learner's achievement is based on their performance, rather than on their potential or their *ability. A learner with high ability might, under some circumstances, perform less well than a learner with lower ability.

Achievement for All (AFA) An initiative to support the achievement of children with *special educational needs informed by the findings of the Lamb Inquiry (2009). This recommended that, rather than focusing solely on improving the learning processes for such children, emphasis should also be given to improving the outcome in terms of the levels of attainment.

(⊕) SEE WEB LINKS
• Presents an evaluation of the initiative.

Action for Employment (A4e) Originally formed in 1986, A4e is now an international organization which helps people to return to work as well as providing a *training and recruitment support service for businesses. The organization works closely with other agencies in supporting and preparing people who wish to re-enter work. Those whom A4e assists include black and non-white British groups, the disabled, and people from disadvantaged areas. The organization also operates *learndirect centres and delivers a variety of *basic skills and *vocational programmes.   VC, KA

(⊕) SEE WEB LINKS
• Provides further details about the work of A4e.

action research A *research methodology in which the researcher investigates practice through cycles of reflection, identification of issues, action, data collection, analysis, and more reflection in order to identify further areas for investigation. The emphasis is on improving practice. Researchers usually investigate their own practice, and may be working alone or collaboratively with one or more co-researchers. Most models of action research encourage collaboration as being optimal at every stage of the cycle. Action research may be narrowly instrumental: simply a method of problem-solving. However, most models emphasize reflection focused on the self of the researcher, the wider context of the research issue, the theoretical background, and the social and political assumptions governing the articulation of the research issue.

There are various kinds of research, all closely related to action research, which use cycles of action, collection of evidence, and reflection on the researcher's own practice. They include reflective practice, action inquiry, action learning, double loop learning, critical action research, and self-study. They differ in the emphasis placed on, for instance, collaboration, the focus on self, or social and political change. These differences in emphasis distinguish different models. All of them unite in having an *epistemological perspective which prioritizes improved practice. Evidence only has to be strong enough to warrant changes in practice in the specific context of the research. Research methods are likely to be qualitative, and are also often creative. 'Small-scale classroom research' and 'practitioner research' are allied to action research but they are not cyclical. Rather, they follow the pattern of identifying a research question, gathering evidence, and using the analysis of the data to formulate conclusions for dissemination.   MG

Further Reading: B. Somekh and S. Noffke *Handbook of Educational Action Research* (Sage, 2008).

(⊕) SEE WEB LINKS
• Provides further information about the structure and uses of action research.

active learning Learning which encourages the pupil or student to engage actively with what is being learned through activities such as *group discussion, role play, or experimentation, rather than passively receiving and memorizing knowledge or instruction from the teacher in order to be able to repeat it accurately, as was the practice in many 19th- and early 20th-century schools. Active learning became the norm in most schools, as the value of being able to reproduce information uncritically and 'parrot fashion' came increasingly under question in the 20th century. However, the facilitation of active learning becomes more difficult the larger the *class size. The implementation of an active approach to learning, therefore, can depend as much on *pupil–teacher ratio as on beliefs about effective approaches to learning.

active vocabulary The range of words which an individual is able to use accurately in their speech (active spoken vocabulary), or their writing (active written vocabulary), or both of these. The active vocabulary does not include words which are only recognized and understood, either by reading or hearing, but not actually used. At most stages of learning of a language, the learner's active vocabulary will be more limited than their comprehension. In other words, their understanding will outstrip their ability to express themselves. *See also* AGE, READING; PASSIVE VOCABULARY.

activity A task or exercise undertaken by the learner, and usually set by the teacher, which has an intended learning outcome. Such activities range from the fairly passive—for example, listening attentively to the teacher—to the dynamic and active—for example, carrying out an experiment, conducting a survey, or painting a picture. The types of activity the learner is required to undertake will be determined by a number of factors, which include the learner's age, the subject matter being learned, and the level of study. *See also* ACTIVE LEARNING; LESSON.

admissions The process of gaining a place at—being admitted to—a school, college, or university. Schools have been required since 2007 to ensure that their **admissions code** promotes social cohesion. This requirement was introduced as a result of evidence that pupils from less advantaged homes were more likely to fail to gain admission to the most popular schools, since these tend to be located in areas of social advantage. Some local authorities, in an effort to address this issue, have introduced the use of an admission **lottery**, where pupils are allocated places by chance rather than by parental *choice. In larger institutions, such as universities and colleges, it is often the title of the department or section which deals with the administration relating to applications, offers, and admissions. *See also* ADMISSIONS APPEAL; SOCIAL CLASS; UNIVERSITIES AND COLLEGES ADMISSIONS SERVICE.

admissions appeal If a child does not gain admission to their first *choice of school, their parents are entitled to lodge an appeal against this decision. Such appeals are heard by independent appeal panels whose membership must exclude all members of the *local authority and the *governing bodies of the schools in question. A decision made by the appeals panel is deemed to be final. The number of admissions appeals made in England annually continues to rise.

adult basic skills *See* BASIC SKILLS; MOSER REPORT.

adult education Courses of study offered for learners over the age of compulsory schooling. Sometimes used synonymously with *evening classes, adult education encompasses a very wide range of provision, including prison education, education in the armed forces, *adult literacy classes, and church-based learning groups, as well as *local authority and *Workers' Educational Association provision. It has a long history closely associated with ideals of social reform, self-help, and self-improvement, particularly among *social classes who could not access adequate schooling or higher education. Direct forerunners of adult education were the 'adult and benevolent evening schools', the 'young men's reformation and mental improvement societies', and the *mechanics' institutes of the 19th century. By the 21st century, however, adult education has lost much of its earlier, radical image. Theory related to the education of adults constitutes in itself a field of academic study, sometimes referred to as **andragogy**, to distinguish it from *pedagogy, the theory related to the teaching of children. It is argued, for example, that some key characteristics can be associated with adult learners, which must be taken into account if they are to be helped to learn effectively. These include:

- their adult responsibilities and commitments, which will inevitably compete for time with their studies;
- their motivation, which has brought them back to education;
- their need to feel they are getting good value, in terms of learning, from the time and money they have invested;
- their level of anxiety at returning to education, which may be much higher than they are willing to disclose.

The education of adults can also necessitate a reconfiguration of the teacher–pupil paradigm into a more egalitarian, negotiated relationship in which it will usually not be appropriate for the teacher to use the same forms of encouragement and sanctions which they might employ with younger learners. *See also* NATIONAL INSTITUTE OF ADULT CONTINUING EDUCATION; RADICAL EDUCATORS.

Further Reading: P. Jarvis *Adult Education and Lifelong Learning: Theory and Practice* (Routledge, 2012).

adult literacy It is estimated that 7 million adults in England possess *literacy skills which are below the level of that expected of 11-year-old pupils. The figures for the UK as a whole are unavailable, but are likely to reflect similar levels. To address this problem the *Skills for Life Strategy Unit was set up in 2000, operating at first within the Department for Education and Skills, and later, following departmental reorganization, within the Department for Innovation, Universities, and Skills. Its aim was to improve literacy (and numeracy) for 2.25 million adults by 2010. It is not clear to what extent this target was achieved. Part of the strategy included the development, begun in 2006, of a series of books, known as **Quick Reads**, designed to engage the interest of adult emergent readers and to encourage them in reading as an enjoyable leisure pursuit. Although simplified, edited versions of popular novels have been in existence for several decades, often aimed specifically at the prison population, in which the level of adult literacy is particularly low, the Quick Reads series takes a rather different approach, commissioning well-known celebrities to write original work which aims to build the confidence of adults who are in the process of developing their literacy skills. *See also* BASIC SKILLS; MOSER REPORT.

((∰)) SEE WEB LINKS
• Provides further information on adult literacy initiatives.

Advanced Extension Award (AEA) Aimed at the most able 10 per cent of *Advanced Level (A level) students, these awards are designed to encourage a critical and analytical approach to the study of a subject. They require the student to study in depth, and are available in a more restricted range of subjects than the standard A level. By making it possible to identify outstanding students, the AEA was intended to make it unnecessary for *universities to develop their own entrance examinations as a response to the increasing number of applicants with good A level results.

Advanced Higher An advanced qualification made up of internally and externally assessed *units, which was introduced in Scotland in 2000/01 to replace the *Certificate of Sixth Year Studies. This is equivalent to level 7 of the *Scottish Credit and Qualifications Framework.   SM

Advanced Level (A level) The generic term applied to the *General Certificate of Education advanced level *examinations taken by some students in Years 12 and 13 of their schooling, and by others, including adult learners, through other educational institutions, such as *colleges of further education. It is the most usual entrance requirement for *higher education, each A level *grade achieved carrying a number of 'points', which, added, must achieve the total specified for entry. Until 2000 the candidate would normally choose two or three subjects to study from a wide range of options. Following the reforms of *Curriculum 2000, the A level curriculum was divided into two stages. During the first year, candidates were encouraged to choose four or five subjects to study at Advanced Subsidiary Level (AS level), and to narrow their choice down to two or three in their second year, following the *assessment of their achievement at AS level. The final assessment was known as **A2**, to distinguish it from the AS stage of the *curriculum. The intention of this structural reform was to broaden the post-16 curriculum. Both students and teachers reported that the increased number of assessments and examinations, as well as the additional subjects for study, was proving onerous. Perhaps as a result, in 2008 assessment in most units was reduced from six to four, with a concomitant revision of content; and synoptic assessment was introduced in all A2 units, requiring candidates to draw on knowledge from across the subject. At the same time a new A* grade was introduced for candidates achieving 90% and above in a full A level. The purpose of this was to offer candidates a greater challenge and a greater reward.

Schools and students receive the results of the A level examinations in August, an annual event widely covered by the national press. For over two decades the results have shown an improvement in performance overall, with more students achieving top grades each year. Perhaps inevitably, this has led to accusations by some of falling standards, and the suggestion that perhaps the A level examinations themselves are becoming easier, rather than students' performance improving year by year. Others argue, however, that such accusations at that juncture each year are ill-judged and do not give sufficient credit to successful students for their hard work and achievement. The debate over this issue of performance and standards remains unresolved. *See also* UNIVERSITIES AND COLLEGES ADMISSIONS SERVICE.

(⊕) SEE WEB LINKS
• Provides current information on A levels and on the points tariff for entry to higher education.

advanced skills teacher (AST) A title awarded to a teacher who was recognized through external *assessment as having excellent classroom practice. The teacher was required to pass a national assessment in order to be appointed to an AST role. This scheme was introduced to reward the very best teachers who wished to remain in the classroom rather than being promoted up the management scale or taking on extra responsibilities for additional payment. Their role included supporting other teachers within their own or other schools; helping colleagues to develop their skills; and sharing excellent practice, approaches, and ideas. The AST role attracted additional payment on a separate pay scale. However, this role and the related pay scale were discontinued in 2013, following the School Teachers' Review Body's recommendation that schools be given more flexibility in using individual teachers' experience and expertise to support professional development within the school, and in deciding how this should be remunerated.   IW

Advanced Subsidiary Level (AS level) The first stage of the *Advanced Level (A level) curriculum, introduced in 2000, following a recommendation in the *Dearing Review (1996) that the existing Advanced Supplementary Level (AS level), which covered about half a full A level syllabus and was assessed against the same criteria, should be retitled Advanced Subsidiary Level, and should be assessed at a lower level which reflected the shorter length of study. Candidates were expected to select four or five subjects, which were assessed after a year. From these they chose the subjects (usually two or three) with which they continued to A2 level. *See also* CURRICULUM 2000.

Advanced Supplementary Level A *General Certificate of Education (GCE) qualification whose syllabus covered about half that of a full GCE *Advanced Level (A level) syllabus and which was assessed against the same criteria, at the same level as a full A level. These AS levels were normally studied over two years, were often taken alongside one or more full A levels, and were designed to allow sixth form pupils access to a broader curriculum. In 2000, following a recommendation in the *Dearing Review (1996), the Advanced

Supplementary was replaced by the *Advanced Subsidiary, which constitutes the first half of the two-year A level programme, and is accordingly assessed against a less demanding set of criteria than the original AS level. *See also* CURRICULUM 2000.

adviser *See* ADVISORY SERVICE.

Advisory Centre for Education (ACE) An independent registered charity offering advice to parents and carers on issues related to state-funded compulsory schooling in England and Wales. Founded in 1960, it provides telephone advice lines as well as printed guidance on a range of topics, including *bullying and *special educational needs. It is particularly active in providing advice on *admission appeals and *exclusions.

SEE WEB LINKS
• The centre's web site provides detailed information about its role and services.

advisory service The education departments of *local authorities usually offer an advisory service to schools in order to support them in meeting national standards in teaching and learning and in school management. The advisory service originally played a major role in providing *continuing professional development (CPD), such as updating on national initiatives, for teachers within the authority; and at one time carried out trial-run 'inspections' to aid schools preparing for imminent *Ofsted inspections. One of its additional functions was to place advisers in schools temporarily to carry out essential roles, such as *head teacher or subject leader, where this is deemed necessary. Advisory services are, however, contracting due to financial constraints, and much of the CPD role is now carried out by private consultancies.

advisory teacher A role, now discontinued, for which a teacher was seconded from a teaching post in order to join their *local authority advisory service and take up an advisory role for local schools in a specific *curriculum area, *key stage, or specific issue, such as *assessment or *inclusion, of which they had expert knowledge and experience. As well as visiting schools and supporting teachers, their remit included organizing and delivering *continuing professional development for teachers in their area of expertise. The role of advisory teacher was largely superseded by the introduction of *advanced skills teachers (AST), who carried out a similar role while remaining based in their own school. With the termination of the AST role, professional development in schools is increasingly provided through commercial consultancy.

AFA *See* ACHIEVEMENT FOR ALL.

affective One of the three **domains** of *knowledge, the others being the *cognitive and the *psychomotor domains. It is used to describe *learning which involves a development or change in attitudes or feelings, and is applied in contexts where such development is an implicit goal, such as spiritual and moral education, or the development of an aesthetic appreciation of art, poetry, or music. Learning in the affective domain is difficult to express in terms of observable outcomes, and difficult to assess, since a change in feelings or attitudes usually cannot be reliably or accurately measured. The term derives from **affect**, in its sense of 'emotion' or 'feeling'.

after-school activity *See* OUT-OF HOURS ACTIVITY.

age, reading The measurement of a child's *reading ability in terms of the average ability expected at a particular age. Thus, a very competent reader at the age of 6 might be deemed to have a reading age of 9. The idea of a reading age in years, however, can be misleading, particularly when related to *adult literacy levels, and does not necessarily correspond to thinking and comprehension age, especially for children with *dyslexia. The very concept of 'reading age' was challenged in the **Bullock Report** as early as 1975, and continues to be questioned by educationalists such as Stierer and Maybin (1994). It is more usual now to express competence in reading in terms of **readability levels** rather than reading age. The *National Literacy Trust defines readability levels by sentence length and complexity of vocabulary, where levels can be calculated for any piece of prose using a simple formula. In schools, *National Foundation for Educational Research tests are now widely used to provide a 'reading quotient', or standardized score. The reading quotient is calculated by dividing the child's reading age test scores by their chronological age. A child's reading age was commonly appended to a child's school *report prior to the onset of the *National Literacy Strategy (1997). Under the National Strategy, children are now expected to reach national levels for reading and writing at each key stage.

Further Reading: Barry Stierer and Janet Maybin (eds) *Language, Literacy and Learning in Educational Practice* (Multilingual Matters in association with the Open University, 1994). This questions the concept of a 'reading age'.

(()) SEE WEB LINKS
- Explains relationship between reading age and children's reading material.
- Provides links to data on reading skills assessment.

age participation rate (APR) The number of a specific age group participating in *further or *higher education as a proportion of the total. A major use of the APR by providers of *post-compulsory education is to calculate trends in the demand for places, both to the institution as a whole and in specific subject areas.

aggregation The adding together of marks awarded for separate pieces of a student's assessed work within an *assessment scheme. In *national curriculum testing or on a programme of study made up of a number of individually assessed *modules or *units, for example, an aggregate summative assessment for the student will be arrived at by a calculation based on all the marks they have been awarded.

aims A statement of intent by a teacher or *curriculum designer, encapsulating what they are setting out to achieve in a lesson, a series of lessons, a *programme of study, or a *syllabus. Aims are phrased in such a way as to make it clear that they refer to the purpose of the lesson; for example, 'to provide the pupils with a clear understanding of the difference between primary and secondary sources of evidence'. They should not be confused with *objectives, which are a statement of what the learner will achieve, and are constructed with the learner as subject. (For example, 'The learner will demonstrate an understanding of . . . '.)

alternative schooling Education which does not conform to that provided in state schools, in terms of either the *curriculum or the approaches to teaching and learning, or both of these. Widely recognized examples of such schooling include provision based on the educational theories of *Steiner, *Montessori, *Malaguzzi, and *Neill. These approaches to schooling are firmly *learner-centred and place an emphasis on *discovery learning and the learner's right to self-determination. Rather than following solely an externally imposed and standardized curriculum, the *lesson planning and teaching in these forms of alternative schooling take into account primarily the learners' needs in relation to their social, emotional, and personal development; take as their starting point those topics which are of direct interest and relevance to the learners; and encourage learner control over the methods and activities employed. This emphasis on individual development rather than upon national standards means that examples of alternative provision such as these may be difficult to reconcile with the requirements of externally imposed targets and testing and standardized curriculum levels. In its most radical form, alternative schooling, such as that provided at *Summerhill School, may take the form of a democratic community of learning where learners and teachers are considered to have equal status.

However, although often associated with radical philosophies of education, alternative schooling can also include private tuition in the pupil's own home, or schooling in a curriculum shaped by ideological or religious beliefs. *See also* EDUCATION OTHERWISE THAN AT SCHOOL; ILLICH, IVAN; REGGIO EMILIA.

amanuensis A person who scribes the dictated answers to questions from pupils or students whose independent writing skills are extremely limited through a learning difficulty, injury, or sensory or physical impairment. If a learner has a temporary or permanent disability, such as a broken wrist or *dyslexia for example, an amanuensis may be provided who will accompany the learner to classes and take notes which the learner is unable to do themselves; or will write an examination or a piece of coursework at the learner's dictation. Permission to use an amanuensis during examinations can be requested from the examining bodies for students who regularly access this type of support as part of their normal provision. Also sometimes called 'scribing', the use of an amanuensis in formal assessments raises a number of questions about validity, arising from the possibility that the candidate's actual ability might be misrepresented.   TB, LE

 SEE WEB LINKS
• Provides detailed information about the use of amanuenses in educational settings.

ancillary staff The staff employed by an educational institution whose responsibilities do not include teaching. Also referred to as non-teaching staff, they include those in technician and administrative roles.

APEL (accreditation of prior experience and learning) *See* ACCREDITATION OF PRIOR LEARNING.

appeals *See* ADMISSIONS APPEAL; CHOICE.

application of number One of the original six *key skills which *General National Vocational Qualification students were required to demonstrate, and one of the three which were formally assessed, the other two being communication and *information technology. It is concerned with skills of *numeracy, and, more specifically, how numeracy is applied in practical situations, both in the workplace and in day-to-day problem-solving and transactions. *See also* FUNCTIONAL SKILLS.

Applied General Qualifications (AGQ) *See* VOCATIONAL A LEVEL.

appraisal A system for assessing the performance and *continuing professional development needs of teachers and managers in *schools, *colleges, and *universities. It normally involves an interview during which the individual's performance is reviewed and their development needs and career trajectory discussed. It may also involve an observation of the teacher's classroom practice. The appraisal of teachers and lecturers are carried out internally by designated staff, usually senior to the appraisee, although some institutions operate a system of peer appraisal. In schools, the appraisal of *head teachers is carried out by *school improvement partners, who make a report to the governing body on the head teacher's performance. *See also* PERFORMANCE MANAGEMENT.

apprenticeship The traditional method of learning the specialist skills and knowledge of a trade or a craft. Apprentices were indentured to a master— someone who had mastery of the trade or craft they required to learn—for a period of seven years. This element of 'time-serving' was criticized in the 1981 *White Paper *A New Training Initiative*, which abolished traditional apprenticeships in favour of *competence-based training where the qualification was based upon the achievement of competence regardless of time served. When the term was reintroduced in 1995 as **Modern Apprenticeship**, it was as a competence-based qualification.

As Modern Apprenticeships evolved, they became more inclusive, expanding to offer a Foundation Modern Apprenticeship for those aiming at an NVQ level 2 qualification, and an Advanced Modern Apprenticeship for those working towards an NVQ level 3 qualification. In 2004 these two routes were renamed 'Apprenticeships' and 'Advanced Apprenticeships' respectively. In the same year, participation in apprenticeships was widened by the introduction of **Young Apprenticeships** for 14–16-year-olds, which enabled pupils in compulsory education to spend up to two days a week in a workplace to learn on-the-job skills, and by removal of the upper age limit of 25 for those wishing to enter an apprenticeship scheme.

Although these various names for 'apprenticeships' were originally designed to distinguish this training route from the original apprenticeships abolished by the New Training Initiative in 1981, the simpler, one-word form is now increasingly adopted, although the training route it describes is very different from what was meant by 'apprenticeships' prior to 1981.

aptitude The potential of a learner to assimilate knowledge, skill, or understanding successfully. This is not quite synonymous with *ability, denoting rather a potential to learn effectively. It is often used in relation to specific areas of knowledge or skill, so that one might speak of an individual having 'an aptitude for scientific enquiry', or 'an aptitude for spot welding', for example. Tests designed to measure such aptitudes are referred to as **aptitude tests**. Although the purpose of these is to assess candidates' potential, they are necessarily based on those candidates' current performance, and therefore the extent to which they are predictive rather than a measure of ability is open to some debate. These tests, however, are more widely used in selection procedures for employment than in assessment for educational purposes.

articulated progression A clearly defined progression route through the qualification system, which enables the learner to choose the appropriate next step in education or training towards their goal, whether it be university entrance or access to a trade or profession. The concept of articulated progression also involves establishing a clear statement of value or equivalence for each qualification. For example, following the introduction of *foundation degrees, it was necessary to establish a clear articulation and progression route from the foundation degree to the *bachelor's degree, which, depending upon the *higher education institution concerned, is now established as involving either a bridging course or direct entry to the final year of the bachelor's degree.

Asperger syndrome A syndrome which current understanding situates on the continuum of *autistic spectrum disorders. It is sometimes referred to as 'high-functioning *autism'; but there are clinicians and others who suggest that it should not be pathologized in this way, arguing that it could be defined as a difference rather than a defect. It was first identified by Professor Hans Asperger (1906–1980) who, in 1978, identified a group of children who had been diagnosed as autistic and yet whose observable characteristics were not consistent with that diagnosis. Unlike those with autism, they demonstrated good—and sometimes excellent—language development and were able to interact with others, albeit preferring to be with adults rather than other children. Other common characteristics included average to high intelligence; narrow and specialized interests; close attention to detail; and some difficulty in recognizing and interacting within social norms, which could manifest as a lack of social skills or as boorish or withdrawn behaviour. This is thought to be the result of their difficulty in accurately 'reading' people and situations. A growing recognition of this syndrome since the late twentieth century has meant that children with

Asperger syndrome can be identified and provided with the appropriate support. A screening instrument known as the Autism Spectrum Quotient, or AQ, can be used with children from the age of four in order to identify their support needs. In the case of pupils with Asperger, these are often around their ability to socialize with and relate to their peers, rather than to do with their academic achievement, which may well be excellent. This is one of the reasons it has been termed a 'hidden disability'.

Further Reading: Simon Baron-Cohen *Autism and Asperger Syndrome* (Oxford University Press, 2008). This provides practical information as well as a clear and accessible account of the current understanding of Asperger syndrome.

((⊕)) SEE WEB LINKS
• Provides links to a variety of information about symptoms and available support.

assertive discipline A systematic approach to managing classroom behaviour, based on the work of Cantor and Cantor in the 1970s which argued that teachers are insufficiently trained in the theory and skills of behaviour management. Based on establishing an expectation of compliance, assertive discipline encourages teachers to respond to negative behaviour swiftly and confidently, with assertion rather than aggression. It suggests that they establish four or five concise rules for good behaviour which they make clear to the class; and that they explain clearly the consequences both of non-compliance and of compliance. Non-compliance will result in sanctions, while compliance will be reinforced by a reward. Proponents of assertive discipline argue that this approach is in pupils' own best interests since it is designed to help them acquire behaviour appropriate to society's demands. *See also* BEHAVIOUR MANAGEMENT.

Further Reading: Lee Cantor *Assertive Discipline: Positive Behaviour Management for Today's Classrooms* (Solution Tree, 2009).

((⊕)) SEE WEB LINKS
• Provides further details about how this approach can be used in schools.

assessment The measurement of a learner's potential for *attainment, or of their actual attainment. The assessment of potential can be carried out through **aptitude tests** or tests of intelligence or verbal acuity. In a general educational context, however, most assessment focuses on the measurement of attainment. This may be *diagnostic, *formative, *ipsative, or *summative. Diagnostic assessment measures the learner's achievement on entry to their course of study in order to identify their current level of achievement, their individual learning needs, and their strengths. Formative assessment is the ongoing process of assessment which takes place throughout the learner's course of study and provides them with the feedback and guidance necessary to enable them to improve their performance. Ipsative assessment is where learners are assessed against their own previous level of attainment. Summative assessment takes place at the end of their course of study, and measures the learner's attainment against the specified learning *objectives of the syllabus or programme. Thus, coursework, *assignments, and other methods of *continuous assessment offer opportunities for formative assessment and a consequent learning from performance which the more traditional style of assessment, involving only summative assessment through an end-of-course *examination, does not allow. A debate continues over the relative merits of end examinations and coursework as methods of assessment, the examination lobby arguing that summative assessment under examination conditions provides a more accurate, rigorous, and reliable measurement of the candidate's ability; while proponents of continuous assessment maintain that the skills necessary to perform well in end examinations may be gender-specific, and that continuous assessment gives a more accurate measure of whether a candidate can attain the required standard consistently over time. Linked to this debate has been the argument about the relative merits of internal and external assessment. Some contend that teachers themselves are best placed to assess their pupils' work, while others, notably the examinations lobby, maintain that assessment by external examiners and assessors is more likely to be both rigorous and reliable.

Three key concepts which apply to assessment are *sufficiency, **validity**, and **reliability**. Sufficiency refers to the requirement that there be sufficient evidence on which to base an assessment decision. Validity refers to the requirement that assessment measures what it claims to measure. For example, an assessment of a candidate's driving skills based on their ability to write an essay about driving would be invalid, as would an assessment of a candidate's knowledge of art history based on their own skill at painting a picture. To be valid, an assessment must measure what it claims to measure. For an assessment to be reliable, the candidate should be awarded the same result, regardless of which assessor is marking their work. For example, a *multiple choice test has a much higher degree of reliability than an essay because the latter may be open to a subjective response from assessors. The use of *assessment criteria and *marking schemes is designed to increase the reliability of assessment; but, to some extent, the question of reliability of assessment will differ from subject to subject, with a higher level of reliability in the assessment of subjects where facts or quantitative data play an important part, such as mathematics and chemistry, and relatively more problems over reliability in subjects which call for a subjective response, such as English literature. *See also* ASSESSMENT INSTRUMENTS; ASSESSMENT PLAN.

Assessment and Qualifications Alliance (AQA) The largest of the three major *awarding bodies responsible for *academic and *vocational qualifications for 18–19-year-olds. It was formed in 1997 as the result of an alliance between three awarding bodies: the City and Guilds of London Institute, which had been responsible for the *assessment and award of a range of vocational qualifications, including teacher training qualifications for the *further education sector; and the Northern and the Associated Examining Boards, both awarding bodies for *General Certificate of Secondary Education and *Advanced Level.

SEE WEB LINKS
• Provides a detailed description of the Alliance's role and function.

assessment criteria A list of requirements against which a piece of work or the performance of a task is measured in order to judge whether it has been successfully completed. An *assessor will use *assessment criteria in order to distinguish between work which is a pass and work which is a fail, and in order to determine what percentage or category of mark to award. The purpose of such criteria is to ensure a degree of objectivity in the forming of an assessment decision. They may be devised and employed within one awarding institution, such as a *university; or, in the case of work leading to national awards, they may be devised and imposed externally by a national *awarding body. In all cases their purpose is to support the standardization and reliability of assessment decisions. *See also* GRADING CRITERIA.

Assessment for Learning (AfL) An approach to *assessment which is applicable to all *key stages and is based on ten underlying principles drawn up by the Assessment Reform Group in 2002. It centres on the processes by which learners find and interpret evidence which enables them and their teachers to decide what stage they are at with their learning, and what they need to do to progress to the next level. AfL encourages *self-assessment by pupils, which helps them to decide how they can improve their own learning. This approach allows pupils a measure of control in their own learning, and one of its central tenets is that assessment should focus on the work, not on the individual. It is based on the belief that it is as important to consider 'how' learning takes place as it is to consider 'what' has been learned. AfL fosters a sense that it is all right to make mistakes, and thereby it develops risk-taking, one of the 'soft skills' which the *creativity initiative aims to foster. Weaknesses are therefore handled constructively so that the pupil is helped to identify for themselves how they might improve. At the heart of AfL is the belief that everyone can make progress. Teachers give feedback to, and receive feedback from, pupils; and this feedback should be used to inform future lesson planning in a way that links teaching more effectively to learning. The use of open questioning and listening to pupils' reasoning while they work are among methods used to help teachers assess understanding and knowledge. AfL is most successful when pupils are shown models of what is expected so that they have an understanding of what is required and can use the model to check their own work against these criteria without fear of criticism. It is essential to provide success criteria which learners understand so that they are clear about the learning goals. The intended outcomes of AfL are that self-esteem increases, and pupils learn to identify their own strengths and weaknesses and the best ways in which they learn. It develops *thinking skills and encourages pupils to reflect on their work and how to improve. The emphasis on *formative assessment is shared between pupil and teacher with the aim of increasing pupil motivation and engagement, as well as learning. AfL is based on a *constructivist approach to learning, and its ten underlying principles are, in summary, as follows:

• lesson planning should incorporate opportunities for formative assessment;
• pupils' full range of achievements should be recognized;
• the focus should be on how, as well as what, pupils learn;

a

- pupils should be encouraged in self-assessment, reflection, and self-management;
- AfL should be central to classroom practice;
- it should also be considered as an essential professional skill for teachers;
- it should encourage a commitment to appropriate goals and involve a clear and shared understanding of the criteria to be met;
- pupils should be given, as part of formative assessment, constructive advice on how to improve their performance;
- assessments and feedback should be conducted sensitively and constructively;
- assessment should always take account of the need to encourage and sustain pupils' motivation to learn.   TB, LE

(⊕) SEE WEB LINKS
- An evaluation of the impact of assessment for learning.

assessment grid *See* ASSESSMENT PLAN.

assessment instruments A means of assessing learners' progress or level of ability. Such instruments may take a variety of forms, including the essay, the short answer test, the *multiple choice test, observation of practice, and presentations. The choice of instrument will usually be dictated by the purpose of the *assessment, the skill or knowledge being assessed, and the characteristics of the learners. For example, the essay may be considered an appropriate assessment instrument to test the comprehension skills of older, more able pupils; while younger, less literate learners might be more appropriately assessed by means of oral question and answer.

assessment outcome The result of an *assessment, whether by *assignment, essay, *test, *examination, or some other means, which is designed to ascertain a learner's current level of knowledge, ability, or achievement. The outcome might be expressed in terms of a simple pass or fail; or it might be graded using categories such as pass, credit, distinction. Alternatively, the outcome might be expressed numerically, in the form of a percentage mark, for example, or in a score out of ten. In the case of assessment for *bachelor's degrees, the outcome is expressed as a class or classification, according to the student's performance, using first, second, and third class, in descending order of merit, to denote the student's achievement. Other ways of presenting assessment outcomes are by using an alphabetical system, as was the case for *Advanced Levels, for example; or by a numerical system such as that introduced to replace it. There is also the system of combining alphabetical grading with plus and minus markers, so that, for example, an A− denotes a slightly better level of achievement than a B+.

In whatever form the assessment outcome is presented—numerical, alphabetical, graded, or classified—the outcome as expressed should be securely grounded in an agreed and transparent set of *assessment criteria so that both assessor and student or candidate are clear about what the assessment outcome means in terms of the student's level of achievement. In order for assessment outcomes to have reliability, a grade B awarded by one assessor for a particular assignment must mean the same in terms of student achievement as a B awarded by a different assessor to a different student for the same assignment.

assessment plan A scheme, grid, or other format which sets out clearly how and where each learning objective is covered by the tasks or questions in a *test, *examination, *assignment, or other means of *assessment, and the relative *weighting given to each in the calculation of a final mark, score, or assessment decision. It should demonstrate that specified outcomes are assessed appropriately, validly, and reliably, and in a sequence compatible with the sequence of teaching. Such grids are required as a matter of course for public examinations such as the *General Certificate of Secondary Education; but individual teachers may also draw up assessment grids for their own use when setting *homework or carrying out assessment in the classroom.

assessor One who assesses candidates' work or performance against pre-specified criteria for the purpose of awarding a mark or grade, or ascertaining whether the required criteria have been met. A distinction is made between an **internal assessor**, who belongs to the same institution as the candidate and is normally responsible for first-line assessment, and an **external assessor**, who comes from outside the institution and whose role is usually to ensure *standardization and reliability of assessment, leading to a specific qualification, between institutions, regionally or nationally.

assignment A task, usually written, which can be used for the dual purposes of *learning and *assessment, and is in the first instance internally assessed. Usually involving some degree of research or preparatory reading, and often consisting of more than one task, an assignment may be set for completion by individual learners, or may require the collaboration of a small group. They are often used as a means of *continuous assessment; and the term is sometimes used interchangeably with *coursework. They were widely used in the first phase of *General National Vocational Qualifications (GNVQs) in the 1990s, when they were presented as a helpful alternative to *examinations for those pupils who did not perform well under examination conditions. In this respect they became the subject of some controversy, considered by some to be an unreliable and insufficiently stringent alternative to external testing. This growing concern led to the introduction into GNVQs of externally set and externally assessed assignments. *See also* ASSESSOR.

assistant head A relatively new post in schools, having been formally established in 2000. The assistant head occupies a rank below that of the *deputy head but senior to that of head of department. The post carries no nationally specified role or set of duties. Instead, these are decided by the individual school according to its circumstances and needs.

Association for Science Education (ASE) A professional body whose aims are to promote science education and to support the professional development of science teachers. Its membership is open to educational professionals, including technicians, involved in science education at all levels and for all age groups, from *pre-school to *higher education. It holds an annual conference, publishes a specialist journal, and provides professional advice on all matters relating to the teaching of science.

((⊕)) SEE WEB LINKS
• Details of publications for science teachers.

Association of Colleges (AoC) An association formed in 1996 to represent and promote the interests of general further education *colleges, *sixth form colleges, specialist colleges, and other *tertiary institutions in England and Wales. Membership is corporate rather than individual. Its board of management consists of 24 chairs and principals of colleges, including one representative of Northern Ireland colleges, and one representative of Scotland's further education institutions. Board members, excluding the chief executive and any co-opted members, are elected to the board by member colleges for a term of four years. The Association holds an annual conference, and its other activities include consultancy and parliamentary lobbying. The Association of Scotland's Colleges (ASC) fulfils a similar function for Scotland's 43 further education colleges. Welsh colleges, in addition to their membership of AoC, are supported by **fforwm**, set up as a charity in 1993 and representing college interests within the principality. *See also* ASSOCIATION OF LEARNING PROVIDERS.

((⊕)) SEE WEB LINKS
• Provides details about the AoC's role.

Association of Employment and Learning Providers (AELP) An association of British providers of post-compulsory education and training, including *Further Education colleges and other training and employment services and organizations concerned with work-based learning, and particularly with apprenticeships. Their aim is to influence and respond to government policy on training and to support high-quality training provision on the job.

((⊕)) SEE WEB LINKS
• Provides details of AELP's aims and activities.

Association of Teachers and Lecturers (ATL) Originally known as the Assistant Masters' and Mistresses' Association (AMMA), this teachers' union changed to its current name in 1993 in acknowledgement of the growing numbers of lecturers from further education *colleges taking up membership. It is affiliated to the Trades Union Congress and has approximately 160 000 members, whose interests it supports through campaigning and negotiation.

((⊕)) SEE WEB LINKS
• Provides a link to the history of the Association from 1884 to the present day.

Association of University Teachers *See* UNIVERSITY AND COLLEGE UNION.

asynchronous learning Usually applied to *e-learning online or other modes of *distance learning, where pupils are undertaking the same course of study but are accessing the learning materials and interacting with their tutors individually and at different times. By contrast, conventional courses of study normally involve **synchronous** learning, which is to say that all learners are participating or receiving input at the same time.

attachment disorder A failure to form normal attachments to parents or carers in early childhood, leading to difficulties with behaviour, relationships and mood control. It is often regarded as a root cause of emotional and behavioural problems in school age children, although there are no consistently agreed diagnostic criteria. Children with attachment disorder find it difficult to manage their emotions and form positive learning relationships. They may be undemonstrative or exhibit control issues presenting in the form of defiant or disruptive behaviour. The disorder manifests on a spectrum from mild difficulty to serious symptoms of insecure attachment, known as reactive attachment disorder (RAD). Within the classroom pupils with attachment disorder may be identified as having *special educational needs.

(((⊕))) SEE WEB LINKS
• Provides details of causes and symptoms.

attainment A level of learning or skill arrived at, as measured against specific targets or criteria, and confirmed by evidence such as test or examination results, or assessment by a teacher. It is part of the vocabulary of the *national curriculum, and, as such, is more often encountered in the schools sector than in further education, where *'achievement' is more commonly used to convey the same meaning.

attainment gap An indicator of economic disadvantage. The gap is that between levels of achievement of pupils receiving free school meals and those whose parents' or carers' income makes them ineligible. The gap is measured at ages 11, 16 and 19. At 16 the attainment gap is a measure of the difference in performance at *GCSE, based on pupils achieving five or more GCSEs at grade C or above and including English and maths. The attainment of pupils on free *school meals is found to be consistently lower; and research carried out by Demos suggests that the overall trend is towards a widening of the attainment gap. *See also* SOCIAL CLASS.

(((⊕))) SEE WEB LINKS
• Sets out the attainment gap between pupils who receive free school meals and those who do not.

attainment test A test which measures the learner's achievement against a set of specified learning *objectives in order to assess how much they have learned. *See also* ASSESSMENT; ATTAINMENT.

attendance It is mandatory that all children aged between 5 and 16 years should receive a suitable education, and to this end parents and guardians are required to ensure that this is the case for their school age children, usually (but not always) by regular attendance at a school. Two registers are maintained by every school, with the exception of boarding schools. One is the admissions register, usually referred to as the **school roll**, and the other is the **attendance register**. It is a requirement of *head teachers to ensure that the attendance register is taken twice each day, once at the beginning of the school day and again in the afternoon. Pupils are marked as present, or as engaged off-site in an educational activity (for example, a field trip), or as absent. For those pupils who are absent, it must be indicated on the register whether that absence has been authorized by the school (for example, in cases of sickness or where some other satisfactory explanation has been provided). Unauthorized absences, which include unexplained or unjustified absences, are closely monitored, and it is a requirement of head teachers that they inform the *local authority of any pupil whose attendance is irregular or who has had a continuous unauthorized absence of ten days. The enforcement of attendance is usually a role carried out by the local authority Welfare Service, whose personnel work closely with the school and family concerned to improve the pupil's attendance. Since 1 March 2001 parents who fail to ensure their child's attendance have been liable to a penalty of up to £2 500, or up to a three-month prison sentence, or both of these. *See also* EDUCATION OTHERWISE THAN AT SCHOOL; TRUANCY.

(⊕) SEE WEB LINKS
• Provides governmental advice on pupil registers and other matters relating to attendance.

Attention Deficit Hyperactivity Disorder (ADHD) A condition presenting as hyperactivity, impulsive behaviour, and the inability to sit still or concentrate. In the classroom, typical features of the condition include the pupil having difficulty in completing tasks, failing to listen to instructions, and exhibiting restlessness which often results in being out of their seat. Becoming distracted and forgetful are also common features, together with poor socializing skills, finding it hard to take turns, and blurting out answers before being asked. ADHD has a negative impact on learning for both sufferers and their peers and may alienate the pupil with the condition from their peers who find it difficult to tolerate such behaviour. ADHD often first becomes noticeable when the child starts pre-school or school and is required to follow routines and rules. It is most frequently diagnosed between the ages of three and seven. Research carried out by the University of Cardiff suggests that there is a genetic component in the disorder, which was previously thought by some to be connected with factors such as inadequate parenting or poor diet.

(⊕) SEE WEB LINKS
• Provides further information about diagnosis and specific educational needs.

audio-visual aid (AVA) Sounds or pictures used to support or reinforce learning. These include such resources as slide projections, DVDs and videos, overhead projectors, sound recordings, radio, and television. Increasing use of electronic resources has led to this term falling increasingly out of use, to be replaced with 'information learning technology'. Nevertheless, in many educational institutions the department or team responsible for supplying or maintaining teaching resources of this kind will still carry the designation 'AV' in its title.

augmentative and alternative communication (AAC) This term is used to describe methods of communication which can add to the more usual methods of speech and writing when these are impaired. AAC includes unaided systems of communication such as signing (for example, *Makaton) and gesture, as well as aided techniques. These aided techniques range from the use of low technology such as picture or symbol charts to the most sophisticated computer technology currently available. A well-known user of a sophisticated high technology device is the scientist Stephen Hawking. AAC can be a way to help someone understand what is being communicated to them, as well as a means of expression. *See also* PICTURE EXCHANGE COMMUNICATION SYSTEM.   TB, LE

( ) SEE WEB LINKS
• Provides a wealth of information about AAC including details of suppliers, publications, assessment centres, and online forums.

authenticity In relation to the *assessment of learning, this term has two distinct usages. **1.** When arriving at an assessment decision, the *assessor must consider whether the work or performance being assessed is genuinely the learner's own, and therefore represents an accurate picture of that learner's ability and achievement. In the case of a pupil who has received substantial covert help with their coursework, or a pupil who has purchased an essay answer from the Internet, the lack of authenticity in their work offered for assessment would invalidate any mark or grade awarded. *See also* PLAGIARISM.
    2. An *assessment instrument may be judged to lack authenticity if it is deemed inadequate to assess the knowledge or skill being assessed; for example, the use of an essay to assess a practical skill. The call for authenticity in this sense was one of the factors which led to the increased use of *continuous assessment and *portfolios of evidence, particularly for the assessment of *General National Vocational Qualifications. Ironically, these means of assessment inevitably raised questions about authenticity in its first sense as set out here. *See also* PLAGIARISM.

autism *See* AUTISTIC SPECTRUM DISORDER.

autistic spectrum disorder (ASD) A continuum of difficulties which impact on three areas of development: social interaction, communication, and imagination. These are commonly referred to as the 'triad of impairments'. The word 'autistic' derives from the Greek word *autos*, meaning 'self'. A person who is on the autistic spectrum has significant difficulty relating to others, and to the world at large. At one end of the spectrum are those cases of severe, low-functioning autism where the individual has little or no language or communication skills. At the other end are those with high-functioning *Asperger syndrome, often highly intelligent, and whose disability is not always immediately apparent. What both ends of the spectrum have in common are difficulties with social communication and a close focus that may manifest in the one as a compulsion to repetitive actions and in the other as a narrow or specialized interest in a specific topic, activity, or hobby. In a learning situation the autistic pupil will normally require substantial support in areas of communication and social interaction. Their social difficulties, even at the highly functioning end of the spectrum, may include avoidance or over-use of eye contact; a lack of interest in their teachers and peers; a tendency to deliver a monologue rather than hold a conversation; uncertainty over how to react to the behaviour of others; difficulty reading the expression of others; and an inability to take into account the point of view of others, which has been seen as a lack of empathy. *See also* ASPERGER SYNDROME.

Further Reading: Simon Baron-Cohen *Autism and Asperger Syndrome* (Oxford University Press, 2008) provides practical information about autistic spectrum disorder.

(⊕) SEE WEB LINKS
• Provides links to a variety of information about symptoms and available support.

autodidact One who is self-taught, having achieved their knowledge or skills through their own efforts, without having gone through the formal processes of further or higher education.

autonomous learner One who is self-motivated to learn and is able to do so without direct supervision and prompting. Most educators in the United Kingdom would claim that one of the aims of education is to produce such learners. This is sometimes expressed as helping individuals to 'learn how to learn'. For autonomous learning to become a possibility, the learner needs to be equipped with appropriate skills, including those necessary for carrying out research, problem-solving, or analysis. For the autonomous learner, the teacher becomes a **facilitator** of the learning process, rather than a source of information or instruction.

Award in Education and Training (AET) *See* FURTHER EDUCATION TEACHING QUALIFICATIONS.

awarding body An organization responsible for the conduct of *assessment leading to recognized awards such as the *General Certificate of Secondary Education (GCSE), and for the issuing of certification. Before 1996 the term applied largely to bodies awarding vocational qualifications, most notably national organizations such as the Business and Technology Education Council (BTEC) and the Royal Society of Arts, which were responsible for awarding qualifications such as the *General National Vocational Qualification. At this time, bodies responsible for general education awards such as GCSEs were referred to as *examination boards. However, in line with the policy of that time to close the gap between vocational and general qualifications, manifested in the replacement of the School Curriculum and Assessment Authority and the National Council for Vocational Qualifications by the Qualifications and Curriculum Authority (QCA) in 1997, mergers took place between the major awarding bodies and examination boards. The University of London Examination and Assessment Council and BTEC

were the first to form a **unitary awarding body**. The RSA awarding body and
the Oxford and Cambridge examination boards formed the Oxford, Cambridge,
and Royal Society of Arts (*OCR) examining board; and the City and Guilds
merged with the Northern and the Associated Examining Boards to form the
*Assessment and Qualifications Alliance. These three awarding bodies are
responsible for academic and vocational qualifications for 18–19-year-olds.
There remain, however, a large number of smaller awarding bodies, each
responsible for qualifications in a specific area, which operate nationally and
regionally within the *further education sector.

The specific operating procedures of awarding bodies vary, but their role will
usually include advising on, or specifying, *curriculum content; devising,
monitoring, and administrating assessments; operating a system of verification
to ensure standardization of *continuous assessment; carrying out *summative
assessment and moderation; and issuing certification of awards.

All awarding bodies, and the qualifications they award, are regulated, in
England by *Ofqual as part of its responsibility for maintaining the reliability
of the *Qualifications and Credit Framework and the *National Qualifications
Framework; in Wales by the Welsh Assembly; in Scotland by the *Scottish
Qualifications Authority; and in Northern Ireland by the Council for the
Curriculum, Examinations and Assessment (CCEA).

B

baccalauréat The national school-leaving qualification in France, which occupies roughly the same status in the French education system as the *General Certificate of Education *Advanced Level occupies in the English system. Often cited, by those who would wish to reform the 16–19 *examination system in Britain, as an example of good practice, *le bac* reflects a broader and less specialized post-16 curriculum, which allows students to combine subjects from the arts, sciences, and humanities. As well as the general, or academic, *baccalauréat*, which prepares students for further academic studies at *university, *lycées* also offer the less prestigious *baccalauréat technologique* and the *baccalauréat professionel*, which focus on vocational skills and knowledge and were designed to prepare the student for direct entry to the workforce. *See also* ENGLISH BACCALAUREATE (EBACC); INTERNATIONAL BACCALAUREATE; WELSH BACCALAUREATE.

bachelor's degree An award conferred for the successful completion of *undergraduate studies. The general field of study is indicated in the title of the degree. Thus, a **Bachelor of Arts (BA)** is awarded for successful undergraduate studies in some branch of the arts or humanities; a **Bachelor of Science (B.Sc.)** is awarded for successful undergraduate studies in a branch of the sciences; and a Bachelor of Education (B.Ed.) is awarded for successful undergraduate studies in the field of education. The conferring of a bachelor's degree marks the elevation of the student from undergraduate to *graduate status. In the case of an *honours degree there are four classes, which are used as grading indicators of the level achieved. These are known as a **first** class, an **upper second** class (sometimes referred to as a **2.1**), a **lower second** class (sometimes referred to as a **2.2**), and a **third** class, the first class degree being the highest and most coveted award. Most bachelor's degrees awarded fall into the second class category. A current controversy exists over the classification of degrees, with some academics arguing that the classifications are not being applied consistently, making it easier to gain a higher classification in some universities than in others. One specific concern expressed has been that a disproportionate number of the bachelor's degrees awarded by some universities fall into the first and upper second class category, thus risking a devaluation of these higher classes of the award. In order to progress to *master's degree level, a graduate will normally be required to have achieved a first or upper second class in their undergraduate studies. A BA or B.Sc. may be awarded with **honours**. Where this is the case, the title of the award is abbreviated as **BA (Hons)** or **B.Sc. (Hons)**. Where the degree is awarded without honours, it is known as an **ordinary** degree, and is usually considered to indicate a lesser academic achievement.

The bachelor's degree title may also be used to refer to someone who holds that degree. So, for example, a graduate who holds a B.Sc. may be referred to as a Bachelor of Science, regardless of their gender. *See also* GRADUATION.

Bachelor of Arts (BA) *See* BACHELOR'S DEGREE.

Bachelor of Education (B.Ed.) An award conferred for the successful completion of undergraduate level studies in education. Following the recommendation in the *Robbins Report (1963) that all teachers should be *graduates, teacher training courses leading to Certificates in Education were largely phased out and replaced, in *universities and *colleges of higher education, by courses leading to a B.Ed. for teachers in the *primary and secondary sectors. Entry requirements usually include English and mathematics at *General Certificate of Secondary Education grade C or above, and two *General Certificate of Education *Advanced Level passes. As well as covering educational theory, *national curriculum, and specialist subjects, these full-time courses for student teachers also require participants to undertake substantial periods of practical teaching practice within schools, the assessment of which contributes towards their assessment for their final degree.

Some universities and higher education institutions also offer part-time B.Ed. courses for teachers already in employment who hold a *Certificate of Education but wish to upgrade their qualification. To accommodate teachers' working lives, such courses usually involve evening or weekend attendance, and are aimed at professionals engaged in teaching or training in the *tertiary sector, the health service, social services, police, and armed forces, as well as teachers in schools.

Bachelor of Science (B.Sc.) *See* BACHELOR'S DEGREE.

Bain Review (2006) This independent report was commissioned by the government in Northern Ireland to examine the provision of education for 14–19-year-olds. It was published as *Schools for the Future* and recommended an end to academic selection and increased collaboration between schools. New schools are to cater for the needs of a geographical area rather than a particular section of the community. Schools will be expected to share lessons and some will become *specialist schools providing expertise in specific areas of the curriculum. This scheme will replace the former grammar school system. The Education Order (NI) 2006 determines these changes and the *Eleven Plus was scheduled to be phased out in 2008. *See also* NORTHERN IRELAND, EDUCATION IN.   JH

(⊕) SEE WEB LINKS
• Provides the full text of the Bain Review.

banding The practice of dividing year groups of pupils in secondary education into bands or sub-groups, according to their *ability or learning needs. Each band may then be divided into a number of separate classes whose members may be selected according to ability within that band, or according to some other criteria, or simply at random. It was common practice in grammar schools in the mid-20th century for the curriculum subjects provided to differ according to band. For example, pupils in the most able band of a girls' grammar school might study Latin, while the middle band might instead be taught an additional modern language, and the least able band might be offered instruction in a practical skill such as 'domestic science' or sewing. Such differentiated (and gender-specific) provision would not be considered acceptable today, although decisions about the number and type of *General Certificate of Secondary Education subjects for which a pupil is entered might well be based on which band they find themselves in.

barriers to learning Events and conditions in pupils' lives which make it difficult or less likely that they will be able to learn effectively; for example, hunger, emotional upset, illness, family separation, and bereavement. On the other hand, barriers might include less obvious factors such as inflexible school systems or an inappropriate *curriculum. *Bullying, too, has a profound effect on some victims' ability to learn. Existing and potential barriers to learning may go undetected, particularly in those cases where the root cause is linked to aspects of young people's lives outside school. Where good home–school partnerships exist, these barriers can more easily be overcome. Barriers to learning may arise unexpectedly and may be of a permanent or temporary nature. For this reason it is important that schools and other educational institutions remain vigilant in order to spot changes in learning and behaviour patterns. This enables appropriate support and interventions to be implemented promptly, and for planning and *assessment to take into account the type and extent of the learner's difficulties.   TB, LE

baseline assessment The instrument for collecting **baseline data** and the method used by teachers to find out a pupil's learning needs, their natural ability, and potential. Tests are given to pupils across an entire year group to establish where each pupil is in relation to a national and institutional norm. The purpose of baseline *assessment is to establish a point from which future measurements and predictions can be calculated. The assessments are not standardized, and different formats may be used in different schools. These tests, such as *Cognitive Abilities Tests, are used to generate a predicted or expected level of achievement for future performance, for example at General Certificate of Secondary Education (GCSE) level. They can also function to highlight specific issues such as whether a pupil should be placed on the *gifted and talented register, or whether they are underachieving in relation to their potential. Teachers can use baseline data to plan effectively for each pupil's learning needs and, for this reason, baseline assessments are usually carried out throughout a pupil's schooling, often starting within six weeks of their entering full-time education. Baseline assessment can also be used on a whole-school level to measure the quality of education which the school is providing, by comparing a pupil's performance with their baseline assessment. The results of baseline assessments are formally registered. The baseline data that are generated form part of each pupil's school records. Subsequent data are then added to this, such as the results of *Key Stage 2 *Standard Tasks and GCSE results. Baselines should be both reliable and valid to enable statistical validity.   IW

baseline data *See* BASELINE ASSESSMENT.

basic skills The Basic Skills Agency (1995–2011) defined basic skills as 'The
ability to read, write and speak in English or Welsh, and to use mathematics at
a level necessary to function and progress at work and in society in general'.
Although initiatives covered all age groups during the time of the Basic Skills
Agency, the term is most commonly used to refer to the skills of adults rather
than of those under 19 years old, where *General Certificate of Secondary
Education and *functional skills qualifications tend to define levels of skill.
    Development of basic skills has been a particular focus of UK government
policy since 1975, when the **Adult Literacy Resource Agency** was created
to support a high-profile *adult literacy campaign. This function was
then taken over first by the **Adult Literacy Unit** (1978–80) and then by the
Adult Literacy and Basic Skills Unit (1980–95).
    The state of adult UK citizens' basic skills has been the subject of several reviews,
the most influential of which is probably that of the committee chaired by Sir Claus
Moser, which published its report, *A Fresh Start: Improving Literacy and
Numeracy*, in 1999. This stated that up to 7 000 000 adults in England have
difficulties with literacy and numeracy inasmuch as that their skills are below level
2 on the *Qualifications and Credit Framework. In 2000 the final report of the
International Adult Literacy Survey, *Literacy in the Information Age*, concluded
that Great Britain ranked in the lower third of the 20 countries that form the
Organization for Economic Cooperation and Development. Both studies relate the
findings to personal socio-economic factors, such as employment, income, and
mental health; and to the consequences for national economic prosperity.
    As a result of the Moser Report, the **Skills for Life Quality Initiative** was
established and given the task of improving basic skills, broadened to include
English for Speakers of Other Languages (ESOL) and information technology
through *widening participation; this included workplace and community
projects, and work with adults with learning difficulties or disabilities.
A key outcome was the development of basic skills-specific qualifications for
teachers, first introduced in 2002; and a system for reporting on the quality
of provision of adult basic skills training. *See also* ADULT LITERACY;
FUNCTIONAL SKILLS.   VC, KA

(⊕) SEE WEB LINKS
• Provides further information on adult literacy initiatives.

Beacon Award A scheme overseen by the *Association of Colleges which
annually rewards those in the *further education sector who have demonstrated
excellence in teaching, learning, and student support. The scheme aims to
celebrate and disseminate good practice. There are a variety of categories in which
Awards are available, including teaching, leadership, community development,
employer engagement, support provision, and equality and diversity.   VC, KA

(⊕) SEE WEB LINKS
• Provides links to further information on Beacon Awards.

behaviour For learners to engage effectively with their learning, it is necessary for there to be a level of cooperation and compliance on their part. Pupil or student behaviour which acts as a barrier to their own learning, and often also to that of their classmates, is of crucial concern to teachers since it can prevent them from carrying out their prime responsibility, which is to support effective learning. Such behaviours are referred to as *disruptive, as they disturb or destroy the learning process. Even one disruptive pupil in a class can have a negative impact on the quality of teaching and learning. While responsibility for decisions about what rules are to be applied within the school lie largely with the *head teacher, it is the teacher in the classroom who has first-line responsibility for applying and enforcing them. The ability to do so has traditionally been regarded as a necessary skill for teachers, known by such terms as 'classroom discipline' and 'classroom control'. A more usual term today is 'behaviour management', which has become a popular focus for *continuing professional development programmes and staff development events. Books for teachers on this topic proliferate, reflecting what many commentators, and particularly the tabloid press, consider to be a continuing decline in standards of behaviour in both primary and secondary schools. Disruptive behaviour is also reported as a growing problem in the *post-compulsory sector, particularly in *colleges of further education, where, in theory, students attend through their own *choice.

A difficulty for teachers in general is the assumption that problems of behaviour have their origins in what is happening in the classroom, and that it is therefore within the teacher's power to address this by changes in approach, lesson content, or their own behaviour. This notion is predicated on a deficit model of the teacher—the belief that teachers can address and solve problems of pupil behaviour by making changes to their own practice and approach. An equally popular 'common-sense' understanding of the issue is based on a deficit model of the learners themselves. This assumes that the pupil or student who presents with non-compliant or challenging behaviour is deficient as an individual and that the solution to the problem lies in changing the individual, modifying their behaviour, or even removing them altogether from the learning situation, either through permanent *exclusion or by some temporary measure.

Many educationalists, psychologists, and sociologists, however, would suggest that the causes of disruptive behaviour and disengagement from learning may arise not from a deficit in the individual teacher or learner, but from wider demographic or socio-economic factors which are beyond any individual teacher's capacity or remit to address, and beyond many individual learners' capacity to overcome. Nevertheless, within their own classroom teachers acknowledge that they have a professional responsibility to do what they can to encourage cooperative and appropriate behaviour which is conducive to learning. The issue of behaviour in schools and colleges is now generally recognized as being closely related to questions of *motivation. Among the effective strategies which teachers use to encourage learner motivation are systems of rewards and sanctions, based on *behaviourist psychology, which in practical terms may mean such strategies as the liberal use of praise for acceptable behaviours and the withholding of 'treats' such as free time at break as a response to disruption or aggression. Alternatively, a strategy based on *humanist psychology may employ determined good humour, a recognition that their teaching needs to take the learner's interests and enthusiasms as a starting point, and the demonstration of a positive attitude towards those misbehaving, though not towards their behaviour. Enthusiastic teachers are also often reported as having fewer problems with disruptive behaviour, perhaps because their enthusiasm engages even the demotivated.

The use of *corporal punishment or beating, once common as a sanction in primary and secondary schools, was made illegal in state schools in 1986, since when teachers have been precluded from using physical force or restraint, except in extreme circumstances such as the prevention of injury. *See also* ATTENTION DEFICIT HYPERACTIVITY DISORDER; ASSERTIVE DISCIPLINE; ZERO TOLERANCE.

Further Reading: L. Cantor *Assertive Discipline: Positive Behaviour Management for Today's Classrooms* (Solution Tree, 2009) gives practical guidance on behaviour management for teachers in schools.

behavioural, emotional, and social difficulties (BESd) There is a
continuing debate over what constitutes a definitive diagnosis of this cluster of difficulties which manifest in the classroom as disruptive or non-compliant behaviour. The three indicators identified by professionals in education and psychology were at one time listed in a slightly different order: *social, emotional and behavioural difficulties (SEBd)*. However, these have tended to be re-ordered in government policy documents, thus coining the current term and shifting the emphasis from *social* to *behavioural*.

The effective learning of students with BESd is impeded on different levels. At a personal level, BESd can be manifested through the destruction of students' own work, pre-empting of failure, a low tolerance of frustration, attention-seeking behaviours, and difficulty with forming relationships. It is common for students with BESd to develop anxieties about going to school. At a verbal level it takes the form of making frequent interruptions, being argumentative or abusive, or even refusing to speak. Non-verbal indicators could be school phobia, destructive and aggressive behaviour, making inappropriate responses to perceived provocation, and difficulty with following rules. At a work skills level the following are typical signs of BESd: students find it difficult to work with others in a learning setting; they are unable to follow instructions or complete tasks; they might possess a short concentration span and have poor organizational skills. It is not uncommon for students with BESd to interrupt and impede the learning of others.

In addition to the above descriptors there is usually evidence of underachievement which does not reflect general levels of ability. Very often the young person is unable or unwilling to accept responsibility for their own actions.

Where there is an escalation of BESd, students will not make adequate progress despite *special educational needs support intervention, and these difficulties become a significant barrier to learning. This is usually an indicator that support and advice should be sought from the appropriate external agencies, and highly individual and differentiated educational plans should be implemented. *See also* ATTENTION DEFICIT AND HYPERACTIVITY DISORDER.

Further Reading: T. Cole, H. Daniels, and J Visser *The Routledge Companion to Emotional and Behavioural Difficulties* (Routledge, 2012).

((⊕)) SEE WEB LINKS
• Provides information on the diagnosis and support of pupils with BESd.

behavioural learning objective A statement of what a learner is expected to have achieved or learned by the end of a *lesson or *programme of study, expressed in terms of observable behaviour. The objective will usually be prefixed, therefore, by a phrase such as 'By the end of the lesson the learner will be able to …'. There should then follow a description of what is expected, including the standard to which it must be achieved. Thus, the sentence 'By the end of the lesson the learner will be able to use the apostrophe correctly and appropriately indicate (*a*) possession and (*b*) abbreviation, and will be able to explain correctly the rules governing apostrophe use' indicates exactly what is to be learned and what behaviours the learner must be required to demonstrate in order that valid assessment of their learning can take place. Such observable objectives can be helpful to the teacher in structuring the lesson, since they indicate not only what is to be learned, but also what learner activities are essential, and how the learning is to be assessed. For this reason, they are often used as a basis on which to construct a *lesson plan, and appear within the lesson plan itself as pre-specified learning outcomes. With the growth of *competence-based education and training in the last quarter of the 20th century, behavioural objectives flourished in the guise of competences in *National Vocational Qualifications. However, useful as they may be in subjects where learning takes the form of observable behaviours, behavioural objectives may be irrelevant or inappropriate in other subject areas, particularly those involving higher-order *cognitive skills, or where learning takes place in the *affective domain. Expressing an understanding of particle physics or an appreciation of Yeats's poetry, for example, in terms of observable behaviours to be assessed would almost certainly prove extremely difficult to do. Moreover, useful as pre-specified outcomes may be in many learning situations, it can be argued that the setting of very precise behavioural objectives inevitably imposes constraints on the teacher and learner alike, and could act as an obstacle to inspiration on both sides. *See also* BLOOM'S TAXONOMY.

behaviourist A school of learning theory which argues that all behaviour can be predicted, measured, and controlled, and that learning is simply a matter of stimulus and response. Of the behaviourists, **Ivan Pavlov's** (1849–1936) is perhaps the most widely recognized name. His experiments with dogs are often cited to illustrate the central behaviourist claim. These experiments involved 'teaching' them to associate a specific sound with their feeding time, so that eventually they began to salivate at the sound alone, having learned to associate this with food. The sound was the stimulus; salivation was their response. The stimulus–response theory was applied not only to animal behaviour; it was also used, for example by John Watson (1878–1958), to explain human behaviour. It is currently viewed by many as a rather reductive and mechanistic view, and one which it would be difficult to apply to the practicalities of teaching and learning in any humane way.

Considered generally to be more relevant to current educational practices is the work of the **neo-behaviourists**, the best known of whom is perhaps **B. F. Skinner** (1904–90). The neo-behaviourists, or new behaviourists, built upon the work of Pavlov and Watson and introduced two additional ideas into behaviourist theory which are of more practical relevance to teachers. One was the suggestion that human behaviour is goal-oriented—that someone learning something may have a sense of purpose in doing so. The other was the importance of **reinforcement** and **behaviour modification**. Reinforcement refers to rewarding a desired behaviour in order to encourage its repetition; and behaviour modification describes the process and result of doing this. Applied to education, it is the idea that a teacher may modify someone's behaviour—that is, teach them something—by rewarding or reinforcing the desired behaviour. Conversely, the teacher might use **negative reinforcement** to discourage undesired behaviour, for example by withholding their attention from a student until they comply with instructions. According to this model, all teaching and learning is a form of behaviour modification.

behaviour management See BEHAVIOUR.

benchmark A target level of achievement, usually derived from national data, and applied on an organizational level. It may be used in relation, for example, to numbers of students successfully completing their qualification, or gaining specific grades. Schools, colleges, universities, and other training organizations may use benchmarking to establish in which areas they need to improve in order to match best practice elsewhere. The term derives historically from workforce monitoring practices in industry. It is said that, in the process of measuring productivity, managers would make a chalk mark on the benches of those workers who were successfully meeting productivity targets, so that other workers could look to them and follow their lead.

Further Reading: M. Dunsworth and D. Billings *The High Performing School: Benchmarking the 10 Indicators of Effectiveness* (Solution Tree, 2009).

Big Brother syndrome A growing tendency among younger learners to voice an ambition for celebrity without notable achievement. Derived from a reality television programme of the same name, the term is now in widespread use by teachers and other professionals involved in work with young people. It expresses a concern not only about values, but also about the difficulties of motivating learners towards academic achievement or useful qualifications which learners themselves may dismiss as irrelevant to their goal of being thrust into a celebrity lifestyle, since their Big Brother role models often make a virtue of having achieved fame despite having little or no academic success at school.

bilingual Having the ability to speak two languages equally fluently. This is often applied to pupils where the language spoken in the family home is other than

English. It is sometimes also applied, although technically inaccurately, to pupils whose first language is other than English and who need substantial support from their school in developing their skill in spoken English. *See also* MULTILINGUAL.

binary system The two-tier system of *higher education which existed between 1966 and 1992 when the *further education sector was expanded to create *polytechnics and other *colleges which delivered higher education separately from, but in parallel with, universities in the higher education sector. The policy for this expansion was set out in the 1966 *White Paper *A Plan for Polytechnics and Other Colleges: Higher Education in the Further Education System*. Because further education was at that time within the strategic control of *local authorities, the creation of polytechnics was heralded by many as representing the final step in the creation of a 'seamless' route of progression from primary school education right through to the awarding of higher degrees, all under the aegis and financial control of the *local education authority. The creation of polytechnics enabled much *wider participation in higher education, although they never achieved equal status with universities in the public perception. The binary system came to an end following the *Further and Higher Education Act 1992, which granted the polytechnics university status and removed them from local authority control. *See also* COLLEGE OF EDUCATION.

bipartite system A system based on selection, where some schools select their pupils by ability while others do not. In England this was typified by the system of *grammar schools and secondary modern schools, where the former selected pupils by ability at the age of 11, and the latter provided for those not selected. The bipartite system is still operated formally through the *Eleven Plus by some *local authorities in England; and continues to operate in practice, if not in name, in areas where oversubscribed schools are able to carefully select their intake. *See also* BUTLER ACT; TRIPARTITE SYSTEM.

Birth to Three Matters A framework of support and learning for children in their earliest years. It provides carers and childcare professionals with advice on, and observation notes for, approaches in four broad areas of learning opportunities, with the aim of developing a strong child, a skilful communicator, a healthy child, and a competent learner. In 2008 it became fully integrated with the *Early Years Foundation Stage, and has led to the setting of standards for early years teachers which are equivalent to those for teachers in schools.   AW

(⊕) SEE WEB LINKS
• Provides further information on current issues.

Black Papers The name commonly used to refer to a series of publications on education which began to appear in 1969 and continued through the early 1970s, whose authors and contributors were politicians, academics, and writers from the political right wing. Their common theme was the claim that educational standards had declined as a result of modern teaching methods, the philosophy of *liberal education, and the introduction of *comprehensive schools. The approach to teaching under criticism in the Black Papers is sometimes referred to as the *Plowden philosophy, against which these Papers levelled three specific accusations. These were that it had led to declining standards of *literacy and *numeracy, declining standards of behaviour, and the danger of pupils being unduly influenced by 'left-wing' teachers. The Papers argued, among other things, for the retention of, or return to, *selection for secondary education.

Further Reading: C. B. Cox and A. E. Dyson (eds) *The Black Papers on Education* (Davis-Poynter, 1971) presents a selection of these papers.

blended learning A combination of modes of learning. It is currently normally used to describe a combination of *e-learning (or some other form of *distance learning) and face-to-face student–teacher contact. Thus, a student undertaking a *programme of study via a blended learning model of delivery will access much of the learning materials and make regular contact with their tutor and other learners online, but will also attend at least one lesson or tutorial—or perhaps a more lengthy weekend or residential course—where tutor and students can all meet in the same place and at the same time. This represents a blend of *asynchronous, *distributed learning with traditional synchronous, non-distributed provision. The inclusion of face-to-face contact is designed largely to overcome one of the problems associated with distributed (online) learning, which is that students can come to feel isolated and demotivated, and may miss the social contact and stimulation which traditional attendance with a group of peers can provide.

(⊕) SEE WEB LINKS
• Sets out the definition and advantages of blended learning for students in higher education.

block release Used mainly in the *further and *higher education sectors to describe a period of time for which an employer 'releases' an employee from their work duties in order to follow a course of study or skills training. The length of time allowed for this may be anything from a few days to several months. During this time, the employee usually continues to be paid their salary or wages; and, in addition, the employer will often pay the necessary college or university fees. The concept of block release originates, and is still associated, with vocational or skills training. In academic or professional contexts, such a release from duties would normally be referred to as a *'secondment'. *See also* DAY RELEASE.

Bloom's Taxonomy A classification of *behavioural learning objectives into **domains** and levels of learning, first developed in 1956 by a group of educational psychologists headed by Benjamin Bloom (1913–99). Their work led them to the conclusion that over 90 per cent of assessment questions which students were required to answer tested only their ability to recall and reiterate information. Three domains of learning were identified: *cognitive, *affective, and *psychomotor. The recall or recognition of facts was classified as occupying the lowest level of the cognitive domain, followed by, in ascending order of complexity and abstraction, comprehension, application, analysis, synthesis, and, identified as the cognitive skill of the highest order, evaluation. Similarly, in the other two domains, a range of skills was identified and categorized according to its complexity. For each level of each domain, a list of behaviours was identified by which that level of skill could be assessed. So, for example, in the cognitive domain, the lowest-order skills—those involving the recall of facts—can be recognized by such examples of intellectual activity as the following: define, label, list, memorize, name, order, recognize, repeat, state; while the highest-order cognitive skills will require the learner to appraise, assess, defend, evaluate, predict, support.

Bloom's Taxonomy is useful to the teacher in formulating learning *objectives and planning learning activities which challenge the learners at the appropriate level. It is also useful in helping them to articulate clearly what behaviours a learner must demonstrate in order for learning to be deemed successful. *See also* KNOWLEDGE.

(⊕) SEE WEB LINKS
• Provides a full table of verbs for each domain and level.

boarding school A school at which some or all pupils are resident during term-time. Most boarding schools belong to the *independent schools sector, although some are to be found under the aegis of *local authorities. In addition, some local authority day schools, not classed as boarding schools, may include a small number of pupils who are **boarders**. The majority of local authority boarding schools are for the education of pupils with a disability or *special educational needs. In most cases, boarding schools in the independent sector follow the *national curriculum and enter pupils for national examinations. The image of the boarding school has recently been popularized among schoolchildren by the cultural phenomenon of the fictional character Harry Potter and his experiences at Hogwarts School.

Boarding Schools' Association (BSA) A body which represents those boarding schools, about five hundred in number, which have accreditation from the Independent Schools Council (ISC). It provides professional development for teachers and governors, and supports research into all aspects of residential compulsory education. It also offers a consultancy service to parents who are considering a boarding education for their child.

(⊕) SEE WEB LINKS
• Provides links to publications available from the BSA relating to boarding and boarding schools.

board of corporation The governing body of a *further education college, which came into use following incorporation in 1993. The composition of the board was changed by the *Further and Higher Education Act 1992, which removed *local authority representation and increased the proportion of representation by local commercial and industrial interests. Members of the board are not required to have a detailed knowledge of the minutiae of the college's provision, but are expected to monitor and take responsibility for the quality of that provision, its funding and finances, and its responsiveness to local and wider community needs. A board will normally operate a number of specialist subcommittees with responsibility for reporting back to the full committee on matters of finance, equal opportunities, and quality assurance, for example. The minimum number of members for a board is twelve and the maximum is twenty, with specified categories of membership within these figures. *See also* COLLEGE OF FURTHER EDUCATION.

(⊕) SEE WEB LINKS

• Links to full text of AoC survey report on FE boards of corporation.

Bologna Process   An initiative launched in 1999 by governments of 29 European Union member countries to create a **European Higher Education Area**. This involves the development of a common structure of higher education, and agreement on equivalence or credit levels of qualifications in order to enable students to transfer their studies and their qualifications between member countries, and to facilitate the mobility of staff. It also requires the recognition of a common structure of higher education study which involves both undergraduate and postgraduate levels. The development of the credit transfer system necessary to facilitate student mobility and progression between member countries is an integral part of the Bologna Process, and is known as the **European Credit Transfer System (ECTS)**. The Process, named after the city where the original meeting of government representatives took place to set the initiative in motion, operates outside the decision-making framework of the EU. All decisions taken require the consent of all participating countries, of which there are now over 40. As well as working towards a common higher education framework, the Process also has the declared aims of improving the quality of higher education across Europe in order to enhance the economy by raising the qualification level of the workforce, and of enhancing the reputation of European higher education and qualifications throughout the world. These economic aims make the Bologna Process a significant factor in the EU's *Lisbon Strategy. The Process also places an emphasis on *'lifelong learning' in the sense of developing provision which will enable the necessary updating of the workforce at every level in order to keep abreast of rapid developments in technology. Since the initial meeting in 1999, ministers representing the member governments have met every two years in a major European city. In 2007 the meeting was hosted by the UK government in London.

  The Process is promoted in UK higher education institutions (HEIs) by a national team of fourteen **Bologna Promoters**, funded by the European Commission. The Promoters' role is to advise HEIs on the implementation of the ECTS and on the implementation of student and teacher mobility between member states. They also provide HEIs with current information about the progress of the Bologna Process. Under the terms of the Process, HEIs are encouraged to develop courses whose content reflects a European perspective, and to engage in partnership activities with HEIs from other member states, including, for example, collaboration in creating joint provision of degrees by institutions in two different member states. *See also* BRUGES–COPENHAGEN PROCESS.

borderline Used to describe a *grade or score arrived at in the *assessment of a candidate's work or performance, which falls on the dividing line between two grades or categories. Thus, if the candidate needed to achieve at least a mark of 40 per cent in order to gain a pass grade, and was awarded 39–41 per cent, they may be said to be a borderline case. Similarly, if the candidate needed to gain 70 per cent in two consecutive pieces of work in order to achieve a distinction, but gained 69 per cent in one and 71 per cent in the other, their work may be said to be a borderline distinction. Such borderline work is often double-marked, *moderated, offered for the consideration of an external examiner, or all three of these, in order to ensure the reliability of the final assessment decision.

Bourdieu, Pierre (1930–2002) A prominent French cultural anthropologist and sociologist whose work covered a wide area of research interests ranging from considerations of cultural taste to the function of education. Bourdieu was interested in how cultural and social understanding and values are transmitted in educational contexts from one generation to the next. Much of the groundwork for his ideas and approach was developed during the Algerian War of Independence (1958–62) when, while serving in the French army, he undertook ethnographic research into Algerian peasant communities. This shaped his desire to focus his approach to research on actual lived experience rather than simply on theory.

One of Bourdieu's principal concerns was to examine the experience and processes of learning. He was interested in how we, as individuals, navigate our lives, making choices, encountering forces which might inhibit these choices, and experiencing hierarchical power relationships which imply symbolic values. This involved an exploration of how unequal and competitive power relationships continue from one generation to the next. Bourdieu sought to find a middle ground between the more objectivist conception of *ideology as a purely external force that constrains and determines human subjectivity of **Louis Althusser** (1918–90), and the emphasis of **Jean-Paul Sartre** (1905–80) upon the power of the agent voluntarily to create meaningful social action, ignoring the influence of constraining external forces.

The two main concepts which distinguish Bourdieu's work are **habitus** and **field**. What is crucial to Bourdieu's theory is that these two concepts work together and, doing so, explain the relationship between the subjective agent and the objectifying external force. 'Habitus' refers to the 'feel for the game' that agents acquire through the lifelong process of learning and socialization: these are the flexible 'cultural competencies' which serve to account for both the stability of the social order and the transformations that initiate cultural change. When a student arrives in a new class at university, she will bring with her a very particular set of cultural competencies learned in various contexts: these might range from her family, to the various cultural texts and genres she has experienced, to perhaps the most immediately relevant, the previous school she attended. If she had been studying English literature, she might perhaps have a feel for how we might study a play or a poem; she might have learned some of the critical terms used. What she will be confronted with on that first day at university is a whole range of cultural competencies yet to be learned.

If 'habitus' accounts for the agent, 'field' accounts for the objectivity of any given situation. According to Bourdieu, society is made up of a structured set of relatively autonomous fields such as politics, economics, and education. Each field is characterized by a set of cultural and political relationships that exist between the positions occupied by the agents within it. For Bourdieu, these fields are not as rigid as a fixed structure but are flexible as they interact with the agents within them. Power relationships are maintained or reproduced, and to an extent transformed, by the agents operating within them. Thus, agents operating in these 'fields' are in competition over the resources available (material and symbolic), and success in competing is dependent on the agent's cultural 'capital' or 'competence'. For instance, in the educational field, there will be other fields within it such as *primary, *secondary, *tertiary, and higher education, and each of these will compete for resources or funding. Even within a particular institution there will be different faculties such as the humanities, the sciences, or business, with academics competing for funding and pre-eminence in their chosen fields.

In *Homo Academicus*, first published in 1984, Bourdieu conducted research into the intellectual landscape of French university teachers, a world in which he, too, worked. He delved into the social background and practical activities of his contemporaries, examining their social origins, how much they published and where, what their connections were within the institution as well as in the media, and what their political involvements were. In doing so, Bourdieu related the issue of reputations within the intellectual map of France to the distribution of power and capital. He was an influential academic in his day, and his methods of research and his ideas about education continue to inform current concerns regarding educational funding and the relationship between education and the needs of the market. He held the post of Director of Studies at the École Pratique des Hautes Études from 1964, and the Chair of Sociology at the Collège de France from 1981.   CH

Brain Gym An educational programme based on using physical movement to develop an integrated and coordinated approach to learning, using not only cognition, but also physical and sensory skills. Known as Educational Kinesiology because of its emphasis on movement, this approach was originally developed in the United States to support the learning of children and adults with learning difficulties such as *dyslexia or *attention deficit hyperactivity disorder. It is used in some schools to help raise standards of pupil learning, *behaviour, and attention; and is also used outside education by some adults as a means of stress management or memory improvement. The idea that such exercises can effectively improve brain function have, however, come under criticism and have been accused of being based upon 'bad science'. The terms 'Brain Gym' and 'Educational Kinesiology' are both registered trademarks.

(⊕) SEE WEB LINKS
• Provides further information on this approach to learning.

brainstorming A means of generating ideas, often by a group of people, whereby immediate responses are written down and collected uncritically and without editing so as not to impede the creative process. These can then be explored and considered at more leisure in order to identify what is useful. It can be used as a *method for teaching and supporting learning, either when learners are working in small groups and recording their own ideas; or when a teacher is working with a larger group, encouraging all to contribute ideas, and writing them on a board or flip chart. There have been objections from some to the use of the term 'brainstorm' on the grounds that it may cause offence to sufferers from epilepsy. Various expressions, including 'thought shower', have been suggested as an alternative. Although 'brainstorm' remains in common usage, teachers may wish to ascertain, before using it, whether such use will cause offence to any of their learners.

British Association for the Advancement of Science *See* BRITISH SCIENCE ASSOCIATION.

British Baccalaureate *See* ENGLISH BACCALAUREAT.

British Council Set up in 1934, and operating under its current name from 1936, the Council's purpose is to promote a wider knowledge of the United Kingdom and of the English language overseas, and to support and develop cultural relations between the UK and other countries. It is funded through the Foreign and Commonwealth Office, and is best known for its work in teaching English as a second language and providing education in developing countries. Its full title is the British Council for Relations with Other Countries.

((⊕)) SEE WEB LINKS
• Provides details of the British Council's role in relation to education.

British Educational Research Association (BERA) An association open to all educational professionals and those working in related fields which aims to promote and sustain a professional research culture with the purpose of informing policy and practice. BERA provides a forum for communication, dissemination, and debate, and supports the professional development of educational researchers. It holds events for researchers, including an annual conference, and publishes current research in the *British Educational Research Journal*.

((⊕)) SEE WEB LINKS
• An account of the history and purpose of BERA.

British Education Index (BEI) A database, updated quarterly, which lists all papers on education which have appeared in British academic *journals, web sites, and periodicals. Papers and articles are analysed and listed according to subject matter. The BEI is also available in hard copy as a quarterly journal and as a CD-ROM. Maintained within the library of

Leeds University and available by subscription only, it is a key resource
in educational *research.

(⊕) SEE WEB LINKS

• A list of the journals indexed by the BEI.

British Science Association (BSA) Established in 1831, previously known
as the British Association for the Advancement of Science, and commonly
referred to simply as the British Association, this registered charity aims to
promote public understanding of science and to ensure that scientific
developments have a positive impact upon society. Its board of trustees acts as
a governing council. In addition to its central office in London, there are
approximately 30 local branches of the British Association throughout the
United Kingdom. Early members of the Association were responsible for coining
the term 'scientist'. Among other activities, it organizes an annual Festival of
Science and a National Science and Engineering Week.

(⊕) SEE WEB LINKS

• An account of the history of the BSA.

Bruges–Copenhagen Process An initiative by governments of the
European Union member countries to create a policy of Europe-wide
cooperation in vocational education and training designed to develop an
enhanced knowledge-based economy and to ensure that the European labour
market is open to all. The Process has two main thrusts: to establish recognition
and transparency in the standards and content of vocational qualifications, and
compatibility between the qualification frameworks of member states; and to
introduce measures for quality assurance in relation to mutually recognized
qualifications. The overall purpose of the Process is to facilitate the mobility of
qualified workers between the member states of the EU, and, to this end, the
measures taken are aimed at making it possible for employers in any member
country to understand clearly the level and scope of the qualifications possessed
by a job applicant from any other participating country in the EU. This emphasis
on workforce mobility makes the Bruges–Copenhagen Process an important
component of the EU's *Lisbon Strategy, which aims to improve the
competitiveness and status of the European economy. The Process itself
originates with an agreement by representatives of EU member states in Bruges
in 2001 to move towards a greater degree of transparency and cooperation over
vocational education and training. This was followed by a signed declaration by
member states in Copenhagen in 2002. The Bruges–Copenhagen Process
followed the example of the initiative established earlier to promote a European
framework for higher education, now known as the *Bologna Process.

Bruner, Jerome (b. 1915) An American psychologist who continues to exert
an influence on education and the development of curriculum theory. In his
work on cognitive psychology, Bruner's interest in the cognitive development of
children and how they represent ideas has drawn him to consider the cultural,
environmental, and experiential factors influencing the process of education, as

set out in his work *The Process of Education* (1960). In the early 1970s Bruner continued his research at Oxford University into the question of infant agency and began a series of explorations into children's language, establishing the concept of LADs (language acquisition devices) and LASSes (language acquisition support systems), which help to explain the nature of cultural–linguistic development. The emphasis on talk as a 'scaffold' to successful learning was influenced by *Vygotsky and demonstrates 'how learning shapes the mind ... [providing] us with the toolkit by which we construct not only our worlds but our very conception of ourselves and our powers' (Bruner 1996).

Bruner sees learning as an active process in which learners construct new understanding based on past knowledge. These accommodated *schemas reflect the cognitive theories of *Piaget but are expanded to encompass the social and cultural aspects of learning. Bruner has more recently worked with the *pedagogistas* in *Reggio Emilia, where children are recognized as competent learners who actively contribute to the emerging curriculum through the encouragement of dialogue, narrative, problem-solving, and documentation—all devices to support the development of the ways in which children and adults make internal sense of the world as a shared construction.

In *The Process of Education*, Bruner presents four key themes: the role of structure in learning and how it may be made central in teaching; readiness for learning and the spiral curriculum; intuitive and analytical thinking (through shared and sustained dialogue); and motives for learning. These themes have been explored further by Donald Schön (1930–97) and Howard Gardner (b. 1943), who have looked at ways in which teachers and schools might create ideal conditions for learners to be able to use their individual *learning style and type of *intelligence to create meaning.

Bruner's cognitive approach to his work in the *early years phase of childhood has made him a key figure in educational theory in the United States and United Kingdom. His three modes of instruction—enactive, iconic, and symbolic—have been interpreted and developed most recently into visual, auditory, and kinaesthetic (VAK) teaching methods, and have informed Gardner's theory of *multiple intelligences.   AW

Further Reading: J. Bruner *Actual Minds, Possible Worlds: The Jerusalem Harvard Lectures* (Harvard University Press, 2009).
S. Smidt *Introducing Bruner: A Guide for Practitioners and Students in Early Years Education* (Routledge, 2013).

BTEC National *See* BUSINESS AND TECHNOLOGY EDUCATION COUNCIL.

bulge A sharp rise in the number of pupils or students reaching a particular stage in the education system at any one time. It was coined as a term to describe the demographic phenomenon following the end of the Second World War, when birth rates rose sharply, creating a succession of unusually large cohorts of pupils which proceeded through the various stages of schooling and *higher education in the 1950s and 1960s. The existing number of teachers and the available classroom space in state schools was insufficient to meet this demand. However, when the bulge had moved through the system and the number of children entering compulsory education began to fall, schools found themselves with a surplus of teachers, while local authorities were, in some cases, forced to close down schools for lack of pupils. Some educationalists saw this as an opportunity for introducing smaller *pupil–teacher ratios for the benefit of the pupils; but in policy terms the problem was viewed as financial and addressed accordingly with a reduction in teaching posts and classroom space.

bullying The Elton Report on discipline (1989) confirmed that bullying in school was widespread. It recommended greater vigilance on the part of teachers to identify and address such pupil behaviour. Nevertheless, bullying has continued to present a problem in many schools and other educational institutions, although it is difficult to quantify, on the one hand because victims are often reluctant to come forward, and on the other because of a continuing lack of awareness about exactly what behaviours constitute bullying. All schools, colleges, and universities are required to have an anti-bullying policy, which will normally also cover the bullying of teachers by other teachers or managers. The policy must conform to the Equality Act 2006, which makes some forms of bullying—for example, on the grounds of sexual orientation or religious beliefs—liable to prosecution. In extreme cases which have been reported, bullying at school has led to pupils attempting or committing suicide. As a result, a number of organizations, such as ChildLine, offer advice and support for victims of bullying, while web sites such as Bullying UK, Donthideit, and the unfortunately named Bully OnLine have been designed specifically to help victims by offering definitions of bullying behaviour and encouraging them to report incidents. Since the use of mobile phones and social networking sites has become widespread, various forms of **cyberbullying** have developed, which are more difficult for teachers to see and prevent. These include the sending of malicious texts and 'trolling'—the anti-social practice of sowing discord through the use of networking sites which may include abusing or encouraging the victimization of individuals. Growing concerns about all types of bullying are reflected in the fact that in 2007 an anti-bullying week was introduced; and that a government web site has been set up to address bullying at school, which presents advice to schools in relation to their mandatory duty to address the issue. This includes reminders that all schools should cover cyberbullying in their anti-bullying policy; that the curriculum should cover instruction in the dangers of new technologies; that schools must monitor all on-site electronic communication, and extend this to off-site communication if this involves a school activity; that they must have a clear policy on phone use within school; that they should employ Internet blocking technologies where appropriate; and that security systems such as firewalls should be in place to prevent information about pupils or staff from being accessed from outside the school.

(((⊕))) SEE WEB LINKS
• Provides definitions of bullying and explains schools' responsibilities in relation to the law.

bunching Used to describe a situation where marks or grades awarded to assessed work show very little variance from student to student, but are closely bunched within a few marks of one another. This could indicate either that the ability of the students within the group being assessed is fairly uniform, or, more worryingly, that the *assessment may be invalid or unreliable. If there is bunching at the lower end of the marking scale, this may indicate a problem either with the selection and recruitment of students, or with the quality of the teaching, or with the effectiveness of the learning.

Burnham scale A single national pay scale for teachers in primary and secondary schools. It takes its name from Lord Burnham, who, in 1919, chaired the committee which devised a national pay scale for teachers in elementary schools. Subsequently, the Burnham Committee was tasked with drawing up a scale for secondary school teachers and for those in further education. As a consequence, the agreement of the single national scale in 1945 was known as the Burnham Agreement.

bursary A grant or financial award offered by an institution such as a *university or private school to help students pay their tuition fees or other expenses related to their course of study. A limited number of bursaries are available at any one institution in any one year, and students must make an application stating their case if they wish to be considered. University bursaries are usually offered to support studies in specific subject areas, or for specific awards, such as a *master's degree. Trainee teachers on school-focused *Postgraduate Certificate of Education *initial teacher training programmes may also access bursaries.

In Scotland eligibility for bursaries may be assessed on individual students' circumstances or may be awarded on successful achievement of an academic standard, and can be available to assist with travel and living expenses, or other costs incurred through study. They are available through individual institutions or through the Student Awards Agency for Scotland (SAAS).

(⊕) SEE WEB LINKS
• Details of bursaries available through the Student Awards Agency for Scotland.

Business and Technology Education Council (BTEC) An *awarding body for the *further education sector formed in 1974 as a result of a merger between the Business Education Council (BEC) and the Technician Education Council (TEC). It now operates under the name of Edexcel and, having taken over the examination of the General Certificate of Education (GCE) *Advanced Level (A level) and General Certificate of Secondary Education (GCSE), formerly carried out by the University of London Schools' Examination Board in 1995, it is now one of the three unitary awarding bodies which offer both *academic and *vocational qualifications in both the schools and the further education sectors. During the 1980s and early 1990s BTEC awards in a range of general vocational areas such as business studies and sports studies formed one of the few alternative progression routes into higher education available to those who did not choose to study for GCE A levels. A BTEC First Diploma claimed equivalence with four or five good GCSE passes, and provided a means of progression to either A levels or a BTEC National Diploma, which some *universities accepted, at distinction level, for the purpose of university entry, as the equivalent of two sound A level passes. On the introduction of the General National Vocational Qualification (GNVQ) in 1993, BTEC initially resisted allowing their qualifications to be subsumed under the GNVQ umbrella; and it is a measure of its reputation that many providers continued to refer to these BTEC qualifications by their original BTEC titles even after they had been endorsed as GNVQs. In some vocational areas, the qualifications remained as BTEC National awards, while others, such as the BTEC National Health and Social Care, have survived the demise of the GNVQ to re-emerge with the original BTEC title.

business education *See* BUSINESS AND TECHNOLOGY EDUCATION COUNCIL; BUSINESS STUDIES.

business studies A *curriculum subject which focuses on business-related topics such as marketing, organizational structures, business legislation, finance, and human resource management. Courses and awards are available at most levels, including at General Certificate of Secondary Education (GCSE), General Certificate of Education (GCE), *Advanced Level, degree, and postgraduate levels. A well-established subject in further education colleges from the 1970s onwards, it has more recently been included in the curriculum of some secondary schools, particularly as an option in Year 12. It is classed as a *vocational subject, and was one of the most popular options for students enrolling on a General Certificate of National Vocational Qualifications in the 1990s. Business is now a key vocational area in the *Applied General Qualifications (AGQs). *See also* BUSINESS AND TECHNOLOGY EDUCATION COUNCIL.

Butler Act The name by which the *Education Act 1944 is popularly known. The reforms enacted in this legislation were largely attributed to R. A. Butler (1902–82), who was at that time President of the Board of Education, and with whose name the Act was associated. This legislation is an important milestone in education policy and reform. It established the three progressive stages or sectors of education with which we are now familiar: *primary, secondary, and *further education. It was also responsible for the introduction of the *Eleven Plus, and the system of selecting pupils at the end of the primary stage of their schooling in order that they should receive the education or training which was judged best suited to their ability and their aptitude. The three routes of schooling provided—the grammar schools, the (secondary) modern schools, and the technical schools—were described as having *'parity of esteem', an early use of this phrase, which has since become a familiar part of policy rhetoric. The Act also replaced the Board of Education with a more powerful **Ministry of Education**, whose Minister was empowered to enforce the statutory duties of *local education authorities. This Act was not superseded until the passing of the Education Act 1988.

BYOD (bring your own device) The practice of encouraging learners to connect their personally owned device, such as smartphone, iPad, or tablet, to the Wi-Fi network of their school, college, or university for the purpose of learning. Also known as BYOT (bring your own technology), this strategy is not simply a response to budget constraints but has clear advantages in terms of supporting learning. It allows the student to learn on the device with which they are most familiar and comfortable; it promotes personalized learning; and it enables students to benefit from the advantages of *blended learning. Drawbacks, however, include issues of equity and security.

campus The grounds and buildings of a school, university, or college. The expressions 'on-campus' and 'off-campus' are used to indicate whether a location or event is situated on university premises or away from them respectively. Some institutions operate across a number of campuses, with students and teachers travelling between different sites. This is sometimes referred to as **split-site provision**. The word 'campus' is the Latin for 'field', and seems to have been first used in its current sense in the United States.

capitation Funding which is calculated literally 'per head'. Prior to the *Education Act 1988 and the introduction of devolved budgets, *local authorities would provide *maintained schools with a capitation allowance for the purchase of resources, calculated on the number of pupils on roll. Devolved funding to schools is also calculated on the basis of capitation.

Career Entry and Development Profile (CEDP) Trainee and newly qualified teachers (NQTs) are required to fill in a CEDP, in consultation with their tutor or mentor, at three 'transition points' in their development. The first is towards the end of their initial teacher training (ITT), the second and third at the beginning and end of the *induction process. The profile sets out their goals, their achievements, and their development needs. The school which employs the NQT can refer to the CDP in order to set objectives for the induction period in order to ensure that the NQT reaches the required induction standards. The statutory requirements for ITT state that all providers of ITT must ensure that trainee teachers have a CEDP and are supported in completing it.

Careers Wales An all-age careers guidance service for Wales which draws together the skills provided by adult guidance networks, including the national telephone helpline *Learndirect and some elements of the **Youth Gateway**, which provides links between education, business, and specialist assessment and support services for young people. The interactive web site has been live since November 2004.   HG

(🌐) SEE WEB LINKS
• The web site for Careers Wales.

case study Although it has a number of meanings outside an educational context, a case study, in terms of teaching and learning, is a *method of developing learners' understanding by enabling them to engage actively with a problem or issue relevant to their studies. It presents an account or a scenario, either fictional or real, which allows the student to apply what they have learned and make sense of it in a realistic context. It may also encourage the student to draw on their own ideas, experience, and *tacit knowledge. The case study is a method or resource which encourages active, rather than passive, learning.

In the context of education *research, however, a case study has a different meaning and purpose, and is usually understood as a means of conducting a small-scale investigation (literally, a study of a specific case) in order to explore a theory or research question.

catchment The area around the school, college, or university from which it draws its learners. The *Education Act 1980 permitted parents to state a preference for the school which their child would attend. The Education Act 1988 required schools to comply with parental preference as long as they had places to offer. These two Acts changed the pattern of enrolment from one in which secondary schools drew their intake almost entirely from the *primary schools in their catchment area, to one in which they may recruit pupils from other areas and even other *local authorities. Conversely, many universities, which traditionally have enrolled students from all parts of the country, are noting, since the introduction of tuition *fees, a rising trend of applications from students living locally, possibly influenced by the fact that it is less expensive for students to remain living in the parental home.

Catholic maintained schools Schools in Northern Ireland which are owned by the Roman Catholic Church through a system of trustees, and managed by a board of governors. The education and *library boards provide funding and direct the employment of non-teaching staff. Teachers are employed by the Council for Catholic Maintained Schools. *See also* DENOMINATION; FAITH SCHOOLS. JH

CAT score *See* BASELINE ASSESSMENT.

Centre for Educational Research and Innovation (CERI) The Centre's purpose is to support the promotion and development of educational *research and the trialling of innovations. Founded in 1968 as part of the Organization for Economic Cooperation and Development, it works to promote cooperation in educational research and development between member countries.

Centre for Excellence in Leadership (CEL) Created in 2003 as part of the *Success for All initiative, CEL's role was to support the development of leadership skills in the *further education and training sector, particularly in further education (FE) colleges, but also in work-based learning provision, offender learning, and adult and community provision. The 2006 *White Paper *Further Education: *Raising Skills, Improving Life Chances* widened its remit to include the introduction of a mandatory qualification for principals of FE colleges, and a strategy for improving quality of provision in that sector. It is now subsumed under the *National College for Teaching and Leadership.

Centre for Policy Studies (CPS) A right-wing pressure group which is often outspoken in its criticism of the education system.

Centre of Vocational Excellence (COVE) A further education (FE) *college or other training provider which is judged to provide high-quality specialist *work-based learning in a specific vocational area. Thus, an FE college might become a COVE for Construction and the Built Environment, for example. The programme was launched in 2001 with the aim of improving the further education sector's capacity to provide *vocational training of a high quality in response to employers' needs.

Certificate in Education and Training (CET) *See* FURTHER EDUCATION TEACHING QUALIFICATIONS.

Certificate of Education (Cert. Ed.) A non-graduate teaching qualification, now applicable only to teachers training for *qualified teacher learning and skills status for the *post-compulsory sector. Courses leading to Cert. Ed. accreditation are normally offered by universities and involve a significant number of hours of practical teaching in a college of *further education or other provider of vocational education and training. The alternative, and competing, qualifications offered within the further education sector itself are the **Certificate in Education and Training** and the **Diploma in Education and Training**. *See also* FURTHER EDUCATION TEACHING QUALIFICATIONS.

Certificate of Secondary Education (CSE) A school-leaving qualification introduced in 1965 as an alternative to the *General Certificate of Education *Ordinary Level (O level) for those candidates for whom O levels were considered too demanding. At the time, it was claimed that a grade 1 CSE was equivalent to an O level for the purpose of progression to employment or to further study. Thus, school-leavers in possession of grade 1 CSEs in English and mathematics were able to use them as equivalent currency to O levels in these subjects. There was a view among many teachers and pupils at the time, however, that a grade 1 at CSE was more difficult to achieve than a grade C at O level. Like the O level, the CSE was replaced in 1988 by the *General Certificate of Secondary Education.

Certificate of Sixth Year Studies (CSYS) Before 2002 a sixth year study qualification was the highest level of qualification available in a Scottish school. Undertaken in the sixth year of schooling, the qualification was roughly equivalent to an English *General Certificate of Education *Advanced Level, but with elements of *undergraduate level study. It was replaced in 2002 by the *Advanced Higher.   SM

certification The awarding of a certificate which confirms achievement in an *examination or course of study.

challenging behaviour *See* BEHAVIOUR; DISRUPTIVE.

charitable status Some private schools have claimed charitable status, which has allowed them to benefit from certain taxation exemptions. However, since 2002 schools which claim such status have been permitted to retain it only on the condition that they can demonstrate that the school operates to the benefit of the public.

chartered teacher Traditionally the term for fully *qualified teacher status in Scotland. Completion of teacher training concluded in the award of a 'parchment'; hence the term 'chartered'.   SM

(⊕) SEE WEB LINKS
• The web site of the General Teaching Council for Scotland, which provides detailed information on achieving qualified teacher status in Scotland.
• Sets out questions and answers about the current chartered teacher grade.

Child and Adolescent Mental Health Services (CAMHS) A community-based service for young people who have mental health difficulties. CAMHS often supports young people together with other members of their families. It is a multi-professional service which includes psychiatrists and psychologists, social workers, and nurses. CAMHS work is linked closely with schools, particularly through educational psychologists and educational welfare staff. It offers support and guidance to young people involved in substance misuse including drugs and alcohol as well as mental health problems. Children between the ages of 0 and 14 are supported by child mental health teams.   TB, LE

child-centred A conceptual framework for education, popularized in the 1960s as a result of the *Plowden Report (1967), in which children's personal, social, physical, and learning needs were to be at the centre of the education process. This was not a new idea and can be traced back to the educational philosophy of *Rousseau, *Dewey, *Montessori, *Isaacs, *Piaget, and *Erikson. Child-centredness identifies children as unique and special who deserve an education appropriate to their individual needs, rather than a prescribed formal curriculum defined by *behaviourist and narrow models of teaching.
    The following notions are central to child-centred education theories:
• education should meet the needs of those being educated;
• these needs are best met if identified with the interests of children;
• the curriculum should be based on experience and discovery;
• rather than being subject- or content-based, educational programmes should focus on activity.

There were, and are, critics of child-centred *ideology who claim that to cater for all individual children's needs might be to embrace learner autonomy to the point of anarchy and an absence of taught and learned curriculum. However, the experiential and active learning *pedagogy of *early years teachers reflects a commitment to encouraging children to be independent, creative, responsible, and autonomous, recognizing their competences and supporting the construction of knowledge through social facilitation rather than didactic teaching. This is reflected in *Reggio Emilia pre-schools and within the *Te Whaariki curriculum. Furthermore, the UK government has embraced child-centred ideology within their *personalized learning agenda and

*Assessment for Learning as set out in the Primary National Strategy (Excellence and Enjoyment, 2003), encouraging teachers to plan for the needs of individual children within their classrooms. *See also* LEARNER-CENTRED.   AW

(∰) SEE WEB LINKS
• Lists the guiding principles of child-centred education.

childminder A registered carer providing play and learning opportunities for children within a home setting. Inspected annually by the Early Years Directorate of *Ofsted against national day care standards, a childminder usually looks after children under 5 in their own home, but can also look after older children before or after school and during school holidays. Childminders have a duty to follow the guidelines for the *Early Years Foundation Stage for children aged 0–5, and the statutory ratio for adult:child as specified in national standards. The majority of childminders are self-employed, but they can be employed by *local authorities to look after vulnerable children at risk of neglect or abuse. Qualifications are not necessary, but many childminders belong to a self-support network and work towards a level 3 Certificate in Childminding Practice.   AW

Children Act 1989 Statutory legislation which defined orders with respect to the welfare of children in the following areas:
• reform of the law relating to children;
• provision for children in need;
• amendments to the law with regards to fostering, children's homes, *childminding, day care, and adoption;
• children in family proceedings;
• *local authority support for children and families, including *looked-after children;
• care and supervision orders and powers of the court;
• protection of children;
• statutory supervisory functions and responsibilities.

This Act brought together, under one framework, a whole raft of legislation with regard to children, young people, and the law over the previous half-century. It was superseded by the *Children Act 2004.   AW

(∰) SEE WEB LINKS
• Provides an overview of the Children Act 1989.

Children Act 2004 This Act superseded the *Children Act 1989 and sets out a legislative spine for the government's wider strategy in England and Wales, for improving children's lives, covering universal and parental responsibility, the *Every Child Matters agenda, services accessed by children, and the targeted services for those with additional needs. The aim of this Act was to legislate for and encourage multi-disciplinary working and delegate responsibility to local authorities to implement the provisions outlined. Following the *Education Act 2005, schools undergoing inspections by *Ofsted were judged not only against quality of teaching but also against the principles set out in this 2004 Children Act.

SEE WEB LINKS
• Provides the full text of the Children Act 2004.

children's centres The centres are places where children under 5 and their families can receive 'seamless' holistic and integrated services and information, and where they can access help from multi-disciplinary teams of professionals. The core offer includes integrated early learning, care, family support, health services, and outreach support for those not attending the centre. High-quality teacher input is also one of the core components of a children's centre. The children centres were at the heart of a government ten-year strategy (2000–10) to deliver better outcomes for children and families. The centres built on the success of Sure Start local programmes, early excellence centres, and neighbourhood nurseries developed since 1997. Children's centres are based in the 20 per cent most disadvantaged *local authority wards in England. With the end of the Sure Start initiative the centres came under threat due to financial restraints, although the National Children's Bureau argues for their continuation.
AW

SEE WEB LINKS
• The web site of the National Children's Bureau which provides information about the debate over children's centres.

choice The issue of parental choice in decisions about their child's schooling has been a key feature of education policy and debate since the 1980s. The *Education Act 1980 permitted parents to state a preference for the school which their child would attend; and the Education Act 1988 took this further by requiring schools to comply with parental preference as long as there were places to offer. These two Acts allow parents to express a choice over their child's schooling, even to the extent that the preferred school might be some distance away and in a different *local authority from that in which the child lives. The principle of choice was an integral part of the introduction of *market competition into the schooling system. By expressing a choice, parents were able to indicate those schools for which there was a market demand, and at the same time provide an incentive to less popular schools to improve their performance in order to be able to compete for pupils. The word 'choice' became prominent in educational policy discourse, appearing, for example, in the title of the 1992 *White Paper *Choice and Diversity*. In September 1995 the *Secretary of State for Education, Gillian Shephard, was quoted as saying, 'We must emphasise the words that people find attractive, such as standards, discipline, and choice' (*The Guardian*, 19 September, 6). The concept of parental choice, however, remains a much-debated one. Those schools which have thrived as a result of market competition, and are fully subscribed or oversubscribed, are now in a position where it is they, rather than parents, who are able to exert an element of choice over which pupils they enter on their rolls. *See also* SCHOOL ADMISSIONS.

CILT, the National Centre for Languages Operates as a centre of expertise whose purpose is to promote and disseminate good practice in the teaching of languages in order to raise levels of capability nationally, across all age groups and sectors. It was established in 2003 as the result of a merger between the Centre for Information on Language Teaching and the Languages National Training Organization as part of the National Languages Strategy. It offers support to businesses and language services, as well as to teachers and learners, and is financed partly by central government grants and public funding for specific projects.

(⊕) SEE WEB LINKS
• Provides further details of CILT's role.

circular The formal means by which the government department responsible for education communicates its guidance to *local authorities. Circulars are signed by the *Secretary of State or the Permanent Secretary.

citizenship Citizenship education became a compulsory part of the *national curriculum in 2002 at *Key Stages 3 and 4, with non-statutory guidelines for citizenship in Key Stages 1 and 2. In September 2013 the national curriculum programmes for citizenship were disapplied, leaving schools free to devise their own citizenship curriculum in line with the needs of their pupils until the introduction of new national curriculum programmes in 2014.

city academy *See* ACADEMY.

City and Guilds *See* AWARDING BODY.

class 1. A collective noun for learners, used to refer to a group of pupils or students taught together. Used in this sense, we find such expressions as 'top of the class' and *'class size'. In secondary schools, the term may be used synonymously with **form**. In schools, classes usually consist of pupils of the same age, except in those minority of *primary schools where *vertical grouping is applied.
    2. May be used synonymously with *lesson, as in 'After break, the pupils have their geography class'.
    3. Denotes level of achievement in an *honours degree, which may be awarded at first, upper second, lower second, or third class. *See also* PUPIL–TEACHER RATIO.

class, social *See* SOCIAL CLASS.

classroom assistant *See* TEACHING ASSISTANT.

class size Recent research designed to discover whether there is a correlation between the number of learners in a class and levels of attainment has produced conflicting findings. Common sense suggests that the smaller the class, the more time and attention the teacher will be able to devote to each individual learner, and therefore the more effective the learning. However, recent government-funded research in the UK calls this assumption into question. For example, a study of pupil progress in over 200 primary schools conducted between 2002 and 2003 found that, although pupils aged 8–11 in larger classes receive less individual attention from the teacher, this has no measurable effect on their attainment in any subject, which is more likely to be affected by the economic circumstances of their home background, children from poorer homes making least progress. Similarly, a government-funded review of international research into the effects of class size on pupil achievement concludes that it has less impact on learning than the level of skill and experience possessed by teachers.

Research carried out in America, on the other hand, suggests that small class sizes in the first four years of schooling can lead to higher attainment by the time the pupil reaches secondary education. A report in the *Economic Journal* (January 2001) on research carried out at Princeton University presented findings which showed that pupils taught in smaller classes during the primary phase of their education were more likely to go on eventually to apply for *higher education, and that smaller classes were of particular benefit in raising the attainment of pupils from impoverished backgrounds and from minority groups. The positive impact of reduced class size on the learning of the very youngest pupils, particularly in literacy, is also reflected in a 2000 research report from the London Institute of Education, based on a study of 300 schools.

Class sizes in state schools in the UK, both primary and secondary, tend to be larger than those in other developed countries, and figures suggest no immediate trend towards reduction, having recently remained fairly static. For example, between 1996 and 2000 the average class size across all state schools was around 28 pupils to every teacher. Between 1985 and 2005, however, the average number of pupils in each class in the UK's fee-paying schools fell from almost 14 pupils to 10. There is no statutory maximum class size beyond *Key Stage 1 in the UK, except in Scotland, where there is an upper limit pledge of 18 pupils per class in primary 1 and primary 3. *See also* INDEPENDENT SCHOOL; PUPIL–TEACHER RATIO.

Further Reading: P. Blatchford *The Class Size Debate: Is Small Better?* (Open University Press, 2003) explores both sides of the debate.

clearing *See* UNIVERSITIES AND COLLEGES ADMISSIONS SERVICE.

Closing the Gap Also known as 'Narrowing the Gap', this is a project which seeks to close the educational achievement gap between children from disadvantaged backgrounds and their peers. Focused largely on research, its aim is to generate evidence-based strategies for effectively raising the achievement levels of socially disadvantaged pupils. *See also* ATTAINMENT GAP; SOCIAL CLASS.

(⊕) SEE WEB LINKS
• Lists relevant research projects and findings.

coach Someone who provides advice to help a learner improve their performance. For example, a pupil might be provided with coaching to help them improve their examination performance or their game of tennis. The distinction between coaching and *mentoring sometimes appears unclear;

and on occasion the two terms are used interchangeably. As a rule, coaching suggests a more restricted role than mentoring, often time-constrained and tightly focused on performance.

co-constructed learning An approach which involves teachers, pupils, and sometimes other professionals working together to develop learning content and processes in schools. In empowering the learner in this way it challenges the concept of teacher as 'deliverer' of the *curriculum and learner as passive recipient. Examples of co-constructed learning in practice might include the implementation of *peer assessment and pupils having a voice in the choice or sequence of project topics.

(()) SEE WEB LINKS
• Provides further examples of the co-constructed learning approach.

Code of Practice (CoP) A framework which provides practical advice to local authorities, maintained schools, early years settings, and others on carrying out their statutory duties to identify, assess, and make provision for children and young people's special educational need (SEN). The first CoP came into effect in 1994 and has been changed, following consultation, to the new Code, which has been effective since January 2002. It includes new rights and duties introduced by the Special Educational Needs and Disability Act 2001. The CoP document includes guidance under the headings of principles and policies, working in partnership with parents, pupil participation, identification, assessment and provision in all educational settings from early years to the secondary sector, statutory assessment of SEN, statements of SEN, and annual reviews. Working in partnership with other agencies is also addressed. Within the foreword of the document is information regarding the status and implementation of the CoP. It describes the implementation and monitoring guidelines, and information about the process of SEN tribunals which deal with appeals from parents. Relevant regulations and guidance on inclusion are also set out. There is also clear instruction concerning the Disability Rights Code of Practice for Schools.

   The advice clearly defines SEN and tracks the development of the CoP through changes in various *Education Acts and *Children Acts. Roles and responsibilities are outlined with regard to principles and policy and working in partnership with parents. The Code also has a comprehensive glossary. All settings which must have regard for the Code of Practice for SEN should demonstrate that they have referred to the framework when developing their own policies and practice for the identification, assessment, and provision for all children and young people who have SEN.

co-education The teaching of girls and boys together in the same school and the same class. Whereas *primary education has generally always been co-educational (although up to the 1950s there were often separate entrance doors for boys and girls), it was often the case in the first two-thirds of the 20th century that boys and girls would attend separate schools for their secondary education. Since the *Education Act 1944 (*Butler Act) the trend has been towards co-educational secondary provision. Some researchers suggest that boys achieve better in mixed (co-educational) classes, while girls may achieve more highly, particularly in science subjects, in single-sex schools. *See also* GENDER.

cognition and learning needs Pupils with cognition and learning needs are those who have difficulty with language, memory, reasoning, organizational or motor skills. They may include those with severe or specific learning difficulties such as *dyslexia; difficulties associated with *autistic spectrum disorder; and physical or behavioural difficulties. Such difficulties entitle pupils to additional or specialist support in schools. *See also* SPECIAL EDUCATIONAL NEEDS (SEN).

cognitive 1. One of the three domains of learning (the others being *affective and *psychomotor) and denoting that area of learning which is to do with **thinking** (cognition) and understanding. *See also* KNOWLEDGE.
2. A branch of *learning theory concerned with how and why learning takes place, which argues that thinking is central to the learning process. **Cognitivists** argue that learning is not, as *behaviourists claim, simply a matter of behaviour modification, but involves the student gaining *knowledge not only through the acquisition of new learning, but also through a process of adapting or discarding old constructs or ideas which no longer fit their developing insight into the world. Cognitivist learning theory argues for a *learner-centred approach to teaching and learning, where the structuring and sequencing of learning is of key importance to the success of the learning experience. It suggests that knowledge is not an object to be dispensed or acquired, but a process. In terms of learning theory, two of the most widely recognized names among the cognitivists are Dewey and Bruner.

Cognitive Abilities Test (CAT) A *test used by some schools to assess the reasoning skills of *Key Stage 3 pupils. The test consists of three parts: verbal, quantitative, and non-verbal reasoning. The verbal reasoning element assesses reasoning processes using the medium of words, and the quantitative reasoning element assesses reasoning processes using numbers. The non-verbal part of the test uses shapes and figures to assess the pupil's reasoning processes, and can therefore be used as an effective way of assessing the ability of pupils with underdeveloped *numeracy or *literacy skills, or pupils with little knowledge of the English language. The results are referred to as pupils' 'CAT scores'. *See also* BASELINE DATA; MIDDLE YEARS INFORMATION SYSTEM; STANDARD TASKS; VALUE ADDED.   IW

cognitive development *See* BRUNER; PIAGET.

collaborative learning A process whereby learners construct shared knowledge, either with peers or with peers and teacher. Some common vehicles for this approach are groupwork and project work. It draws on *Bruner's theory that most learning is a communal activity, and on a range of more recent research which suggests that learning is more effective when approached in this way rather than through didactic methods.

collaborative provision *Programmes of study which are run jointly by more than one institution, as is the case, for example, when two or more schools pool their sixth form teaching in order to offer pupils a wider choice of options; or as might also be the case where one institution teaches and assesses a programme of study validated by another. This latter example might apply where a *college or an overseas institution offers a course which is validated, verified, and partly taught by a *university.

collective worship It is a statutory duty, under the School Standards and Framework Act 1998, for all *maintained schools to provide a daily act of collective worship for all pupils except those who have been withdrawn from this through the wishes of their parent or guardian. This is usually provided through a daily assembly which must be of a broadly Christian character. The exact nature of the provision is agreed between the *head teacher and the governing body and set out in a school policy.

(⊕) **SEE WEB LINKS**
• Provides information about the collective worship policy.

college 1. A generic term popularly used to refer to institutions providing *post-compulsory education, including *colleges of education, *colleges of further education, and *sixth form colleges. Following the American usage, the expression 'going to college' may also be employed by some to denote 'going to *university'.
   2. An administrative or nominal subdivision of a university, which may have considerable autonomy, in the case of *collegiate universities, or may operate in a similar way to the **house** system in some secondary schools in providing students with a team or sub-group with which to identify.
   3. A colloquial term in Scotland for any form of further or higher education.

college of education Teacher training colleges were renamed colleges of education following the recommendation of the *Robbins Report in 1963. Many of these later closed or merged with *polytechnics or *colleges of further education when teacher training places were greatly reduced in the 1970s. Those which remained often did so in partnership with a university which validated their awards, or became autonomous **colleges of higher education**.

college of further education A *tertiary institution offering a wide curriculum which provides *vocational education and training from *entry level up to *foundation degree level across a broad range of areas, and can also include *basic skills programmes, *General Certificate of Education *Advanced Level programmes, teacher training for the sector, and *adult education and community education. Many were originally known as **technical colleges**. The *Further and Higher Education Act 1992 removed colleges from local authority control and funding and established them as independent corporate bodies which received funding through the *Further Education Funding Council, a function currently served by the *Learning and Skills Council. The removal of colleges from local authority control and the granting of their right to manage

their own budgets became known as incorporation. Colleges' role as centres of
skills training was defined in the *Foster Report of 2005. Since 2007 fully
trained teachers in the sector can be awarded *qualified teacher learning
and skills status. *See also* COLLEGE SELF-ASSESSMENT; FURTHER EDUCATION;
PARITY OF ESTEEM.   VC, KA

college of higher education *See* COLLEGE OF EDUCATION.

collegiate university A *university in which the separate colleges, while
subject to university regulations, have a high degree of autonomy in relation
to management of their funds and property and their admissions procedures.
Oxford, Cambridge, and Durham are collegiate universities.

Common Assessment Framework (CAF) A generic assessment tool
available to all practitioners in statutory agencies and voluntary organizations
across England working with children and young people. Its use is aimed at
children and young people, including unborn babies, who have been identified
as having additional needs for which either short- or long-term support is
required. The intention is that assessments are carried out early and effectively,
with involved professionals fully aware of all issues affecting the child or
young person, planning and working together to address these additional
needs. When a CAF is in existence, a lead professional will be allocated to
coordinate the team around the child or young person, and act as the single
point of contact for parents or carers. The CAF has a standard form (although
some local areas may have modified this) considering three areas: the
development of the child, parents and carers, and family environment.
It replaces some existing assessments but sits alongside specialist assessments
such as statutory assessment for *special educational needs and universal
health checks.   TB, LE

Common Entrance Examination An examination for pupils applying to
enter an *independent school between the ages of 11 and 13. Not all independent
schools apply this as an entry condition, some preferring to set their own entry
*examinations. It is not a public examination, although pupils from state
schools can apply to sit it. It is usually conducted in the candidate's own school.
See also PREPARATORY SCHOOL.

**Common European Framework of Reference for Languages
(CEFRL)** A set of descriptors relating to levels of language ability, which apply to
any language and can be used as stage markers in language acquisition and use.
Disseminated widely from 2001 and translated into about 30 languages, the
CEFRL is an established and worldwide means of providing *benchmarks in
language ability, and is used to underpin the teaching and certification of
language skills in most countries of the European community. It provides a
framework consisting of learning objectives at six progressive levels, A1, A2, B1,
B2, C1, and C2, together with associated competence descriptors in speaking,
reading, writing, listening, and interacting. The descriptors are generic in that
they can be applied to any language. In order to address language-specific

learning issues, however, specifications are under development to provide CEFRL frameworks for each European language, both national and regional. These are known as **reference-level descriptors (RLDs)**. The project for the development of RLDs for English language learning is known as English Profile, and is led by bodies including Cambridge University's Research Centre for English and Applied Linguistics, and the *British Council. *See also* ENGLISH FOR SPEAKERS OF OTHER LANGUAGES.

(∰) SEE WEB LINKS
• Provides details on the development of RLDs for English.

communication and interaction needs Pupils, such as those with an *autistic spectrum disorder or those whose language skills are slow to develop, and who therefore have difficulty interacting with others, may be identified as having communication and interaction needs. These are part of the spectrum of *special educational needs for which there is the entitlement to specialized support in schools.

(∰) SEE WEB LINKS
• Provides information on ways to address this range of needs.

community college This may take a number of forms, but is often the name taken by a large secondary school which opens up some of its provision and resources to adults in the local community both during the day and in the evening.

community education A concept and practice often linked to *adult education, and involving the provision of courses and educational events outside the *school or *college premises in public or private buildings within the community. This type of provision is also referred to as 'outreach', since it reaches out to the community rather than requiring people to travel to the institution. *See also* WIDENING ACCESS; WIDENING PARTICIPATION.

community of practice A group of people with a shared interest whose interaction serves to increase their knowledge, understanding, or skill. The term was coined by **Etienne Wenger** (b. 1952) who argues that learning is primarily a social activity which arises from our participation in everyday life. Communities of practice are formed wherever people learn together and from one another in a shared endeavour. So, for example, students who meet for a coffee and discuss their latest project are developing a shared fund of knowledge and ideas; just as teachers discussing assessment issues in the classroom are, at the same time, developing their professional knowledge and expertise. The learning is not necessarily intentional, and need not be the primary reason for the group's interaction. Wenger's thesis is that, where people share a common interest or concern—which he terms the 'domain' or 'shared domain of interest'—their social and/or professional interactions have the potential to increase their understanding of it. The emphasis on **practice** is crucial in distinguishing what is meant here from a group with simply a shared interest. A community of practice learns, through its interaction, to improve its performance, whether this be in skills, knowledge, or understanding. Schools, colleges, and universities are all contexts in which communities of practice could be expected to operate. *See also* COLLABORATIVE LEARNING.

SEE WEB LINKS
• The Wenger web site provides a comprehensive introduction to communities of practice.

community school *See* COMMUNITY COLLEGE.

compensation The process whereby a candidate's poor performance in one aspect of an *examination or other *assessment procedure may be made up for by their high level of performance in one or more aspects. This is sometimes applied, within university regulations, in the classification of degrees.

competence The ability to perform to a specified standard. The introduction of competence-based vocational qualifications, which was signalled in the 1981 *White Paper *A New Training Initiative*, brought with it a number of changes in the way training and assessment were understood and applied. Where previously gaining a qualification might have been based on time served, or courses attended and examinations passed, it was now based firmly on what the candidate could do; and so the emphasis moved from teaching skills to assessing them. Thus, a candidate for a vocational qualification might be assessed at the point of enrolment, found to be already competent, and awarded their qualification. The introduction in 1986 of National Vocational Qualifications (NVQs) and the national framework of vocational qualifications established competence-based assessment as the dominant model in vocational education and training. This gave rise to a number of debates, which can be summarized as follows: How does the competent/not competent model of assessment allow for a differentiation to be made between the candidate who is barely competent and the candidate who is very competent indeed? What part do experience and theoretical understanding play, if any, in the competence model? How many times should the candidate be required to demonstrate competence before the assessor can be sure that an assessment of 'competent' is reliable?

An occupational, competence-based qualification is made up of units, each of which contain a number of statements of competence, each with performance criteria defined in terms of standard and range. They describe the skills and knowledge that a candidate must be able to demonstrate in order to be judged competent. The teaching profession has resisted the introduction of competence-based teacher training programmes, arguing that many of the areas of skills, knowledge, and understanding necessary in an effective teacher cannot be described in terms of observable behaviours and require a developmental rather than *instrumental model of learning and assessment. However, the professional standards for teachers in the *further education and training sector introduced by Lifelong Learning UK in 2007 bore a close resemblance to a competence model.

comprehensive school A non-selective model of secondary school which began to replace the former system of secondary moderns and selective *grammar schools in the 1970s. The *Education Act 1976 required *local authorities to make all secondary provision comprehensive; but this was repealed by the Education Act 1979, leaving pockets of selective secondary education in some local authority areas in England. The term 'comprehensive' was used originally to indicate that such schools would provide a secondary education for all pupils in their area. Comprehensive education has been the subject of much debate among educationalists and others, with some claiming that the loss of grammar schools has impeded rather than encouraged social mobility and that comprehensive schools have resulted in a general 'dumbing down' in terms of academic achievement. Others, however, support the argument for comprehensive education on the grounds of equity and social cohesion. Nevertheless, the rise of *academies in the 21st century could be seen as a loss of confidence in the original comprehensive system.

In Scotland the majority of state schools are comprehensive and are referred to as **high schools** or *academies. Selective education is provided through the independent schools system. In Wales, too, almost all schools were comprehensive by the end of the 1980s. In Northern Ireland, however, selection lingered longer and became the focus of the Burns Report.

(( )) SEE WEB LINKS
• Presents the argument for comprehensive schools.
• Presents the argument that comprehensive schools have failed to promote equity and social cohesion.

computer-assisted assessment The application of computer technology to assessment processes such as delivery of the task, test, or questions, and collection and collation of learner responses, but where the *marking may be done by a teacher or assessor. This latter is what differentiates it from **computer-based assessment**, where both delivery and marking are done solely by computer.

computer-assisted learning (CAL) A mode of teaching and learning in which learning material is presented via a computer, and the learner is able to interact with them. *See also* E-LEARNING; INFORMATION COMMUNICATION TECHNOLOGY.

conditional offer An offer of a place made to an applicant by a *university which is conditional on their achieving specified grades, for example in the *General Certificate of Education *Advanced Levels.

constructivist A view of education which challenges the belief that learning is something which can be delivered by means of a teacher transmitting facts or knowledge to a class of passive recipient learners; but rather that knowledge, meaning, and understanding are actively constructed by learners by a process of development, which builds on what they already know, causing them to change and adapt and invent ideas. In practical terms, in a classroom where teaching is informed by constructivist theory, the teacher's role is not to *deliver facts, but to continuing education   64

provide learners with the stimulus and experience which then allows them to
pose their own questions, hypothesize, explore, predict, and investigate
knowledge for themselves. The **cognitive constructivist** view is that meaningful
learning requires an active construction of meaning, in which we make sense of
new information by testing it against, and assimilating it into, what we already
know, often thereby achieving a higher level of thinking and understanding.
Notable proponents of this view are Dewey, sometimes referred to as the
originator of this approach, Bruner, and Piaget. **Social constructivists**, notably
*Vygotsky, argue that key elements for successful learning are participation
in social interaction, and the processes of thought facilitated through
language and dialogue; and that the construction of learning is influenced by
the historico-social context in which the learner lives. There are a number of
schools of constructivist thought, but all share an emphasis upon the active
role of the learner in constructing his or her own reality.

continuing education Education which continues throughout life, both
through formal institutions and by other means, as a continuous process of
personal development. It is often linked with *adult education in the phrase
'adult and continuing education'. *See also* LIFELONG LEARNING.

continuing professional development (CPD) The continuation of a
teacher's professional development beyond their initial training, qualification,
and *induction. This may take many forms, including attendance on short
courses for updating skills or knowledge; longer programmes of study such as
*diplomas and postgraduate degrees in education; staff development events held
within the teacher's own institution; conferences; *mentoring; and peer
assessment. CPD is a requirement of teachers in schools and for all those
teaching in *further education colleges. Many universities offer CPD courses and
qualifications for teachers.

continuous assessment *Assessment of student's work which takes place
throughout the duration of their course, usually through *assignments or other
*coursework. It involves no terminal *examination, and is sometimes accused
of lack of rigour for this reason. However, continuous assessment may also
involve some element of external *testing and externally marked assessment, as
was the case with some *General Certificate of Secondary Education continuous
modules. Assessment may be *formative, as well as providing a *summative
assessment of the student's *attainment.

co-operative learning A specific type of *collaborative learning in which
pupils or students work together in a small group on a structured activity, but
are assessed individually on their contribution to the task, as well as being
assessed as part of the group as a whole. *See also* ASSESSMENT.

core skills *See* KEY SKILLS.

core subject A subject which is central to the *curriculum and must be
studied by everyone. In the *national curriculum, the three core subjects are

English, mathematics, and science. In Welsh-speaking schools Welsh is also a core subject. In contexts other than the national curriculum, too, core subjects, as opposed to optional subjects, are usually those which are mandatory.

corporal punishment Abolished under the *Education (No. 2) Act 1986. Teachers may still use reasonable force to restrain a pupil in order to prevent injury or damage to others or to property, but may not use force as a form of punishment. *See also* BEHAVIOUR.

correspondence course A *programme of study undertaken through written correspondence, where the learner and tutor communicate solely through means of the postal service. This type of *distance learning, typified by the early days of the *National Extension College, has been largely overtaken by technology and *e-learning, although *Open University programmes and others still retain some features of this type of provision. Correspondence courses are still to be seen advertised commercially by private individuals or companies offering specialized skills, such as writing for children or memory enhancement.

Council for Catholic Maintained Schools (CCMS) The Council for Catholic Maintained Schools promotes and directs Catholic education in Northern Ireland. It is funded by the *Department of Education, Northern Ireland. It is responsible for the employment of teachers in *Catholic maintained schools and acts in an advisory capacity. JH

Council for Irish-Medium Education (Comhairle na Gaelscolaíochta) This body was set up in 2000 by the *Department of Education, Northern Ireland, to promote and develop Irish-medium education and schools in the province. JH

SEE WEB LINKS
• Explains the aims and function of the Council.

course a discrete *programme of study which follows a predetermined *syllabus or specification, and may lead to a qualification or some other form of certification. Courses of study vary in duration, short courses lasting only days, while a degree course may take three or four years to complete. From a usage point of view there is a lack of clarity about the distinction between 'course' and 'programme', some institutions using the two interchangeably, while others use the term 'course' to refer to a subdivision of a lengthier programme of study, such as that leading to a degree.

coursework Assessed work which is completed by the student during the process of their course of study. It is usually the case that the *assessment outcomes for their coursework will count towards the student's final mark or grade. If the course involves no terminal *examination or end test, the coursework alone will form the basis of the final assessment outcome. This model is known as *continuous assessment, and is often employed for the assessment of *modular *programmes of study. Where an end examination or test is also used, the student's performance in their assessed coursework will constitute a fixed proportion of their final and overall mark or grade. Coursework may be set at regular intervals during the course of study, often, although not always, in the form of written *assignments; or it may take the form of an ongoing project on which the student works for part or all of the duration of their course. It may be *internally assessed by the student's own teachers or institution, or externally assessed by an *awarding body; or the process may involve a combination of both of these, with specified pieces of coursework, or a representative sample of all coursework, being scrutinized by the awarding body, while the remainder is assessed internally. This latter is the type of model which operated until recently in the assessment of *General Certificate of Secondary Education (GCSE) coursework. As well as providing a means of *summative assessment by contributing to the student's final and overall mark or grade, coursework has the advantage of providing the student with *formative assessment, since it is a means of giving feedback on their current level of attainment and of identifying areas of weakness which need to be addressed. Detractors of coursework-based assessment, on the other hand, accuse it of lack of *academic rigour and of being open to *plagiarism and other forms of inequity which render it unreliable in comparison to invigilated and time-constrained examinations. There is also some evidence to suggest that continuous assessment of coursework may most benefit female candidates, who are thought to perform less well, on the whole, in terminal examinations than their male peers. Current policy trends suggest a growing emphasis on the desirability of a return to assessment, for example at *Advanced Level, by end examination only. Nevertheless, coursework remains part of the assessment process in key qualifications throughout secondary and tertiary education, from GCSEs, Advanced Levels and *diplomas, to *master's degrees.

 SEE WEB LINKS

• Sets out the advantages and disadvantages of assessing learner attainment through coursework.

crammer The colloquial term for a private college which prepares students aged 16+ for public *examinations and other entry qualifications though short courses, often in school holidays. Such colleges are so called because of the relative shortness and intensive nature of the courses they provide.

creative curriculum A learning provision in which educational creativity is central rather than peripheral or 'bolt on'. The National College for School Leadership (NCSL), in 2007, set out descriptors for a creative curriculum. These included the suggestion that it should encourage imagination; allow for reflection and choice; give freedom to fail; encourage *collaborative learning and *co-constructed learning; employ a range of teaching strategies; promote understanding of the *personal, social, and spiritual aspects of the curriculum; and enhance the professional development and sense of self-worth of the teachers involved. This latter point is an important one, since it is based on the belief that the implementation of such a curriculum can be a significant factor in motivating teachers as well as learners, and enhancing their sense of job satisfaction.

Creativity itself is an area of proficiency not currently measured in schools by existing methods of testing or measures of progress, but which might manifest itself in abilities and skills such as self-confidence, risk-taking, resilience, teamwork, questioning, and challenging. These are sometimes referred to as **soft skills**, which some employers are eager to see acknowledged as part of pupil assessment. Finding a way to measure these aspects of creativity without extinguishing them, however, clearly presents more substantial problems than the testing of academic ability and understanding.

(⊕) SEE WEB LINKS
• Provides a full list of the NCSL descriptors.

credit 1. Recognition of achievement. In *further and *higher education, a student may accumulate credit, for example in the form of a number of *modules successfully completed, each of which carry a number of credit 'points'. The accumulated credits may be used to gain a recognized qualification, such as a certificate, diploma, or degree. This is sometimes colloquially termed as 'cashing in credits'. A candidate may also transfer credits from one institution to another, adding those gained in one institution to those gained in the next. This is known as 'credit transfer'. **Credit accumulation and transfer (CAT)** is the term used for both parts of this process. The *Qualifications and Credit Framework is designed to facilitate this process by clarifying levels, equivalence, and credit value of qualifications and their component units or modules.

2. A *grade awarded for successful achievement in an *examination or other *assessment, indicating attainment beyond the minimum level of a pass. It is the highest level of *Standard Grade qualification in the exam taken by students aged 15 or 16 in Scotland. The three levels are Credit, General, and Foundation. Students will usually sit two levels at the same time; hence Credit students will also sit General papers and those taking General level will sit Foundation papers.

(⊕) SEE WEB LINKS
• Provides guidance on Standard Grade.

Credit and Qualifications Framework for Wales (CQFW) A structure developed from a joint project initiated in 2001 by the *Higher Education Funding Council for Wales and the Further Education Funding Council for Wales (since merged with the Assembly Department of Education) to cover all post-16 learning. From 2005 all accredited learning, including mainstream qualifications offered in Wales, has gradually been brought into a single unifying structure, the CQFW. The Framework merges the concepts of volume of learning achievements (credit) and the demands made by the learning on the learner (level) to create a system that is able to embrace all types and styles of learning. Major objectives are to assist in removing barriers to progression, to allow the accumulation of credits to meet the needs of individuals, and to offer parity in the recognition of achievement for learners of all ages, whether they are learning in the workplace, in the community, or at school, college, or university. *See also* WALES, EDUCATION IN.   HG

criterion-referenced Describes methods of *assessment which assess the candidate against a fixed set of criteria, rather than by comparison with the performance of others (*norm-referenced) or by comparison with their own earlier performance (*ipsative). *Competence-based assessment is an example of the straightforward use of criterion-referencing.

cross-curricular If a topic, activity, skill, responsibility, or initiative is applied not just to one subject but across the *curriculum as a whole, it is described as 'cross-curricular'. For example, in schools, *literacy is a cross-curricular issue, relevant to, and embedded in, every subject. A *literacy coordinator, therefore, has a cross-curricular responsibility.

cultural studies An area of study and research which emerged across Europe and America during the 1960s. The Frankfurt Institute for Social Research, founded in the 1920s, became highly influential in the development of the subject. In Britain cultural studies first emerged as a discipline within education at the Centre for Contemporary Cultural Studies (CCCS) at the University of Birmingham in 1964. Richard Hoggart (1918–2014) was the first director. Other notable directors and academics associated with the centre include Raymond Williams (1921–88), E. P. Thompson (1924–93), Stuart Hall (1932–2014), and Dick Hebdige (b. 1951).

In the early years of the CCCS, the modus operandi of these theorists was to acknowledge the growing significance of popular culture and the media in people's lives. Initially, figures like Hoggart, Williams, and Thompson espoused what was to become known later as culturalism, which, as much as anything, was a changing attitude to what was deemed worthy of study. In 1948 F. R. Leavis had written *The Great Tradition*, outlining a series of classic texts which would form the canon of literary texts that encapsulated what was valuable in British culture. By the 1960s Hoggart et al. began to use the same analytical tools of English literature, but, instead of the classics, applied them to the study of ordinary, everyday people. From this moment on, just as much cultural significance could be attributed to a pop song by Petula Clarke as to a poem by W. H. Auden.

Although the earlier members of the CCCS, especially Hoggart, largely viewed the mass media as something which polluted ordinary working-class culture, later theorists such as Hall, Hebdige, and McRobbie, having been influenced by the lessons of the Frankfurt School, structuralism, and Marxism, began to see popular culture as an area of conflict and resistance. The media, and culture in general, could be viewed as a site for the unequal distribution of power of producers and consumers, but also where subcultures like punk could emerge and form identities from the detritus of consumer culture.

Although cultural studies remains a successful area of study and research in global higher education, after nearly 30 years of research, study, and left-wing radicalism, the CCCS was shut down in 2002.   CH

currency **1.** A qualification, or credits towards a qualification, are said to have currency if they are generally recognized and accepted.

2. In *assessment, and particularly the assessment of skills, the currency of a candidate's achievement or level of competence is an important factor. For example, they may possess experience or a qualification in *information technology which they gained many years before, and which does not therefore attest to their ability to work with current systems.

curriculum The content and specifications of a *course or *programme of study (as in 'the history curriculum'); or, in a wider sense, the totality of the specified learning opportunities available in one educational institution (as in 'the school curriculum'); or, in its very widest sense, the programme of learning applying to all pupils in the nation (as in 'the national curriculum'). It has been observed, with some irony, that the word is the Latin term for a track around which competitors race for the entertainment of others. This metaphor is an interesting one in that it suggests a Darwinian view of formal education as a competition in which there are winners and losers. This is a construct at odds with the thinking of educators such as *Freire and *Rogers. *See also* CREATIVE CURRICULUM; NATIONAL CURRICULUM.

curriculum, common A *curriculum which applies to all learners in a school, or to all learners in all schools in a region or country. Commonality lies in the fact that all learners will have the same learning experiences and have covered the same topics in common. The *national curriculum is an example of a common curriculum in that it applies in all *maintained schools and ensures that pupils share a common experience of learning and assessment at each stage of their education.

curriculum, compulsory A *curriculum which every learner is required to follow. A curriculum may be compulsory within an institution, or may be a statutory requirement for all pupils. The *national curriculum is an example of a compulsory curriculum since it must be applied in all appropriate *maintained schools.

curriculum, core The parts of a *curriculum which are compulsory and common to all. The term is generally used when other parts of the curriculum are optional, so as to identify the central, or 'core', curriculum content which must apply to every learner.

curriculum, entitlement A term used to describe a *curriculum of worthwhile knowledge, understanding, and experience to which every pupil should be entitled. It was coined by *Her Majesty's Inspectorate of Schools in the 1980s and was predicated on a model of education which was *liberal rather than *instrumental.

curriculum, hidden Learners may, in the course of their exposure to the formal curriculum, also learn or acquire knowledge, skills, or attitudes which were not part of the formal intended learning outcomes. This incidental or accidental learning is referred to as the hidden curriculum, since its processes are not apparent and its outcomes are unplanned. It may be positive, as in the case of pupils acquiring the social skills modelled by their teacher; or it may be negative, as when they 'learn' that arriving late can effectively delay the start of the lesson. The term is also used by some to describe the extracurricular activities provided by the school.

curriculum, national *See* NATIONAL CURRICULUM.

curriculum, negotiated Used to refer to the content, coverage, and outcomes of a course of study which has been agreed through consultation between the teacher or institution and the learners themselves. Curriculum content specified by legislation (for example, the *national curriculum) or by an *awarding body is not open to negotiation in this way. However, within those formal restrictions, there may be some narrow scope for negotiation in terms of choice when, for example, selecting a text to be studied from a list of options. This, however, does not, strictly speaking, constitute a negotiated curriculum, since the term implies a wider degree of learner choice over what is to be covered and achieved. Thus, a negotiated curriculum is usually associated with *learner-centred education, where the curriculum is constructed around the expressed needs and interests of the learners themselves.

curriculum, spiral A curriculum whose structure allows for topics or skills to be revisited and repeated, each time in more detail or depth as the learner gains in knowledge, skills, and confidence. This curriculum model is consistent with an *ipsative approach to learning.

curriculum development The review of a whole *curriculum or of specific subjects or *cross-curricular themes for the purpose of revising or improving, or even replacing, it. In its widest sense, curriculum development encompasses all those professional activities which teachers, researchers, and other educationalists undertake in order to improve and support the curriculum, from the development of innovative teaching materials or methods, to the formulation of new learning outcomes or syllabuses.

Curriculum for Excellence** (CfE)* Published in November 2004, this document sets out the values, purposes, and principles for education in *Scotland for pupils aged 3–18. It describes the characteristics which education should aspire to encourage, suggesting that schools should produce successful learners who are also confident individuals, effective contributors to society, and responsible citizens. The *Curriculum for Excellence* was drawn up as the result of a review of the Scottish education system begun in 2003, following the 2002 report ***Educating for Excellence, which cited the need for a review of the *curriculum and the need to create a single, coherent curriculum for age 3–18 'with space for children to achieve and teachers to

teach'. It also sets out a timetable for engaging with the teaching profession
and reviewing the curriculum.   SM

(⊕) SEE WEB LINKS
• Details of the *CfE* process, progress, and objectives.

curriculum planning Creating, designing, and organizing a curriculum,
either for one institution or on a national level, for example in the case of the
curriculum for a nationally available qualification.

Curriculum 2000 (C2K) A broadening of the post-16 curriculum based partly
on the recommendations in the 1996 *Dearing Review of Qualifications for 16–19
Year Olds*. Implemented in 2000, it revised the traditional structure of General
Certificate of Education (GCE) *Advanced Level provision, by introducing the
requirement for students to choose four or five subjects at *Advanced Subsidiary
Level in their first year of studies, preferably spanning a range of arts and
science subjects; and only in their second year to narrow their focus, dropping
some of their AS subjects and continuing with the rest at A2 level. Curriculum
2000 also introduced *key skills across the post-16 curriculum, for those studying
GCEs as well as those on *vocationally related courses. During the pilot year
2000/01 difficulties were reported by both students and teachers over the volume
of *assessment. Assessment procedures were subsequently reviewed and
simplified, and the inclusion of key skills made optional.

cyber-bullying *See* BULLYING

day nursery A facility providing care and education for children aged 0–5, either full-time or part-time. They are usually open from 8 a.m. to 6 p.m., all year round. The day nursery has to be registered with *Ofsted and is inspected every year by the early years team of its local Health and Social Care Trust. At least half the staff must have a childcare qualification. Day nurseries vary in size, but most take 25–40 children who are grouped together according to age; children aged 0–5 in England follow the *Early Years Foundation Stage curriculum. There are different types of day nursery including those with private, community, voluntary, work-based, and local authority status. Some day nurseries take children up to age 8 as part of 'wraparound care' for school age children. For children under 2, there is a staff ratio of one adult to three children; for those aged 2–3, one adult to four children; and for 3–5-year-olds, one adult to eight children. Most day nurseries operate a key worker system, which supports a child's attachment to a significant adult.   AW

(⊕) SEE WEB LINKS
• Provides detailed information and key questions for parents to consider in choosing a day nursery for their child.

day release Used widely in the past in the *further education sector to describe the arrangement whereby trainees in employment attend a *college or similar training organization for one day a week to develop their *vocational skills and gain an appropriate qualification. The employer releases them from work for that day, on the condition that they attend such training, and, in addition, the employer normally pays their fees. The term is now less frequently used, having been replaced by the expression **off-the-job** training. This change of terminology followed the introduction of *National Vocational Qualifications (NVQs), which provided greater opportunities for what was referred to as **on-the-job** training and assessment. Prior to the introduction of NVQs, the curriculum for day release students often included a lesson of *liberal studies as well as training in the vocational knowledge and skills relevant to their employment.

dean A title which has two distinct meanings in *higher education. It may be used to confer status on a head of department or *faculty, in which case the full title will indicate this, as in 'dean of faculty'; or it may indicate a senior member of a *university who is responsible for matters of student discipline.

Dearing Report on Higher Education (1997) Entitled *Higher Education in the Learning Society: The National Committee of Inquiry into Higher Education*, the Report followed a comprehensive review of *higher education and presented 93 recommendations. These included the introduction of student contributions towards their tuition *fees of up to 25 per cent; the introduction of a new national framework of higher education qualifications, to be monitored by the Quality Assurance Agency for Higher Education; and the setting up of an *Institute for Learning and Teaching in higher education to accredit the professional development of teachers and lecturers in the sector. It also suggested, as one of the nine underlying principles on which the Report was based, that learning should be responsive to the needs of employment and should develop those skills which are valued in the world of work. In this sense the 1997 Dearing Report contributed heavily to the debate about the purposes of higher education. *See also* VOCATIONAL.

Dearing Review of Qualifications for 16–19-Year-Olds (1996) The government brief for this Review was that Sir Ron Dearing and his team should advise on how the existing system of post-16 qualifications might be revised in order to encourage greater *parity of esteem between *General Certificate of Education (GCE) *Advanced Level (A level) and parallel *vocational and pre-vocational routes. The brief included a government admonishment that A levels should not be discarded or undermined. The Secretary of State for Education, Gillian Shephard, writing to Dearing on 10 April 1995, instructed him that 'Our key priorities remain to ensure that the rigour and standards of GCE A levels are maintained.' This proviso made any radical overhaul, such as the introduction of a *baccalauréat system, out of the question. The Committee was also tasked with suggesting ways to build on development in *National Vocational Qualifications (NVQs) and *General National Vocational Qualifications (GNVQs); to increase participation and achievement; to prepare young people better for work and for higher education; and to ensure value for money. Dearing himself described the purpose of the Review as being one of breaking down barriers between academic and vocational courses and thereby promoting parity of esteem between the two.

Describing the scale of the task, Dearing pointed out on page 1 of the Review's published report that, 'In spite of action taken by the government to bring clarity into the structure of vocational qualifications, the world of education and training between the ages of 16 and 19 remains intelligible only to specialists.' The proposals which emerged from the Review included the following:

- a common framework across NVQ, GNVQ, *General Certificate of Secondary Education (GCSE), and A level, comprising four levels: entry, foundation, intermediate, and advanced;
- the renaming of Advanced GNVQs as 'Applied A levels';
- a National Advanced Certificate which would comprise two A levels, or an Advanced GNVQ, or a level 3 NVQ;
- a National Advanced Diploma, comprising the same qualifications as the Certificate, but awarded to pupils who have also covered four general areas

of study, such as science, languages, arts, and 'community' studies, such as
business or psychology;
- able pupils to be offered units of degree courses while still at school;
- *key skills to be offered across the framework;
- *awarding bodies to make joint arrangements for awards of GCSE, A level,
  and GNVQ;
- a marrying of the roles of the School Curriculum and Assessment Authority
  (SCAA) and the *National Council for Vocational Qualifications (NCVQ).

It is clear that many of these proposals were aimed at encouraging a broadening
of the curriculum and parity between the different routes through the post-16
education system. Many of the Review's recommendations, including the new
Diploma and Certificate, and the renaming of GNVQs, were not implemented.
The reorganization of the awarding bodies and the merger of the NCVQ and
SCAA did go ahead, however, as did the introduction of key skills across the
curriculum. Critics of the report from the academic community argued that
Dearing's proposals did not go far enough, while the press criticized the same
proposals for their possibly detrimental effect on the status of A levels,
claiming that they were too radical.

deep learning A student approach to learning which aims to achieve a
holistic understanding of the topic in question and to grasp and analyse any
underpinning principles or theory. This is in contrast to a **surface learning**
approach which focuses on memorizing surface facts and details with a view to
answering teachers' factual questions correctly or presenting 'correct' answers
in a test or *examination. Deep learning, unlike surface learning, involves critical
analysis and reflection and is typified by a willingness to question, rather than
just accept, the knowledge and ideas being taught. This is particularly relevant
to *higher education, where teachers are expected to design their lectures and
seminars in a way which will encourage their students to take a deep approach
to learning.

deficit model A perspective which attributes failures such as lack of
achievement, learning, or success in gaining employment to a personal lack of
effort or deficiency in the individual, rather than to failures or limitations of
the education and training system or to prevalent socio-economic trends. For
example, the argument for the introduction of youth and adult training schemes
in the 1981 *White Paper *A New Training Initiative* included the suggestion that
because people lacked skills there were no jobs for them, and that therefore
this deficit must be addressed by appropriate training. The implication here was
that unemployment arose from a deficiency in the unemployed themselves,
rather than from economic trends. The deficit model of teaching, in which the
teacher provides the learning to make good a deficit, stands in direct contrast
to the belief that the teacher's role is to draw out learners' *tacit knowledge
and understanding through questioning and facilitation.

The deficit model perspective is also apparent in the view expressed in some
discourses about learner *attainment and *behaviour which suggest that it is
a deficit of some kind in the teacher's performance which leads to such

problems, and that learner attainment and behaviour can therefore be improved simply by changing the teacher's behaviour or by enhancing their skills through professional development. An application of the deficit model, as can be seen from these examples, is often indicative of an oversimplified view of the issue in question.

degree A qualification awarded by a *university or other institution of *higher education to candidates who have successfully completed a course of studies. Degrees are awarded at foundation level (*foundation degree), undergraduate level (*bachelor's degree), postgraduate level (*master's degree), and *doctorate level. In Scotland most undergraduate university students embark on a four-year degree, at the end of which they will achieve a master's degree of MA or M.Sc. Students also have the option to complete their studies at the end of the third year, however; in which case successful candidates will receive a bachelor's degree (BA or B.Sc.) or may be awarded an ordinary or general degree.

degree classification *See* BACHELOR'S DEGREE.

deliver Commonly and increasingly used as an alternative to 'teach' to describe what *teachers do. It is not, however, quite synonymous with 'teach' since its metaphorical roots suggest a process in which something—in this case learning—is simply handed over intact from teacher to student. To 'teach', on the other hand, usually implies a more complex activity, which may involve strategies such as *Socratic questioning, group facilitation, the *motivating and management of learners, *assessment, *evaluation, and so on. The metaphor of 'delivery' also suggests that the lesson itself originates from a source outside the teacher, who simply presents it to the learners; whereas in most cases teaching also involves the teacher in the preparatory planning and *research, as well as in interaction and dialogue with learners. 'Deliver' is also used in the sense of to 'deliver' a lecture, which implies the presentation to an audience of a pre-prepared text, slides, or other material, and again suggests a process of one-way communication from lecturer to learners.

demand-led The provision of education or training courses on the basis of what is currently most in demand, either locally or nationally. In the *lifelong learning sector, where this term is most commonly found, *further education colleges and other providers must respond to the training demands of local employers and businesses, since their funding from the *Learning and Skills Council is dependent on their ability to do this. The curriculum of universities and other institutions of *higher education may also be demand-led, in the sense that courses which show a consistent pattern of under-recruitment may be discontinued and new courses created in response to perceived *market trends. The concept of demand-related funding in this context is closely bound up with the market model of education and training.

Demos A think-tank founded in 1992 whose recommendations sometimes include those on matters relating to education, and particularly in the curriculum area of *citizenship. Its political philosophy is situated to the left of centre.

denomination Most English, Welsh, and Scottish schools tend to be non-denominational, and thus religious observance and study are not a compulsory part of the curriculum. In Scotland those which are denominational tend to be Roman Catholic. These denominational schools follow the same curriculum as non-denominational schools and must accept students who do not follow the religion of the school. *See also* RELIGIOUS EDUCATION; SCOTLAND, EDUCATION IN. SM

Department for Business, Innovation, and Skills (DBIS) The government department responsible for *higher education, including universities, and for *further education and training. Established in 2010, it replaced the Department for Innovation, Universities, and Skills. The retention of a separate department for matters relating to *post-compulsory education and training could be seen to reflect a continuation of the policy to encourage *parity of esteem between academic and skills routes, since it signals a differentiation by sector, rather than by whether the provision is general or vocational. The linking together of higher education and the business agenda here under one government department suggests that, in policy terms, higher education is seen primarily as instrumental in supporting the economy, rather than as a good in and of itself.

(⊕) SEE WEB LINKS
• Department's web site which provides details about policy, roles, and current developments.

Department for Education (DfE) The government department responsible for schools and children's services, created in May 2010, following a change of government to replace the Department for Children, Schools, and Families. It has oversight of three key executive agencies: the *Education Funding Agency; the *National College for Teaching and Leadership; and the **Standards and Testing Agency**. Its remit with regard to children's services continues the linking of responsibilities for matters relating to children's health and child poverty with those for education in schools, which was begun with the creation of its predecessor and which signalled a more coordinated approach to social provision and safeguarding for children, in line with the aims expressed in the document *Every Child Matters*.

(⊕) SEE WEB LINKS
• Department's web site which provides details about policy, roles, and current developments.

Department for Education, Culture, and the Welsh Language The Department of the Welsh Assembly which is now responsible for policy and funding for all areas of education, training, and *lifelong learning with the exception of *higher education, which remains with the *Higher Education Funding Council for Wales. The Department operates through five groups: Children and Schools; Qualifications and Curriculum; Lifelong Learning and Skills; Higher Learning; and Culture, Welsh Language, and Sport. From April

2006 an expanded Department has included the work of the Further Education
Funding Council for Wales and the responsibilities previously held by the
Qualifications, Curriculum, and Assessment Authority for Wales.   HG

Department of Education, Northern Ireland (DENI) The DENI
manages and directs the central administration of education in Northern Ireland.
It is responsible for the strategic planning and management of education, the
content and delivery of the curriculum, the allocation of funding to the
Education and *Library Boards, and the capital costs for most schools. The
DENI is headed by the Minister for Education, whose principal adviser is the
Permanent Secretary. Two Deputy Secretaries and the Chief Inspector of the
Education and Training Inspectorate support the Permanent Secretary.   JH

**Department of Education's Education and Training Inspectorate
(DEETI)** This body carries out school inspections in Northern Ireland, reporting
to the *Department of Education, Northern Ireland. It is responsible for
monitoring standards of learning and teaching.   JH

Department of Employment and Learning (DEL) The Northern Ireland
government department responsible for employment, apprenticeships, further
education, and higher education. One of its functions is the funding of
universities and other institutions of higher education. This means that, unlike
England, Wales, and Scotland, Northern Ireland does not have a separate
higher education funding council.

(⊕) SEE WEB LINKS
• Provides details of the role and responsibilities of DEL.

deputy head A senior member of school staff whose role is normally to act as
second in command to the *head teacher, and to stand in for them in their
absence. The precise duties and detail of the post will differ from school to
school, but will often involve liaison between the head teacher and the teaching
staff as well as acting as a member of the senior management team of the school.
In larger schools there may be two or more deputy heads, each with a specific
whole-school responsibility, such as *curriculum management or pupil
*achievement and *behaviour. Increasingly, deputy head posts are being
replaced by that of *assistant head, usually at a lower salary.

Derrida, Jacques (1930–2004) Jacques Derrida was a highly influential
Algerian-born French philosopher who came to prominence in the late 1960s
and early 1970s with the publication of *Of Grammatology* (1967), *Writing and
Difference* (1967), and *Margins of Philosophy* (1972). He came to be one of the
most controversial thinkers of the 20th century owing to his wide-ranging
theories regarding the instability of language and the consequent impossibility
of truth claims. Responding to structuralist thought, which had been based
on the differential *semiotic theory of Ferdinand de Saussure, Derrida introduced
a neologism, *différance*, which brought together 'difference' and 'deferral'.

Meaning, according to Derrida, is constantly deferred as ever-changing discursive contexts unravel a never-ending chain of signifiers.

The term that he is widely associated with is 'deconstruction'. Derrida was always keen to stress that deconstruction was not something that was used as a method to 'take apart' that which is studied; for him deconstruction is something that already happens within texts. For Derrida, institutions such as *schools, *colleges, and *universities were contexts where various and competing discourses could be observed, and it was in the space where these discourses clashed that one could observe dissonances that questioned the naturalness of the underlying presuppositions that informed educational policy and practice. For instance, it could be argued that the importance of increasingly commercial value placed on education could be at odds with the search for 'truth' in the various disciplines.

Latterly, Derrida discussed the future role of the humanities in *The Future of the Profession, or, The University Without Condition* (2003). Here, Derrida likened the university to a kind of supplementary body which, although increasingly a part of the commercial world, could still carry out the critical pursuit of truth. Although Derrida, in much of his work, had rejected the concept of ultimate and universal truths (something which fired animosity among his contemporaries), he did not reject, and indeed advocated, a more critically reflective search for truth; the focus on critical reflection must be continuous, as truths, according to Derrida, tend to exclude.   CH

deschooling A term coined by Ivan Illich (1926–2002) in his book *Deschooling Society* (1971), in which he argues that schooling and education are by no means necessarily synonymous. He suggests that the function of schools is as much about social control as it is about learning; and that most of what is valuable in our learning takes place outside such institutions. He further argues that schools are not only an inefficient means of providing education in that they generate excessive bureaucracy and expense, but that they are also socially divisive.

descriptor *See* GRADE; LEVEL.

descriptor of need *Special educational needs are categorized into four main areas. These are:

- cognition and learning, which is about specific or moderate learning difficulties, severe, and profound and multiple learning difficulties;
- behavioural, emotional, and social development needs;
- communication and interaction needs, which refer to speech and language and communication needs as well as autistic spectrum disorders;
- sensory and/or physical needs, which include visual, hearing, and physical impairment and also multi-sensory impairment.

These categories are used to identify a student's main areas of need. They are set out in detail in chapter 7 of the Code of Practice for Special Educational Needs (revised), DfES/581/2001. *See also* ASPERGER'S SYNDROME; AUTISM; LEARNING DIFFICULTIES.   TB, LE

detention A strategy for behaviour management used by schools, which takes the form of keeping pupils 'detained' under the supervision of a teacher in a classroom at break, lunchtime, or after school. Its purpose is to impress upon pupils the negative consequences of unacceptable behaviour, in this case the forfeiting of their free time. If pupils are to be detained after school, the school is obliged to give parents or carers a day's notice of the fact. In the past, pupils were often required to undertake some punitive activity during their detention, such as the writing of 'lines', a sanction famously satirized and subverted in the opening sequence of the cartoon series *The Simpsons*. These days it is more usual for schools to use detention time constructively; for example, by taking the opportunity to provide pupils with support for completing coursework. Detention is one of the few sanctions, short of *exclusion, open to schools for the management of pupil behaviour.

Determined to Succeed (DtS) A Scottish policy designed to develop enterprise in education. DtS aims to promote young people's self-confidence, self-reliance, and ambition to achieve goals in work and in life.   SM

(((⊕))) SEE WEB LINKS
• Documents policy expectations for local authority delivery.

Developmental Coordination Disorder (DCD) A disorder in which a child has poor motor control and core stability. The ability to carry out fine and gross motor skills with fluency and accuracy is lacking and the child appears clumsy. The condition can be greatly ameliorated by practising a skill repeatedly (skill practice). The term DCD is often closely linked and incorrectly used interchangeably with *dyspraxia, causing confusion.   TB, LE

Dewey, John (1859–1952) An American educational philosopher who was a major influence in *progressive education and was recognized for developing an approach based on practical experiences which he called **instrumentalism**. Focusing on intellectual and social issues in education, he believed that schools should enable problem-solving skills in students rather than providing an instructive menu of *rote learning. He believed that students should be autonomous decision makers and individuals able and prepared to make judgements, and should become citizens, although this in no way represented a denial of the rights and academic status of teachers. He encouraged teachers to develop a learning cycle: to plan, implement, and review through observation and reflection; to watch for social change; and then to support their students in active citizenship.

As Director of the University of Chicago's Laboratory School, he developed the notion of educational *ideology as an experimental science, and, through observations of the teaching–learning dynamic, wrote his most important texts: *The School in Society* (1899) and *Democracy and Education* (1916). Dewey espoused the concept of learning by doing, which was never really integrated into American public (i.e. state) schools even though his ideas were popular at the time. It is interesting to note that his philosophy underpinned the child-centred *pedagogy of the *Plowden Report (1969) and has been embraced more recently by *early years educators in the UK, New Zealand, Australia, Scandinavia, and Italy, where ideological beliefs conceive the child to be an active, competent, and social learner—one who, through social interaction and experiential education, constructs their own understanding of the world.

Dewey proposed that the role of teachers was to harness the interest shown by students and plan for an emergent curriculum to exploit their natural drive to learn. *See also* LEARNER-CENTRED. AW

Further Reading: J. Dewey *Democracy and Education* (Start Publishing, 2012).

diagnostic test A test whose purpose is to evaluate a learner's strengths and areas for development. It is not a test in the sense of a *formative or *summative *assessment of the learner's attainment, but rather a means of discovering what level of support or challenge the learner will need. A diagnostic test is often a first step in developing an *individual learning plan. It is usually carried out when the learner enters their course of study, and its results are sometimes referred to as the learner's 'entry behaviour', or starting point.

dialogic teaching A strategy practised most commonly in primary education, but used also in secondary schools, in which learning takes place through dialogue between teacher and pupils and between pupils themselves. This is designed to place an emphasis on speaking and listening as well as on thinking skills, clear lines of enquiry, and pupil engagement. In operational terms this may mean teachers encouraging pupils to give extended, rather than brief, answers and to pose their own questions. It may involve allowing pupils the time to reflect upon questions and answers before responding, and calling upon named individuals for answers, rather than encouraging the classroom 'bidding' process of raised hands. However, the dialogic approach is more than the sum of these sorts of strategy. It demands that there be a balance in the pupil–teacher dialogue so that the teacher's input does not dominate; and it relies upon a positive teacher–pupil relationship, which may be reflected in a number of ways, including the utilization and arrangement of classroom space. In these ways and more, dialogic teaching recognizes and builds upon the cognitive potential of classroom talk.

The pedagogy underpinning this approach to teaching places an emphasis on five principles: reciprocity, or the sharing of ideas between teacher and pupils; cumulation, or the careful building of arguments or lines of enquiry by linking the ideas of all those contributing to the dialogue; cooperation and collectivity, with pupils working together with the teacher or in groups; supportiveness, which encourages all to feel accepted and included; and purpose, in that the dialogue is intended to achieve specific educational goals.

Evidence from pilot projects in London and Yorkshire suggests that dialogic teaching supports inclusive learning, in that it encourages quieter or less able learners to contribute with confidence. It originally formed part of national strategies for *primary education and *Key Stage 3.

Further Reading: R. J. Alexander *Education as Dialogue: Moral and Pedagogical Choices for a Runaway World* (Dialogos, 2006).

differentiation The practice of acknowledging and allowing for different levels of *attainment in a group of learners. This may be done through differentiation by activity, which involves the teacher in planning and providing different activities for learners who may be working at a higher or lower level of attainment than the majority. These are known as **differentiated activities**. It may also be applied to the assessment of learners, through differentiation by outcome, where multi-level assessment tasks are set which allow learners to respond at a level appropriate to their ability or attainment. Another means of differentiated assessment is to set different tasks or questions for different ability groups, as has been the practice in the examination of some *General Certificate of Secondary Education subjects. Two terms associated with differentiation in schools are 'enrichment', which is the provision for more capable learners to study a subject or topic in more depth; and 'extension', which is the provision for accelerated progress through all or part of the curriculum.

Further Reading: D. Guiney and T. O'Brien *Differentiation in Teaching and Learning: Principles and Practice* (Continuum, 2001).

diploma An award conferred on successful students at the end of their course of study. These may be at any level of the qualification framework, from *postgraduate diplomas to diplomas of completion for non-academic courses. The term is also used to refer to the document itself which the candidate receives, attesting to their achievement. *See also* DIPLOMA 14–19.

Diploma 14–19 A qualification for 14–19-year-olds, introduced in 2008, to run alongside the *General Certificate of Secondary Education and the *General Certificate of Education *Advanced Level. The 14–19 Diploma combined theoretical and practical learning, including work experience, and was aimed at young people of all ability levels. One of its purposes was to bridge the gap between vocational and academic routes. It constituted part of a wider reform of education for 14–19-year-olds discussed in the 2005 *White Paper *14–19 Education and Skills*, which set the target that all young people should possess *functional skills in English and mathematics by the time they leave school. It is interesting to compare the purpose and role of the Diploma with those attributed to the *General National Vocational Qualification when it was introduced in 1992. The Diploma was closed by the *Department for Education in 2013 and is no longer offered.

(((🌐))) SEE WEB LINKS

• Provides access to an archived summary of the 2005 White Paper *14–19 Education and Skills*, which set out the rationale for the Diploma.

Diploma in Education and Training *See* FURTHER EDUCATION TEACHING QUALIFICATIONS.

directed time **1.** Time teachers are expected to be available for non-teaching duties such as meeting parents or attending meetings.

  2. Time on the learners' *timetable during which they are required to study but without input from a teacher and, usually in the case of older learners, without supervision. It is 'directed' time in that clear instructions are provided by the teacher beforehand about the specific task or tasks to be undertaken as well as the total study time required. A typical period of directed study might involve the learner in carrying out a library task, such as research; or in reading and analysing a given text or texts. It is a strategy often used in *further and *higher education where the age of the learners does not require that they be closely supervised.

director of studies Used to describe a variety of roles in schools, colleges, and universities, so that the precise definition will depend upon the institution and the context concerned. In a large school this title may denote the senior member of staff responsible for coordinating the teaching and learning. In some institutions it might be used to indicate responsibility for a particular *curriculum area and involve duties of the sort associated with a departmental head. In *higher education it is often used as a term for the principal supervisor of a doctoral research student, to distinguish them from other members of the supervisory team. The title may therefore, according to context, indicate a whole-institution responsibility, a departmental leadership role, or small-team academic leadership.

disadvantaged A learner may be disadvantaged by their social, economic, physical, or family circumstances. Where any one (or more) of these is the case, there are implications for the learner's specific educational needs, and how they can best be met. The concept of disadvantage is linked to that of deprivation, in the sense that social or economic deprivation can result in individuals or sections of society being disadvantaged educationally and therefore in terms of their life chances in general. *See also* SOCIAL CLASS; SOCIAL JUSTICE.

disapplication Used to describe instances where an exception is made to the statutory requirement to apply the *national curriculum to the education of all pupils. For example, in the case of 14-year-olds undertaking a *vocational course which replaces a part of their *national curriculum *Key Stage 4 studies, that part of the national curriculum is said to have been **disapplied**.

discipline 1. A field of academic study, such as chemistry or English, which constitutes an area of teaching and research within *higher education and in the academic community as a whole.
  2. The control exerted by a teacher over the *behaviour of the learners. 'Discipline' in this sense is less frequently used now than the alternative expressions: **classroom control** behaviour improvement, and behaviour management, perhaps partly because of associations with *Foucault's usage of the term to denote social and political manipulation.

discovery learning An approach to learning in which the learner is allowed to explore and become actively engaged with concepts, objects, or the physical environment in order to develop their understanding of it. In this process, the teacher is a facilitator rather than an instructor, and it is their role to organize a rich or appropriately resourced learning environment and to encourage the learner's self-directed curiosity and problem-solving skills, rather than to demonstrate or provide 'correct' answers or procedures. Discovery learning is a *learner-centred approach, theoretically underpinned by a *humanist philosophy of education, according to which the planning and teaching of lessons should take into account the learners' needs in relation to their social, emotional, and personal development, and should take as their starting point those topics which are of direct interest and relevance to the learners. The principles of discovery learning for the education of young children were set out by *Piaget, who, while stressing the need for the teacher to adopt a non-directive and relatively non-didactic role, nevertheless emphasized the importance of peer interaction in the process of such learning as a means of encouraging the child to engage with and consider viewpoints which perhaps conflicted with their own (a process known as **socio-cognitive conflict**) in order to develop their ability to review and revise their own understanding. Piaget argued that, while children might refine and evaluate their own ideas as a result of socio-cognitive conflict with peers, they would tend to adopt uncritically and too easily the ideas of teachers and other adults where these conflicted with their own. In the latter case the result would be conventional instructional learning rather than learning constructed by the child through their own discoveries.

discrimination *See* EQUAL OPPORTUNITIES ACT 2006; SOCIAL JUSTICE.

disruptive Children and young people who have difficulty forming relationships owing to persistent antisocial *behaviours such as lying, breaking of rules, aggression, stealing, defiance of authority, and cruelty may have **disruptive behaviour disorder**. Many children will show some of these behaviours occasionally but it is the pattern of consistency which suggests a mental health disorder. 'Disruptive behaviour disorder' is an overarching label for a range of conditions including **oppositional defiant disorder** and **conduct disorder**. A coordinated approach to dealing with the disorder involving the child or young person's school, family, and other professionals is necessary, via a combination of treatments embracing therapy (*see* CHILD AND ADOLESCENT MENTAL HEALTH SERVICES), specialist parent training, and possibly medication. *See also* PUPIL REFERRAL UNIT.   TB, LE

dissemination Sometimes referred to as the **sharing of good practice**, dissemination is an integral part both of *curriculum development and of teachers' own professional development. Ideas and examples of good practice may be disseminated through conferences, web sites, academic papers and other publications, national bodies and committees, local authority advisory services, or in-service professional development programmes. Dissemination may take place within a school, college, or university, or between institutions on a local or national level.

dissertation A lengthy piece of academic writing based on research undertaken by the candidate and submitted by them in partial fulfilment of the requirement for an award, usually as postgraduate level, such as that of a *master's degree. It is a term sometimes used interchangeably with *thesis, although in most universities it is used to assess candidates at a level lower than that of *doctorate.

distance learning A mode of learning designed to be undertaken without frequent or regular direct face-to-face contact between student and teacher. It is also sometimes referred to as *distributed learning. It usually involves the production and distribution of learning materials by the supporting institution to the student, either in hard copy or, as is more normal today, by electronic means. Students are provided with tutorial support, which takes place by telephone, email, or other electronic means, possibly with occasional face-to-face meetings and short periods of attendance, such as a weekend or summer school. The *Open University is perhaps the best-known provider of this mode of learning in the United Kingdom, although many universities and colleges also run their own programmes. In Scotland the University of the Highlands and Islands (UHI) Millennium Institute provides access to graduate level study through a partnership of colleges and research institutions for students in the highlands and islands. *See also* E-LEARNING.

(⊕) SEE WEB LINKS
• Describes the operation of the UHI and the courses it offers.

distributed learning A mode of study in which students are following the same programme of learning but do not come together as a group in the same location. It is a term which is now applied to *distance learning. The rapid growth of information communication technology to support learning and teaching has facilitated the development of distributed learning through electronic networks and web sites. *See also* ASYNCHRONOUS LEARNING.

divergent thinking A process which seeks a number of possible solutions to a question, rather than assuming, as is the case in **convergent thinking**, that there can be only one correct answer and only one way to arrive at it. Some educationalists have suggested that the ability to apply divergent thinking indicates a predisposition towards success in arts subjects rather than in sciences, since it is regarded as a creative, rather than an analytical, skill. *See also* LATERAL THINKING.

doctorate The highest *postgraduate degree award made by a university or other institution of *higher education. The degree of Doctor of Philosophy (Ph.D. or D.Phil.) is awarded following the candidate's successful completion of a *thesis, which they must also successfully defend at a *viva voce examination. Higher doctorates such as Doctor of Literature (D.Litt.) are awarded in acknowledgement of the recipient's body of published works. Once awarded the doctorate, the successful candidate is entitled to be called 'doctor' if he or she so wishes.

don A colloquial term for university lecturers or teachers. It was originally applied only to those who were Fellows of an Oxford or Cambridge college, and indicated a person of rank. It has since entered the colloquial Australian vocabulary as a synonym for 'expert'.

Down syndrome A genetic condition caused by the presence of an additional copy of chromosome 21 at conception, affecting roughly one in every thousand babies in the United Kingdom a year. Why an additional copy of the chromosome is present is unknown, although the incidence increases with maternal age, especially when the mother is over 35. Developmentally, a degree of *learning difficulty is associated with the syndrome, although the severity of this can differ considerably from individual to individual. Most children with Down syndrome will encounter delay in speech and language acquisition and reach motor milestones at a later age than the norm. Frequently children of school age will be in receipt of a *statement of special educational need, but increasingly they are being educated in mainstream schools, where they will particularly benefit from teaching strategies designed to develop language and communication skills, social skills, and psychomotor skills. Despite myths and prejudices to the contrary, many children and young adults with Down syndrome have considerable potential for going on from education to gain employment and lead independent lives.

A number of medical conditions such as heart deformity, thyroid gland problems, and cataracts are associated with the syndrome, and it is essential, therefore, that such learners have access to good health care if they are to enjoy their experience of education and maximize their potential.

SEE WEB LINKS

• Provides useful information on Down syndrome for professionals in the fields of education, medicine, and social care.

Dunning Report (1977) The Report sets out the findings of the Dunning Committee, which recommended that all pupils should be given the opportunity to take courses leading to the *Scottish Certificate of Education and that both examinations and internal assessment by teachers should play a part in determining awards. It also advised that all pupils should be assessed in a way which would enable them to demonstrate positive achievement. Together with the *Munn Report, this document was the basis of the focus on equality of access to education in the Scottish education system after 1977. *See also* SCOTLAND, EDUCATION IN; SCOTTISH LEAVING CERTIFICATE.   SM

dyscalculia A specific learning difficulty in mathematics. Many of the characteristics found in *dyslexics are also found in people with dyscalculia. Errors will be made when writing and reading numbers. The position and reversal of digits is common, so that, for example, 127 can be written as 721. Difficulties in sequencing creates problems with turn-taking. Spatial problems such as confusing left and right may be present. People with dyscalculia will also struggle with life skills such as understanding time and money and personal organization. Seemingly straightforward mathematical processes are often beyond a person with dyscalculia and present tremendous obstacles to them.   TB, LE

dyslexia A specific learning difficulty which affects the ability to recognize words fluently and/or accurately; causes problems with spelling, auditory short-term memory, phonic skills, multi-tasking, remembering instructions, and organizational skills. Spelling is erratic, with letters of a similar shape such as *b* and *d* being mixed up. Words and letters may be written back to front. Learners with dyslexia can find it hard to keep their place when reading, as print seems to be shifting on the page. Because they have problems with phonological processes, blending and sequencing to sound out a word becomes problematical. As a result of these difficulties with reading, the dyslexic learner may find their functional vocabulary and general knowledge restricted. However, dyslexia is by no means an indicator of lack of academic ability or intelligence. Indeed, Albert Einstein is said to have been dyslexic. Educational psychologists will not diagnose a pupil as dyslexic before the age of seven, after which it is possible to assess the pupil's cognitive strengths and weaknesses and suggest further support if appropriate. In schools, colleges, and universities learners who have been diagnosed as having dyslexia are provided with additional support, including being allowed additional time to complete tests, examinations, and homework. Difficulties with reading are not always synonymous with dyslexia, however, but could arise from other causes such as impaired sight or hearing, cognitive impairment, or emotional problems. Dyslexia affects between 3 and 10 per cent of the population. It is neurobiological in origin and may run in families. *See also* DYSCALCULIA; DYSPRAXIA.

dyspraxia A coordination disorder causing specific difficulty in planning an action or movement (fine or gross motor), sequencing the movements required, and performing the action in a smooth and controlled way. A child with dyspraxia is likely to have difficulty with planning movements in physical education, undertaking basic motor skills such as catching a ball and climbing, recording their knowledge on paper, and organizing themselves. They are likely to have an average or higher than average IQ and good general knowledge, but this is not reflected in their school work owing to difficulties with organization and handwriting. Dyspraxia is often linked with *developmental coordination disorder and with *dyslexia. TB, LE

early intervention Professional agencies working together to respond to the additional needs of pre-school or school age children without delay. These needs may be due factors within the child, e.g. disability, or situations surrounding the child and their family, e.g. social issues. For every child identified as requiring multi-agency support, a lead professional should be allocated to take responsibility for co-coordination. Early intervention may be directly focused on the child in the form, for example, of support from a specialist pre-school teacher, or it may involve professionals working together to address issues surrounding the child. Early intervention is firmly routed in the *Every Child Matters agenda. *See also* COMMON ASSESSMENT FRAMEWORK. TB, LE

early years A crucial stage of life in terms of children's physical, intellectual, emotional, and social development and well-being, internationally recognized as the years 0–8, when growth is both rapid and differential. A significantly high proportion of learning takes place between the ages of 0 and 6, and it is a period of time when children need particularly high-quality care and learning experiences from attuned adults and an appropriate environment. *See also* EARLY YEARS FOUNDATION STAGE. AW

Early Years Foundation Stage (EYFS) A framework setting out the national standards for the learning, care, and development of children from birth to the age of 5 which was launched in 2007 and became a requirement for all schools and *early years providers from September 2008. It superseded previous statutory guidance for the *Foundation Stage, as well as the *Birth to Three Matters framework and the previously existing frameworks applying to day care and childminding for under-8s. The framework makes it a requirement for all providers to teach *literacy and *numeracy skills to under-5s, so that, by the age of 5, children have acquired sufficient knowledge of *phonics to write simple words, and to begin to form simple sentences in writing. Under the terms of the framework, children should also be taught to understand simple concepts of addition and subtraction. In addition, it requires carers to base their planning of learning activities on their structured observations and assessments of children's learning, play, and behaviour in order to ensure that such activities are appropriate to the child's stage of development. These assessments can then be shared with parents, carers, and appropriate professionals.

The introduction of this framework gave rise to some controversy and earned it the nickname 'the nappy curriculum'. Opponents include many teachers and academics, particularly those engaged with the *Montessori or *Steiner approaches to early years education, who express fears that its introduction of formal literacy and numeracy instruction to very young children runs counter to the developmental needs of this age group. Opposition was also expressed at the failure of the framework to make opportunities for outdoor play a mandatory requirement, and at its raising the pupil–adult ratio limit in some cases from the previously required 8:1 to 13:1. Supporters of the framework, on the other hand, argue that it allows flexibility and encourages providers to employ more qualified specialist staff.

Economic and Social Research Council (ESRC) A body to which educational researchers in universities and other institutions of *higher education may apply for funding for *research projects. This is because, in an academic context, education is included as one of the social sciences. Applications for funding are considered not only against criteria relating to research design and originality, but also according to whether they focus on issues which have been identified as being of priority concern in the field.

Edexcel *See* AWARDING BODY.

educability The extent to which an individual or group is considered able to benefit from a programme of education. It is a term laden with assumptions, and is used with caution by educationalists, many of whom prefer to take the approach that almost everyone is capable of learning if the learner's level of capability, rather than the requirements of the *syllabus or *curriculum, is taken as a starting point.

Education Act Legislation relating to innovation and reform of the education system, its provisions, funding, inspection, curriculum, and assessment is agreed by Parliament in the form of Education Acts. These are normally preceded by a *White Paper, which sets out the arguments for the policy to be enacted; or by a *Green Paper, which calls for consultation over some aspect of the policy prior to legislation. Over the past century or so there have been a number of landmark Acts which have signalled significant changes in key aspects of the education system. Examples of these may be summarized as follows:

Education Act 1902	Made the Board of Education centrally responsible for educational provision; created *local education authorities
Education Act 1918	Raised the school-leaving age to 14
Education (*Butler) Act 1944	Reorganized education into three sectors we recognize today as primary, secondary, and further education
Education Act 1979	Made the development of a comprehensive system of secondary education by local authorities optional rather than mandatory (by repealing an earlier Act of 1976), thus enabling some authorities to retain a selective system

Education Act 1980	Gave parents the right of representation on schools' governing bodies; required local authorities and governing bodies to demonstrate transparency in relation to examination results and admissions policies; introduced the concept of parental *choice
Education Act 1986	Abolished corporal punishment in schools; required every local authority school to have a governing body, and gave added responsibilities to governors
Education Reform Act 1988	Introduced the *national curriculum and the option for schools to apply for *grant maintained status
Education (Schools) Act 1992	Introduced the requirement for schools and local authorities to publish *league tables based on examination performance; instigated four-yearly inspections of schools by *Ofsted
*Further and Higher Education Act 1992	Enabled polytechnics to adopt university status
Education Act 1996	Section 19 of this Act requires local authorities to provide appropriate education for children of compulsory school age either at school or otherwise than at school; forms of alternative provision are now known as *education otherwise (than at school)
Education Act 1997	Brought together general and vocational qualifications under one regulating authority by replacing the *School Curriculum and Assessment Authority and *National Council for Vocational Qualifications with the unitary *Qualifications and Curriculum Authority
School Standards and Framework Act 1998	Created *education action zones; empowered local authorities and the Secretary of State to intervene in the case of *failing schools; replaced the *grant maintained schools initiative with *foundation schools
Education Act 2002	Was amended at a late stage to include a specific duty on state schools and local authorities to have arrangements in place for safeguarding children. This amendment is contained in section 175, and came into force later (June 2004)
Education (Scotland) Act 2004	Addressed the issue of educational support in Scotland's schools
Children Act 2004	Superseded the *Children Act 1989 and set out a legislative spine for the government's

wider strategy in England and Wales, for improving children's lives, covering universal and parental responsibility, the *Every Child Matters agenda, services accessed by children, and the targeted services for those with additional needs

Education Act 2005
One of the longest Education Acts since that of 1944. Introduced a system of shorter, sharper inspections, with small Ofsted inspection teams visiting schools for no more than two days; schools to be judged not only by quality of teaching but also against the outcomes of the *Children Act 2004 and how they promote pupils' well-being; replaced the Teacher Training Agency with the **Training and Development Agency**; encouraged local authorities to exert local leadership, but with effectively less funding

Education and Inspections Act 2006
Enabled schools to become trust schools; local authorities regained some of their strategic role; introduced specialized *diplomas for 14–19-year-olds; merged inspectorates to become the Office for Standards in Education, Children's Services, and Skills; extended the power of the *Learning and Skills Council to providing support for under-16s

Child Care Act 2006
Legislated for the duties, regulations, and inspection arrangements in England and Wales for childcare providers, simplifying the Ofsted Child Care Register Standards

Apprenticeship, Skills, Children, and Learning Act (2009)
Set out the role of the *Office of Qualifications and Examinations Regulation (Ofqual)

Education Act (2011)
Expanded the *academies programme; made reforms to the *Ofsted inspection regime and to *student loans; and gave free *early years provision for disadvantaged 2-year-olds. Its key emphasis, however, was on *discipline in schools, with powers given to teachers to search pupils for banned items such as drugs and weapons. It provided additional protection for teachers from false allegations by pupils, and replaced *exclusion appeal panels with **review panels** which are not empowered to force schools to reinstate excluded pupils.

See also EQUAL OPPORTUNITIES ACT 2006.

(⊕) SEE WEB LINKS
• Provides full-text version of the White Paper *The Importance of Teaching* (2010), the proposals of which are enacted in the 2011 Act.

education action zone (EAZ) A partnership between a group of schools which also involves local businesses, parents, and the *local authority for the purpose of raising educational standards in areas where such standards are cause for concern, and particularly in areas of social deprivation. Each zone consists of around 15–25 schools and receives about £1 million extra funding each year, 75 per cent of which comes from central government; the remainder of the funding is raised by the zone itself from its business and commercial partners in the private sector. Each zone is managed by a project director and run by an action forum of local partners. EAZs were introduced under the provisions of the Schools Standards and Framework Act 1998, and each is supported for a maximum of five years, after which it becomes an *Excellence in Cities action zone or an **Excellence Cluster**.

Educational Institute of Scotland (EIS) Founded in 1847, the EIS is the oldest teaching union in UK. It has over 59 000 members and represents around 80 per cent of teachers in Scotland, working in nursery, primary, secondary, and special education, right through to further and higher education. *See also* TEACHERS' UNIONS.   SM

(⊕) SEE WEB LINKS
• Provides information about the union's activities and events, including links to tweets.

educational psychologist Psychologists often employed by the local authority who specialize in the psychology of children, particularly as it relates to motivation and learning. They provide diagnoses of emotional or behavioural difficulties and of specific learning needs and disabilities. Training for educational psychology usually requires that the applicant hold a first degree or equivalent in psychology, or, in the case of graduates in other disciplines, have attended a bridging course in psychology before commencing their formal educational psychology training. It is also normally expected that an applicant to the profession will be a qualified teacher with at least two years' teaching experience.

Education Funding Agency (EFA) An executive agency of the *Department for Education, established in April 2012, to manage the funding for all state-provided education for learners aged between 3 and 19 years. In addition to *maintained schools and *sixth form colleges, it funds provision for learners with a disability or learning difficulties up to the age of 25; monitors and funds *academies; and supports building site maintenance for schools and sixth form colleges. Funding for education is allocated to *local authorities. The EFA has offices throughout England, in London, Coventry, Sheffield, Darlington, Manchester, Nottingham, and Bristol.

SEE WEB LINKS
• Provides details of EFA's role and responsibilities.

Education, Health, and Care Plan (EHCP) *See* STATEMENT OF SPECIAL EDUCATIONAL NEEDS.

Education Maintenance Allowance (EMA) A regular weekly payment of up to £30 made to young people over the age of compulsory education who went on to some form of further education or training. Introduced as a pilot scheme in a limited number of local authorities in England in 1998, the EMA was originally conceived as a means of encouraging 16-year-olds from low-income families to stay on in education or training. After the initial three years of the scheme it was widely adopted, and was also launched in Scotland in 2004. Payment is made directly into the student's bank account. Because payment of the allowance is contingent on the student's regular attendance, some teachers in further education have found it an effective source of motivation for students, although others claim that, while it encourages attendance, it does not necessarily improve students' motivation to engage with their learning when they are there. It was discontinued in England in 2010, but remains in place in Northern Ireland, Scotland, and Wales.

SEE WEB LINKS
• Provides details of eligibility and of the results of Scottish pilots such as that in East Ayrshire in 2002.

education otherwise than at school (EOTAS) Section 19 of the Education Act 1996 states that *local authorities must provide appropriate education for children of compulsory school age either at school or otherwise than at school. Placements must be appropriate to the needs and ability of the child (including any special educational need), in line with local authority policy and their requirement to use public resources efficiently, and agreed with the child's parents. Education Otherwise, also referred to as 'alternative provision', encompasses a range of provision including *pupil referral units, hospital schools, home tuition, further education *colleges, *work experience, private or voluntary sector schools, teenage pregnancy units, and *National Vocational Qualifications. Parents may also take the decision to educate their child otherwise than at school by electing to pay for an independent school place or by providing education at home. *See also* HOME EDUCATION.   TB, LE

Education Reform Act 1988 (ERA) Introduced originally as the Great Education Reform Bill (colloquially referred to at the time as Gerbil), this Act marked a major milestone in education provision, introducing for the first time a *national curriculum with core subjects (English, science, mathematics, and religious education) taught to all pupils. It also introduced the need to promote the cultural, moral, and spiritual development both of pupils and in wider society as a whole; and it began the process of delegating responsibility for school finance away from local authorities to the schools themselves, introducing the concept of *grant maintained schools. *Further education colleges were removed from local authority control, and their governing bodies were required to have less local authority representation but to ensure representation by local employers. In this way the Act illustrates two major themes which were to continue through education policy for the next two decades: the diminishing of local authority control over educational funding, policy, and practice, and the introduction of *market values into educational provision. *See also* EDUCATION ACT.

Education Scotland A Scottish government executive agency, established in 2011 to support quality and improvement in Scottish education. It works in partnership with *local authorities and other bodies to support *curriculum implementation, encourage the professional development of teachers and educational leaders, provide independent evaluation of provision, and give evidence-based advice on policy and practice. Although directly accountable to the Scottish government, it operates independently and is not politically aligned to any party. Its chief executive is responsible for its performance within the terms of the **Education Scotland Framework** document.

((()) SEE WEB LINKS
• Provides a link to the Framework document which defines Education Scotland's role.

Education (Scotland) Act 2004 This replaced sections of the Education (Scotland) Act 1980, which dealt with additional support for learning. The Education (Additional Support for Learning) Scotland Act 2004 sought to change the way in which children and young people's educational support was identified, planned, and recorded. Key changes included the replacement of *special educational needs with additional support needs; the introduction of new duties on education authorities and other agencies; measures to improve integrated working; greater rights for parents and young people along with provisions for avoiding and resolving disputes; and the introduction of a coordinated support plan.   SM

Education Welfare Service (EWS) A service which acts on behalf of the *local authority to ensure that parents fulfil their legal obligation to provide their child with an appropriate education. Its officers, known as education welfare officers (EWOs), education social workers, or attendance advisers, work with families and with schools to address cases of persistent *truancy and other problems of non-attendance. Parents or carers can be served with a notice or school attendance order if EWOs discover a child is not receiving an education. EWOs also support families of pupils who have encountered difficulties at school, or where home circumstances are causing disruption to the child's education.

educator Used as an alternative word for 'teacher', particularly in the context of adult and community education, where the emphasis is upon facilitative rather than didactic teaching. The relationship implied between educator and

learner (or 'educatee') is a more equal or egalitarian one than that between
teacher and pupil; and one through which both parties expect to learn and to
develop their understanding. This is particularly the case where education is
aimed at bringing about economic change or social justice, as, for example, in
the work of Paulo *Freire. The term may also be used in order to distinguish
the concept of a teacher as one who encourages individual development and a
spirit of enquiry from that of one who delivers standardized training or a
prescribed curriculum in line with the *objectivist model of teaching. Thus,
an educator has come to mean more than simply a transmitter of knowledge
or skills.

e-learning Learning facilitated by the use of computers, using the Internet, an
institution's intranet, or material on disks. The term is an abbreviation of
'electronic learning', and is an aspect of *information communication
technology. As a form of *distance learning, it is often described as 'distributed,
*asynchronous learning'—distributed in the sense that learners are not all in one
location, and asynchronous in that they are not learning at the same time.
Although this mode of learning has a number of advantages, such as allowing
large groups of learners anywhere in the world to network through chat rooms or
to discuss issues between themselves and their tutor through online discussions,
it also presents some potential barriers to learning. For example, it requires
learners to have functional levels of literacy in both the traditional sense and with
regard to *information technology; and it does not provide face-to-face contact
with the tutor or teacher (except perhaps through a webcam), or between the
learners themselves. The removal of this social aspect of the educational
experience does not appeal to all learners. The dynamics of e-learning have led to
the development of a slightly different terminology for this mode of teaching and
learning. E-learners are often referred to as 'participants' rather than students;
and the teacher managing the learning programme may be referred to as the
'e-moderator', facilitator, or tutor. Group discussions in e-learning, which allow
the thread of each participant's contribution to be reviewed and summarized, are
known as **threaded discussions**. Salmon (2004) presents a model of e-learning
which consists of five steps in the course of which the tutor or e-moderator
progresses from being proactive and directive to being responsive and
supportive, while the learner progresses from being dependent and reactive to
independent and proactive. Where an e-learning approach is used as only part of
a programme of learning, combined with provision for face-to-face contact with
tutor and other students in a conventional attendance mode, this is known as
*blended learning.

Further Reading: G. Salmon *E-Moderating: The Key to Teaching and Learning Online*
(Kogan Page, 2004).

element In *National Vocational Qualifications (NVQs) statements of
*competence are broken down into their constituent parts, the smallest of which
is an element of competence. It is against these elements of competence that the
NVQ candidate is assessed. A number of elements make up a *unit of

competence. Units, but not their constituent elements, may be awarded separately as part of a process of credit accumulation.

elementary school Prior to the 1944 Education Act (*Butler Act), elementary schools were the standard educational provision for pupils aged 5–14. They were replaced by the system of primary and secondary schools with which we are more familiar today.

Eleven Plus A *test or *examination once commonly taken by pupils at the age of 11 to determine their progression route into secondary education. Administered by *local authorities, the Eleven Plus could take the form of an examination in English, mathematics, and general knowledge, or of a test which aimed to measure the *intelligence quotient (IQ) of pupils. Those who achieved highest scores gained entry to *grammar school or grammar technical school; the rest were destined for technical or secondary modern schools. When this system of *selection at the age of 11 gave way in most authorities to a system of non-selective, *comprehensive education following the *Education Act 1976, the Eleven Plus was largely discontinued, except within those authorities with a strong Conservative council, such as Lincolnshire and Kent, where the policy of retaining their grammar and secondary modern schools was enabled to continue by the Education Act 1979, which made the abolition of selection optional rather than mandatory, and meant that the testing for selection at the age of 11 continued to be used in some authorities into the 21st century.

The accuracy of the Eleven Plus as a predictor of future achievement has been widely questioned. In addition, it is now argued that two key factors cast doubt on its validity and reliability as a method of assessment. One concerns doubts raised over the use of blanket IQ testing, with its assumptions of implicit cultural and ethnic norms. Another arises from the recognition that testing for selection tended to favour boys, since their scores were often adjusted in cohorts where fewer boys than girls achieved a 'pass', in order to balance the numbers of boys and girls progressing to grammar schools. *See also* BUTLER ACT; INTELLIGENCE TEST.

emeritus A title awarded to *professors, and sometimes to *readers, on their retirement, in acknowledgement of their continuing outstanding contribution to their area of work. Their title then becomes 'emeritus professor' or 'emeritus reader' of whatever is their specialist field.

emotional intelligence A theory developed in the 1970s and 1980s by Howard Gardner (b. 1943) and others, and popularized by Daniel Goleman (2005), which suggests that the ability to think and act from a position of awareness of one's own emotions and with sensitivity to the emotions of others is a form of intelligence which is undervalued in comparison to cognitive or intellectual *intelligence, as measured by traditional *intelligence tests. Purely cognitive intelligence, argues Goleman, is of limited use in forming and sustaining relationships, and in conducting most social interactions, where our feelings—emotions or intuitions—need to come into play. This idea can usefully be applied to the teacher–learner relationship. The emotionally intelligent teacher would typically have a knowledge of their own strengths and weaknesses; be able to exert control over their own emotions; recognize the emotional needs of others; and demonstrate honesty and integrity. In this sense, emotional intelligence could be said to be integral to the *humanist ideal of the teacher, as presented by, for example, Carl *Rogers. This form of intelligence is also increasingly regarded as a subject which may be taught in schools, as witnessed by publications such as Maurice Elias and Harriett Arnold's *Educator's Guide to Emotional Intelligence and Academic Achievement: Social-Emotional Learning in the Classroom* (Sage, 2006). The complex set of skills and qualities described by proponents of the emotional intelligence theory goes far beyond the common misunderstanding of emotional intelligence simply as a willingness to display one's emotions, and emphasizes the central role which self-knowledge plays in our personal development and social interactions.

Further Reading: D. Goleman *Emotional Intelligence* (Bantam Books, 2005).

(⊕) SEE WEB LINKS
• Provides details of the emotional intelligence theory and links to critical analyses.

employability The extent to which an individual possesses the skills and qualities required by employers in a suitable employee. These will usually include the *key skills of communication and *numeracy, and qualities such as willingness and an ability to interact appropriately with others, as well as *vocationally specific skills. In an era when much education and training policy is driven by the imperative to build a more highly skilled workforce, the notion of employability has become increasingly relevant to the prevalent understanding of education's purpose.

employer engagement Also referred to as **employer links**, this is a catch-all term for the initiatives, particularly in *vocational *further education and training, aimed at involving local employers in the planning, development, delivery, and evaluation of learning programmes. It is closely associated with the first theme of the *White Paper *Success for All* (2002), 'meeting needs, improving choice', which acknowledged that existing provision at that time did not uniformly meet the requirements of local employers, and that ways to improve collaboration and communication between employers and education and training providers should be developed.

Many further and *higher education institutions have responded to this challenge by creating business units to centralize responsibility for employer links and engagement, and to separate this aspect of provision from that which is publicly funded; others devolve it to individual departments, a strategy which may enable them to avoid internal competition or potential communication problems. Typically, local partnerships are formed with business links and chambers of commerce, as well as relevant local and regional boards. The *governing bodies of education providers offer a universally used forum for engagement, in addition to other formal opportunities. *See also* NEET; WORK-BASED LEARNING; APPRENTICESHIP. VC, KA

employer-led A phrase used to describe the origins of national occupational standards in many spheres of work; and also to identify the influence which has shaped some aspects of education and training policy. Standards which are employer-led are those which are identified by employers through common agreement as being necessary for carrying out skilled work in their vocational area, and are then set as the national standard at a number of levels of skill. Policies which are said to be employer-led are those which are drawn up in response to needs expressed by employers in terms of the skills required of potential employees. At a national level an employer-led approach could be said to include the introduction of a *National Vocational Qualification framework in 1986, and the setting up of the **Learning and Skills Council** in 2001.

England, education in Responsibility for education and *training is divided between two specialized governments departments, each headed by a Secretary of State: the *Department for Education (DfE), with a remit for compulsory education and children's services; and the *Department for Business, Innovation, and Skills (DBIS), with a remit for science, *further and *higher education, and skills training.

Education in school is compulsory from the age of 5, although more than 50 per cent of under-5s attend some form of *pre-school provision, and the *Early Years Foundation Stage sets out a curriculum for children aged 0–5. The age for leaving education has risen from 16 to 17 in 2014, and to 18 in 2015. Since the beginning of the 21st century the majority of 16-year-olds have remained in some form of education or training at least until the age of 18. Those who have not have become known by the acronym *NEETs (not in education, employment, or training).

In most *local authorities there is a system of *primary schools and secondary schools, with transfer to secondary school being made at the age of 11. In some authorities, however, a system of *first, *middle, and secondary schools operates, with middle schools providing for 8–12-year-olds. Most secondary provision is in the form of *comprehensive schools, although a small minority of local authorities have retained a system of *selection at 11 through the *Eleven Plus examination, according to the results of which pupils are allocated a place at either a *grammar school or a non-selective school in their local authority area. *Academies, which are nominally non-selective, are currently the fastest-growing type of secondary school.

A *national curriculum was introduced in 1998, consisting of four *key stages, for ages 5–7, 8–11, 11–14, and 14–16, at the end of each of which pupils are assessed. At the end of Key Stage 4 the *assessment for most pupils takes the form of the *General Certificate of Secondary Education (GCSE), which was originally conceived of as a school-leaving examination, but is now seen more as a means of selection to determine the next stage in pupils' progression. A performance measure, known as the *English Baccalaureat (EBacc), acknowledges the attainment of candidates who achieve grade C or above in English, mathematics, history or geography, two sciences. and a classical or modern foreign language. Progression from this stage may be into a school sixth form or a *sixth form college to study for *General Certificate of Education *Advanced Levels (A levels) or *Vocational A levels or to a *college of further education for more vocationally focused education or training. Some pupils may take the option to incorporate some vocational elements at the beginning of Key Stage 4.

At 18 many students use their A level or equivalent qualification to progress to *university or some other form of *higher education. Others may proceed to employment or further *skills training. The creation of a more highly skilled workforce has been the goal of successive governments since the last quarter of the 20th century. Adult and *continuing education may take the form of re-skilling or up-skilling for work, of personal development, or of learning for leisure. Only the first of these qualifies for subsidized funding. Providers of *adult education include the *Workers' Educational Association (WEA), local authorities, and further education colleges. *Ofsted is responsible for the inspection of primary, secondary, and further education provision, and of teacher training provision in higher education. Other higher education provision is subject to inspection by the *Quality Assurance Agency.

English as a Foreign Language (EFL) Taught both overseas and in the United Kingdom to learners for whom English is not their first language, and whose permanent place of residence is not the UK. It is this latter fact that distinguishes it from *English for Speakers of Other Languages, which is intended for those who have made their home in the UK. The *British Council takes a leading role in the provision of EFL overseas. *See also* ENGLISH FOR SPEAKERS OF OTHER LANGUAGES.

English as an Additional Language (EAL) *See* ENGLISH FOR SPEAKERS OF OTHER LANGUAGES.

English Baccalaureat (EBacc) A performance measure at *General Certificate of Secondary Education (GCSE) which certifies that the candidate has achieved grade C or above in English, mathematics, history or geography, two sciences, and a classical or modern foreign language. It is not a separate qualification, but rather an acknowledgement of achievement across the breadth of the *Key Stage 4 curriculum. The purpose for its introduction, proposed in the White Paper *The Importance of Teaching* (2010), was to encourage a broad range of achievement, mirroring the principle of the French *baccalauréat. It has been used as an indicator of schools' performance since 2011 and has clear implications for schools in providing pupils with appropriate advice and guidance on subject choices. It should not be confused with the English Baccalaureat Certificate which was proposed in 2013 as a replacement for GCSEs, but quickly abandoned in the face of widespread opposition.

((⊕)) SEE WEB LINKS
• Provides detailed information on the subjects required for the EBacc designation.

English for Speakers of Other Languages (ESOL) The provision of English language learning for those with other first languages who have settled in the UK. The *Adult ESOL Core Curriculum* of 2001 outlined the skills, knowledge, and understanding that non-native English speakers need to demonstrate as set out in the National Standards drawn up by the Basic Skills Agency. The adult ESOL curriculum, which relates to **Adult Literacy Standards** and *English as a Foreign Language, separates the skills of speaking and listening, to reflect the tendency for ESOL students to understand more than they can speak. ESOL learners constitute a diverse group of students in terms of the disparity in their cultural, educational, linguistic, and economic backgrounds. ESOL practitioners are therefore required to meet the challenge of planning and delivering differentiated but inclusive teaching and learning sessions. Teachers of ESOL have, since 2004, been required to gain specialized practitioner qualifications at level 4 on the *Qualifications and Credit Framework. *See also* BASIC SKILLS.   VC, KA

enhanced resources school A mainstream school which receives additional funding to meet the needs of pupils with a particular *special educational need or disability. A typical example of enhanced resource provision would be for pupils with hearing impairment. Schools in any key stage could have enhanced resourced status. Funding is received from the *local authority to be managed by the school to enhance staffing, teaching, and learning resources, the learning environment, and access to the curriculum. Pupils are generally taught with peers in lessons with additional adult support and appropriate equipment, but may receive specialist teaching in small groups or one-to-one within the resource base.   TB, LE

enquiry-based learning Sometimes described as 'learning by doing' or 'problem solving', this is an approach to learning which encourages the student or pupil to engage actively and analytically with an investigation or enquiry. This may take the form of a small-scale enquiry, for example, or a case study. It is *learner-centred in the sense that the student or pupil has the freedom to make decisions about the direction their enquiry will take, and to draw on their own existing knowledge or skills in order to extend them.

( ) SEE WEB LINKS

• Provides a link to a PDF document which sets out the definitions and purposes of enquiry-based learning.

enrichment A programme of activities designed to provide additional stimulus for more able pupils, or to give additional support to pupils from areas of social and cultural deprivation by providing some of the activities, resources, and stimuli not available to them in their home environment.

entitlement All students have a right or entitlement to a broad and balanced curriculum. Prior to the Education Act 1970, children with severe learning difficulties or disabilities were the responsibility of the Health Service and often labelled as ineducable. They had no access to school or qualified teachers. Schools can use the flexibility they now have to develop a curriculum which responds to the strengths and needs of all students. This would include award-bearing vocational and entry level courses at Key Stage 4. For younger children it requires appropriate differentiation of the *national curriculum to ensure they receive their entitlement to learn at their own level alongside their peers. Students should be given the opportunity to express their own hopes and aspirations for their future. TB, LE

entry level The lowest level of the *National Qualifications Framework, and based on a level of achievement below that of *General Certificate of Secondary Education. Foundation level qualifications are available in a range of subjects from the vocational, such as that in hairdressing, and the vocationally related, such as life skills, to national curriculum subjects such as science.

epistemology The study and understanding of knowledge. Teaching and learning depend on an often implicit understanding of what knowledge is. So does educational *research. Epistemology addresses the issue of what counts as knowledge. Theories of knowledge draw distinctions between knowledge understood as being, for instance, implicit or explicit; practical or theoretical; of things or of people; and of skills or of facts. Further distinctions are drawn between human wisdom and understanding as opposed to information. Only the latter can be stored or coded as facts and symbols. Some epistemologies take it that knowledge is independent of power and ethics, while others (for example, **postmodern**, **poststructural**, **feminist**, and social epistemologies) take these to be central. How these distinctions are articulated affects how questions are posed and answered about: how knowledge is recognized *as* knowledge, ways of getting it (methodology), and its relation to reality, truth, certainty, and cultural differences. All of these questions, including what counts as knowledge, are themselves dependent on *ontology, which addresses the issue of what exists. If the real is taken to be articulated as propositions that something is the case ('knowledge that'), then knowledge is held to be justified true belief. However, this formulation is inadequate if knowledge is held to include skills ('knowledge how') or to include understanding of social meanings which vary with social–cultural context **(relativism)**. MG

equal opportunities *See* SOCIAL JUSTICE.

Equal Opportunities Act 2006 This Act replaced the Equal Opportunities Commission, the Commission for Racial Equality, and the Disability Rights Commission with a unitary **Commission for Equality and Human Rights**. The Act requires public authorities to promote equality between men and women, and between girls and boys, and to explicitly prohibit sexual harassment. It also makes it unlawful for any individual, collective body, or organization to discriminate on the grounds of religion and belief; and it enables provision for the prohibition of discrimination on the grounds of sexual orientation. The Act represents an important step in anti-discrimination, and is of direct relevance not only to classroom practices, but also to the regulations and policies of all educational institutions. In semantic terms it is significant as a move away from the concept of 'equal opportunity' in favour of an emphasis on the *social justice constructions of 'equality' and rights. *See also* EDUCATION ACT.

Erikson, Erik (1902–94) A developmental psychologist and psychoanalyst
known for his theory on the social development of human beings. Through
his association with Anna Freud, and his study for a certificate in *Montessori
education, he became interested in the influence of culture and society on
child development, and his book *Childhood and Society* (1950) is considered
a classic text by educators, psychologists, and sociologists. For those
professionals working with the *early years, Erikson's theory of the **eight ages
of man** shows how children develop the foundation for emotional and social
development and mental strength through social interactions with significant
adults, and thus are able to assimilate the culture of their own community.
The attachments made with adults help to internalize culture, essentially
when the child is supported to 'pass through' each of the developmental
stages which define each individual child's personality. The stages, therefore, are
based on psychosocial development rather than, as *Piaget's are, on *cognitive
stages, which Erikson might argue are dependent on a child's well-being. Erikson's
theory, based on attachment to adults, suggests that it is essential for a child to
develop trust and empathy in order to be able to achieve higher levels of social
functioning. This reflects a similar notion to *Maslow's hierarchy of needs.
Erikson further states that these stages are epigenetic; that is, they are
predetermined and sequential. The confidence and self-esteem gained through
the success of the child overcoming each stage of psychosocial 'crisis', Erikson
suggests, should not be rushed, but can be revisited. In the early years, it is
critical for significant adults to help children develop trust, autonomy, and initiative
by offering real and practical tasks that the child will be able to accomplish and
which will therefore enable them to develop confidence. Requiring children to
learn, work, or carry out tasks beyond their stage of personality development,
Erikson argues, could have the effect of denying the child an opportunity for
their needs to be met, and may result in negative outcomes for the child, their
schooling,and their later successful participation as adults in society. Erikson was
Danish by parentage but became an American citizen. He is thought to have
coined the term 'identity crisis'.   AW

🌐 SEE WEB LINKS
• Provides an explanation of Erikson's wider work.

Estyn [Welsh *verb* 'to extend'] The office of Her Majesty's Inspectorate for
Education and Training in Wales, funded by the National Assembly for Wales but
independent from it. For Wales it is the equivalent body to *Ofsted in England.
Estyn is responsible for school inspections and for reporting on school
achievement for all levels of compulsory education, as well as for pre-schools,
government-funded training programmes, and colleges of further education,
including adult education. Stated objectives are to deliver high-quality inspection
of individual education and training providers, and related services, and to
provide advice, based on inspection evidence, to inform the Welsh Assembly
in the formulation and evaluation of education and training policy.   HG

🌐 SEE WEB LINKS
• Provides links to current issues and reports.

European Qualifications Framework (EQF) A system of cross-referencing equivalence of vocational qualification coverage and level across member countries of the European Union. Officially adopted by the European Parliament in 2008, its purpose is to encourage the flexibility and mobility of the European workforce and to encourage lifelong learning.

(⊕) SEE WEB LINKS
• Provides further details about the EQF.

European Quality Assurance Reference Framework (EQARF) A framework initiative in operation since 2009 to promote high standards of *vocational education and training (VET) by establishing parity in quality management for VET across Europe. It is informed by the drive to establish equivalence of competence and qualification from country to country in order to promote workforce mobility and an internationally shared confidence in the quality of VET. Arising from the aims of the Copenhagen Declaration, the EQARF has been formally adopted by the European parliament. *See also* QUALIFICATIONS AND CREDIT FRAMEWORK.

(⊕) SEE WEB LINKS
• Explains how the Framework is implemented.

evaluation The measuring of the effectiveness of a lesson, course, or *programme of study, often based upon, among other sources of evidence, the views and responses of the learners concerned, which constitutes qualitative evidence, as well as upon a quantitative assessment of the impact the course or lesson has had on learners' levels of *attainment. As well as participating in formal evaluations carried out for institutional purposes of quality assurance, teachers are encouraged to evaluate their own performance in planning, teaching, assessing, and supporting learning through a process of reflection on their professional practice. Evaluation is a process quite distinct from *assessment. While student attainment may be assessed, it is the effectiveness of the processes which have contributed to their learning which are the focus of evaluation, although this may include using assessment data on attainment as one source of evidence.

evening class Traditionally, a *lesson, or course of lessons, in the *post-compulsory sector, conducted after 5 p.m., and sometimes associated with leisure or cultural activities, such as yoga, holiday Spanish, local history, or the study of literature. Such classes are aimed primarily at adults, and are often held in colleges of *further education or on school premises. Although at one time subsidized by *local authorities, students are now required to pay the full cost of fees for attending such non-vocational provision. As a result, evening classes are currently declining in number, and are recruiting a narrower demographic, largely confined to those who can afford the increased fees. Vocationally related courses which are scheduled for evenings are usually run at this time because they are aimed at adult learners in employment who cannot attend during standard 9–5 working hours. The vocational content of such courses makes them eligible for funding. *See also* ADULT EDUCATION; WORKERS' EDUCATIONAL ASSOCIATION.

Every Child Matters This policy strategy was a shared programme of change to improve outcomes for all children and young people. At the time of its commencement (2004) it took forward the then UK government's 'vision of radical reform' for children, young people, and families and was set out in response to an inquiry regarding the death of **Victoria Climbié** in 2000. She was a child murder victim whose death led to major changes in child protection policies as a result of the **Laming Report** (2003) and to shared working agreements between the professional agencies (health, education, social services, probation) who may support children and their families. Every Child Matters applied to all children from 0 to 19, with the aim of improving educational achievement and reducing the levels of ill health, teenage pregnancy, abuse and neglect, crime, and antisocial behaviour. The shared outcomes—being healthy; staying safe; enjoying and achieving; making a positive contribution; and achieving economic well-being—are embedded in legislation (the *Children Act 2004), which was shared across all government services, and underpinned by an integrated inspection framework (*Common Assessment Framework) to ensure all services work together effectively and share information. Following the change of UK government in 2010, support and funding for the initiative, and the use of its terminology, went into decline.   AW

(((●))) SEE WEB LINKS
• Explains the background of this policy.

evidence-based teaching (EBT) The use of teaching methods and approaches which professional research has found to be effective. EBT links to the concept of **visible learning**. Because research findings can sometimes be contradictory, EBT draws on systematic reviews or meta-studies of available research which offer an evaluative synthesis of available research findings on a particular aspect of teaching and learning. In this way, key indicators are identified and the quality, reliability, and transferability of the findings are appraised. A range of such systematic meta-studies are available; some are aimed at teachers and some at academics. Two examples of the former are provided below.

Further Reading: J. Hattie *Visible Learning for Teachers* (Routledge, 2011).
G. Petty *Evidence Based Teaching: A Practical Approach* (2nd edn) (Nelson Thornes, 2009).

(((●))) SEE WEB LINKS
• Web site of the EBT network, providing details of EBT principles and practice.

examination A means of formal *summative assessment, usually involving time-constrained tasks, which assesses the *knowledge, *skills, or understanding of the candidate. Conduct of candidates and the regulation of start and finish times are usually monitored and enforced by one or more **invigilators**. The major national examinations in England, Northern Ireland, and Wales are the *General Certificate of Secondary Education and the *General Certificate of

Education (GCE) *Advanced Level (A level). In Scotland they are the *Standard
Grades, the *Highers, and the *Advanced Highers. These public examinations are
externally assessed by *external examiners, although schools and other
institutions may set their own examinations, for example when presenting
pupils with mock A levels, in which case the examination is internally assessed
by the candidates' teachers. Proponents of the examination system claim that
it has advantages over *continuous assessment in that it is a more reliable,
objective, and stringent means of *assessment. Opponents, on the other hand,
argue that examinations impose anxieties and false constraints which may
adversely affect candidates' performance, and that such restraints, being
unrealistic, undermine the examination's validity. Some researchers claim
that examinations disadvantage female candidates while *continuous
assessment disadvantages male candidates. Whatever the facts of the matter,
recent policy developments have shown a resurgence of emphasis on
assessment by examination and a reduction in continuous assessment by
coursework in both the GCSE and the GCE A level. *See also* COURSEWORK;
ACADEMIC RIGOUR.

examination board **1.** *See* AWARDING BODY.
   2. A formal board convened at a *university or *college to consider students'
assessment results and approve the mark, grade, or qualification awarded.
Such boards consist of course leaders and their teams, external examiners,
administrative staff, and a senior member of the institution in the role of chair.
In most cases, all assessment decisions on *undergraduate and *postgraduate
courses are subject to the approval of the examination board.

examination terminology Traditionally termed '**rubric**', *examination
terminology refers to the instructions to candidates found in examination
papers. An ability to understand and comply with these instructions is obviously
essential to the candidate's successful performance, and a failure to notice
or comprehend them could seriously disadvantage the candidate involved.
For this reason, many secondary schools now include guidance on examination
terminology in their preparation of pupils for the public examinations such
as the *General Certificate of Secondary Education and the *General
Certificate of Education *Advanced Level.

examiner, external **1.** In schools and colleges, the assessor responsible for
marking external examinations and other assessments. They are external in that
they represent the *awarding body and not the institution in which the candidate
has been taught.
   2. In *higher education the external examiner's role is to ensure that standards
of achievement are being maintained in line with those in other institutions,
and to this end an academic from another higher education institution is
usually chosen for this role. In the examination of candidates for a *doctorate,
the external examiner is selected in their capacity as an authority in the
candidate's field.

examiner, internal An examiner who assesses an internally set examination or piece of coursework, who teaches in the school, college, or university attended by the candidate, and may even be one of the candidate's teachers.

Excellent Teacher Scheme (ETS) A scheme designed to recognize the achievements and skills of excellent teachers by drawing upon their expertise to help other teachers to improve their effectiveness. Excellent teacher status was introduced in April 2006 as a means of rewarding teachers who wish to pursue their careers further without going into a management role in schools. In order to apply externally for an ET post, teachers must meet prescribed ET standards which are part of the government **framework of professional standards for teachers**. The government estimated that 5 000 teachers would apply for this route in the first year; in fact, by 2008 fewer than 40 teachers in all had qualified for excellent teacher status. Several reasons have been suggested for this, including the level of the fixed salary offered, the reluctance of teachers to put themselves forward as 'excellent', and the then alternative route of *advanced skills teacher, which offered a higher salary and the opportunity to carry out professional development work in other schools. As a consequence, in 2008 the Secretary of State for Children, Schools, and Families accepted a recommendation by the **School Teachers' Review Body** to review the pay scale for excellent teachers with a view to raising the upper pay limit.

(⊕) SEE WEB LINKS
• The 2009 review of the scheme by the Institute for Policy Studies.

exclusion The barring of a pupil from attending school, either temporarily (up to fifteen school days) or permanently. *Behaviour for which pupils may be permanently excluded includes *bullying, carrying weapons, acts of violence, supplying drugs, sexual misconduct, and persistent non-compliance. Pupils who have been excluded from secondary schools may be provided by their local authority with a place in a *pupil referral unit, where they can continue full-time with their education, although this will not necessarily include full coverage of the *national curriculum.

experiential learning Sometimes called 'learning by doing', this type of learning allows the pupil or student to learn through practical experience rather than through formal instruction by the teacher. The emphasis is on practice rather than on theory. To some extent a belief in the efficacy of experiential learning underpins the provision of *teaching practice for trainee teachers and of *work experience for trainees on vocational programmes.

external verifier *See* VERIFICATION.

extracurricular Organized activities which fall outside the formal school, college, or university *curriculum may be described as extracurricular. This would include, but would not be restricted to, such things as whole-school drama productions, sports matches with other schools, hobby clubs, and theatre visits.

extramural department A university department which provides courses, usually in *adult education, for members of the local or wider community, often outside the university *campus. Its literal meaning is 'outside the wall'. Such provision has declined since the withdrawal of public funding from *liberal (non-vocational) adult education.

extrinsic motivation *See* MOTIVATION.

faculty A subdivision of a *university or *college according to subject or field. For example, a university might consist of a number of faculties, including perhaps faculties of science, humanities, education, and so on. The term itself refers both to the academics—the teaching and research staff—working within that subdivision, and to the organizational subdivision itself. Thus, it may be used either as a collective noun, or to indicate a part of the institution's organizational structure, usually managed by a head—or dean—of faculty.

Fade or Flourish Subtitled *How Primary Schools Can Build on Children's Early Progress*, this report, funded by the Esmée Fairbairn Foundation in 2006, presents evidence to suggest that the educational and social benefits of an *early years, *pre-school education can be lost if not consolidated in the *primary phase.

(⊕) SEE WEB LINKS
• Provides link to the text of the report.

failing school *See* SPECIAL MEASURES.

faith schools Schools, both *primary and secondary, which are provided under the aegis of a recognized religious faith. Although the most common faith schools are those supported by the Church of England and the Roman Catholic Church, the range of such provision reflects a multi-*denominational, multicultural society and includes a rapidly growing number of Muslim schools. All newly established faith schools are required to liaise closely with other schools, including other faith schools, in their geographical area. The 2001 *White Paper *Schools: Achieving Success* recommended that, in order to avoid insularity or inter-faith conflict, the interests and sensibilities of the whole community be taken into consideration by those establishing a faith-specific school.

falling rolls A decline in the number of pupils entering a school. Although this can be a problem for individual schools, it has also been seen as a national trend since the final quarter of the 20th century. Some of its consequences can be seen in the closure or amalgamation of schools. The introduction of a quasi-*market in education following the *Education Reform Act 1988 required schools to compete for pupils by introducing the concept of parental *choice to replace the system of local authorities allocating school places on the basis of *catchment areas. This proved an effective strategy for reducing school places overall in the face of falling rolls, since it led to failure and closure of less popular or more isolated schools.

family grouping *See* VERTICAL GROUPING.

FAS *See* FETAL ALCOHOL SYNDROME.

feedback A technical term taken from communication theory which, when applied in an educational context, refers to a formal response from teacher to learner about their work or progress; or from learner to teacher in answer to a question, problem, or task which has been set. In the first case, a teacher's feedback to the learner can take the form of either a spoken or a written appraisal of the learner's performance, including advice on what areas need to be improved and which should be regarded as strengths. This may be referred to as *formative assessment. In the second case, learners who have been set a task, individually or in groups, may be asked to 'feed back' their findings or conclusions to the teacher and the rest of the class, for the purposes both of providing the teacher with an opportunity for the *assessment of students' learning, and also of providing an opportunity for peer learning, where students learn from one another. This process is also known as **debriefing**. If learners are asked to evaluate a lesson or module or course, their spoken or written responses are again referred to as 'student (or learner, or pupil) feedback'.

feeder course A programme of study which prepares the learner, directly or indirectly, for entry to a specific and more advanced course. For example, a *further education college may enrol students onto intermediate or advanced level vocational courses with a view to encouraging them to progress onto a *foundation degree taught in the same college.

fees Payment charged by a university, college, or non-maintained school for tuition and, in some cases, accommodation. Schools which charge fees are sometimes referred to as 'fee-paying'. In England tuition fees for undergraduate students in *higher education were at one time normally paid by the student's *local authority, but are now charged to the student themselves. Although government *loans are available to ease the immediate financial burden on the student, many find it necessary to take on part-time employment to meet the cost of their higher education, and as a consequence have less time to spend on their studies. It was partly for this reason that tuition fees for Scottish students in higher education in Scotland were abolished in 2000. English students studying in Scotland pay a fixed-rate tuition fee, while Scottish students studying in England are required to pay the standard tuition fee demanded by their institution.

In Wales all students, as elsewhere, are eligible for a loan. Unlike the arrangements in England, variable fees were not introduced in Wales until autumn 2007.

fellow In a general educational context this most often refers to someone who holds a funded *research post in an institution of *higher education, and is known in full as a *research fellow. These are usually fixed-term contract posts created for the furtherance of specific research projects. The funding may come from within the university or college itself, or from an external partner organization or sponsor, which may give its name to the fellowship. The term may also be used to indicate membership of a professional or academic group, as in 'Fellow of the Royal Institute of British Architects' (FRIBA). It is also a title given to senior members of Oxford or Cambridge colleges who, as well as their teaching duties, contribute to decision-making on academic and administrative matters relating to their college.

fetal alcohol syndrome (FAS) One of a spectrum of conditions known as **fetal alcohol spectrum disorders** (FASDs) which can develop in a baby before birth as a result of its mother's alcohol consumption during pregnancy. Children with this syndrome have a range of learning difficulties arising from cognitive impairment and impeded physical growth. These can include *Attention Deficit Hyperactivity Disorder and delayed language acquisition. The characteristic features of a child with FAS, which may include a small head, small eyes and drooping eyelids, may lead to socializing difficulties with which the pupil will need additional support.

(((⊕))) SEE WEB LINKS
• Provides a full list of indicators and other symptoms.

field study A project, investigation, or activity carried out 'in the field', outside or away from the learner's school, college, or university. Its purpose is to allow learners to investigate questions or subjects which cannot be fully or satisfactorily studied in a classroom or workshop. Subjects such as geography, archaeology, and architecture can be taught more effectively by providing learners with access to a wider environment where the focus of study may be examined in context.

field trip An organized visit for pupils or students under teacher supervision for the purpose of carrying out a *field study or some activity relevant to their curriculum. Such trips might take the form of a visit to a museum or art gallery, or of activities such as abseiling or canoeing. In the case of younger learners, parental permission must be formally given, and expectations about standards of learner behaviour clearly articulated. For all field trips, observance of health and safety measures are of central importance. The responsibility of teachers for pupils' safety and behaviour on such trips means that *pupil–teacher ratios must reflect the need for close supervision. In recent years there has been a growing reluctance among some teachers to take part in out-of-school visits such as field trips for fear of litigation.

first The highest classification of a *bachelor's degree, the others being an upper second (2.1), lower second (2.2), and third class. Possession of a first class degree has traditionally been one of the prerequisites for progression to postgraduate-level study, although 2.1s are now also widely accepted for this purpose. Published figures are open to the interpretation that a first class degree may be more readily attainable at some institutions and in some subjects than others, based on a comparison between candidates' *General Certificate of Education *Advanced Level scores and subsequent degree classification attained.

first degree A degree taken at the end of *undergraduate studies. It is described as a 'first' degree in order to distinguish it from higher degrees such as those at *master's and *doctorate levels, which may be taken subsequently. First degrees are awarded by universities and some other institutions of higher education. *See also* BACHELOR'S DEGREE.

first school Provides education for pupils aged 5–8, who go on to continue their education in a *middle school. The first and middle school system operates within some local authorities in place of the more commonly found infant and junior provision, and was introduced following recommendations in the *Plowden Report (1967). The system is claimed by some professionals in education to ease the difficulties of *transition experienced by some pupils in moving from one stage of their education to the next.

folio A piece of extended work completed during a Scottish *Standard Grade or *Higher course which is marked externally but counts as a *National Unit in a National Qualification. *See also* SCOTLAND, EDUCATION IN.   SM

foreign language assistant (FLA) Native speakers of the appropriate language employed in the language departments of schools, colleges, and universities to assist in the teaching of a modern foreign language, particularly by providing a model of practical language skills and accurate pronunciation. FLAs are often recruited from students studying English at a university in the country of origin, in which case their experience in a British school is expected to aid the development of their own English language skills. Their status and terms of employment within schools and other institutions is not equivalent to that of qualified teachers, and they are paid on a different scale. In United Kingdom schools they are organized through the Education and Training Group.

Forest School Outdoor education, using forests and woodland as a learning environment to support learners' acquisition of social, personal, and practical skills. This pedagogical approach, with its emphasis on inspiring learners and building their confidence and self-esteem, applies to all age groups, from pre-school children to adults. The woodland environment is also used as a context in which to develop *functional skills such as mathematics and communication. The Forest School has been presented as an effective alternative learning environment of particular benefit to children who exhibit challenging *behavior or suffer from *Attention Deficit Hyperactivity Disorder. Originally developed in Wisconsin, USA in the 1920s, the idea of Forest Schools spread to Europe and was incorporated into the pre-school curriculum in Denmark in the 1950s. Reaching the UK in the 1990s, Forest School pedagogy has been widely adopted and is supported by the **Forest Education Network** and **Forest Schools Wales**.

SEE WEB LINKS
• Explains the Forest School philosophy and provides details of training for Forest School practitioners.

formative assessment *Assessment which is designed to provide feedback to the learner in order that they may improve their performance. In this sense it helps to 'form' the learner. Its very purpose demands that formative assessment be part of the learning process rather than a terminal assessment event which takes place at the end of the course of study. *Continuous assessment, for example through *assignment work, is formative, as are week-by-week teacher assessments of class work and *homework. The key feature of effective formative assessment is that it provides the learner with clear constructive feedback. The distinction between formative and *summative, or end, assessment was pointed out by Scriven in 1967. *See also* ASSESSMENT FOR LEARNING.

Further Reading: M. Charles *Formative Assessment for Teaching and Learning* (Sage, 2014).

Foster Report (2005) The publication of the findings of the **Foster Review of Further Education**, the full title of which is Realising the Potential: A Review of the Future Role of Further Education Colleges. It represents a significant landmark in the history of *further education (FE) since it offers the definition of the purpose of the sector, which was to inform the 2006 *White Paper *Further Education: *Raising Skills, Improving Life Chances*. The vision it puts forward is of FE as the cornerstone of skills training. In paragraph 57 of the Report this is set out clearly as follows: 'A focus on vocational skills building is not a residual choice, but a vital building block in the UK's platform for future prosperity. It gives FE colleges an unequivocal mission and the basis of a renewed and powerful brand image.' This 'unequivocal mission' was not welcomed unanimously by educationalists within FE, some of whom retained a vision of the sector which included its role as provider of the 'second chance' for those seeking to re-engage with a general, rather than an instrumental, education. The Report is notable for its employment of a *market-related vocabulary in a context of education and training, as illustrated in the extract above; and also for its introduction of a new metaphor for FE, describing it as a 'middle child' occupying a position between the schools sector and *higher education, and sometimes suffering neglect as a consequence.

SEE WEB LINKS
• Provides link to full text.

Foucault, Michel (1926–84) A French social theorist, philosopher, and historian, and one of the most influential poststructuralist thinkers of the 20th century. Like *Derrida, Foucault's ideas caused controversy as they questioned long-held opinions regarding the nature of identity, truth, and how power operates. As a historian, Foucault challenged the received methods of historical investigation, proposing the idea that the dominant method of narrating a linear story of Western development was one of exclusion, which tended to silence those thus marginalized. But, arguably, the most important aspect to Foucault's work, as it relates to education, was his focus on the concept of **discourse** and its role in the formation of identity.

Throughout Foucault's major works, including *Madness and Civilization* (1961), *The Birth of the Clinic* (1963), *Sex and Sexuality* (3 vols, 1984), and especially *Discipline and Punish* (1975), he concentrated on showing how the concept of the individual is a political subject, one that is formed in the very particular discourses of certain, usually institutional, contexts. Here, the term 'discourse' is used to mean language in context. According to Foucault, power flows in a complex web which defines what we can know and how we can express knowledge of our 'selves' and the world around us. In educational institutions, whether as students or teachers, we are constituted as subjects; the discourses available in that context define what can be said and known, and what is excluded or rendered 'invisible'. In the modern world, suggests Foucault, it is no longer possible to have a unified theoretical concept of power as in Marxism. Power is localized and particular.

Foucault's ideas, and particularly the emphasis he places on the function of **surveillance**, have proven influential in educational theory. In contemporary culture surveillance does not simply refer to the ubiquitous surveillance camera, but also to the way we are in various ways encouraged to observe and discipline ourselves and others. Many have linked these ideas to the cultural significance placed on achieving educational qualifications, the importance of measuring success, the emphasis on self-assessment, and the compilation of *portfolios of evidence and learning journals, as well as the stigmatization and consequences of not gaining qualifications. *See also* IDEOLOGY.   CH

foundation course An introductory course, or one at a basic level, designed for beginners who are unfamiliar with, and lack the 'foundations' of, a subject. Students may take a foundation course as a first step in their progression to more advanced qualifications. In the vocabulary of the *Qualifications and Credit Framework, 'foundation' has a measurable meaning in terms of level, and refers to the most elementary, or 'entry', level of *National Vocational Qualification, a level below that at which most trainees will commence their training. In the context of the *Open University, too, 'foundation course' has a very specific meaning, in this case referring to the first, more general, stage of studies which some students undertake before going on to focus on their chosen degree subject.

foundation degree A two-year degree course, usually taught in *university or a *college of further or *higher education, and focusing on a vocationally related area of study. Introduced in 2001, this degree can be awarded in the arts (Foundation Degree Arts, FDA), the Sciences (Fd.Sc.), or in specific vocational fields such as law (FDL) or engineering (FDE). Further education providers offer foundation degrees in partnership with a university or other institution of *higher education; and successful students can go on to 'top up'

their qualification by additional study in higher education to achieve an *honours
degree. The foundation degree was introduced primarily as an additional
means of building a more highly skilled workforce, and its implementation has
involved cooperation between employers, trainers, and professional bodies,
as well as colleges and higher education institutions. It was designed to recruit
primarily from those in the 20-30 age group of the population who have not
engaged with higher education through more traditional routes.

foundation school A school which has ownership over its own premises.
Foundation status became an option for schools from 2001. For some schools
it presented an alternative route to some degree of independence from *local
authority control at a time when *grant maintained status became discontinued
since it enables schools to operate with a high degree of autonomy in the
implementation of admissions procedures and the recruitment and appointment
of teaching staff. The governing body of a foundation school has ownership
of, and is responsible for, school buildings and land. Alternatively, a trust or
foundation may be set up to undertake this responsibility. In the latter case
the school is known as a **trust school**. *See also* ACADEMY.

(⊕) SEE WEB LINKS
• Provides a link to further information about foundation schools.

foundation subjects *National curriculum subjects which are compulsory
at various *key stages, other than the core subjects of English, mathematics, and
science; in Key Stages 3-4 they also include technology, physical education,
and a modern foreign language; and in Key Stages 1-3, history, geography,
art, and music. In Wales, Welsh is an additional foundation subject in all
*maintained schools. From September 2014 foreign languages became
foundation subjects at Key Stage 2.

(⊕) SEE WEB LINKS
• Sets out a current list of foundation subjects for each key stage.

4children A national charitable organization whose aim is to ensure an
integrated approach to children's services, in which schools, social services,
and the medical profession work together in the best interest of children. It
is responsible for *children's centres, and works closely with the *Department
for Education in developing policy and best practice for children and family
services.

(⊕) SEE WEB LINKS
• Explains the charity's role and aims as they relate to children in schools.

14–19 agenda The focus on the development and implementation of
education provision for 14-19-year-olds in the UK in the first decade of the 21st
century. Following the final report in 2004 of the committee chaired by Mike
Tomlinson, which proposed a radical reform of qualifications for students at
*Key Stage 4 and in 16-19 education, the government published the *White Paper
14-19 Education and Skills in February 2005. This White Paper, and its

accompanying implementation plan, identified several proposals aimed at 'improving choice, improving chances', with the accent on enhancing employability. These included a commitment to raising the levels of skills in English and mathematics; the development and ensured local provision of vocational diplomas which would replace the hundreds of individual qualifications offered by *awarding bodies and would—alongside *General Certificate of Education *Advanced Levels—allow progression to *higher education as well as to employment; the provision for candidates to achieve qualifications at the appropriate level for their ability rather than their age, with the intention of encouraging providers to challenge individual students; and a more robustly supported approach to disengaged students.

A distinctive Welsh programme was put in place in Wales to provide structured learning pathways tailored to individuals, designed to motivate and enthuse young people, balanced by real-life learning experiences and opportunities to develop essential skills. This programme was linked with the *Welsh Baccalaureate qualification and began as a pilot in September 2004. The programme was supported by the **Learning Coaches Scheme**, whereby students are given guidance by adults trained to help with the development of study skills and to make choices which reflect the aptitude and potential of the individual learners. *See also* APPRENTICESHIP; FUNCTIONAL SKILLS; SKILLS AGENDA.

14–19 Curriculum and Qualifications Reform *See* TOMLINSON REPORT (2004).

14–19 Diploma *See* DIPLOMA 14–19.

Freire, Paulo (1921–97) An international educationalist based in Brazil, Paulo Freire's philosophy grew from his experiences of teaching adult literacy to the underprivileged poor of Latin America. Freire called for a change from more formal, teacher-controlled education to that constructed by the learners themselves. In his seminal work *Pedagogy of the Oppressed* (1970) he used the phrase 'the banking concept' to describe formal education, which he felt restricted teachers to delivering a curriculum highly prescribed by those with governmental power. In contrast, Freire sought to develop an awareness among underprivileged learners that they should consider their social and cultural backgrounds as the starting point for their literacy learning, with the intended outcome that they would recognize ways they could transform their learning and their lives for themselves. Although his original focus was on adults and the oppressed, the outcomes of his writing and the subsequent influence have extended well beyond this. Because of the political implications of his approach he is classed as a *radical educator.   VC, KA

Further Reading: P. Freire *The Pedagogy of the Oppressed* (1970; Penguin, 1972).

Froebel, Friedrich (1782–1852) A German educator and originator of the *kindergarten, who argued that young pupils should not be constrained by a formal, regimented curriculum structured according to specific age groups. Instead, he advocated that pupils be provided with the opportunity to develop as individuals, and not be subjected to *rote learning. His philosophy of teaching and learning underpinned provision in **Froebel schools**, of which the first in England was established in 1851; and in 1892 the **Froebel Educational Institution** for the training of teachers was opened in London. Froebel's approach to education continues to inform much of *pre-school and *early years provision in Great Britain.

SEE WEB LINKS
• Provides a bibliography and suggestions for further reading.

full-time equivalent (FTE) A measurement used in the calculation of teaching-related resource needs in *further and *higher education, where a proportion of students are enrolled on a part-time basis. For example, two part-time students attending for 50 per cent of a full-time timetable may be deemed to be the equivalent of one full-time student in terms of teacher contact hours, or in terms of their required attendance in hours or days. This makes it possible to calculate the total number of students enrolled in terms of full-time places or their equivalent, an important calculation in terms of institutions' levels of external funding.

functional literacy The level of literacy necessary to cope with the demands of everyday adult life, and to function effectively both socially and in the workplace. While difficult to define in absolute or universal terms, national levels of functional literacy have been a subject of concern in a number of *White Papers, which have raised the issue of pupils leaving compulsory education without having acquired the literacy skills necessary to secure employment or to contribute fully to society and to the economy. Part of the reason for the introduction of *key skills across the 16–19 curriculum in 2000 was to address this problem by providing continued support in literacy skills beyond the age of 16. *See also* FUNCTIONAL SKILLS.

functional skills Qualifications in English, mathematics, and *information communication technology (ICT) in the UK, which are available from entry level to level 2 on the *Qualifications and Credit Framework. The introduction of **Functional Skills awards** was announced as part of the *14–19 Education and Skills* White Paper of 2005. They were developed for all learners aged 14+ to improve *numeracy, *literacy, and ICT skills nationally, to strengthen the practical skills necessary for employment, and for access to further and higher education. They were designed to build on the literacy and numeracy strategies at primary schools as will as the secondary school *Key Stage 3 strategy, and to be a mandatory component of all learning programmes at Key Stage 4 and beyond. Functional skills are integral to the English, mathematics, and ICT curriculum at Key Stages 3 and 4, and are a component of *apprenticeships. The term functional skills has replaced that of *key skills and Skills for Life in England. Their equivalent in Scotland are **core skills**; and, in Wales, **essential skills**.

SEE WEB LINKS
• Provides examples of on-screen tests for functional skills.

Further and Higher Education Act 1992 Approved by Parliament in March 1992, this piece of legislation marked a turning point in the provision of *post-compulsory education. It was an enactment of the proposals set out in the 1991 *White Paper *Education and Training for the 21st Century*, one of the most far-reaching of which was that colleges of *further education, *sixth form colleges, and *tertiary colleges were to be removed from the control of local education authorities (LEAs). The colleges were to be funded through Further Education Funding Councils, of which there was one for England and one for Wales. This transformation of the further education colleges into corporate bodies became known as **incorporation**, and brought about major changes in the employment conditions of lecturers in further education. Existing lecturers were required to sign new contracts involving them in longer hours and shorter holidays in return for progression in pay. Those who were unwilling to relinquish their original conditions of service remained on the old pay scale with their salaries frozen. All new appointments were made under the revised terms and conditions. This matter of contracts caused widespread discontent among lecturers in the sector, and a deterioration in the relationship between lecturers and senior management. Incorporation also marked the real beginning of a quasi-*market in further education, as colleges whose provision had previously been managed and agreed strategically under the aegis of the LEAs began to operate as individual corporate organizations. Competition for students often involved offering courses and qualifications which duplicated provision in neighbouring colleges and sixth forms. The necessity to compete in a crowded market created a situation in which stronger (larger, better resourced, or more entrepreneurial) colleges thrived at the expense of others which were less favoured by the market, which inevitably led to some college closures and mergers in the years following this legislation. Moreover, by allowing schools to bring an element of *vocational education into the *post-16 curriculum with the introduction of *General National Vocational Qualifications (GNVQs), the Act was also responsible for creating further competition between schools and colleges for attracting or retaining pupils at 16. Many 11–16 schools used the introduction of GNVQs as an opportunity to open vocational sixth forms, thereby enabling them to retain pupils after *Key Stage 4 who would otherwise have gone on to further education college or joined the sixth form of a neighbouring 11–18 school. In a number of ways, therefore, the Act was responsible for pushing the secondary and tertiary sectors of education firmly into the world of competition and market forces, with the declared purpose of raising standards of provision. In a similar vein, it also brought about a reform of the careers advisory service by requiring *local authorities to put this service out to tender.

In terms of higher education, the Act abolished the *binary system (or binary divide), allowing *polytechnics to assume the title of 'university', and introducing the *Higher Education Funding Council, with separate councils to fund higher education in Scotland and Wales. The Act encouraged the implementation of an alternative, vocational route at 16—a route described as having *parity of esteem with *General Certificate of Education *Advanced Levels—and at the same time an expansion in higher education provision. In this way it ensured a *progression route for students wishing to use vocational qualifications to gain entry to university.

Further and Higher Education (Scotland) Act 1992 This Act reviewed Scottish Further and Higher Education. Its main proposal was the creation of a new funding agency, the **Scottish Higher and Further Education Funding Council**, thus creating a single body to oversee strategic developments at both higher and further education levels.   SM

further education (FE) A sector which encompasses all *post-compulsory education and training, with the exception of *higher education. Although a semantic distinction is made between further and *adult education, FE in its broadest terms encompasses this, too. The terminology for the sector has been subject to a number of recent developments, particularly in government policy documents, which refer to it variously as the skills sector, the *lifelong learning sector, the learning and skills sector (although this does not apply in Scotland), and the post-compulsory education sector. It is associated with *vocational education and skills training, which, following the *Foster Report (2005), has been confirmed as the primary focus of further education *colleges. Traditionally, however, it has been widely regarded as the 'sector of the second chance', providing an opportunity for learners who have not succeeded within the school system to re-engage with their education, including preparing for public examinations such as the *General Certificate of Education *Advanced Level at colleges of further education. Referred to as the 'Cinderella sector' by Kenneth Baker when Secretary of State for Education in the 1980s, it has often been regarded as a relatively low-status provision in comparison with sixth forms on the one hand and *higher education on the other, largely because of its association with vocational skills training. Three decades later, in the Foster Report, it is referred to as a 'middle child', a metaphor which suggests that as a sector it still remains to some extent undervalued.

further education teaching qualifications Professional qualifications for teaching in the *further education (FE) sector were extensively revised from September 2013. Three *Qualifications and Credit Framework (QCF) levels of qualification are available. For intending or beginner teachers there is the introductory **Award in Education and Training** (AET) which is awarded at QCF level 3 (the equivalent of GCE A level) and carries 12 credits on that framework. For teachers who are teaching a minimum of 30 hours there is the **Certificate in Education and Training** (CET) which is awarded at level 4 and carries 36 credits. **The Diploma in Education and Training** (DET) is aimed at teachers who have, or aspire to have, substantial teaching responsibilities. It is awarded at QCF level 5 (degree level) and carries 120 credits. In addition there is a specialist DET which provides training in specific curriculum or professional areas, such as *literacy, *English for Speakers of Other Languages, or teaching learners with a disability. These qualification did not replace, but ran alongside, the existing FE teaching qualifications known as PTLLS, CTTLS and DTTLS, normally awarded by *universities. The Education and Training

Awards, however, were designed to be delivered by and within FE colleges. They are validated by *awarding bodies such as *City and Guilds. It is interesting to note the use of the word 'education' in the title of these qualifications. It seems likely, however, that this move away from the vocabulary of 'learning and skills' represents a semantic distancing rather than a conceptual shift.

 SEE WEB LINKS

• Provides links to information about qualifications at all three levels.

Gaelic schools Education in Gaelic is available in around 60 Scottish primary schools, the majority of which are located in the Highlands and Islands of Scotland. As Scotland's longest-established language, Gaelic features in both primary and secondary schools to a varying degree, both as a subject and as a teaching language in class, and there are separate qualifications and examination courses available in this language. *See also* SCOTLAND, EDUCATION IN.   SM

games **1.** An alternative terminology for physical education which forms part of the curriculum of compulsory education, and is sometimes referred to as 'organized games'.

  2. A *method of teaching which involves an element of simulation or competition, and which may be used to encourage learners to engage more actively with the area of study. These learner activities can take simple form such as word games, or may be complex and extend over several lessons or periods of study if they take the form of simulations with learners playing allotted roles. Computer games, too, can be used as learning tools. Although they have the advantage of making learning vivid and engaging, games can have the disadvantage of being time-consuming when compared to more traditional teaching methods such as exposition. They tend, therefore to be used rather less frequently than alternative methods, particularly when the curriculum is full and time-constrained. A further disadvantage is the danger that learners will view such activities as entertainment and fail to recognize the *objective or intended learning outcome. When incorporating games into their *lesson plan, therefore, teachers have to ensure that the purpose of the activity is explained clearly to the learners and is followed by a discussion or plenary in which the learning outcomes are discussed and clarified.

Gardner, Howard *See* MULTIPLE INTELLIGENCE.

gender A term used to differentiate between males and females resulting from social and cultural influences as opposed to purely biological ones. Increasingly the use of the term is taken to be inclusive of issues that relate especially to boys and men as well as to those which relate mostly to girls and women. Theories of gender range through those which: emphasize cultural conditioning (liberal feminism), take a psychoanalytic stance, stress large-scale power relations in society (socialist or Marxist feminism), or draw attention to discursive relations (postmodern and poststructuralist approaches). The phrase 'doing gender' is becoming more common. It refers to a conception of gender as learned through performance and which helps to constitute personal identity. Since the 1980s the realization that gender always intersects with race, religion, *social class, and so on has led to an understanding that it is more appropriate to talk of femininities and masculinities rather than a unitary femininity or masculinity. However, there remain dominant conceptions of both, which are reinforced in educational institutions, partly through the elision of sex, gender, and sexuality. This is one function of playground insults which refer to sexuality. For many young people, 'gay', for instance, is widely perceived as a term of abuse, even by those who have no particular prejudice against lesbian, gay, or bisexual people.

There is a wide range of issues in education which are gender-related. They apply not only to students, but also to everyone else involved, including teachers, governors, and policy-makers. Furthermore, they apply to the structures of education, within and outwith schools, universities, and colleges. They also apply to policy at local and national level. Policy has an influence on educational structures and gender relations. Some policy is intended to influence gender reform directly. Finally, informal as well as formal education is accessed and experienced differently by males and females.

Gender is a special case of *social justice and so is directly related to equality of outcome, equality of opportunity, and the formation of identity in education. Gender is often specifically addressed in equal opportunities policies to be found in schools, colleges, and universities. Areas where issues of equality of opportunity arise include those of *curriculum, *pedagogy, and *assessment.

It has become rare for girls or boys to be formally excluded from particular areas of the curriculum. However, subject choice at school and later is still strongly correlated with gender. Post-16, males predominate in physics, technology, and sport, while females are over-represented in biology, languages, and the humanities. As students are increasingly expected to make choices earlier in their educational careers, these differences are intensifying and have consequences for available employment. Currently 60 per cent of working women are clustered in 10 per cent of occupations. The hidden curriculum is also inflected by gender. Attitudes and aspirations are differentiated by gender, with girls generally expecting to work harder but having fewer career aspirations—but, of course, this is strongly mediated by social class.

Pedagogies appear to be gender-differentiated, although, as with everything else, they also depend on other markers of difference such as social class and ethnic heritage. For instance, research shows that boys tend to prefer more competitive and individualist ways of learning while girls tend to prefer more collaborative, cooperative methods. The difference in preferred pedagogy is particularly evident for some subject areas. There is evidence that girls prefer science to be related to the everyday and that the role of speaking and listening is highly significant in raising boys' literacy. Assessment strategies are similarly gender-differentiated, with boys excelling in end-of-session *examinations and girls shining in *coursework and *continuing assessment. It must be emphasized that these are generalizations which hide large variations. Many middle-class boys excel in every area and by every means, and many working-class girls underachieve whatever the subject and however assessed.

Equality of outcome has become a hot issue for schools. Both boys and girls continue to improve in their performance as measured by national tests. However, the girls, in general, now outperform the boys at all levels, especially in literacy, although less so in physics and chemistry. This underachievement of boys has caused widespread concern in the press and in policy circles.

Gender issues affect teachers as strongly as students. There has been much concern expressed about the alleged feminization of teaching, even though the proportion of women teachers has changed only slowly over decades. Men are still over-represented in senior positions in schools, colleges, and universities. Even where there are senior women, management styles are increasingly masculine as a result of the intensification of work and the stress on *performativity found in all sectors of the education system.

Educational *research has identified a number of underlying gender issues, especially those related to personal identity. The significance of motherhood and the ways it intersects with teaching is one such issue. Another is citizenship, where the traditional model of a good citizen has been male. The current emphasis on the significance of parental involvement in schools is another area where there are gender issues, since the 'parent' is often tacitly assumed to be a mother. *See also* INCLUSION.   MG

General Certificate of Education (GCE) In 1951 two levels of public examinations were introduced: the GCE *Ordinary Level and the GCE *Advanced Level (A level). The former was designed as a school-leaving examination to replace the *School Certificate. It remained in place through the *raising of the school-leaving age to 16, until it was replaced in turn by the *General Certificate of Secondary Education in 1988. Its international reputation, however, has led to continuing demand for the qualification overseas, particularly on the Indian subcontinent. As a result, the award is still offered, for example by the Cambridge examining board.

The GCE A level remains the 'gold standard' examination for 18-year-old school-leavers, and still fulfils its original purpose as a preparation, and a means of selection, for university and other types of *higher education, although it now constitutes one of several routes into higher education for 18- and 19-year-olds since the introduction of *vocational A levels and other general vocational qualifications.

General Certificate of Secondary Education (GCSE) Introduced in 1988 to replace both the *General Certificate of Education *Ordinary Level and the *Certificate of Secondary Education with one unified examination syllabus. Nevertheless, the GCSE still originally offered the opportunity for *differentiation by task through the introduction of *tiering, an approach which was discontinued under the reforms announced in 2013, as was the regulation that allowed for GCSE candidates to be assessed in all subjects through a combination of *coursework and end *examination. Pupils' assessment at GCSE marks the culmination of their *Key Stage 4 studies. The grading criteria and syllabus now conform with *national curriculum level descriptors and *programmes of study in each subject area. In England, the eight pass grades, from A* to G, each carrying a number of points used in the presentation of secondary schools' performance tables, are to be replaced from 2017 in English language, English literature, and mathematics by numerical grades 1 to 9, with 9 being the highest grade achievable, in order to enable greater *differentiation at the top of the scale. The rationale presented for this reform was the concern that the high number of candidate achieving an A or A* grade created difficulties for universities in their selection processes. Numerical grading will apply to the remaining GCSE subjects from 2018. There is also the intention to draw comparisons with the achievement of pupils in countries such as South Korea where attainment levels in mathematics, for example, are known to be far ahead of those in England. The discontinuation of tiering and modular coursework means that all pupils will sit the same examination at the end of their two years' study, which many have seen as a return to the *GCE O level model. An *English Baccalaureat is to be awarded to candidates achieving grade C or above in English, mathematics, history or geography, two sciences, and a classical or modern foreign language. This is not a separate qualification, but a measure of performance.

(⊕) SEE WEB LINKS

• Summarizes recent developments in GCSEs.

general education An education designed to support the development of the learner as an individual, rather than to equip him or her with specific, vocationally related skills. In this sense, a general education may be defined as developmental rather than instrumental. It is a term which is often used in differentiating an academic route, such as that represented by *General Certificate of Secondary Education and *Advanced Level, from a *vocational route, for example through the various levels of *National Vocational Qualifications. A general education may be described as 'broad', in contrast with the acquisition of narrowly focused skills for work. For historical reasons, a general education still tends to be accorded a higher status in some quarters than a vocational education or training. Various general vocational initiatives such as the *14-19 Diploma and the Applied GCSE, while designed to have a broad vocational focus, were nevertheless often presented as consistent with a general education curriculum, perhaps in the same sense that led to the choice of name for the *General National Vocational Qualification (1992-2007), suggesting that, while the contexts used are vocational, the skills and understanding developed, such as *literacy, *numeracy, analysis, and synthesis, are transferable and general. *See also* LIBERAL EDUCATION; PARITY OF ESTEEM; TAUNTON REPORT.

General National Vocational Qualification (GNVQ) Introduced in 1992 to provide a third qualification route which bridged the gap between the *academic or *general education provided by the General Certificate of Secondary Education (GCSE) and *General Certificate of Education *Advanced Level route in schools, and the vocationally specific training

provided by National Vocational Qualifications (NVQs) in *further education.
Introduced initially in the 1991 *White Paper *Education and Training for the 21st
Century*, GNVQs were intended to be taught in schools and to cover 'broad
occupational areas'. Their introduction, according to the White Paper, had a
number of purposes. They were to provide an alternative route to both
employment and *higher education; to allow progression to and from NVQs;
and to 'be of equal status with academic qualifications'. This last point proved
difficult to achieve, despite repeated government claims about *parity of esteem.
Nevertheless, within two years of its introduction the GNVQ was being offered at
*Foundation, Intermediate, and Advanced Level in five broad occupational areas
in many schools and colleges. Intermediate Level was taken to be broadly
equivalent to four good GCSEs, while the Advanced Level was, for the purposes
of progression to higher education, accorded equivalence with two A Levels.
At all levels *assessment was initially by *continuous assessment. This in itself
created some difficulties in establishing the status of the Advanced award; and
over time the assessment regime was developed to include more rigorous
external assessment and testing. Candidates succeeded in gaining university
places through the GNVQ route, and one of the strengths of its curriculum—the
inclusion of *key skills—was later (2000) extended to all 16–19 provision. In 1999–
2000 Advanced GNVQs were restructured to increase their compatibility with
modular A Levels and, as part of the *Curriculum 2000 reforms, became known
as Vocational Advanced Levels. Foundation and Intermediate GNVQs remained
an optional component of the Key Stage 4 curriculum in schools, and were
included in the calculation of pupil attainment points. Their withdrawal was
announced in November 2003, and they were phased out between 2005 and
2007, to be replaced by successor qualifications, again with a broad vocational
focus, such as *National Certificates, National Diplomas, Applied GCSEs, and
now the **Applied General Qualifications (AGQ)**, developed and regulated by
the same unitary *awarding bodies which were previously responsible for
awarding GNVQs. *See also* VOCATIONAL A LEVELS.

general studies 1. A *General Certificate of Education *Advanced Level
(A level) and *Advanced Subsidiary Level subject which was originally designed
to introduce breadth into A level studies, particularly for candidates taking
exclusively science subjects. It requires the candidate to demonstrate an
appropriate level of literacy and fluency in their written English as well as an ability
to give informed consideration to a range of topics, including current affairs.

2. An alternative title for the programme of *liberal studies which
formed part of the curriculum for vocational students in *further education
in the 1960s and 1970s.

General Teaching Council (GTC) There were originally four separate
Councils for the four principalities of the United Kingdom. Although the Council
for England (GTCE) ceased to operate in 2012, the other three continue. The
purpose of each Council is to monitor professional standards of teachers, and
to establish a code of conduct, to be enforced through a disciplinary committee.
The Council for Scotland (GTCS) has been in existence since 1965, and was one

of the first teaching councils in the world. It has wider powers than the other two, including the power of approval for programmes of teacher education and training. Its 50 members including elected teachers, appointed representatives of *local authorities, and those nominated by Scottish government ministers to represent the interests of parents, employers, and teachers of children with special educational needs.

A Council for Wales, Cyngor Addysgu Cyffredinol Cymru, (GTCW) was set up in 1999, with 25 members and a chair. In Wales teacher representation is proportionately higher than it was in England, with twelve elected teachers, nine nominees of teaching unions appointed by the National Assembly for Wales, and four direct appointees of the Assembly. All qualified teachers in the state sector must be registered with the Council, which is responsible for investigating and hearing cases of misconduct or incompetence. The Council advises the Assembly on policy in relation to teaching issues such as *continuing professional development, recruitment, retention, and supply. It also administers funding programmes for the Welsh Assembly to meet the professional development needs of teachers.

A Council for Northern Ireland (GTCNI) was set up in 2002. It has 33 members, of whom fourteen are teachers elected by the profession. Five members are nominated by the Northern Ireland Teaching Council, ten by other stakeholders such as employers and *higher education, and four are appointed by the *Department of Education for Northern Ireland.

(((⊕))) SEE WEB LINKS
- Provides information about the GTCNI's role and activities.
- Provides information about the GTCW's purpose and functions.
- Provides details of the GTCS's role and functions.

generic criteria Criteria for *assessment which apply across a range of subjects, topics, or assignments, and which are related to the level of study rather than to its content. For example, students' work which is being assessed at *master's level will be assessed against criteria specific to their focus of study, but also against the generic criteria which are applicable to all master's level study, such as the ability to cite and reference sources correctly.

Gestalt A theory of learning based on the idea that the teacher should view the student's experience of learning as a whole, rather than as the sum of a series of stimuli; and that the learner achieves understanding by a process of reorganization of their existing ideas, thereby discovering how one fact might relate to another, or how gaps in their pattern of understanding might be filled. The word itself is German, and means a perceptual pattern or configuration which cannot adequately be described in terms of its component parts but must be perceived as a whole. Gestalt psychology was to some extent a reaction against the *behaviourists and neo-behaviourist definitions of learning. A key figure was Kurt Koffka (1886–1941), who taught for most of his career in the United States of America. Like other Gestaltists, he argued that during learning the human mind goes through a process of drawing on previous experience in order to reorganize its perceptions, a process which is infinitely more complicated than a series of stimulus–response interactions. The idea of wholeness is implicit both in the way the learning process is construed and as a significant event when learning leads to insight and the learner suddenly perceives 'the whole picture'. This theory of learning reminds teachers to encourage learners to make their own connections and discoveries in order to find solutions to the questions they are exploring. In this sense it contrasts sharply with approaches based on *rote learning.

Further Reading: K. Koffka *The Growth of the Mind* (Transaction, 1980) presents the Gestaltist argument against a behaviourist approach to child psychology and the process of learning.

gifted and talented A term applied to pupils who have abilities which are developed to a level significantly above that of their year group, or who are judged to have the potential to develop such abilities. It is recognized that such pupils need to be taught in a way and at a level that challenges them; and to be presented with tasks which stretch and motivate them. This understanding has been reflected in government education policy. A **Gifted and Talented Programme** was introduced in 2000 as part of the *Excellence in Cities initiative; and was applied initially in 495 secondary schools and with older children in 400 primary schools. In 2002 a National Academy for Gifted and Talented Youth was established for 11–16-year-old pupils. Based at Warwick University, it follows a similar model to that used in provision for talented children in America. In 2005 the *White Paper *Higher Standards: Better Schools for All* set out the aim that every pupil should have the right to a *personalized curriculum designed to enable them to reach the full potential of their ability. In the case of gifted and talented pupils, this implies not only greater challenge within the classroom, but also the provision of opportunities to develop their abilities and talents further outside school at a local and national level. The same 2005 White Paper also required that every secondary school and every cluster of primary schools has a trained leading teacher for gifted and talented education; and was instrumental in the setting up of a **National Register** to improve the identification and tracking of gifted and talented pupils' attainment and performance. Regional Partnerships work collaboratively with schools to improve overall provision for gifted and talented learners through self-evaluation. Schools are able to evaluate their own provision for gifted and talented pupils by measuring their provision and practices against the **National Quality Standards in Gifted and Talented Education**.   IW

Gittins Report (1967) Published under the title *Primary Education in Wales*, the Report presented the findings of an examination into *primary education in Wales and of the *transition of pupils to the secondary phase. Like the *Plowden Report, it argued for a system of *first and *middle schools to help ease the difficulties of transition. It also argued for the inclusion of Welsh into the curriculum of all Welsh schools as either a first or second language. *See also* WALES, EDUCATION IN.

governors Since the *Education Act 1980 the law has required that all *maintained schools have a board of governors which represents parents and teachers as well as drawing membership from the local community and volunteers with appropriate management skills. The Education Act 1944 (*Butler Act) made it mandatory for the duties and responsibilities of schools' governing bodies to be defined in an instrument of government, and their role to be set out unequivocally in their articles of government. This was a means of clarifying the respective responsibilities and roles of the *head teacher, the *local authority, and the governing body itself. Training for governors is not compulsory, but governors are strongly encouraged to take advantage of the **National Strategy for Training and Support**, which provides a national training programme for new governors, as well as training for chairs and clerks to the board. Governing bodies are encouraged to provide induction training for new members.

Governors are responsible for ensuring that the school provides an adequate quality of education and that standards of attainment within the school are maintained and, if necessary, raised. They are responsible for the selection of the *head teacher, together with whom they define the school's aims and policies. They are responsible to parents, to the wider community, and to funding bodies for the school's performance; they make decisions about the school's budget and staffing; they are responsible for ensuring that the *national curriculum is taught, and for deciding ways in which the school will encourage pupils' spiritual, moral, and social development.

The number of governors on a school's governing body varies according to the size of the school. Membership may include representation from community and business interests, the Church, and charitable trusts, as well as from parents and from teachers at the school. Membership is normally for four years. In the case of *special schools, the governing body may include representation from health authorities and from relevant voluntary or charitable organizations.

(⊕) SEE WEB LINKS
• Explains the content and aims of governor training.

grade The category of mark awarded in the *assessment of a candidate's performance. This may constitute part of a *continuous assessment or represent the result of a final assessment such as an *examination. Grade categories may be descriptors, such as pass, *credit, or distinction; or they may be referred to by letter, as in the General Certificate of Secondary Education (GCSE) grading system; or by numerical category, as in the case of *bachelor's degrees. Normally, each grade occupies a range of percentage marks, and therefore the grade awarded is based on the percentage mark achieved. It is usual for the assessor to refer to *grading criteria, in the form of **grade descriptors**, for guidance in coming to an assessment decision.

Often, and particularly in GCSEs and *General Certificate of Education *Advanced Level, the grade achieved may be crucial to the candidate's progression to the next stage of their education. In some cases, where the grade awarded in these public examinations falls significantly below that predicted by the candidate's school or college, a **grade review** may be requested, which involves the double-checking of the examination result in question. *See also* GENERAL CERTIFICATE OF SECONDARY EDUCATION.

grading criteria Descriptors setting out in detail what a candidate must achieve in order to be awarded a specific *grade. These are drawn up for the benefit both of the candidate themselves, who is thereby provided with a clear guidance on what must be achieved in order to attain the required grade, and of the assessor, for whom they provide a means of making an accurate and reliable *assessment decision.

graduate The term may be used as a noun, indicating someone who has successfully completed their *undergraduate studies and been awarded a *bachelor's degree; or as a verb, indicating the achievement of that graduate status, as in 'She graduated last week'. It may also be used as an adjective, in describing the level of study undertaken, as in 'Since she graduated she has enrolled on a graduate course in education studies'. *See also* GRADUATION.

graduated approach Students who do not make adequate progress may be identified as having special educational needs (SEN). The student is placed on the school SEN register. This should be done with the knowledge and agreement of parents and the child. There are varying levels of intervention which can be implemented. A graduated approach to intervention enables a wide range of strategies to be applied to the diverse needs on the SEN continuum. School-based interventions are known as School Action and School Action Plus. At School Action teachers identify students who need support that is different from, and in addition to, the normal strategies for differentiation and support already in place. A lack of adequate progress might trigger the input from other professionals, and at this stage the student moves to School Action Plus on the register. If students still do not make adequate progress after having had interventions at both these stages, it may be necessary to request a statutory assessment, which may or may not result in a *statement of special educational needs being issued.   TB, LE

Further Reading: Department for Education and Skills *Code of Practice for Special Educational Needs (Revised)* DfES/581/2001 (DfES, 2001).

Graduate Teacher Programme (GTP) A programme of teacher training which allowed *graduate trainee teachers to gain their teaching qualification while working in schools. Although originally aimed at mature entrants to the profession, age discrimination legislation prevented recruitment on this criterion alone. The training took between three months and a full academic year to complete and could be undertaken in any *maintained school in England or Wales (other than schools in *special measures and *pupil referral units) which was prepared to employ the trainee as an unqualified teacher. Applicants were required to hold *General Certificate of Secondary Education qualifications in English and mathematics at grade C or above (or the equivalent), as well as a recognized degree. The GTP was discontinued at the end of the academic year 2013 and replaced by the *School Direct training programme.

Graduate Teacher Training Registry (GTTR) Until 1992, graduate applicants for initial teacher training, and those in the final year of their undergraduate studies, registered with the GTTR as part of their application process for a place on a *Professional Graduate Certificate of Education programme. They listed in order of preference a choice of higher education institutions where they wish to undertake their training, and these applications were then processed by the GTTR, just as the *Universities and Colleges Admissions Service (UCAS) processes applications for undergraduate courses. Indeed, the GTTR is now incorporated into UCAS, where it continues to operate as a vehicle for *initial teacher training applications.

graduation The gaining of *graduate status through successful completion of undergraduate studies. This is usually marked by a **graduation ceremony**, attended by dignitaries of the awarding institution as well as by the graduates and their families and friends. This provides a formal occasion for the awarding of certificates and other honours, and the event itself is often referred to in brief as a 'graduation'. The term has been taken up and used in a wider context, so that now we may speak of pupils 'graduating' from school, or from one phase of schooling to another. In all contexts it indicates the progression from one grade to a higher one.

grammar school Originally, a school which focused on an education in the classics, and specifically upon the grammar of Latin and Greek. Following the *Education Act 1944 (*Butler Act), *local authorities were empowered to set up secondary schools inspired by this model, and the name became attached to the selective schools in the *tripartite secondary system designed to cater for the needs of the most academic pupils. Selection of pupils was carried out at the end of *primary schooling through the *Eleven Plus examination, which was believed to identify the type of schooling most appropriate to each child. Those not selected for grammar schools were allocated places at a secondary modern school or, in some local authorities, a technical school. Following the *Education Act 1976, the Eleven Plus was largely discontinued, except within those authorities with a strong Conservative council, such as Lincolnshire and Kent, where the policy of retaining their grammar and secondary modern schools was enabled to continue by the Education Act 1979, which made the abolition of selection optional rather than mandatory. In most of England, however, the selective system was gradually replaced by *comprehensive schools in the 1970s and 1980s; and by the early 1990s there were few grammar schools remaining. These do continue to exist, however, alongside secondary modern schools, in some local authorities, such as Lincolnshire.

grant maintained school (GMS) Schools which were allowed to opt out of *local authority control, under the provision of the *Education Reform Act 1988, and receive their funding directly from the Department for Education and Employment. They were part of a move by the government of the time to introduce *market forces into educational provision. As a result of the School Standards and Framework Act 1998, the option of **grant maintained status** was discontinued, and was replaced by the *foundation schools initiative in 2000.

Great Debate The ongoing debate about standards in education, which is widely held to have been launched in 1976 by James Callaghan, then Prime Minister, in a speech at Ruskin College, Oxford. In the speech, calling for a public debate on education, he drew attention to the need for school-leavers to possess the appropriate levels of literacy and numeracy required of them by employers. One of the consequences of the Ruskin speech was the publication of the *Green Paper *Education in Schools: A Consultative Document*, which was published later that same year. The eventual introduction of *key skills into the post-16 curriculum is often attributed in part to the concerns raised in the process of the Great Debate.

((⊕)) SEE WEB LINKS
• Provides the full text of the Ruskin speech.

Greats The title given to an undergraduate course of study in classical history, philosophy, and languages at Oxford University.

Green Paper A consultative or discussion document in which the government sets out its proposals for future policy for debate and discussion before a final policy decision is made. Like *White Papers, Green Papers are a type of command paper and may be the subject of statements or debates in the House of Commons. Following the consultation triggered by the Green Paper, the government normally publishes a White Paper setting out firmer recommendations.

Examples of recent key Green Papers relevant to education and children's welfare include the following:

1998	*The Learning Age*
	Meeting the Childcare Challenge
2001	*Schools: Building on Success*
2002	*14–19: Opportunity and Excellence*
2003	*Every Child Matters
2005	*Parental Separation*
	Youth Matters
	Offender Learning
2006	*Care Matters*
2007	*Raising Expectations: Staying in Education and Training Post-16*
2012	*Support and aspiration: A new approach to SEN and disability*

((⊕)) SEE WEB LINKS
• Provides links to summaries or full text PDF versions of education Green Papers.

group discussion A method of teaching and learning where learners discuss a given topic. This may be done as a whole group, led by the teacher; or may take the form of small-group discussion at the conclusion of which each group feeds back its ideas to the class as a whole.

group size *See* CLASS SIZE; PUPIL–TEACHER RATIO.

guidance In Scottish schools this is the term given to the personal support available to students set out in the **National Review of Guidance** (2004). All education authority secondary schools in Scotland have at least one principal teacher with responsibility for guidance. In primary and special schools this is a designated member of senior staff or management. This role may also encompass responsibility for *personal and social development. SM

half-term A holiday for *pupils, usually of a week's duration, in the middle of each *term of the school year. The summer half-term holiday usually coincides with the Spring bank holiday; the autumn half-term falls at the end of October; and the date of the spring half-term depends upon the length of that term and when Easter falls, but is usually sometime in February. While most schools have half-term holidays, they are less commonly found in further education, and not at all in universities.

hall of residence Living accommodation for students on or near the *campus of a university or college. A hall will usually contain a number of single or double rooms furnished to provide both sleeping accommodation and a desk at which to study. There is also normally a kitchen facility, although many halls also include a common dining room in which student meals are provided.

halo effect The tendency of *assessors to be influenced by their previous evaluation of a learner's standard of work when arriving at an assessment decision. Therefore, if a teacher has already come to the conclusion that a learner produces good (or poor) work, so the halo effect theory goes, the mark or grade they award, even though it might be in an unrelated subject, may be in danger of reflecting this prejudgement, rather than being based entirely on the standard of the actual work being assessed. This effect can also apply to their perception of learner behaviour, in line with the old saying 'Give a dog a bad name . . . '.

Hawthorne effect The tendency of learners to perform better when being closely observed by the teacher. The effect is so called because it derives from research into the performance of workers in an American factory bearing that name. Close observation by the teacher is clearly easier in some circumstances than others; for example, when *class sizes are smaller. In such a case, a question is inevitably raised for educational researchers about whether it is the close observation or in fact the *pupil–teacher ratio, or a combination of both, which accounts for the improvement in performance. *See also* MOTIVATION.

head of house A pastoral role in those secondary schools which operate a 'house' system. The teacher who is appointed head of house has pastoral responsibility for all pupils in that house, much as a *head of year has in schools which do not operate a house system. Perhaps the most famous heads of house currently are the fictional ones responsible for the pupils in the four houses at Hogwarts School in the *Harry Potter* books.

head of year In most secondary schools this is a pastoral role which also involves leading a team of year tutors and monitoring the progress of pupils within that year group. The head of year normally also has responsibility for liaising with parents and carers, and with other agencies, over issues relating to the welfare of pupils under their care. The post carries responsibility points which are reflected in the calculation of the post-holder's salary. *See also* HEAD OF HOUSE.

headship development The *National College for Teaching and Leadership offers a number of programmes for the professional development of *head teachers and aspiring head teachers. For those aspiring to headship, such as *deputy heads and *assistant heads, it offers the *National Professional Qualification for Headship (NPQH), a programme of three essential and two elective modules. Successful graduates of the NPQH may go on to join the **Head Start** programme, which is also available to new head teachers within the first two years of their appointment. The college also offers a **Black and Minority Ethnic (BME) Head Teacher and Deputy Head Teacher Internship** programme for experienced BME deputy or assistant head teachers who are also graduates of the NPQH. Some universities and other higher education institutions accept evidence of successful completion of programmes such as the NPQH as grounds for accelerated entry onto *postgraduate programmes in education. *See also* CONTINUING PROFESSIONAL DEVELOPMENT.

(((⊕))) SEE WEB LINKS
• Provides links to the range of headship development programmes.

head teacher The senior leadership role in primary and secondary schools. Together with the governing body, the head teacher has responsibility for much of the management of the school, including, since the *Education Reform Act 1988, management of the school's budget. The role of head teacher has developed over the past quarter of a century from one largely concerned with leadership and curriculum issues, to one which focuses also on management, finance, and marketing. This development has been reflected and supported by the extensive provision of professional development programmes for headship. *See also* HEADSHIP DEVELOPMENT.

hearing impairment A general descriptor to denote all levels of hearing loss from minor to profound. Some children and young people with profound hearing loss or with additional impairments may be educated in specialist schools; but most learners with a hearing impairment attend mainstream education where they are entitled to additional support in schools, colleges, and universities. This may take a variety of forms including, for example, the provision of an *amanuensis for support with note-taking or an interpreter for alternative forms of communication such as signing; specialist speech or auditory training; sign language instruction for their teachers and classmates; or the use of specialist amplification systems. *See also* SPECIAL EDUCATIONAL NEEDS; AUGMENTATIVE AND ALTERNATIVE COMMUNICATION.

(((())) SEE WEB LINKS)

• A Canadian web site providing a resource guide for classroom teachers supporting learners with a hearing impairment.

Her Majesty's Inspectorate (HMI) The Inspectorate was founded in the 19th century and its role was gradually expanded from its early function of overseeing public spending on the education of the poor to its late 20th-century remit of inspecting the standards of teaching and learning in all maintained schools and local authority funded colleges, and providing professional development courses for teachers. The Education (Schools) Act 1992 established a new inspection regime under *Ofsted. Thereafter the number of HMI inspectors was reduced, and their role became one of training, monitoring, and advising Ofsted inspectors, and sometimes acting as lead inspectors. *See also* HER MAJESTY'S INSPECTORATE OF EDUCATION.

Her Majesty's Inspectorate of Education (HMIE) In Scotland HMIE operates as an executive agency of Scottish government ministers under the terms of the Scotland Act 1998. The Inspectorate operates independently and impartially while remaining directly accountable to ministers. The core business of HMIE is inspection and review in order to improve the quality of education and raise attainment. The HMIE inspects and evaluates pre-school education, primary and secondary schools, teacher education, community learning and development, further education, and the education functions of local authorities in Scotland. Schools are rated on a scale of one to six, from unsatisfactory to excellent. These inspections are the equivalent of *Ofsted inspections in England and Wales. *See also* HER MAJESTY'S INSPECTORATE.

SM

heuristic play Heuristic learning encompasses the notion of exploratory play which is self-directed by the infant and young child. Eleanor Goldschmied uses the specific term 'heuristic play with objects' to explore 'a large number of different objects and receptacles with which [children] play without adult intervention' (Goldschmied and Jackson 1994: 128). Commonly, the objects are placed in a **treasure basket** within reach of where very young infants are seated, and high levels of concentration, engagement, and persistence are observed as the children explore the nature of the presented objects. The adult acts as observer, having first selected a range of natural, everyday objects or combinations of objects, to stimulate particularly the child's senses and their development of *schema.

AW

Further Reading: S. Ridall-Leech *Heuristic Play* (2nd edn) (Practical Pre-School Books, 2013).

hidden curriculum *See* CURRICULUM.

Higher Equivalent to *Scottish Credit and Qualifications Framework level 6, this is a qualification taken by students in Scotland who have achieved passes in *Standard Grades at *Credit level or completed a course at Intermediate level 2. Highers are required for entry into *further or *higher education study, and therefore their level is roughly equivalent to that of *Advanced Levels (A levels) elsewhere in the United Kingdom. For the purpose of university entry, three Highers are usually taken to be the equivalent of two A levels in terms of coverage and entry points. Students will normally complete an average of five Highers over a year. *See also* ADVANCED HIGHER. SM

higher degree An award at a higher level than a *bachelor's or *first degree. This includes *master's degrees and *doctorates. An applicant to study for a higher degree will normally be required to hold a good first degree at either first class or upper second class level for entry to a master's programme; and usually to have successfully completed a master's degree for entry to doctorate level. Higher degrees are awarded by *universities and some other institutions of *higher education.

higher education Programmes of study which lead to advanced qualifications such as those at *National Qualifications Framework (NQF) level 5 or 6 and above, such as *degrees and diplomas. These are usually offered in **higher education institutions** (HEIs) such as *universities, but may also form part of the provision of *further education (FE) colleges, as in the case of *foundation degrees. The higher education sector is largely comprised of universities and *university colleges, and is distinct from the further education sector in terms of funding and purpose. The *provision* of higher education, however, is an area in which there is some overlap, since HEIs may accredit FE colleges to deliver some higher-level, vocationally related courses.

In Scotland higher education institutions include thirteen universities, the Open University in Scotland, one university college, two colleges of higher education, two art schools, one conservatoire, and the Scottish Agricultural College. The universities developed in three stages: the ancient universities (St Andrews, Glasgow, Aberdeen, Edinburgh) date from the 15th and 16th centuries; four others (Dundee, Strathclyde, Heriot-Watt, Stirling) achieved university status in the 1960s; and the newest group (Glasgow Caledonian, Napier, Paisley, Robert Gordon, Abertay) achieved university status in the 1990s. Students can be accepted to university on completion of their Higher examinations at the end of Year S5; however, Scottish students wishing to attend an English university may often go on to complete Advanced Highers in Year S6.

Higher Education Funding Council for England (HEFCE) The body which distributes funding for teaching and research to support *higher education provision in colleges and universities in England. HEFCE was set up as a non-departmental body in 1992, following the *Further and Higher Education Act of that year which awarded polytechnics university status. Separate councils were established for Wales (*Higher Education Funding Council for Wales)

(Cyngor Cyllido Addysg Uwch Cymru) and Scotland (the *Scottish Funding Council). Universities in Northern Ireland (NI) are funded through the NI **Department of Employment and Learning**. Although the HEFCE does not form part of any government department, it operates within the framework of policies set out by the *Secretary of State for the department responsible for higher education.

(⊕) SEE WEB LINKS
• Explains the role of HEFCE.
• Summarizes the work of the Scottish Funding Council.

Higher Education Funding Council for Wales (HEFCW) (Cyngor Cyllido Addysg Uwch Cymru) An Assembly-sponsored body established in May 1992 under the *Further and Higher Education Act, responsible for funding the higher education sector throughout Wales; it also has the power to fund higher education in *colleges of further education. Its key strategic aims are widening participation; encouraging excellent student learning and support; delivering improved research performance in the sector; encouraging more productive links between higher education and the public and private sectors; supporting high-quality *initial teacher training provision; and developing a strong emphasis on collaboration and reconfiguration in higher education in Wales.   HG

Higher Education Wales (HEW) The national council in Wales of Universities UK, established in 1996 to represent the *higher education sector in Wales. Membership includes all the heads of universities and higher education institutions in Wales, and the Welsh director of the *Open University. HEW promotes and supports higher education in Wales, representing the interests of its members to the National Assembly, to Parliament, to political parties, and to European institutions and bodies, with whom it negotiates on behalf of Welsh higher education. It also provides an expert resource on all aspects of higher education to stakeholders, including Assembly Members and Welsh MPs, the Welsh and UK media, business leaders, and industrial entrepreneurs.   HG

Higher National Certificate (HNC) A vocationally related national qualification, usually offered by colleges of *further education as a part-time programme of study for those already in employment who wish to gain further qualifications. It is available in a wide range of subjects, from business and finance to engineering. Applicants are usually required to have five *General Certificate of Secondary Education passes at grade C or above, including English and mathematics, and at least one pass at *General Certificate of Education *Advanced Level. *Assessment is by *assignment, and the award is accredited in England and Wales at *National Qualifications Framework level 4. In Scotland an HNC is equivalent to level 7 on the *Scottish Credit and Qualifications Framework.

Higher National Diploma (HND) A vocationally related national qualification, usually offered by colleges of *further education as a two-year full-time programme of study, available in subjects such as business and finance and computing. Applicants are usually required to have *General Certificate of Secondary Education passes at grade C or above in English and mathematics, or the equivalent *key skills, as well as a total of around 80 *Universities and Colleges Admissions Service (UCAS) points. HNDs can be 'topped up' by additional study by those students wishing to gain a relevant *honours degree. The award is accredited in England and Wales at *Qualifications and Credit Framework level 4. HNDs now form part of the *foundation degree framework. In Scotland an HND is equivalent to level 8 on the *Scottish Credit and Qualifications Framework.

Higher Still An alternative name for the Scottish *Advanced Higher.   SM

Highlands and Islands Enterprise *See* SCOTTISH ENTERPRISE, HIGHLANDS AND ISLANDS ENTERPRISE.

high school At one time used as a title by some grammar schools (as in 'girls' high school'), non-selective schools, and independent schools, it is still used in Scotland in the term **junior high school**, a school which offers both primary and secondary provision. Pupils may also associate the term with the American secondary schooling system, with which they have become familiar through popular television series.

home education Some parents exercise their statutory right to give their child of compulsory school age (5–16) full-time education within the home. In the United Kingdom it is education that is compulsory and not attendance at school. Any home education programme of work, however, must be relevant to the age, needs (including any special needs), ability, and aptitude of the child, but is not required to conform absolutely to the *national curriculum. There is no financial support available to home educators, and the education they provide is subject to *local authority monitoring and inspection. *See also* EDUCATION OTHERWISE THAN AT SCHOOL.   TB, LE

(⊕) SEE WEB LINKS
• Provides guidance on home schooling.

home–school agreement An agreement drawn up by the school's *governing body, in consultation with parents and the head teacher, setting out a statement of the school's values and aims, and the role and responsibility of parents and carers in supporting these by ensuring that their child meets the required standards in respect to *behaviour, attendance, and the completion of homework. Parents and carers are requested and encouraged to sign the agreement, although doing so is not a mandatory requirement. The main purpose of the agreement is to improve standards of behaviour and *attainment, and to encourage and enhance cooperation between school and home. The agreement became a requirement for all schools under the provision of the School Standards and Framework Act 1998. There is so far insufficient evidence to confirm whether the introduction of the agreement has had any direct impact on the level of parental cooperation.

(⊕) SEE WEB LINKS

• Provides a link to the full text of guidance for governing bodies and local authorities on home-school agreements.

home tuition Sometimes referred to as 'private tuition', it is the provision of additional support for learning, outside school hours, usually engaged and paid for by the parents or carers in the case of young learners, or by the learners themselves if adults. Home tuition may be sought in subjects in which the learner is having difficulties at school or college, and is often designed to supplement and reinforce the teaching they are receiving elsewhere. It is particularly sought by parents to prepare their children for public examinations, such as the *General Certificate of Secondary Education in core subjects such as English and mathematics. *See also* EDUCATION OTHERWISE THAN AT SCHOOL.

home tutor A teacher employed by a *local authority to teach pupils who cannot, for whatever reason, attend school. Instead, the pupils are taught in the home. *See also* EDUCATION OTHERWISE THAN AT SCHOOL.

homework Tasks related to their school studies which pupils are expected to complete outside school hours. All schools are required to have a homework policy, which is drawn up to promote the partnership between school and home and to extend and build upon learning undertaken in school. Many schools post their homework policy on their web site. In 1998 the government published guidance on the type and extent of homework that pupils could be reasonably expected to undertake at each stage of their education. According to this, pupils in *primary schools may be expected to spend 10–30 minutes a day on homework, which should focus on literacy and numeracy skills. For secondary pupils the coverage extends across the curriculum and the recommended duration is 90 minutes a day in *Key Stage 3, rising to a maximum of two and a half hours a day in Key Stage 4. *See also* HOME–SCHOOL AGREEMENT.

homework club Run after school hours in local libraries, and sometimes in schools, *homework clubs are intended to provide pupils with a safe environment conducive to study, which may also offer support for computer and Internet access. They are available to pupils aged 7 years and over. Schools and *local authorities provide parents and carers with information about the location of their nearest homework club.

honorary degree A *degree awarded by a *university or other higher education institution to individuals who are not students of that institution, but who have gained wide recognition for their achievements in a worthwhile field. The award is usually made formally at a *graduation awards ceremony by the chancellor, vice-chancellor, or some other dignitary of the institution.

honours degree A degree which indicates a higher level of achievement than a *foundation degree or a pass degree, and may require the student to study to a greater depth or breadth. A candidate who has achieved an honours degree may indicate this by the inclusion of the abbreviation '(Hons)' after their qualification; for example, Mohammed McPherson BA (Hons). Unlike a pass degree, an honours degree award is divided into different classes which are used as grading indicators of the level of achievement the student has attained in their undergraduate studies. These classes are **first** class, **upper second** class (sometimes referred to as a **2.1**), **lower second** class (sometimes referred to as a **2.2**), and **third** class, the first class degree being the highest awarded. Most honours degrees awarded fall into the second class category. *See also* BACHELOR'S DEGREE.

humanist A philosophy which views the individual and their potential for development as the essential starting point for theorizing about, or implementing, systems of teaching and learning. A humanist approach to education focuses on the learner as an individual, taking their interests, enthusiasms, and goals as the basis upon which to organize or facilitate their learning experiences. Learning is not seen as an end in itself, but rather as a means towards enabling the individual to realize their full potential, referred to by some humanist theorists such as Abraham *Maslow and Carl *Rogers as achieving **self-actualization**. In the education of young children the philosophy and activities of the *Reggio Emilia schools or of the *Montessori method are examples of this approach, encouraging children to develop their curiosity by facilitating their exploration of their current interests and their creativity, rather than imposing a mandatory and uniform curriculum. A. S. *Neill's *Summerhill School, too, provides an example of a humanistic approach in its creation of a democratic community of learning where pupils and *teachers have equal status, and pupils are empowered to exercise choice over whether and what they will learn. What these approaches have in common is that they are *learner-centred, the learner acknowledged not only as the starting point of the education process, but also as taking responsibility for their own learning. The teacher or *educator is regarded, according to this model, as a facilitator of learning, rather than as a dispenser of knowledge or skills; and the learning process itself takes into account not only the academic needs of the learner, but also their emotional, creative, psychological, and developmental needs.

A humanistic model of education operates on the belief that achievement is its own reward and that personal satisfaction at having learned or understood or created something will motivate the learner more effectively than the *extrinsic rewards and sanctions favoured by *behaviourists. For this reason even the 'reward' of praise is treated cautiously, since it could lead to a craving for teacher approval, displacing the learner's *intrinsic enjoyment of learning. The humanistic approach places an emphasis upon recognizing and valuing the dignity and self-worth of every individual learner, and upon developing the self-concept of the learner. It starts from the assumption that the learner must feel positive about themselves and about their ability to improve and progress towards the realization of their full potential; and that, in order to do this, they must have a clear and accurate understanding of their own strengths and weaknesses.

In practice, a humanistic method of education is one in which an emphasis is placed on *discovery learning and the learner's right to self-determination. It places little or no emphasis on externally imposed attainment standards, targets, and testing, and may indeed be seen as antithetical to a rigid, mandatory, standardized curriculum. The teaching is student-centred, and takes into account the learners' social, emotional, and personal development. The curriculum takes as its starting point topics which are of central interest to the learners, and allows for learner control over the learning activities employed. Learners are encouraged to monitor and evaluate their own progress.

There are clear difficulties in operating such a model on a whole-school basis in the UK, not least because of the demands of the *national curriculum. A humanistic approach, however, may be applied to individual lessons, or may constitute the preferred teaching style of individual teachers. When the terms 'humanist' or 'humanistic' are used in this microcosmic sense, they imply a limited application of this approach, and one which is consistent with, and accommodated within, the statutory requirements of the national curriculum framework.

humanities A collective term for a range of academic disciplines or fields, all of which draw upon a knowledge of the development, achievements, behaviour, organization, or distribution of humanity. These include literature, history, philosophy, and some aspects of geography. In its widest sense it is used to draw a distinction between 'hard' sciences and other subjects. When this is the case, education and the social sciences may also be included in the category of humanities.

ideology One of the most important and widely used conceptual categories, not just in education, but also in other areas such as the media, politics, economics, and other arenas of cultural activity. There are many competing definitions of the term as its use has been determined by various contexts. At its most basic level, it can be used to refer to a set of beliefs and ideas which inform the practices of a profession such as teaching. These ideas will inform all aspects of the training of a teacher and reflect the values placed on education in any particular context. Ideologies represent what appear to be 'common-sense' ideas—ideas which are taken for granted and rarely questioned or analysed critically—such as acceptance of the power relationship inherent in interactions between teacher and pupils. It is in addressing assumptions such as these where an understanding of the concept of ideology gains a more critical edge, particularly in relation to ideas or practices which are taken for granted but which may function to exclude, or render 'invisible', certain groups or types of learners.

Ideology was originally exclusively a Marxist term, and was used to imply a body of ideas and attitudes which not only bound a society together but were used to mask or conceal the material reality of people's lives. In the 19th century, Karl Marx (1818–83) conceived a theory which offered a historical account of how society and culture replicated unequal distributions of power and wealth. It offered a base–superstructure model of how capitalism reinforced class distinctions. The most significant part of this model was the base, which comprised the mode of production (technology) as well as the relations of production (the difference between workers and those who own the means of production). The superstructure comprised all the other aspects of life such as education, the arts, politics, religion, and the family. It was through areas such as education that an ideology (or a body of ideas which supported capitalism) would communicate, for Marx, a 'false consciousness'. In classical Marxian thought, people are understood to be born into a pre-existing ideology and to live in a condition of conflict between their material lives and the ideologies which determined their identity.

One of the most influential definitions of ideology since the 1960s came from the Marxist academic Louis Althusser (1918–90). Althusser developed Marx's concept of ideology by arguing that it was through the way language functioned as a structure that ideology gained its significance. Like many other contemporary theorists, Althusser benefited from Ferdinand de Saussure's (1857–1913) concept of *semiotics, and the structuralism that was its outcome, by suggesting that people gained their identity from pre-existing structures that dominated every aspect of their lives. He called these structures **ideological state apparatuses**, one of which was education. According to Althusser, ideology was not just a set of ideas which bound people together; it also represented the everyday material practices of our experiences. Meaning and identity were communicated at the level of the sign, and any object or gesture—not just verbal or written language—could operate as a sign. Thus, although the architectural features of a school building may at first seem neutral and value-free, they carry with them ideological assumptions built into the structure of its design. Similarly, the way *lecture theatres and classrooms are designed can tell us about the hierarchical relationship between teacher and pupil; the teacher's position at the front might hint at the unidirectional flow of knowledge. In the same way, the categorization of knowledge into the arts, sciences, business, and other fields is reflected in the faculty system, which houses separate disciplines in different buildings. According to this theory, all 'texts' speak to an implied reader: in a school situation, all the texts in the institution, including the building, the textbooks, the posters on the wall, and the teacher, address the pupil and 'hail them into being'; the moment the student reads these texts, they adopt a particular identity which comes with an associated set of ideological attitudes and values. This process is called **interpellation**.

Although poststructuralist ideas in the late 1960s about the instability of language led theorists such as Michel *Foucault to doubt the possibility of a unified, stable set of beliefs which bound people together, ideology still has its Marxist connotations today. It became a central concept for those academics working at the Centre for Contemporary *Cultural Studies. Referring to ideology and the related concept of hegemony (the resolution of conflict by power through rhetoric or persuasion), theorists such as Stuart Hall (1932–2014) and Dick Hebdige (b. 1951) studied practices of production and consumption in the media, proposing that oppositional ideologies could exist which countered more dominant ideologies.

Ideology is a concept which has been used to refer to power relations outside the issue of class: the various feminisms have used the term when discussing the inequalities that are a consequence of a patriarchal systems and beliefs. Similarly, postcolonial theorists analyse the consequences of colonial ideologies. The term today permeates all subject areas in the arts, humanities, and social sciences, and has become an important critical tool in higher education.   CH

Illich, Ivan *See* DESCHOOLING.

inaugural lecture When an academic is promoted or appointed to the post of *professor, and occasionally *reader, in *higher education, they are usually expected to deliver an initial lecture which is open to all and which allows them to introduce and expound upon their existing body of work or their current research in their specialist field. This event is known as their inaugural lecture.

inclusion A term used to describe and promote policies, strategies, and practices which aim to enable all learners to participate fully in education. As widely conceived, inclusion is closely connected with *social justice concerns for equality and rights for all. In this conception it often refers to **social inclusion**, which is concerned with reducing inequalities between the relatively disadvantaged sectors of society and the relatively advantaged. In this sense it may refer to race, *gender, *social class, disability, learning difficulties, religious belief, or some other category or group. It is contrasted with exclusion. *Exclusion may be imposed. It may also take the form of self-exclusion, as in *truancy, or as in the self-exclusion of the middle classes from mainstream educational institutions. More narrowly conceived, the term 'inclusion' can refer especially to pupils and young people with *special educational needs. Such pupils have traditionally been excluded—or excluded themselves—from classrooms, mainstream institutions (schools, colleges, and universities), and the curriculum. The 1994 Salamanca Statement is widely credited with promoting a view of special education as an equality or social justice issue rather than as a response to a *deficit in individuals. Consequently, 'inclusion' rather than 'integration' has become the preferred term, implying that the school must change to 'fit' the pupil rather than the pupil to fit the school. However, the concept of inclusion continues to be contested. Tensions arise because there are contradictory educational policy imperatives both for inclusive education and for competition and selection. Moreover, policy approaches to inclusion may prioritize the supporting of individual children, making schools inclusive at a systems level or, more politically, challenging discrimination. Underlying these tensions are different kinds of explanatory framework within special education: individual pathology, social theory, critical theory, and social justice perspectives.   MG

(⊕) SEE WEB LINKS
• The text of the Salamanca Statement.

inclusive education Access to mainstream education, including equal opportunities for progression, for students with learning difficulties or disabilities. It reflects the principle that all learners, regardless of their learning difficulty or disability, should be able to take part in education or training to enhance their quality of life and lead to their improved integration into wider communities. The *Tomlinson Report (1996) set out suggestions of ways in which to improve the organizational culture of learning and training institutions in order to ensure that they respond positively to applications from students with difficulties and disabilities, and are able to acknowledge and address their needs. In recent years the terms *inclusion and *'widening participation' have, in *further education particularly, been used interchangeably to encompass the improvement of learning opportunities for all. However, 'widening participation' derived originally from the main theme driving the *Kennedy Report (1997), which aimed to ensure that all UK citizens over the age of 16 would have equal access to further and higher education.

inclusive learning *See* INCLUSIVE EDUCATION; TOMLINSON REPORT (1996).

independent learning An approach to learning in which pupils are encouraged to be self-regulating. It is one of a number of approaches, such as *pupil-centred and *personalized learning, which have in common the elements of empowering learner initiative and encouraging the pupil's sense of ownership of their learning. Contrary to what the name suggests, independent learning does not necessarily involve individual learners working alone or without teacher support. Indeed, it is often employed in the form of groupwork. Research suggests that successful independent learning depends upon pupils' pre-existing levels of cognitive and meta-cognitive skills, as well as on adequate resourcing of *information and communication technology, and positive teacher-learner relationships.

(⊕) SEE WEB LINKS
• Provides information about the advantages and disadvantages of independent learning.

independent schools Sometimes referred to as **public schools**, these include both preparatory, or 'prep', schools, which prepare pupils for the *Common Entrance Examination at 13 or for the *Eleven Plus in those areas where it still exists; and private secondary schools. They are fee-paying.

In Scotland, too, independent schools are fee-paying, and provide education for the age of 3–18. Again they are known as private or 'public' schools although they do not receive any public funding. All are registered with the Scottish Education Department and receive regular inspections from HM Inspectorate of Education. As they are not managed by the education authority, these schools are not required to teach the Scottish national curriculum although in practice nearly all pupils are entered for the same public examinations as in state schools. However, after standard grade examinations, some schools choose to follow the English *Advanced Level system as opposed to Scottish *Highers. *See also* INDEPENDENT SCHOOLS INSPECTORATE.

Independent Schools Inspectorate (ISI) The body responsible for the inspection of *independent schools, private colleges of *further education and English language schools in England and Wales. It reports directly to the *Department for Education on whether and to what extent independent schools are meeting the statutory requirements for education of pupils between the ages of 5 and 18 years.

(⊕) SEE WEB LINKS
• Provides links to ISI reports on individual schools and a guide to ISI reporting in general.

index for inclusion A document produced by the **Centre for Studies in Inclusive Education (CSIE)**. It outlines a series of indicators of *inclusion which form guidance for developing policy, practice, and culture. The CSIE promotes a move away from segregated education. The index for inclusion describes how good education and good social sense uphold human rights. There is a **Charter for Inclusion** which was first written in 1989 and was rewritten in 2002. Typically, schools will use the index to support self-review and to identify *barriers to learning. It contains comprehensive definitions for inclusion. The index upholds the rights of all individuals to be educated

locally and recommends the training of staff to support the development
of an *inclusive ethos and practice. TB, LE

individual education plan (IEP) A plan of action designed to meet the
individual *special educational needs of a learner in order to help them to
maximize their learning. It sets out teaching and learning strategies identified
as best meeting the child's individual needs, sets targets, and identifies
provisions and outcomes. All these may be additional to, or different from,
those of other learners in the class. In this sense the IEP is an instrument
of *differentiation. It ensures that teachers, support workers, and other
professionals are aware of the learner's needs and targets and the strategies for
achieving them. The plan has no legal status and therefore local authorities are
neither compelled to produce them nor to ensure that they are implemented.

(((•))) SEE WEB LINKS
• Provides information on the application of IEPs.

individual learning 1. The practice of allowing students to learn at their own
pace and according to their own preferred *learning style, and to cover those
areas of the *syllabus or lesson which are necessary to their learning. It is an
approach which necessitates the teacher having a clear understanding of the
starting point and learning needs of each student, and is part of the wider
practice of *differentiation. In this approach, which is widely used in the teaching
of *basic skills, for example, students may have their own **individual action
plans** and learning *objectives.
2. The practice of encouraging pupils to work separately on individual tasks,
for example using *work cards, rather than working as a group or class. This
alternative meaning does not necessarily imply the practice of differentiation.
See also INDIVIDUAL LEARNING PLAN; PERSONALIZED LEARNING.

induction 1. The process by which pupils or students are introduced to their
educational institution, their *course, or their subject. This may take a variety
of forms, from a simple welcome and an introductory lecture, to a full week or
more of organized activities. A thorough induction will be designed to ensure
that learners are able to find their way about the school or *campus; that they
have met key members of teaching staff; have been introduced to the *aims
and structure of their course; have been made aware of the institution's rules and
regulations; and have been informed about the learner support services
available. In many universities the induction of new students takes place in the
week before other students return to resume their studies after the summer
break. This is known as **freshers' week**.
2. The process by which a newly appointed teacher is introduced to their
school. This particularly applies to newly qualified teachers (NQTs) in their first
year of teaching, for whom the induction period is set as a full three *terms; that
is, an entire school year. This induction replaces what was known formerly as
the 'probationary year'. During this time, the NQT's timetable should allow them
at least 10 per cent non-class-contact time in order to focus on their professional
development. During this process they will normally have the support of an

induction *mentor. At the end of the three terms a decision will be taken by the local authority, based on evidence from the induction tutor and *head teacher, as to whether the teacher has met the required **induction standards**.

induction mentor *See* INDUCTION; MENTOR.

induction standards *See* INDUCTION.

infant school A school for children aged 5–7 which teaches *Key Stage 1 of the *national curriculum. It may form part of a larger *primary school or operate as a separate institution. Some infant schools have *pre-school facilities attached for children below the age of compulsory schooling.

information communication technology (ICT) 1. An area of the *curriculum concerned with the uses of technology. Although it is sometimes used interchangeably in schools with the term *information technology, ICT is widely recognized as denoting the study of the applications and use of the technology, for example through the exploration and creation of electronic toys and models, and through the production of electronic music. Since the introduction of the *national curriculum, ICT has been a compulsory subject for all pupils, but was disapplied for pupils in *Key Stages 1 and 2 from September 2012. **2.** Also used to refer to resources for supporting learning, such as computers, televisions, or audio equipment. **3.** The title given to one area of *functional skills, and thus constituting part of the 14–19 curriculum.

(⊕) SEE WEB LINKS
• Sets out the advantages and disadvantages of ICT for the learner.

information learning technology (ILT) The term used in *post-compulsory education, particularly in *colleges of further education, to refer to the use and applications of technology by teachers to support and enhance students' learning. It includes such resources and strategies as *virtual learning environments, *e-learning, and *blended learning programmes. *See also* INFORMATION COMMUNICATION TECHNOLOGY (ICT).

(⊕) SEE WEB LINKS
• Discusses the impact of ILT on teaching and learning in Northern Ireland FE colleges.

information technology (IT) The study of computing, microelectronics, and the storage and transmission of data. Once a generic term for all aspects of this field of study, its most common usage now is in referring to the study of the software and hardware which computer technology employs, for example in subjects such as computer studies, rather than to the use or application of that technology, which now comes under the curriculum area of *information communication technology. Both have become an important part of the school curriculum following the publication of the Stevenson Report in 1997, which argued for a greater emphasis on IT in schools in order to hasten the development of an IT-literate workforce.

initial teacher education (ITE) Courses of training which lead to
*qualified teacher status (QTS). The traditional model of undergraduate
teacher training combines a course of academic and professional study in
institutions of *higher education (HE), such as *universities, with periods of
practical experience in schools or colleges, and the award of a *Postgraduate
Certificate of Education (PGCE). For graduates entering the teaching
profession there are a number of routes, all incorporating practical experience
in schools that have been approved for the purpose. Graduates with no
relevant postgraduate work experience can join a **Schools Direct Training
Programme (SDTP)** on which they may be entitled to financial support in
the form of grants and bursaries. Graduates with a minimum of three years'
work experience may enter an SDTP and earn a salary during their training.
SDTPs, as well as leading to QTS, may in some instances also include the
award of a PGCE. Experienced teachers without QTS but who have a degree
may gain qualified status through the Assessment Only (AO) route. This
requires them to present evidence of their experience and proficiency; to
successfully pass the *professional skills tests in literacy and numeracy; and
to have their teaching assessed in a school by an accredited provider, usually
a university. Experienced teachers who have trained and qualified overseas
may also gain QTS via this route, although those who have qualified in
Australia, New Zealand, Canada, and the USA may not be required to do
so. Historically, teacher training for schoolteachers took place in teacher
training colleges, which were renamed **colleges of education** following
the recommendations of the 1963 *Robbins Report. Many of these
eventually became incorporated into university departments of education.
See also NEWLY QUALIFIED TEACHER.

(((⊕))) SEE WEB LINKS

• Provides more detail about the various routes for initial teacher training.

in-service education of teachers (INSET) Now often referred to as
*continuing professional development, INSET is the provision of professional
education, training, and updating for teachers already employed in schools
or colleges. It takes a wide range of forms, from formal provision such as
part-time study for a postgraduate degree in education, to development days
in school run by the teachers themselves. Such days are sometimes still referred
to colloquially as 'Baker days' after Kenneth Baker, who, as *Secretary of State
for Education under the 1980s Thatcher administration, instigated the inclusion
of five non-contact days (days when teachers are in school but pupils do not
attend) each academic year for the purposes of INSET. Professional development
may take the form of attendance at conferences, day events in school
presented by staff or visiting consultants, *webinars, or short courses run for
or on behalf of the *Department of Education. Providing INSET was originally
part of the role of *local authority advisory services, but is now increasingly
outsourced to educational consultancies.

inspection The process by which an independent, external evaluation of an educational establishment's effectiveness is carried out. National inspectorates across the UK are:

- Ofsted
- Independent Schools Inspectorate
- Education and Training Inspectorate
- Estyn
- Her Majesty's Inspectorate of Education

In addition to facilitating the improvement of education providers, the process is designed to provide information about the performance and provision of schools so that parents can make an informed choice about where to have their children educated. Inspection is also intended to set the standards expected of education providers, monitor the progress of improving providers, provide guidance for specific areas of development and encourage providers to evaluate their own performance. After an inspection, a report identifying the strengths and weaknesses of the provider is made available to the general public via the relevant inspectorate web site. *See also* ESTYN; INDEPENDENT SCHOOLS INSPECTORATE; HER MAJESTY'S INSPECTORATE; HER MAJESTY'S INSPECTORATE OF EDUCATION; LEAD INSPECTOR; OFSTED; STANDARDS.   IW

(⊕) SEE WEB LINKS
- Provides access to recent examples of Ofsted inspection reports.

Institute for Learning (IfL) Formed in 2002, the Institute provides a professional body for teachers in further, adult, and work-based learning and training in the UK. Its aims are to support the professional needs of practitioners and to raise their status across the learning and skills sector. The 2004 government reform proposals set out in *Equipping Our Teachers for the Future* named the IfL as the body responsible for awarding certification of qualified teacher learning and skills (QTLS) status to all new teachers entering the *lifelong learning sector from September 2007. As a result of the reforms in teacher training within the sector leading to QTLS, the IfL took on an extended role.   VC, KA

(⊕) SEE WEB LINKS
- Provides information about IfL's role.

instructor Someone who works as a trainer or teacher but does not hold a recognized teaching qualification and does not have *qualified teacher status or *qualified teacher training and skills. The term is more closely associated with skills training than with education, and may carry its own qualifications, as, for example, in the case of a driving instructor. It is a term also used to refer to those with a formal teaching or training role in the police and armed forces.

instrumental Describes learning which is undertaken not for its own sake but for some other purpose. For example, all vocational education is instrumental in that its purpose is to prepare the learner for a specific line of work and to improve their chances of employment. The increasing emphasis on skills for work in the 14–19 curriculum indicates a general trend towards the instrumental, as opposed to **developmental** or *liberal, model of education, as does the concept of *employer-led education and training.

instrument of government Under the terms of the Education Act 1944 (*Butler Act), every secondary school is required to have an instrument of government which clearly records the name of the school and the constitution of its *governing body. Since 1980 *primary schools have also been included in this requirement.

integrated community school (ICS) The pilot programme was launched by the Scottish Office in 1998 with the aim of promoting social *inclusion and raising education *standards by developing schools with increased support for vulnerable children. These schools were to be focused in disadvantaged areas and to undertake close liaison between community and social agencies as well as with parents. Full development of this policy began in 2002 with the aim that by 2007 all schools would be using an integrated community schooling approach to education.   SM

(∰) SEE WEB LINKS
• Contains the full report on ICS.

integration As described in the *Warnock Report (1978), integration was the original concept of educating children with special needs alongside their peers in mainstream schools. The Report detailed three types of integration: locational, social, and functional. Where a *special school or unit shared their campus with a mainstream school, it was seen as locational integration; social integration was where pupils with special needs were taught separately but joined each other at social times of the day; and functional integration was where children with special needs joined their peers for the full educational experience. The terms 'integration' and '*inclusion' are not to be confused as they describe entirely different philosophies. Integration is a situation in which children with special needs are deemed to benefit from fitting into a largely unaltered routine and procedure of a mainstream school, whereas inclusion is a process benefiting the whole school community. *See also* INCLUSIVE EDUCATION.   TB, LE

intelligence Usually defined as a measure of cognitive skill and the ability to solve problems, intelligence has been a topic of debate precisely because it has been open to a range of definitions and has fuelled theories of a contentious nature about the question of genetic inheritance. The theory that there exists a general intelligence factor, or 'factor g', was first proposed in 1904 by the British psychologist Charles Spearman (1863–1945), who based his claim on statistical analysis. The concept of a factor g has underpinned all subsequent psychometric models of intelligence, and has been used to fuel the controversial argument that genetic inheritance plays a major role in determining an individual's intelligence. Traditional understandings of intelligence were

brought into question in the 1980s by Howard *Gardner's (b. 1943) theory of
*multiple intelligences. Nevertheless, the assessment of 'intelligence' continues
to play an important role in some areas of educational and psychological
measurement and testing.

The origins of such testing is generally accredited to the work of the French
psychologists Alfred Binet (1857–1911) and Théodore Simon (1873–1961),
published in 1905, which was designed to identify pupils aged 3–12 who would
find learning difficult and would therefore need a different teaching approach
or additional support. This led to the development of the Stamford–Binet
intelligence scale (1916), which remains in use today, when psychologists from
Stamford University in the United States translated and revised the assessment
tasks designed by the two French psychologists. Building on this work, the
American psychologist David Wechsler (1896–1981) developed what became
known as the Wechsler scale for the psychometric measurement of intelligence.
Like the Stamford–Binet model, Wechsler's approach was to use *standardized
testing, individually administered and assessed by professional psychologists,
to arrive at a score referred to as the individual's intelligence quotient (IQ). This
led to the development of tests designed for ease of administration to large
groups, both in educational contexts and in the armed services, often for the
purposes of *selection, such as the *Eleven Plus test.

The contentious and fiercely argued debate over the extent to which
intelligence is an inherited or an acquired factor is yet to be resolved. There are
claims that psychometric intelligence tests have been misused or misinterpreted
to substantiate erroneous claims that specific ethnic and racial groups are
inherently less intelligent than others. This theory of genetic determinism has
been used, particularly in the United States, to support the argument against
government programmes of intervention designed to compensate for the social
and environmental deprivation of some groups of the population. There are
also fears that it could be used to argue the case for eugenics, the process of
human genetic selection. The genetic determinism model of human intelligence
was encapsulated in a controversial book entitled *The Bell Curve* (1994) by the
Americans Richard Herrnstein and Charles Murray, who further argued that
there was a correlation between low intelligence scores and antisocial
behaviour. The title of their work refers to the shape of norm group scores,
which, when entered on a graph, create a shape which is sometimes referred
to as a bell-shaped curve, widest in the middle since most scores fall into the
average range, with relatively few very high or very low. The first British
educational psychologist, Sir Cyril Burt (1883–1971), also made claims that
intelligence was an inherited factor. Following his death, accusations were
made that some of the data on which he had based these claims may have been
fabricated. Recent research, however, has cast doubt on these accusations.

Also vigorously debated is the question of whether birth order affects
intelligence levels. Research evidence on the whole has suggested that it may
do in some cases and that the number of siblings, as well as birth order, may
have some effect on intelligence levels. An early researcher, statistician, and
psychologist, Francis Galton (1822–1911), in his book *English Men of Science:*

Their Nature and Nurture (1874), claimed to have discovered a correlation between birth order and high achievement, first-born sons tending to achieve eminence in their field. However, his results did not take account of female children, so that a first-born son might in fact be one of the last of his siblings, provided those born earlier were all girls. Further studies appear to confirm Galton's thesis, first-born children being disproportionately represented among psychologists, composers, Nobel Prize winners, and other eminent personalities. In 1973 Lillian Belmont and Francis Marolla published research findings which suggested that first-born children score best in an intelligence test, with performance declining in line with children's place in the birth order; and that children with many siblings tend to score less well, regardless of social class, although still exhibiting differences according to birth order.

However, controversy still surrounds the validity of intelligence testing; that is, whether they indeed measure what they purport to measure. Some current researchers, such as Howard Gardner, suggest that such tests measure only a small part of intellectual performance, and do not make allowance for the cultural or social contexts in which those tested find themselves. Test questions can be based on assumptions about cultural or social norms which those being tested may not recognize or share. This factor alone can provide an explanation for why some ethnic or cultural groups consistently score less well in standardized intelligence tests. Moreover, Gardner suggests that we should understand intelligence as a multiple array of responses to our multifaceted environment, rather than as a singular cognitive or intellectual skill; and researchers such as Daniel Goleman also currently argue that our concept of intelligence should be expanded to embrace other facets, such as *emotional intelligence. The concept of multiple intelligences is also known as **MI theory**, and encompasses the idea that we possess moral intelligence (the ability to distinguish between right and wrong), and social or interpersonal intelligence (the ability to understand other people and how best to work with them). A further broad definition of intelligence was posited by Robert Sternberg in *Beyond IQ: A Triarchic Theory of Human Intelligence* (1985), who defines it as the set of abilities we use in order to attain our life goals, including practical and creative abilities as well as the capacity for analytical thinking.

Interesting claims have been made recently about the possibility of increasing children's intelligence scores by playing them recordings of music by Mozart. This idea is based on work published in 1993 by researchers at the University of California, who found that students' IQ scores temporarily rose by 8 or 9 points and their performance in spatial–temporal tests improved after listening for ten minutes to a Mozart sonata. This has become known as the 'Mozart effect', and has been treated with caution in scientific circles. One explanation which has been offered for this phenomenon is that listening to the music may result in raised levels of intellectual arousal, and therefore in increased readiness to respond to testing.

Further Reading: J. Hawkins and S. Blakeslee *On Intelligence* (Times Books, 2010) discusses the distinctions between human and artificial intelligence.

intelligence test (IQ test) A test designed to measure someone's level of *intelligence in terms of their intelligence quotient (IQ). This may be administered to individuals as part of an assessment of their learning potential, or to whole groups, often for the purpose of identifying and selecting those with the highest scores, as was the case in the implementation of *Eleven Plus testing. Testing may, for example, take the form of a requirement to complete such statements as *Finger is to hand as —— is to foot*, or of the requirement to identify matching shapes. There is evidence to suggest that such tests are generally accurate predictors of an individual's future educational achievement, although not all would agree with this contention, citing cases of individuals who have scored badly in IQ tests but have gone on to become high achievers, scholastically or in some other field.

Most IQ tests are standardized in that they require the examiner and the candidate to follow a clear set of criteria in the way the test is administered, worded, and assessed. The purpose of this is to try to ensure that the only variable will be the responses of the candidate. However, critics of this means of testing argue that such standardization does not resolve the issue of cultural and ideological differences in candidates' backgrounds, which may lead some groups to interpret the content or context of questions differently from others. Tests are usually *norm-referenced in order that the results will show how an individual has performed in relation to other members of the same group. In the case of the *Eleven Plus, for example, a child's performance was measured against that of other 11-year-olds. Standardized measures are designed so that the norm group scores, when drawn on a graph, are distributed in a curve, which is sometimes referred to as a bell-shaped curve, which is widest in the middle because most candidates' performance will be average, with relatively fewer scoring very high or very low. IQ tests use the number 100 to denote an average score. Thus, if a child scores higher than 100, they are said to be of above average intelligence; and if they score below 100, they are deemed to be performing at below average intelligence.

IQ testing can be traced back to the work of Alfred Binet (1857–1911) and Théodore Simon (1873–1961) published in 1905, who were tasked by the French government of the time to discover a means of identifying pupils with learning difficulties. This led to the development in 1916 at Stamford University of the Stamford–Binet intelligence scale, still in use today, building on the work of the two French psychologists. Later, the Wechsler scale for the psychometric measurement of intelligence was developed by David Wechsler (1896–1981). Like the Stamford–Binet model, this used *standardized testing which was individually administered and assessed by professional psychologists. This led to the development of tests which were designed specifically for ease of administration to large groups, both in educational contexts and in the armed services, often for the purposes of *selection.

interactive whiteboards A teaching resource which can be used in the same way as an ordinary whiteboard but which also for example saves, orders, or highlights text and allows what is written to be printed or electronically disseminated. *See also* INFORMATION LEARNING TECHNOLOGY.

interdisciplinary Describes a course of study which draws on more than one academic *discipline to create a structured perspective on topics which are common to both. Thus, one might draw on the disciplines of education and sociology to examine the topic of cultural deprivation, for example.

internal assessment The formal *assessment of learners' work or performance which is carried out by teachers within the learners' institution, who are referred to for this purpose as **internal assessors**. It is used in courses which have some element of *continuous assessment, and is normally subject to a process of *moderation. If the assessment contributes towards a national or externally validated award, it will also normally be subjected to *verification by the relevant *awarding body. Proponents of externally set and marked *examinations often claim that internal assessment is insufficiently robust and possibly unreliable; while its proponents argue that it can provide a more accurate evaluation of a candidate's abilities and *achievement, measured over time and removed from the artificial pressures of the examination room. *See also* ASSESSMENT.

internal assessor *See* INTERNAL ASSESSMENT.

internal verification *See* VERIFICATION.

International Baccalaureate (IB) A qualification for pupils aged 18, available at some schools in the United Kingdom and overseas, successful completion of which qualifies pupils for entry to higher education in the UK and in other countries which recognize the qualification. Referred to colloquially as the 'International Bac', it covers a broad curriculum of six subjects which include languages, mathematics, and a science. It may be offered at some schools as an alternative to *General Certificate of Education *Advanced Levels. *See also* BACCALAURÉAT.

(⊕) **SEE WEB LINKS**
• Provides detailed information on the IB.

interpretivist *See* RESEARCH.

intervention 1. A strategy for raising or accelerating the achievement of pupils. Often used to support the acquisition of English as an Additional Language (EAL), intervention takes the form of a teacher working with an individual or, more normally, a small group. This specialized role is known as **intervention teacher** and the learning sessions may be referred to as **intervention classes**. Intervention is also used to support pupils in key areas of the *curriculum such as mathematics and English where they are identified as underachieving in relation to targets.
    2. Following the assessment and identification of *special educational needs (SEN) it is necessary to implement intervention strategies for support which enable students to make progress. Intervention must make full use of SEN provision and match the needs of the student. There are varying levels of intervention. Regular reviews are required to measure progress and plan the next

stage of intervention, or indeed to reduce the level of additional support where adequate progress has been made. *See also* GRADUATED APPROACH.

3. A term used in action *research to indicate the point at which the teacher–researcher implements a change of approach or practice in order to evaluate the subsequent effect on an identified aspect of teaching and learning.

intrinsic motivation *See* MOTIVATION.

invigilate To supervise during an *examination in order to ensure that no cheating takes place and that candidates are supplied with the necessary writing materials. An invigilator will also keep track of time for the candidates, and notify them when the time allowed for the examination has elapsed and they must cease their efforts. They are often also responsible for distributing examination papers and collecting completed scripts.

ipsative A type of *assessment in which the learner's current level of achievement, skill, knowledge, or understanding is assessed against their own previous level, rather than against fixed criteria or a norm. It can also describe a process of learning in which the same content is covered more than once, but at an increasingly challenging level, as happens within a *spiral curriculum model. This is known as an **ipsative process**.

IQ *See* INTELLIGENCE.

Isaacs, Susan (1885–1948) An English *early years educator who ran an experimental school in Cambridge called the Malting House from 1924 to 1927. One of Isaacs's enduring legacies for teachers of very young children is the key skill of narrative observation to document the learning responses of children to environmental and cognitive encounters within an emergent curriculum, through both indoor and outdoor activity. Using observation, Isaacs noted the interests and inquiries of children and allowed experiential learning to further children's quests for constructing their own knowledge and understanding. She claimed that children should be able to express their feelings openly and needed the freedom to explore, take risks, and learn through play. Following the educational theories of John *Dewey, she valued the joy of discovery. This led to one of the better-known stories about her approach to *discovery learning, which involved her response to a group of young children wanting to find out whether a pet rabbit had gone to 'heaven' after burying it. Her answer was to allow the exhumation of the rabbit's remains in order, she explained, to satisfy the children's thirst for knowledge. This incident is often cited as testimony to the progressive nature of her headship and her approach to learning. Isaacs claimed that any testing or assessment of achievement would not demonstrate a child's true ability; and she was one of the first critics of *Piaget's theory of developmental stages. The guidance for the original *Foundation Stage of the national curriculum supported Isaacs's philosophy that parents are the most important educators in a child's life, establishing the importance of significant adults in child development; and this philosophy is equally reflected in the pedagogic principles underpinning the subsequent (2007) *Early Years

Foundation Stage. After establishing the Malting House, Isaacs went on to lecture in early childhood education at the Institute of Education at the University of London. AW

Further Reading: P. Giardello *Pioneers in Early Childhood Education: The roots and legacies of....Susan Isaacs* (Routledge, 2013) provides an account of Isaacs' work in the context of that of other early childhood educators.

S. Isaacs *Intellectual Growth in Young Children* (Routledge, 1930) is the original publication which sets out Isaacs' educational philosophy and principles.

Jisc The purpose of this committee is to promote and facilitate the use of *information and communication technology (ICT) in education and research. Originally known by the title Joint Information Systems Committee, it manages research and development programmes, funds ICT-related development projects in institutions of *further and *higher education, encourages innovation, and provides resources and advice to support ICT and *e-learning across *post-compulsory education and training.

(⊕) **SEE WEB LINKS**
• Provides links to current Jisc projects.

journal, academic A discipline-specific publication through which academics and other researchers can publish and disseminate their work, the academic journal normally takes the form of a collection of articles, research papers, or reviews which have been submitted to the journal's editorial board. In most cases papers being considered for publication are submitted for scrutiny and appraisal by recognized academics or authorities in the appropriate field, who may recommend that the paper be accepted as it stands, or that specific revisions be made, or that the paper be rejected for publication. This process of refereeing is known as **peer review**. Publication in refereed journals is one of the **outputs** encouraged by the Research Assessment Exercise (RAE), and is therefore a goal for many teachers in *higher education. For academics wishing to publish their research, a clear hierarchy of journals exists, with international refereed journals being considered the most prestigious. This hierarchy is reinforced by the assessment framework applied by the RAE. There is, therefore, considerable competition to place papers for publication, particularly in high-profile international journals, as an RAE approaches. For teachers and other academics in the field of education, a key publication is the British Educational Research Journal, which is the journal of the *British Educational Research Association.

journal, reflective Teachers, and particularly student teachers, often find it useful to keep a journal or diary in which to reflect critically and analytically on their teaching in order to see what they have learned from it and how they could use this to inform future planning and to contribute to their *continuing professional development. The keeping of such a journal might involve daily reflections, but more usually the journal will be used to record and reflect on **critical incidents**, which are situations or events of particular professional significance. In order to contribute effectively to a teacher's professional development, journal entries would be expected to do more than simply describe events, and should involve some element of action planning for future practice. The keeping of a reflective journal is particularly encouraged in programmes of teacher training, and it is used extensively within the *action research model of education research.

Further Reading: G. E. J. Bolton *Reflective Practice: Writing and Professional Development* (Sage, 2010) explores the application of written reflection to professional development.

junior school The name usually given in England to schools catering for pupils aged 7–11, delivering *Key Stage 2 of the *national curriculum. In some cases these are combined with an *infant school under the leadership of one *head teacher to provide continuous primary education through Key Stages 1 and 2 until pupils progress to secondary school at the age of 11. *See also* ENGLAND, EDUCATION IN.

Kennedy Report (1997) The Kennedy Report *Learning Works* represents the findings of the committee chaired by Dame Helena Kennedy which investigated patterns of participation in, and access to, *further education, and is a significant document which helped to drive the *widening participation agenda. As a result of the Report, a national strategy was implemented which aimed to ensure that all UK citizens over the age of 16 would have equal access to further and *higher education. The main themes of the Report were that learning was central to national and individual economic prosperity and social cohesion, and that equity dictated that all should have the opportunity to succeed. Furthermore, it was suggested that a dramatic shift in policy was needed to widen participation in post-16 learning, and to foster a culture in which continuing learning was considered a natural facet of adult life. Dame Helena's task was to reach under-represented groups and non-traditional learners and to define the critical role of the further education sector in the process. The Report defined further education as 'everything that does not happen in schools or universities'. The notion of widening participation has been superseded to a great extent by that of *lifelong learning, which continues to address common barriers that adults have in accessing education, such as pressure of work; family and social life; financial constraints; and cultural and language issues.

The issue of *widening participation specifically for learners with learning difficulties or disabilities was explored by the *Tomlinson Report (1996). VC, KA

(()) SEE WEB LINKS
• Provides the full text of the Kennedy Report.

key skills These were defined as communication, application of number, information technology (IT), working with others, improving own learning and performance, and problem-solving. They formed a part of the post-16 curriculum. Recognition was given to all six, but only the first three were externally assessed. Their inception can be traced back to a document entitled *A Basis for Choice*, produced by the *Further Education Unit in 1979, which advocated a core entitlement for all students in *further education which should include communication, numeracy, and personal skills, arguing that these were the **core skills** demanded by employers. In 1990 the *National Curriculum Council listed six core skills, the development of which should form a part of the post-16 vocational curriculum. These were communication, numeracy, IT, problem-solving, personal skills, and a modern foreign language, and corresponded to the core skills being promoted at that time by the *Technical and Vocational Education Initiative. In the same year there was a recommendation from the **Schools Examination and Assessment Council** that core skills should also become a part of the *Advanced Level curriculum. This recommendation was repeated in the *Dearing *Review of Qualifications for 16–19-Year-Olds* (1996), in which core skills were identified as one of the strengths of the *General National Vocational Qualification curriculum. The skills were referred to in this document as 'key' skills, and this terminology was used in the Key Skills Qualification (in communication, application of number and ICT) which was available as part of the post-16 curriculum in schools and colleges. In 2013 the Key Skills Qualification was discontinued and key skills were replaced in England by *functional skills, in Northern Ireland by **essential skills**, and in Wales by **essential skills Wales**.

key stage (KS) The four chronological stages into which the *national curriculum programmes of study are divided. These are: Key Stage 1 for ages 5–7; Key Stage 2 for ages 8–11; Key Stage 3 for ages 11–14; and Key Stage 4 for ages 14–16. Within the schools sector, education for 16–19-year-olds is sometimes referred to unofficially as 'Key Stage 5', although in reality schooling for this age group falls outside the bounds of the national curriculum.

kinaesthetic *See* LEARNING STYLES.

kindergarten Although widely used to describe any school or class for the youngest of school age children, this term originates in a system of provision aimed specifically at very young children and based on the educational theories of Friedrich Froebel, who believed that children will best develop holistically through the medium of play. In German the term translates literally as 'children's garden'; in other words, a place of play.

Kingman Report (1988) The *Report of the Committee of Inquiry into the Teaching of English Language*, chaired by Sir John Kingman. It failed to conclude, as some expected it to, that the teaching of English should place more emphasis on the formal rules of grammar. The Report did argue, however, that 'the working of a democracy depends on the discriminating use of language on the part of all its people'.

knowledge What is known. According to *Bloom's Taxonomy, education engages with three domains of knowledge. One is the *cognitive domain, concerned with what students know and understand. The other two are the *affective, which is concerned with the development of attitudes and feelings; and the *psychomotor, which focuses on the development of physical skill, and is concerned with students' knowing how to perform a task. The term 'knowledge' in its broadest sense can be used to encompass all three of these. In its narrowest sense it can be taken to mean a body of information in the form of bare facts, such as that possessed by someone who is able to name capital cities correctly or cite the dates and sequence of monarchs. A fictional exponent of this latter interpretation of knowledge is Mr Gradgrind from Charles Dickens's novel *Hard Times* (1854), who claims that education is all about 'Facts, facts, facts', and whose name is now synonymous with this point of view. Knowledge in this limited sense is about recall and *rote learning. Most educators today would argue that, in many contexts, the acquisition of facts alone is of limited value without the development of some level of understanding. In simple terms, this would involve moving beyond the 'who', 'what', and 'when' to the 'how' and the 'why'.

The contrast between rote learning and understanding is not confined to the cognitive domain. In the psychomotor domain, too, a learner may gain the ability to undertake a task (that is, know how to perform it), without necessarily developing an understanding of why it should be done that way. So, for example, a student may be taught to assemble the ingredients for a loaf of bread, and to knead and bake an edible loaf, without understanding the purpose of including yeast, or how a raising agent works. With the addition of that understanding, their knowledge of how to bake bread would be of a different order. A further question concerning the psychomotor domain, widely debated during the growth of *competence-based training, was that of *sufficiency: how many times must a student perform a task correctly before we can reliably judge that they have succeeded not by chance but that they genuinely know how to do it?

More problematic still is the measurement of a student's knowledge in the affective domain. The question raised here is about the relationship between the acquisition of knowledge and the development of 'right' attitudes or feelings. In the education of health or care workers, for example, it remains unclear whether such curriculum requirements as empathy or *emotional intelligence can be taught or accurately assessed; or, indeed, in what sense such attributes can be construed as a form of knowledge.

For educators, an abiding question has been that of how knowledge is acquired. For example, much of *Piaget's work was concerned with how children move through different stages of learning. Theories of *learning which are currently used to explain knowledge acquisition also draw heavily on the work of psychologists of the *behaviourist, cognitivist, and *humanist schools.

Underlying all this is the philosophical question which asks how we can reliably know anything at all, and what the distinction is between knowledge and belief. The relativism associated with postmodernism suggests that all knowledge is culturally, socially, and politically constructed, rather than absolute. This is most clearly illustrated by the teaching of history, where the distinction between knowledge and interpretation can be problematic, and may be influenced or decided according to current hegemonies. This leads us to wider ideological questions such as who decides what is legitimate or worthwhile knowledge and how *curriculum content is chosen. Teaching and learning depend on an often implicit understanding of what knowledge is. *Epistemology—the theory of knowledge—addresses the issue of what we count as valid knowledge, and what types of 'knowing' we marginalize or reject, and why.

knowledge about language (KAL) An understanding of, and ability to employ correctly, the rules which govern language, such as phonetic rules, spelling, syntax, and grammar. In the context of the *national curriculum, KAL is normally integrated into the pupil's learning experience across all subjects, rather than formally taught through structured exercises in English grammar, as used to be the practice up to the middle of the 20th century. The theory is that a learner will draw upon the knowledge they have gained about their first language when they begin to learn a new one. Their ability to name the parts of speech, such as nouns and verbs, for example, will facilitate their study of a second language by providing a frame of reference and a set of underlying grammatical rules.

((⊕)) SEE WEB LINKS
• Provides information about the application of KAL.

Kolb, David (b. 1939) An American educator specializing in the field of organizational behaviour as well as education. His name is, perhaps, synonymous with the experiential learning model he developed in collaboration with Roger Fry in the 1970s, which is discussed in his book *Experiential Learning: Experience as the Source of Learning and Development* (1984). This concept had already been the subject of much discussion, and Kolb acknowledges the work of influential educationalists of the 20th century, such as *Piaget, *Dewey, and *Rogers. Kolb and Fry's 'learning cycle', which draws on the work of Kurt Lewin (1890–1947), presents a model of the relationships between 'concrete experience, reflective observation, abstract conceptualization, and active experimentation' in the learning process. They postulate that the cycle can begin at any of the four stages, and, as it is rarely completed in one tour, would be more properly represented as a spiral. They argue that it follows from this premise that the most effective learning will take place where individuals have an equal and balanced response to each of the stages, but acknowledge that most people have preferences for certain aspects of the cycle. This leads to the recognition of *learning styles; in Kolb and Fry's model, each of the four styles they identify is based on a preference for two of the stages, as shown in the table.

Kolb's work has attracted much attention; it was, for instance, the basis for the commonly used learning styles inventory launched in the UK by Peter Honey and Alan Mumford in 1982. Like the Honey and Mumford inventory, it has been criticized as failing to take sufficient account of reflection, cultural influences, and the acquisition of knowledge. However, Kolb's strenuous argument that individuals differ in the ways that they learn has ensured that his work continues to have influence.   VC, KA

((⊕)) SEE WEB LINKS
• Provides discussion of experiential learning critiques of David Kolb's theory.

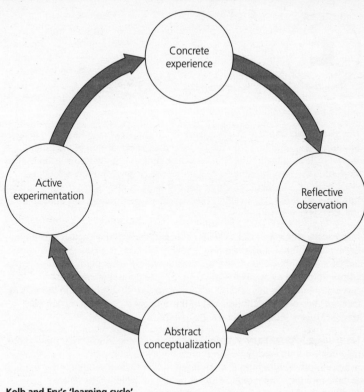

Kolb and Fry's 'learning cycle'

Kolb and Fry's four learning styles

Learning style	Preferences
Converger	Abstract conceptualization and active experimentation: practical, unemotional, rational
Diverger	Concrete experience and reflective observation: imaginative and aesthetic, interested in people and the ideas of others
Assimilator	Abstract conceptualization and reflective observation: theoretical, interested in abstract connections and ideas
Accommodator	Concrete experience and active experimentation: practical, adventurous, intuitive

language across the curriculum A forerunner of the *National Literacy Strategy (NLS), and based on the premise that, as advocated in the Bullock Report of 1975, all teachers, whatever their subject, should also see themselves as sharing the responsibility for helping pupils to develop English language skills across the curriculum, either directly or by modelling good practice. The introduction of the NLS in 1997 represented a formalizing of this approach. *See also* LITERACY HOUR.

language deficit A lack of skills in spoken and written English which may have a detrimental effect on a pupil's ability to learn. The concept of language deficit has been used to explain underachievement particularly in those pupils whose home circumstances might tend to leave their language skills underdeveloped. In this sense it is an explanation closely linked to theories of cultural and social deprivation and to the concept of *social class. *See also* LITERACY HOUR; NATIONAL LITERACY STRATEGY.

language laboratory A specialized room, equipped with electronic audio resources, for the teaching and learning of spoken languages. Each student is provided with headphones and can listen to, repeat, and assimilate the language at their own pace, from tapes, CDs, or online recordings. The teacher facilitates and supports learning by interacting with individual students through a central control which allows them to instruct, correct, and encourage students, and to monitor their progress. Such facilities are found in further and higher education, but rarely in schools. Developments in *information communication technology have made possible increasingly sophisticated applications for language laboratory use. The language laboratory is classed as a teaching resource, rather than a *method of instruction.

language school A school which recruits mainly overseas students of all ages, and offers courses at various levels in written and spoken English as a second language. Such schools are usually privately owned and employ teachers, often on short, fixed-term contracts, who have a qualification in Teaching English as a Second Language, but do not need to have *qualified teacher status. *See also* ENGLISH AS A FOREIGN LANGUAGE.

languages in primary schools *See* NATIONAL LANGUAGES STRATEGY.

lateral thinking A concept and technique popularized by Edward de Bono (b. 1933), which approaches problem-solving by considering the question from a number of angles other than the obvious one. In that it avoids convergent thinking, it may sometimes be equated with its opposite, divergent thinking, and is best described as a form of reasoning which does not proceed in the usual series of logical steps, but requires creativity on the part of the thinker. The following is a typical question which has been used to encourage lateral thinking in order to arrive at an answer. *John and Mary lie dead on the floor. Part of the carpet has been soaked by water and there are pieces of a broken glass bowl lying beside the bodies. The room is locked and its only living occupant is a cat. How did John and Mary die?* The answer, of course, is that they are goldfish! This sort of puzzle requires the thinker to recognize the automatic assumptions about 'the way things are' (for example, that human names must denote humans) which deflect us from considering other possible interpretations. Thus, lateral thinking is regarded as an aspect of creative thinking, and is often included in the teaching of *thinking skills.

Further Reading: E. de Bono *Lateral Thinking: a Textbook of Creativity* (Penguin, 2009).

later life learning As *lifelong learning has become associated increasingly with retraining and with learning for employment, those people concerned with learning for its intrinsic satisfactions and sheer joy have searched for a term which makes a distinction. Members of the *University of the Third Age in particular, since they are by definition out of the labour market, have emphasized the value to individuals and the community of continued learning throughout life, including learning undertaken during retirement. To this end, they have coined the term 'later life learning' to refer not only to learning for and by older people but to learning which is usually shared and pursued for its own value to human beings, for example in terms of personal growth and development. In doing so they reject what they see as the reductive view of *instrumental education aimed at preparation for employment which is often the focus of contemporary government policy and funding. In this sense, later life learning is a concept which draws upon the theory of *liberal education.

Launchpad schools An initiative announced in 2002 in which 30 schools drawn from the primary and secondary sectors were chosen to pioneer government strategies to reduce the workload of teachers. The initiative received £4 million in government funding; provided every teacher in the chosen schools with a networked laptop computer and Internet access; gave head teachers professional support in devising strategies to reduce workloads; and enabled schools to appoint extra support staff, including classroom assistants, and technicians to support the teaching of *information technology.

lead inspector The inspector responsible for leading the team formed to carry out an *Ofsted *inspection. Their leadership responsibility includes compiling the pre-inspection briefing, which is based on scrutiny of the school's self-evaluation and will identify possible issues for inspection. It may also include a pre-inspection visit to the school; meeting parents and governors; attending frequent meetings with the head teacher and other members of the *senior leadership team to discuss the progress of the inspection; meeting all staff where possible, briefly, at the start of the inspection; coordinating the inspection; collating the report; and giving feedback on the inspection finding to the head teacher. *See also* SELF-ASSESSMENT REPORT.

league tables *See* PERFORMANCE TABLES.

Learndirect A network which delivers careers advice, vocational qualifications, and work-based *e-learning programmes for businesses. The qualifications it offers include teaching qualifications for the *further education and training sector and *apprenticeships, as well as specific skills training, *functional skills, and programmes in modern foreign languages. Learning takes place in the workplace, in local centres, and online. Learndirect Scotland is funded by the Scottish government, and provides information about access to educational and training courses in Scotland.

((⊕)) SEE WEB LINKS
• Provides details of courses, qualifications, and modes of learning.

learner-centred An approach to teaching and learning in which the learner, their interests, enthusiasms, and aspirations are taken as the starting point of the education process, and the learner is credited with taking responsibility for their own learning. The *teacher or *educator is regarded, according to this model, as a facilitator of learning, rather than as a dispenser of knowledge or skills; and the learning process itself takes into account not only the academic needs of the learner, but also their emotional, creative, psychological, and developmental needs. Based on a *humanistic model of education, the learner-centred (or pupil-centred) approach owes much of its underlying philosophy to theorists such as *Rogers and educators such as *Malaguzzi. The lesson planning and teaching takes into account the learners' needs in relation to their social, emotional, and personal development, and allows for learner control over the learning activities employed; and the curriculum takes as its starting point those topics which are of direct interest and relevance to the learners. In a learner-centred approach, learners are encouraged to take some responsibility for monitoring and evaluating their own progress.

In its most radical form it implies a democratic community of learning where learners and teachers have equal status, and learners exercise a choice over whether and what they will learn. It is an approach to education which emphasizes *discovery learning and the learner's right to self-determination. From a philosophical point of view it sits uneasily with externally imposed targets and testing and with a standardized curriculum. It is commonly (and to some extent inaccurately) used, however, simply to describe a style of teaching in which the learners are actively engaged with their learning rather than adopting the role of passive recipients of knowledge. In this sense it is construed as the opposite of teacher-centred learning, in which the teacher takes the active role and the learners are required merely to be receptive. *See also* PUPIL-LED LEARNING.

learning Learning, rather than teaching, is the central purpose of education. It is usually defined as a change in someone's behaviour, *knowledge, level of

skill, or understanding which is long-lasting or permanent and is acquired
through experiences rather than through the process of growth or ageing. In this
sense it is difficult to draw a clear distinction between what is learned through
education or training and what is acquired through conditioning or exposure
to propaganda. Some educationalists, therefore, would prefer to link
definitions of learning to the concept of self-actualization or personal
development, situating the process in a *humanist context rather than a purely
*behaviourist one. *See also* MOTIVATION.

learning and skills sector One of several terms used to describe the
*post-compulsory sector of education and training which covers all provision
except that offered by *universities and other institutions of *higher education.
The sector is funded through the *Skills Funding Agency under the aegis of the
*Department for Business, Innovation, and Skills and includes a wider range
of provision than that traditionally covered by the term 'further education',
since it also includes sixth form provision and *adult education. It is a
terminology not in use in Scotland. *See also* FURTHER EDUCATION; LIFELONG
LEARNING.

learning difficulties (learning disabilities) Most types of learning difficulty
can be categorized as either specific or non-specific disability. Specific learning
difficulties most commonly include conditions such as *dyslexia and *attention
deficit hyperactivity disorder; *dyscalculia, verbal *dyspraxia, and dysphasia
also belong to this category. Specific learning difficulties affect a particular aspect
of learning rather than the overall abilities of students. A dyslexic student,
while experiencing significant difficulties with reading and writing, may also
enjoy high levels of academic achievement in a range of subjects. It is important
not to assume that a student with a specific learning difficulty is less able than
others. There are those students who underachieve and are simply classed as less
able and as having special needs. These are the students whose learning
difficulties might be classed as non-specific or general. The impact on
development and progress can result in social immaturity, which impedes the
ability to develop age-appropriate friendships, problems with written and
spoken language, difficulty in grasping new concepts, poor concentration, which
makes listening and acquiring new skills difficult, and poor organizational
skills. Whether specific or non-specific, learning difficulties are also described
as being moderate (MLD) or severe (SLD). A generalization of thought
concerning the distinctions used to be that students with MLD cope well at
school, with low levels of intervention needed, and will acquire some level
of qualifications, while those with SLD will be educated in special schools
without ever having achieved the most basic skills. The latter description is
applied to students who are unlikely to achieve level 2 of the *national
curriculum by the end of *Key Stage 4.

Further categorization applies to students whose *cognitive development is
significantly behind that of students of the same age, and who may also have
additional sensory or motor disabilities. These are students with profound and
multiple learning difficulties (PMLD). Students with PMLD may also have

communication difficulties. It is more usual for students with PMLD to be educated in *special school settings. The needs of students with PMLD are complex and require high levels of support and intervention. Schools will engage with other outside agencies such as physiotherapists, speech and language therapists, and medical professionals.

Whatever category of learning difficulty applies, it is essential that reasonable adjustments are made in order to afford the students maximum access to an appropriate curriculum so that they achieve their full potential by setting realistic expectations which challenge and stimulate the students. TB, LE

(⊕) SEE WEB LINKS
• Provides details and definitions of learning disability.

learning difficulty assessment (LDA) A learning difficulty assessment (LDA) is carried out to determine the continuing needs of learners who have a statement of *special educational needs and will be leaving school between the ages of 16 and 19 to enter *higher education, *further education, or skills training. *Local authorities have a legal duty to ensure that the LDA is carried out and that it focuses specifically on the programme of continuing support necessary to facilitate the learner's increased independence and aspirations.

(⊕) SEE WEB LINKS
• Provides an explanation of how LDAs are applied in the context of learners with an *autistic spectrum disorder.

learning mentor First introduced in 1999 as part of the **Excellence in Cities (EiC)** initiative, learning *mentors are employed to work with learners in schools and colleges in order to help them to overcome barriers to learning and engage more fully with the learning process. This may involve anything from building motivation to giving practical assistance with literacy issues or note-taking skills. A 2003 report from *Ofsted, *Excellence in Cities and Education Action Zones: Management and Impact*, concluded that in 95 per cent of the schools surveyed, the mentoring programme had had a positive impact on the school as a whole, as well as on the behaviour and learning of individual pupils. The learning mentor is now one of a number of support staff roles in schools. Requirements include a good level of general education, including literacy and numeracy, and Disclosure and Barring Service (DBS) clearance to confirm suitability for working with children and young people.

learning objective *See* OBJECTIVE, LEARNING.

learning organization An organization in which its members, whatever their level or status, are working continuously as individuals or teams to increase their effectiveness and to achieve outcomes about which they hold a set of shared values. This theory, originally applied in the context of large companies, suggests that if the personnel within an organization are each themselves committed to learning, then that organization will be the better equipped to adapt in response to constant demands for change. This idea is clearly of particular relevance to educational organizations such as schools, colleges, and universities which operate in an environment of rapid and continuous policy-driven change. The concept of the learning organization also involves the idea of continuous improvement, a policy goal which is urged upon educational institutions through, for example, *Ofsted and the *Department for Education. One aim of the learning organization, therefore, is that each individual within it also continues to learn and develop. To this end, it will adopt a model of continuing professional development (CPD). We can see this reflected in national policy in, for example, the key areas of reform set out in the 2006 *White Paper *Further Education: *Raising Skills, Improving Life Chances*, which include a regulatory CPD provision for all teachers in the further education sector.

Further Reading: P. Senge *The Fifth Discipline: The Art and Practice of the Learning Organisation* (Doubleday, 1990).

(⊕) SEE WEB LINKS
• Explores the concept of the learning organization.

learning styles A concept based on the theory that some students learn in a different way from others and so need to be taught in a way that makes it easy for them to learn. Where their preferred learning opportunities are not provided, students may perform less well and therefore mistakenly be assumed to be underachieving through lack of ability. Three widely recognized categories of learning styles are visual, auditory, and kinaesthetic. The majority of people are **visual learners**, who use mainly their sight to gather information. They cope well in lessons with lots of written, pictorial, and diagrammatic styles of presentation. Visual learners struggle where there is an emphasis on giving information orally. **Auditory learners** prefer spoken explanations to expand any graphical information presented to them. The use of technological aids such as voice recorders can be as effective as the teacher's voice. **Kinaesthetic learners** prefer to learn through activity. They enjoy movement and space. A great benefit to kinaesthetic learners is to be able to watch another person demonstrate what they need to do before trying themselves. Kinaesthetic learners enjoy hands-on activities. Most people possess elements of all three learning styles. This makes a *multi-sensory approach to teaching the most likely to engage all students most of the time. An approach to learning styles which has been widely used in schools and colleges is that of Honey and Mumford whose 1986 work drew on *Kolb's theories to present a learning styles questionnaire designed to allow individuals to identify whether they were **activists, theorists, pragmatists**, or **reflectors**. This approach has come under criticism in academic circles for encouraging the application of an over-simplified taxonomy of learners' characteristic needs when over-used or approached uncritically by teachers and organizations. *See also* KOLB, DAVID.

Further Reading: A. Pritchard *Ways of Learning: Learning Theories and Learning Styles in the Classroom* (David Fulton Books, 2008).

(⊕) SEE WEB LINKS
• Provides further details of Honey and Mumford's learning styles theory.

learning support assistant *See* TEACHING ASSISTANT.

Learning Support Unit (LSU) An integral part of a school's approach to supporting pupils who have become disengaged, and who have challenging *behaviour. LSUs provide individual support programmes which may include one-to-one or small-group teaching for pupils identified as having emotional and social difficulties. Ideally pupils will follow their usual curriculum programmes of study within the support unit. Some pupils may need a support package to be put in place which enables them to carry on studying while they address their behaviour issues. Though the support is carried out away from mainstream lessons, best practice exists where all staff are aware of the ethos of the LSU and work in partnership with support staff to reintegrate pupils as quickly as possible. Some LSUs are not on the same site as the school. It is preferable that a unit is part of a school's *inclusion faculty.

Pupils who are typically supported in an LSU will be those who find it difficult to accept sanctions and who challenge authority. They may be aggressive or possess poor social communication skills. Difficult family circumstances resulting in low self-esteem and poor confidence levels are common among pupils supported in LSUs. Such pupils are quite often victims of bullying or other forms of abuse and have very poor attendance levels. LSUs are often a 'safe haven' where pupil can rebuild their confidence. There should be clear exit and entry criteria and procedures for referrals to LSUs. The units must not be seen as 'sin bins' or 'dumping grounds' for *disruptive pupils. Support in LSUs should be short-term and planned. The work of LSU staff will be closely linked with parents and carers and with professionals from other agencies, particularly with social care workers and behaviour support services. *Child and adolescent mental health workers are often involved with pupils in LSUs.   TB, LE

learning theory Sometimes referred to as 'the psychology of learning', the body of theory about how and why learning takes place draws heavily on the work of schools of psychology as diverse as the *behaviourists, on the one hand, and the *humanists, on the other. It underpins much of the professional practice of teachers in all sectors of education since it may be drawn upon to answer the key question, How do learners learn best? Of course, there is no definitive answer to this, but rather a range of theories, any one of which will be more applicable in some situations than in others. The *Gestalt approach, for example, as exemplified by the work of Kurt Koffka (1886–1941), argues that the stimulus-response model of the behaviourists and neo-behaviourists is an over-simplification of what we mean by learning and that between stimulus and response learners go through a cognitive process of organizing and reorganizing their perceptions. Human learning, therefore, cannot be simply seen as a response to stimuli; nor can it be understood by breaking it down into constituent stages. According to the Gestaltist view, learning must be seen as a complex whole, in which previous experience, new data and the reorganization of ideas can lead to the creation of new understandings and insights. Hence the expression 'gestalt', a German word meaning a perceptual pattern or configuration which cannot be described in terms of its constituent parts. Another approach to learning theory is that of the **Cognitivists**, such as John *Dewey (1859–1952) and Jerome *Bruner (b. 1915), who argue that learning is about the progressive accumulation of new knowledge, in tandem with the adaptation or discarding of old knowledge which is no longer consistent with the learner's growing understanding of the world. Further examples of theory include, for example, the concept of *learning styles and the child-centred approaches of *Montessori and *Steiner.

However, for the teacher, the application of a theory is only useful if it works. As professionals, they are encouraged to formulate their own theoretical grounding based on their experience of professional practice and their accumulated propositional knowledge. This may be formalized through the process of *action research or other forms of continuing professional development. *See also* COGNITIVE; MASLOW, ABRAHAM.

Further Reading: A. Pritchard *Ways of Learning: Learning Theories and Learning Styles in the Classroom* (David Fulton Books, 2008).
B. R. Hergenhahn and M. H. Olson *An Introduction to Theories of Learning* (Prentice Hall, 2005).

Learning Through Landscapes (LTL) A charitable body whose aim is to encourage outdoor learning experiences for children in order to stimulate their interest in nature and the environment and to help develop their social skills. Known in Scotland as **Grounds for Learning** and in Wales as **LTL Cymru**, LTL also aims to build learners' motivation to engage with key curriculum subjects such as mathematics by providing opportunities for active learning out of doors. *See also* FOREST SCHOOLS.

SEE WEB LINKS
• Explains the opportunities provided by LTL.

lecture A *method of teaching used mainly in higher education, where students are taught in large groups, often in specially designed **lecture theatres**, which are tiered so that all students have a view of the teacher (or *lecturer) and whatever resources or visual aids are being used. The advantage of the lecture is that it allows a large number of students to be taught in a relatively short length of time. It is therefore cost-effective in terms of human resources. From an educational point of view, however, it does have some disadvantages, including the fact that the lecture format does not easily allow for student–teacher dialogue, and that it requires students to possess sophisticated note-taking skills if they are to benefit fully from the process. The very term 'lecture theatre' itself goes some way towards setting expectations of the respective roles of lecturer and students, since it implies that the lecture will be a performance on the part of the lecturer, thereby casting students simply as an audience. The model of learning implicit in this scenario is a very restrictive one, predicated on the student as the passive recipient of learning. Moreover, the lecture, as a method which lends itself well to teaching in the *cognitive domain, is less effective for other types of learning such as the acquisition of practical skills. It could also be argued that anything capable of being said in a lecture could as easily be presented in written form for students to read at their

leisure, thereby dispensing with the teacher–student contact altogether.
On the other hand, an interesting lecture, well delivered, may both inspire and
motivate its audience.

The term is also used in a less precise way in both *further and *higher
education to mean any type of *lesson, as in the sentence 'Lectures begin at
nine o'clock', where the 'lectures' in question may, in fact, be seminars, practical
laboratory sessions, or lessons in a normal classroom.

lecturer 1. A generic term for a teacher in *further or *higher education.
In further education there are three lecturer grades: lecturer, senior lecturer,
and principal lecturer. In *universities the grading continues to *reader and
*professor. Post-1992 universities and *colleges of higher education usually
conflate the lecturer and senior lecturer grades into one, which is the equivalent
on the pay scale to the standard lecturer grade in the older universities. Although
further education colleges still refer to their teaching staff as lecturers, the
national standards for *qualified teacher status in the sector monitored by the
*Institute for Learning refer to them throughout as 'teachers'.

2. One who delivers a *lecture. *See also* PAY, TEACHERS'.

Leitch Report (2006) Lord Sandy Leitch was tasked by the UK government
in 2004 to review the UK's long-term skills needs. The final Leitch Report,
Prosperity for All in the Global Economy: World Class Skills, was published by Her
Majesty's Stationery Office for Her Majesty's Treasury in December 2006. Apart
from its aim to advise on ways to restore the UK's position as a major leader in
the skills needed to compete globally, the Report also presents suggestions for
strategies designed to help increase productivity and employment rates in the
UK, with the effect of reducing poverty and inequality. The Report recommended
that the UK strive to become a global leader in skills by 2020, benchmarked
against the most economically developed countries of the Organization for
Economic Cooperation and Development. To achieve this, the Report set out
a number of 'stretching objectives' which would double education and training
attainment levels required by 2020. These include: increasing the achievement
of *basic skills to 95 per cent of the adult population for functional *literacy
and *numeracy; exceeding 90 per cent of adults vocationally qualified to at
least level 2 on the *National Qualifications Framework (NQF); shifting the
balance from NQF level 2 to level 3 and increasing the number of those on
apprenticeship schemes to 500 000 a year; and raising the number of
adults who will be qualified to level 4 and above to 40 per cent, with
29 per cent committed to further progression.   VC, KA

((∰)) SEE WEB LINKS
• Provides link to full text of the 2006 review of the Leitch Report.

lesson A means of dividing up both the school or college day and also the
steps or components of the learning process. In schools and colleges, lessons
are usually between 40 and 60 minutes long, and may sometimes run end to
end in a 'double lesson' for those subjects where lengthy activities are essential,
such as art, *games, and practical sciences. A summary of what lessons are

being taught where and when is set out in the *timetable. For the teacher, the
lesson represents a unit of planning and preparation. For each lesson a *lesson
plan is drawn up which sets out the aims, the learning *objectives, the topic
or topics to be covered, the activities and *methods to be used, the methods
of *assessment, the resources required, and the arrangements made for
*differentiation by task or by assessment. Each lesson constitutes a subsection
of the *scheme of work which is drawn up from the programme of study,
*syllabus, or course specification, so that, taken together, the complete sequence
of lessons for the duration of the course of study in one subject is a process of
translating these into learning activities and tasks in order for the specified
learning outcomes to be achieved and assessed.

lesson plan A detailed plan, usually drawn up by the teacher, encapsulating
the content and sequence of the *lesson. A typical lesson plan sets out the aims,
the learning *objectives, the topic or topics to be covered, the activities and
*methods to be used, the methods of *assessment, the resources required, the
arrangements made for *differentiation by task or by assessment, and the
ways in which the lesson will cover generic aspects of the curriculum, such as
literacy or social, moral, and spiritual development.

   The lesson plan has a number of functions. Primarily it serves to formalize the
planning process, which in turn provides a means of ensuring that the
curriculum is fully covered. In a practical way it serves as a prompt or reminder
for the teacher in terms of how activities will be sequenced, what resources
will be required, and so on. Lesson planning is also a developmental process,
helping the teacher to think through issues such as the balance between
teacher and learner activity; the learning needs of specific individuals and
small groups; the provision of a sufficient variety of activities to ensure learner
engagement; the most effective ways of presenting unfamiliar topics; and so on.
It also contributes to the professional process of reflection and evaluation, in that
the teacher is able to review how well the plan succeeded in its implementation,
and which aspects they might wish to review and revise when the lesson is
taught again. The plan also plays an essential part in quality assurance, and
is regarded as a useful piece of documentation for the purpose of inspections and
internal quality reviews.

   Many schools and colleges require teachers to use a standardized lesson
plan format. This usually takes the form of a grid, and is designed to ensure
that all components of the lesson, such as inclusion, differentiation, and
mandatory curriculum requirements, are included.

level Refers both to the standard of achievement within a specific curriculum,
and to the status of qualifications in a national framework. Thus, a pupil will
be assessed as having attained a specific level as defined by the *national
curriculum; and the same pupil may eventually go on to gain a degree, which is
a qualification at level 6 of the *National Qualifications Framework. As well as
applying to these curricular and national levels, the term may also be used
within an individual institution to refer to stages in an education programme,

where, for example, students going into their second year of a programme of study may be said to be progressing from level 1 to level 2.

level descriptor A definition of specified outcomes in terms of what the learner should be able to do, know, and understand at each *level of an attainment or qualification framework. Such descriptors are used for each level of *attainment in the *national curriculum.

level of attainment The descriptions of what a pupil who is working successfully at that level is achieving in each subject of the *national curriculum. Pupils are assessed by teachers in school at each stage in order to ascertain the level of attainment at which each is working. For the purpose of *standard tasks (SATs) results, there are seven levels, level 7 indicating the highest attainment and level 1 the lowest (although exceptionally, pupils may be awarded a level 8 for outstanding attainment). Some schools continue to use subdivisions within the levels themselves, indicated, for example, thus: 5a, 5b, 5c, where 'a' represents a higher level of achievement than b, and so on. Attainment levels do not apply at *Foundation Stage. At *Key Stage 1 pupils are expected to work at between levels 1 and 3 and to have attained level 2 by the end of that stage. At Key Stage 2 they are expected to work at between levels 2 and 5, and to have attained level 4 by the end of that stage. At Key Stage 3 they are expected to be working between levels 3 and 7, and to have attained level 5 or 6 at the age of 14. *See also* LEVEL DESCRIPTOR.

(⊕) SEE WEB LINKS
• Provides a summary for parents on levels of attainment.

liberal education Originally, and literally, an education which *liberates* the pupil or student from errors in their thinking by encouraging the acquisition of genuine knowledge through a process of rational thought and reflection. The liberal knowledge thus gained is seen as quite distinct from the types of learning which are acquired through practice or whose purpose is to equip the learner with the ability to carry out particular tasks or activities. This distinction, which draws on Plato's theories of education and the acquisition of knowledge, may be expressed in today's terms as the difference between the acquisition of 'knowledge for its own sake' and the acquisition of instrumental knowledge designed for a specific end such as skills for employment. A liberal education, then, is one which is not designed to equip the learner for a job or the means to earn a living, but one which presents education as a 'good' in itself. The current differentiation in status between *academic and *vocational provision and qualifications, sometimes referred to as the 'academic–vocational divide', has its roots in this historical idea that the most valuable and genuine knowledge is liberal—or *liberating*—knowledge, gained purely for its own sake. The educational ideal formed the basis of school and university provision for the sons of 'gentry' in the 18th and early 19th centuries. The curriculum was made up largely of Latin and ancient Greek, its only purpose being to produce 'gentlemen of culture'. A curriculum which diverged from this liberal model, for example by introducing an element of instrumentalism, such as science or modern languages, which might better equip the learner with skills needed to earn a living, was considered suitable only for classes below the level of gentry, whose circumstances meant they might have to take paid employment. This class distinction between the provision of liberal and instrumental knowledge reinforced the idea that a liberal education was inherently of higher status. Instrumental, or useful, knowledge became closely associated with 'trade' and the artisan classes and with narrowness of purpose, while liberal education maintained its elite status and later became associated with a broad and life-enhancing curriculum and with the principles of *learner-centred education which aims to support the development of individual potential. This distinction was illustrated clearly in the 1960s and 1970s by the provision of an additional and eponymous *liberal studies curriculum for students on skills training courses in technical colleges (now *colleges of further education), designed to broaden their minds and enhance their experience of learning.

A liberal education is associated with the acquisition of knowledge which is theoretical rather than practical, reflective rather than instrumental, and valued for its own sake rather than acquired for some use. It is often understood today to be synonymous with a **general education** or **academic education**, inasmuch as these terms, too, are used to express the opposite of 'vocational' in the context of educational provision. It is, however, as much an ideal or a philosophical construct as it is a type of curriculum. To describe a model of education as 'liberal' is not only to state something about its purpose and curriculum content, but is also implicitly, and unavoidably, to ascribe a value to it.

liberal studies Part of the curriculum of *further education colleges in the 1970s and 1980s intended to contribute breadth to the education of students on *vocational courses by introducing topics such as literature, letter-writing, and sociological debate into their timetable. Its purpose derived from the *liberal education model, which regarded a purely vocational, or skills-based, curriculum as restrictive and mechanistic. It was aimed at developing the 'whole person', and represented the view that education should operate as a means of developing individual potential, aspirations, and enlightenment. By the 1990s liberal studies (or **general studies**, as it was sometimes known in this context) had been widely replaced by the teaching of communication and numeracy skills, later defined as *key skills, with the more instrumental purpose of providing students with the skills demanded by employers and building a more literate and numerate workforce.

Because of the 'bolt-on' nature of much liberal studies provision, it was sometimes viewed both by students and their vocational teachers as irrelevant and even risible. Something of this is captured in Tom Sharpe's comic novel *Wilt* (1976), which famously satirizes the contradictions of liberal studies provision in the 1970s.

library boards As part of the educational system in Northern Ireland there are five education and library boards which are the local education authorities and library authorities for their areas. They are: Belfast Education and Library Board, South Eastern Education and Library Board, Southern Education and Library Board, North Eastern Education and Library Board, and the Western Education and Library Board. Funds are allocated to the boards by the *Department of Education, Northern Ireland, and their responsibilities include: advising on the curriculum; enforcing school attendance; providing milk and meals, free books, and pupil transport; employing teachers in *controlled schools; and employing non-teaching staff in controlled and *maintained schools.   JH

lifelong learning 1. Originally used by educationalists to denote the idea that education is an essential part of life and an ongoing pursuit, rather than something which begins and ends with compulsory education, it has more recently become associated with workforce training. Rapid developments in technology, together with changes in employment patterns, have resulted in a greater demand for retraining and for higher qualifications in order for learners to compete in the job market. As this trend has developed during the 1990s and the early years of the 21st century, so the phrase 'lifelong learning' has become more frequently used, particularly in *White Papers on education and training, to indicate skills training and programmes leading to vocational qualifications.
  2. Used to refer to the post-compulsory sector, particularly work-based training and further education, which are sometimes known collectively as the 'lifelong learning sector'. This term has, however, become associated with a set of policy initiatives instigated by the Labour governments of 1997–2010 which were subsequently overturned, beginning with the dissolution in 2011 of **Lifelong Learning UK (LLUK)**, the sector skills council set up in 2005 to regulate the professional development of teachers and trainers in the *post-compulsory sector and to manage what had become known as the 'LLUK standards' for teacher training. The terminology employed to describe the sector has since begun to revert to some of its previous, non-politicized aliases: *further education (FE); further education and training (FET); vocational education and training (VET); or post-compulsory education and training (PCET). *See also* LATER LIFE LEARNING; LEARNING AND SKILLS SECTOR.

( ) SEE WEB LINKS
• Provides links to key themes in lifelong learning.

link course A programme of study involving the collaboration of two or more institutions, which forms a 'link' in order to provide full coverage of the curriculum. These courses may represent collaboration between a *college of further education and a *university, where the student attends some classes in each institution or the teaching is shared between the two. More usually the link course is one run collaboratively between a secondary school and a further education college for the benefit of pupils who wish to include an element of vocational study into their *Key Stage 4 *curriculum. Since the publication of the 2005 *White Paper *14–19 Education and Skills*, this has become a more widely accepted practice. In colleges such pupils are sometimes referred to as 'link students'. *See also* 14–19 AGENDA.

Lisbon Strategy Aimed at building a competitive European economy with enhanced employment and a cohesive social structure by the year 2010, the Lisbon Strategy was the result of the Lisbon European Council summit of 2000. It is of direct relevance to education since the strategy's goal was recognized by heads of member states to be largely dependent on a review and modernization of the education and training systems of European member states. This process of change and modernization, where necessary, is carried out by the member states themselves and is not therefore an imposition by the European Union (EU) but rather a mutually agreed strategy. The collective element is in the dissemination and sharing of good practice and in the setting of agreed goals. These are closely linked to those set out for higher education in the member states as part of the *Bologna Process, and those adopted for vocational education and training in member states as a result of the *Bruges–Copenhagen Process. The three major goals of the Lisbon Strategy, to be achieved by a target date of 2010, were: an improvement in the effectiveness and quality of education and training systems within the EU; the accessibility of those education and training systems to all within the EU; and the accessibility of those systems to learners and trainees in the rest of the world.

(((**⊕**))) SEE WEB LINKS
• Provides details of the Lisbon Strategy.

literacy The ability to read and to write at a standard appropriate both to the individual's needs and to society's expectations. Standards of literacy, particularly among school-leavers, have been a matter of concern to educationalists, governments, and employers. At a policy level the problem has been addressed in a number of ways, including the introduction of *key skills across the post-16 curriculum; the introduction of a *National Literacy Strategy for schools (1998–2011); additional resources to support *basic skills provision for adults; and the reintroduction of phonics into the primary curriculum. A number of explanations have been offered for inadequate standards of literacy. These range from criticism of trends in teaching methods to the influence of video games and the semantic short cuts of mobile phone texting. *See also* ADULT LITERACY; FUNCTIONAL LITERACY.

literacy coordinator A teacher with whole-school responsibility for ensuring that the *literacy skills of pupils are supported and developed in lessons across the *curriculum. The literacy coordinator role was originally created to play a significant role in supporting the implementation of the *national literacy strategies in schools and monitoring their effectiveness. The national strategies were in place between 1996 and 2011, but the literacy coordinator role has survived their termination and remains a key post at both primary and secondary levels. Coordinators are often responsible for leading sessions of *in-service education of teachers to enable them to become familiar with national

curriculum materials and revisions of policy; and for supporting the
*senior leadership or senior management team in monitoring provision
for literacy in all subjects.   IW

literacy hour Although discontinued after 2010 under the incoming
coalition government, the literacy hour remains a significant marker of the
*National Literacy Strategy (NLS) introduced in 1998. While the NLS framework
explained *what* should be taught, the *literacy hour was the *means* of teaching
it. It was a compulsory part of *primary education which required primary
teachers to deliver a daily literacy lesson according to a recommended structure.
Pupils were taught for the first half of the lesson as a whole class, and for the
second part of the lesson they worked in groups or individually, with the
teacher focusing on supporting one group. The lesson ended with the pupils
sharing and reflecting on what they had learned. What was taught could vary,
but the general aim of the literacy hour was to raise the standard of pupils'
reading, writing, spelling, grammar, and communication skills. The
recommended structure of a literacy hour was as follows:

Section 1 (15 minutes)	Whole-class guided reading
Section 2 (15 minutes)	Whole-class word- or sentence-level work
Section 3 (20 minutes)	Group or individual work while the teacher works with one or more ability group
Section 4 (10 minutes)	Whole-class plenary session IW

LL M Master of Laws, a higher degree awarded by a university or other higher
education institution at *master's level. The successful candidate is entitled to
use the letters 'LL M' after their name.

loan, student Loans for full-time students on non-postgraduate courses
were introduced by the 1990 *Education (Student Loans) Act, and were offered
at an interest rate level with the rate of inflation, while at the same time student
eligibility for financial help through the social security system was withdrawn.
Previously, undergraduates' *fees were in most cases met by their *local
authority. As this financial support was withdrawn, the proportion of 'top-up'
fees necessary was increased, so that students in England without *bursaries
or other sources of income are now expected to fund their tuition fees and
living expenses through a combination of student loan and parental support or
part-time work. In 2000 the loan system was extended to include part-time
students on low incomes. The loans are administered through the Student Loans
Company (SLC), a public sector organization, which also manages the collection
of repayments from students no longer in higher education. The amount of the
loan for which the student is eligible depends upon their course and place of
study, their individual circumstances, and where they live. The SLC administers
loans for tuition fees, for maintenance (living expenses), and for additional
support in cases where the student has dependants, a disability, or a learning
difficulty. Loans are paid in equal amounts at the start of each academic *term
directly to the university or college. In addition, students from low income

backgrounds may be eligible for maintenance bursaries or grants which do not
have to be repaid.

Loans are repaid, at an interest rate of 3 per cent plus inflation, through the
income tax system, with repayments not beginning until the ex-student is
earning over £21 000 per annum. The repayment, which is deducted monthly
through income tax at a rate of 9 per cent of all income over that minimum,
is thereby scaled to the loan-holder's income, a system known as
income-contingent repayment. Nevertheless, opponents of the loans system
argue that it discourages young people from lower-income families from
applying for higher education, and is therefore socially divisive. In Scotland,
where tuition fees were abolished in 1999, student loans are assessed and
awarded through the *Student Awards Agency for Scotland.

((⊕)) SEE WEB LINKS
• The Student Loan Company web site provides further details of financial support for
  students.

local authority (LA) The locally elected governing body of a town, county, or
district, whose remit includes the support of *maintained schools. The arm of
local government responsible specifically for education was until recently
referred to as the **local education authority**; but the erosion of LA powers
during the 1980s and 1990s, including the introduction of *grant maintained
schools and the removal of further education colleges and polytechnics from
their remit, saw a reduction in LAs' role of strategic planning, funding, and
*inspection. The introduction of compulsory competitive tendering for LA
*advisory and inspection services, introduced by the Local Government Act 1988,
further reduced the LAs' power and influence in relation to the schools in their
area of operations. This has resulted in a change of terminology which reflects,
on the one hand, the recentralization of education policy-making, and, on the
other, the delegation of powers such as budgetary control to the schools.
Nevertheless, LAs still retain considerable responsibility for supporting schools
in their area, particularly in the drive to raise standards of achievement and
to implement national policy initiatives such as reform of children's services.
In these areas, they are required to work closely with central government.
Scottish maintained schools are funded by local authorities, of which there are
32. Currently the Scottish government pays an annual grant to LAs, who then
decide how much of the grant will be allocated to education. Schools may
then spend money as they see fit, within certain guidelines.

((⊕)) SEE WEB LINKS
• Explains the local authority's role and function in relation to education.

Local Management of Schools (LMS) A reform introduced in 1988 by
the *Education Reform Act, which delegated financial responsibility and
budgetary control of individual schools from the *local authority to the schools
themselves. Part of its purpose was to introduce *market competition between
schools in the belief that this would drive up standards of achievement and
provision more effectively than the system of strategic planning operated until that

time by local authorities. The reform had far-reaching effects, particularly on the role and responsibilities of the *head teacher, who now became responsible for balancing a substantial budget and for developing an effective marketing strategy, as well as for providing leadership on curricular and pedagogic issues.

London allowance An additional payment included in the salaries of teachers who work in London and its immediate area in recognition of the higher living costs associated with the capital. Lecturers in colleges and universities also receive a London allowance, although it is substantially less than that of teachers in schools. *See also* PAY, TEACHERS'.

longitudinal study Often used in educational *research, this type of study involves tracking individuals or groups over a period of time in order to monitor and record developments in their learning, circumstances, or achievement. A famous example of a longitudinal study is the television series *Seven Up!* (1964–   ), which follows the development of a group of individuals from the age of 7 into adulthood, reporting on developments in their lives at successive seven-year intervals.

looked-after children These are children who are in the care of the *local authority. Children come into care either through a court care order, where the court has satisfied itself that the child is at risk of 'significant harm' (section 31 of the Children Act 1989), or on a voluntary basis, when parents cannot cope for one of any number of reasons, such as extreme complex needs of the child or parental illness (section 20 of the Children Act 1989). Government statistics show that at any one time around 60 000 children are looked after in England, with the highest percentage being children subject to a care order. The local authority must have regard to their education and plan for minimum disruption to the child's life. Children are normally placed with foster parents or put in the care of relatives, although a small number, particularly those with challenging behaviour, are placed in care homes. Many children encounter several placements. Where possible, the care system aims to return children eventually to their families. The educational achievement of looked-after children is behind government expectations for children of the same age, and a government public service target has been set to address this issue, along with the issue of placement instability.   TB, LE

lower school Used in a variety of ways to differentiate between age groups of pupils in a secondary school. Schools with sixth forms may use it to refer to the majority of its pupils, those in Years 7–11. Alternatively, it might be used to indicate Years 7 and 8 only, while Years 9, 10, and 11 are referred to as 'middle' and 'upper' school. Its original usage was in public schools, where it was a term used for the younger pupils.

MA *See* MASTER'S DEGREE.

McCrone Committee of Inquiry Undertaken in 2000 and resulting in the McCrone Report, the Committee of Inquiry carried out a comprehensive review of Scottish education. Prompted in part by threats of industrial action by teachers, the Report focused on improvements to the profession. Its recommendations included those relating to teachers' career structure, working conditions, and pay. It also made recommendations about minimum class sizes, the necessity for stable positions for probationary teachers, the effective use of classroom assistants, and the need to monitor teacher workload. The subsequent implementation of the Committee's recommendations has had far-reaching effects on the working conditions of teachers in Scotland.   SM

McQualifications A nickname given, initially by the press, to qualifications which are awarded by employers and subsequently recognized formally. The nickname arises from the publicity given to the first of these cases early in 2008, when a qualification awarded by a chain of fast food restaurants to its managers who had followed a structured in-house training programme was awarded *National Vocational Qualification status at level 3 by the QCA, equivalent to *Advanced Levels. The significance of this development is in its recognition of the contribution which employers can make to the vocational education and training system, which is claimed by some to mark a liberalization in the provision of *vocational training. The sensationalist and in some cases scornful response to this development in the press and elsewhere may be indicative of an enduring view of vocational qualifications as invested with a lower status or value than their academic or general equivalent.

maieutic The *Socratic method of questioning which is designed to elicit the learner's *tacit knowledge. Learners are guided, by careful questioning, to come up with answers they had not consciously known they possessed.

mainstream Used to describe a 'standard' school in the state sector, supported by the *local authority. The majority of schools are mainstream, catering for the local community.

maintained school A school financially supported by the state; that is, maintained from public funds. These are more usually referred to as '*state schools'.

maintenance grant Money awarded to students for the purpose of subsidizing their living costs, such as accommodation, fares, and meals, but not intended for the payment of fees. In the past, *local authorities' education departments would have a discretionary fund from which such awards were made, either in cases of hardship, or where the applicant's case met the necessary criteria. These have been replaced by the introduction of *loans for students in *higher education. *See also* BURSARY.

major When undergraduates are studying for a degree which combines more than one subject, one of which is their chief field of study, that specialist subject is referred to as their major subject. As well as serving as an adjective, the term can be used as a noun to refer to the subject or to the student themselves, so that, for example, a student studying English literature, with philosophy and history as subsidiary subjects, will be an English major, for whom English is their major. In addition, it can be employed as a verb, as in 'She will major in English'.

Makaton A simple language based on signs for everyday words but incorporating facial expressions, symbols, and gestures as well as speech. Makaton has a core vocabulary consisting of everyday concepts such as 'drink' and 'toilet'; this is supplemented by a resource vocabulary consisting of over 7000 words grouped in topics. A *national curriculum resource pack is available. Makaton is a universally recognized form of communication used for children and adults with *learning difficulties in the UK.   TB, LE

Malaguzzi, Loris (1920–94) An Italian educator whose work is closely associated with the *Reggio Emilia approach to early childhood education. As a middle school teacher in the Reggio Emilia district of Italy in the immediate aftermath of the Second World War, Malaguzzi was instrumental in founding an approach to young children's education which is based on mutual respect and reciprocity between teacher and child, and the philosophy that teaching and learning embodies a relationship of equality and democracy, rather than a power relationship in which the teacher dominates.

Born in Correggio in the province of Reggio Emilia, Malaguzzi was educated at the University of Urbino, where he gained a degree in pedagogy, and at the National Research Centre in Rome, where he was awarded a degree in psychology. Following the Allied liberation of Italy from fascist rule, in 1946 he became involved in the setting up of pre-schools organized and run by parents in Reggio Emilia, and in 1950 he established the Municipal Psycho–Pedagogical Centre in which he practised as a psychologist until the 1970s. In 1980, working as a consultant for the Italian Ministry of Education, he founded the Gruppo Nazionale Nidi-Infanzia (National Early Years Centre) in Reggio Emilia to promote child-centred education, and went on to travel Europe and the United States promoting his approach to *early years education. His travelling exhibition *The Hundred Languages of Children* (originally entitled *If the Eye Jumps Over the Wall*) was instrumental in bringing his educational philosophy to a wider audience of teachers and parents worldwide. Opening with the words 'Il bambino e fatto di cento' (literally, 'The child is made of a hundred'), Malaguzzi's manifesto goes on to say:

'The child has a hundred languages (and then a hundred hundred hundred more) but they steal ninety-nine. The school and the culture separate the head from the body. They tell the child to think without their hands, to do and make without their head, to listen and not to speak, to understand without joy, to feel love and awe only at Easter and Christmas. They tell the child to discover the world that is already there.'

This extract encapsulates several key points of Malaguzzi's beliefs about the education of young children: that children and their viewpoint are to be taken seriously; that education should not be defined in terms of what the state or the teacher decides should be taught; that it should not be subjected to categorization in the form of *curriculum subjects; but that it should arise from a response to the child's creativity and search for meaning. Indeed, asked whether he advocated curriculum planning, Malaguzzi is said to have responded that in his view this, like lesson planning, would simply lead to 'teaching without learning' and to the humiliation of the child. His ideas on education drew upon, and were influenced by, the work of an eclectic range of philosophers, educationalists, artists, and psychologists, who included key educational thinkers such as *Bruner, *Dewey, *Erikson, *Piaget, and *Vygotsky.

In describing his approach, Malaguzzi employs two metaphors which are useful in helping us to understand his educational philosophy. One presents the educative process as the tossing of a ball back and forth between child and teacher, an exchange in which both players are equal and in which they cooperate equally in the play and development of ideas. Another is of teacher and child embarking together on a journey downriver, rather than standing on opposite banks watching the river flow.

In acknowledgement of his contribution to the philosophy of early years education, Malaguzzi was awarded the Ygdrasil-Lego Prize by Denmark in 1992, and the Kohl Award in Chicago in 1993. He died at home in Reggio Emilia in 1994.

managed learning environment (MLE) The information systems and processes of an organization which contribute in any way to the learning of its students, and to the recording of their achievements. These will typically include the monitoring of attendance and student progress towards pre-set goals, and the tracking of support and guidance. An MLE allows any stakeholder in a student's career to access appropriate and necessary information on that student, within the confines of the law, and with appropriate restrictions according to role. An MLE can also include a *virtual learning environment in its framework.   VC, KA

management The *Education Reform Act 1988 resulted in a shift of much of the responsibility for the management of schools from the *local authority to the schools themselves. This was known as *Local Management of Schools (LMS). Part of the purpose for this reform was to encourage *market competition between schools. This was considered to be a more effective way of ensuring that standards of provision would rise than the previous system of strategic management by local authorities, which encouraged cooperation and collaboration between schools. Under LMS the management of the school became largely the responsibility of the *head teacher and the *governing body. They were required to manage the school's budget and business strategy as well as academic and curriculum matters. Some commentators (e.g. Ball 1994) suggest that one effect of this was to create a fundamental divergence between the agenda of school managers, concerned with market competition and balancing budgets, and that of teachers in the classroom, whose priorities were centred on *pedagogic issues. The tension between these two agendas would become apparent in situations where, for example, financial constraints imposed by management on staffing levels led to larger class sizes, thus raising concerns among the teachers about the quality of the pupils' learning experience.

A parallel situation arose when the *polytechnics were removed from local authority control following the *Further and Higher Education Act 1992, which also granted them *university status. Managers of these new universities were required to take control of multi-million-pound budgets and to enable the new university to compete, as a business, within the *higher education 'market'. Here again, this raised questions about the purpose of the organization and the potential contradictions inherent in, on the one hand, ensuring financial growth and, on the other, providing a public service.

Subsequent funding policy and continuing emphasis on market competition has had an impact on the role of management across all educational sectors. One notable consequence has been a growth in the use of business and management terminology within the education sector. Another has been the creation of new roles and titles, such as 'school manager', 'senior management team', 'finance director', and 'human resource manager'. Thus, the overall trend since the 1980s has been for head teachers, *principals, vice-chancellors, and their respective governing bodies to become increasingly involved in the management of business strategy and financial growth as well as the management of education in its pedagogic sense.

All this has been reflected in the range of professional development programmes and qualifications in the field of management which are now available to leaders and aspiring leaders of educational institutions. The acquisition of management skills as a route to promotion within the teaching profession has become widely recognized and acknowledged, and is reflected in the increasing numbers of classroom teachers from all sectors choosing to enrol for continuing professional development qualifications such as a postgraduate diploma or *master's degree in **Education Management**. *See also* MANAGERIALISM.

Further Reading: S. Ball *Education Reform: A Critical and Post-Structural Approach* (Open University Press, 1994).

managerialism The operation of an organization for the benefit of its managers, or in such a way that its activities and development are prescribed by managerial concerns and financial constraints. The word originates from the world of business and commerce, and is one example of the business terminology which has colonized the vocabulary of education since the 1980s. Associated with managerialism, particularly in *colleges and *universities, is the practice of addressing issues of human resourcing as purely business or financial, and the emphasis on *performance indicators, which takes precedence over individual scholarly activity or learning for its own sake. Within an educational context the term is most often used in a pejorative sense, and managerialism has been described by critics as the misapplication of private sector strategies to address public sector issues. *See also* MANAGEMENT.

mandatory award Before the introduction of the student *loans system, *local authorities were required to award grants to eligible *higher education students in order to pay their university or college fees. Eligibility depended on the type of course being undertaken. The award was mandatory for some forms of higher education, for example for *initial teacher training and first degrees, where this was the student's first experience of this course of study. In some cases the award would also include some funding towards the student's maintenance costs. Eligibility for this was ascertained through means-testing, either of the student's parents or, in the case of adult students, of the students themselves. With the introduction of student loans, mandatory awards began to be phased out. *See also* MAINTENANCE GRANT.

market Perhaps more properly 'quasi-market' as applied to education, this term refers to a political, social, and economic context in which competition is encouraged between schools, between colleges, and between universities for student numbers, excellence of results, and a reputation for delivering 'value for money'. The ideology of the free market as expounded by Friedrich Hayek (1889-1992) began to shape Conservative thinking radically in the mid-1970s. Hayek argued against socialist ideals of collective planning—a role which, in educational terms, could at that time be said to be embedded as a function of the local education authorities—claiming that such measures are doomed to failure in the face of the complexity and unpredictability of society and human nature. The market mechanism, it was argued, would lead to survival of the fittest through competition. In terms of education, a free market ideology is based on three propositions: that provision must reflect the public will; that schools, colleges, and universities which are responsive to the public are likely to survive; and that unpopular institutions will be forced to change or close. Critics of the free market in education address their arguments to one or more of these propositions, their main criticism being that changes brought about by the market will not necessarily be driven by genuine educational issues. For example, the public might be less concerned with educational excellence than with *league tables, tradition, or conformity of behaviour. Critics also argue that the market creates a situation in which favoured schools are able to exercise choice over the pupils they accept, thus reinstating *selection by the back door and subverting the claim that a free market in education will increase parental choice. Proponents of the application of a market model to educational provision argue that it functions to drive up performance standards, including cost-effectiveness and academic achievement.

Further Reading: M. J. Sandel *What Money Can't Buy: The Moral Limits of Markets* (Penguin Books, 2012).

marking The process of *assessing and grading learners' written work, usually carried out by a teacher or examiner as a part of their duties. It is a means whereby both teacher and learner can ascertain whether, and to what level, learning has taken place. At a minimum, the marker will indicate whether an answer is correct or incorrect. A more detailed form of marking will award points for each answer out of a possible total set out in a **marking scheme** and based on the stipulated *assessment criteria. The marking of *examinations does not normally involve providing the candidate with any direct *feedback on their work, apart from an overall score or grade. For non-examination work and coursework, however, it is normally expected that the marker will communicate clearly to the learner the strengths and weaknesses of their work, and what they need to do to improve it. Sometimes a process of **double marking** is implemented, whereby the learner's work is assessed separately by two markers. Instances when this might be used include when the initial marking results in a *borderline mark or grade, or the work to be marked is worth a large proportion of the overall *assessment (as in a dissertation, for example), or where the first marker is undecided about the mark to be awarded. Alternatively, a process of **blind double marking** may be undertaken, where the second marker does not know what mark the first marker has awarded. Marking is usually, and of necessity, carried out by teachers and lecturers outside lesson times, and can constitute a substantial part of their workload. *See also* MODERATION.

Maslow, Abraham (1908–70) An American psychologist whose theory of a hierarchy of needs leading to self-actualization is often used to illustrate and explain issues relating to learners' *motivation. It suggests that individuals' basic needs for safety, food and drink, and a sense of belonging and self-worth must be met before they will begin to address their higher-order needs, such as the desire to learn and to fulfil their potential for achievement. Translated into practical terms, Maslow's theory suggests that teachers will find it useful to pay close attention to such issues as whether their students are comfortable and whether their anxieties have been addressed, since any obstacle to their well-being may also prove to be an obstacle to their learning. Maslow is a major figure in the *humanist school of psychology, sometimes referred to as the Third Force, to distinguish it from the schools of *behaviourist and Freudian psychology, which have also contributed to our understanding of learner motivation.

Further Reading: A. Maslow *Motivation and Personality* (Harper and Row, 1987) provides a detailed account of Maslow's ideas on motivation.

master's degree A higher degree, which occupies the next level beyond the *bachelor's degree and sits at level 7 in the *National Qualifications Framework. A master's degree in education is abbreviated as M.Ed.; in science as M.Sc.; and in the arts as MA. To gain entry to master's level study, an

applicant will usually be expected to have a good *first degree, awarded at
either first or upper second class. The master's curriculum often involves
the candidate in acquiring research skills, and is normally assessed by
*dissertation or *examination, or both of these. Exceptional students may
progress from an M.Ed., M.Sc., or MA to the more demanding and far
more specialized Master of Philosophy (M.Phil.) or Doctor of Philosophy
(Ph.D. or D.Phil.). *See also* DOCTORATE.

matriculation **1.** An examination taken in the first half of the 20th century
by candidates wishing to gain a *university place. It also came to be used to
describe the achievement of candidates who passed five subjects across a
required range with a credit grade in their *School Certificate examination, since
this achievement exempted them from the matriculation examination at most
universities. When School Certificate was replaced by *General Certificate of
Education (GCE) *Ordinary Levels in 1951, candidates were required instead
to pass two GCE *Advanced Levels to achieve matriculation.
    2. The name given to the ceremony at which new students are entered into the
university register at the universities of Oxford, Cambridge, and Durham.

mature student In further and higher education, as defined by the
*Universities and Colleges Applications Service (UCAS) and for the purposes of
government initiatives for up-skilling or retraining, a student over the age of 21
is referred to as a mature student in order to distinguish them from those who
form the majority in that sector; in other words, 16–19-year-olds in further
education, and 18–21-year-olds in higher education. 'Mature' in this case is
indicative only of the students' relative age and should not necessarily be taken
to imply anything about their developmental *stage or general behaviour.
Mature students may gain access to further and higher education through
specialized routes (for example, *Access courses) and without meeting the
same specified entry requirements as younger applicants.

mechanics' institutes Adult educational establishments for working men
(and sometimes working women) which were set up in the second quarter of
the 19th century. The establishment of the institutes at this juncture in the
country's industrial development reflected employers' needs for a skilled
workforce at least as much as it served to meet the workers' aspirations to
learning and self-improvement. The institutes provided elements of a general
education as well as work-related skills. Classes were held in the evenings, and
those who attended usually came there straight from a long day's work. This
provision was the forerunner of several aspects of today's *post-compulsory
provision: the work-related classes combined with studies based on a *liberal
education model becoming features of *further and *adult education in the
1960s and 1970s; and the impetus to self-improvement being reflected in the
opportunities for academic study such as those provided by the *Workers'
Educational Association. The terminology surrounding them lingered long
after the mechanics' institutes had ceased to exist. As late as the 1960s,

centres which offered *adult education evening classes were often referred to as 'evening institutes'.

The suspicion by some educators and political activists of the time that the original institutes might be a covert means of creating a docile workforce was one of the factors that fuelled the growth of the 19th-century *Radical Education movement. The radical educators were concerned that the education being offered to the artisan was little more than a process of indoctrination designed to stifle enquiry and discourage questioning about the worker's status and conditions. This debate over what constituted 'useful knowledge' was also a debate about the purposes of education and about what it meant to be educated. A hundred and fifty years later the debate continues.

memory The ability to recall information, experiences, and feelings accurately; or to copy or re-enact procedures correctly. As well as enabling formal learning to take place, memory is the means by which the individual creates a coherent story of their life and experiences, and may therefore be said to be part of what constitutes the self. In both its narrow and wider sense, therefore, memory is central to the learning process. An important concern for educators has been the distinction between short- and long-term memory, and the question of how long a lesson should be remembered for it accurately to be said that learning has taken place. This concern can be illustrated, for example, by the case of the candidate 'cramming' for an examination, who retains what they have learned long enough to write it down in the examination room, but then promptly forgets it. Educators who define learning as a process which brings about a permanent change in the individual might argue that this candidate's failure to memorize in the longer term means that he or she has not learned in any real sense. Memory, therefore, may be said to be inextricably bound up with our understanding of what it means to learn. *See also* ROTE LEARNING.

Further Reading: C. Fernyhough *Pieces of light: The new science of memory* (Profile Books, 2013).
J. K. Foster *Memory: A Very Short Introduction* (Oxford University Press, 2008).

mentor A more experienced colleague who offers support, guidance, and advice, usually to someone new to a role or organization. The word derives from the name of a character in Homer's *Odyssey*, a wise and trusted friend, Mentor, who promises to look after and teach Odysseus' son while Odysseus himself is away at the Trojan wars. This captures very well the dual role of mentoring, which involves elements of both teaching and caring. Student teachers on *teaching practice are usually allocated a mentor; and it is common practice for newly appointed teachers and lecturers to be mentored during their first year at a *school, *college, or *university. Mentoring is also widely used in the professional development of those in managerial roles in all sectors of education. The mentoring relationship itself has been found to work best when it is based on trust, rapport, and a shared agenda. This is not always easy to achieve in a context where mentors are allocated and neither mentor nor 'mentee' has any choice in the decision, as is often the case with newly appointed and student teachers. The role of the mentor in education frequently includes responsibility for assessing and giving feedback on the performance of the 'mentee'; a function which some argue is closer to that of a **coach** than a mentor. Where institutional mentoring schemes are in place, these are often integral to the policy of operating as a '*learning organization'.

In *colleges of further education the role of mentoring newly appointed teachers or those with professional development needs is often one of the duties expected of staff who have achieved advanced teacher status. *See also* LEARNING MENTOR.

Further Reading: J. Gravells and S. Wallace *Dial M for Mentor: Critical reflections on mentoring for coaches, educators and trainers* (Critical Publishing, 2012).

((())) SEE WEB LINKS
• Sets out the benefits of mentoring.

merit A grade awarded for work in an examination or other type of *assessment which denotes achievement at a level greater than that of a simple pass. Other terms used in a similar way are *credit and **distinction**.

meritocracy A society ruled by those chosen not for their wealth or birth, but for their intellect or talents. A term coined by Michael Young (1915–2002) in *The Rise of the Meritocracy, 1870–2033: An Essay on Education and Equality* (1958), it came to be used, not in the satirical or darkly prophetic sense originally intended, but to describe a society worth aspiring to—one which might be achieved through selective education. The idea of creating a meritocracy, therefore, was used as an argument to support developments such as the use of *intelligence tests and the *Eleven Plus examination to separate talented pupils from the less talented in order to enhance their educational opportunities. Young himself, towards the end of his life, expressed some concern over what he saw as a wilful misunderstanding, particularly by policy-makers, of a term originally coined to describe the social structure of a fictional future—a dystopia in which social divisions of wealth and power have become all the more difficult to challenge because the idea of meritocracy not only allows those with power in society to argue that they deserve their position because they have achieved it through merit, but also increasingly assimilates the potential leaders of the underprivileged into the meritocracy itself, leaving the poor as an underclass further disempowered and disfranchised.

meta-cognitive strategy A plan or approach which learners can use to solve problems, improve recall and understanding, or organize information. It has been found to be particularly helpful to students with a range of learning difficulties as it can aid the efficient retrieval of information or skills. *Mnemonics are a common form of meta-cognitive strategy.

((())) SEE WEB LINKS
• Provides a detailed explanation of meta-cognitive strategies and how they are applied in teaching and learning.

meta-narrative The French philosopher Jean-François Lyotard (1934–98) claimed that two major myths, or meta-narratives, have shaped and legitimized Western thinking for two centuries but are now no longer believed. These are the Myth of Liberation—the idea that history is the account of progress towards an achievable state of freedom and equality; and the Myth of Truth—the idea that any 'truth' can be objective, knowable, or verifiable. This claim, which is central to postmodernist philosophy, clearly questions our understanding of the purposes of education. Implicit within the current concept of education is the belief that it is an instrument for progress, not only of individuals but of society as a whole; and that the endeavours of science and the *humanities will result in the discovery of further 'truths' about ourselves and the human condition. In this sense it could be argued that education is still embedded in, and perpetuates, the meta-narratives which postmodernism brings into question.

method A strategy, activity, or procedure for teaching or supporting learning. Some common teaching methods include: *lecture or exposition, *group discussion, *case study, demonstration and practice, role play, simulation, debate, *field trips, and learning through *discovery. A teacher's choice of method will be informed by factors such as the nature of the subject and topic to be taught; the ability of the learners and their level of *motivation; the time available; the need for *inclusion and *differentiation; the degree to which the learners need to be actively involved; and the teacher's own preferred teaching style. A number of different methods may be employed within one lesson to provide learners with changes of activity, or one method may take up the entire lesson, as in the case of a lecture. A skilled teacher will be spoken of as having 'a repertoire of methods', indicating a confident flexibility of approach.

methodology *See* RESEARCH.

Michaelmas Term Also known as the Autumn Term, it is one of the three *terms into which the academic year is traditionally divided, the other two being the Spring Term and the Summer Term. The Michaelmas Term runs from September or October to December. Its duration depends upon the institution in question, but is usually between eight and twelve weeks. It takes its name from the feast of St Michael the Archangel, traditionally known as Michaelmas Day, which falls on 29 September, thus marking (approximately) the beginning of term. It is the traditional name for the Autumn Term at the universities of Oxford and Cambridge (where the Spring Term is known as **Hilary** and the Summer Term as **Trinity**), and has subsequently been adopted by some other institutions.

microteaching A method used in the development and initial training of teachers whereby the teacher or trainee teacher teaches for a very short time, usually only ten or fifteen minutes, under the supervision of a *tutor, to a '*class' of their peers. The micro-lesson is then analysed by teacher, 'class', and tutor, sometimes with the help of a media recording. Its purpose can be to encourage reflective practice, to build confidence, to address specific

skills, or to try out unfamiliar strategies, *methods, or material in a safe
learning environment.

middle school A school for pupils aged 9–13/14. It is part of an arrangement,
recommended in the *Plowden Report and introduced by some *local authorities
in the 1960s, in which compulsory schooling begins with a *first school which
takes pupils from age 5 up to the age of 8 or 9, at which point they progress to
the middle school. Secondary schooling, therefore, begins at 13 or 14 rather than
at 11 as is the case in the more usual structured progression of *infant, *junior,
and secondary provision. The middle school system was first introduced in the
West Riding of Yorkshire in 1963, and became more widespread partly as a
measure to address a school accommodation crisis brought about by the
introduction of comprehensive education. The middle schools themselves
were seen as a way of introducing a comprehensive model, since they avoided
the traditional change of school at the age of 11 and the *selection process it
entailed. Because of changing demographics and the reforms of post-16
education which have resulted in more pupils staying on at school in Years 12
and 13, the number of middle schools is currently in decline.

Middle Years Information System (MidYIS) Provides tests which
are used nationally by secondary schools to gauge the potential of their
*Key Stage 3 pupils. Schools choose whether or not to participate in this type
of standardized assessment. Tests results can be used by secondary schools as a
baseline for *value added measures. They are also used to predict *General
Certificate of Secondary Education grades. MidYIS tests provide an alternative
baseline to Key Stage 2 *Standard Task results, which are the outcome of
specific learning and instruction rather than innate potential. In addition,
MidYIS produces baseline tests for Years 7, 8, and 9. These tests are assessed
externally by MidYIS and results are returned to the school shortly afterwards.
See also COGNITIVE ABILITIES TEST; YEAR 11 INFORMATION SYSTEM.   IW

mind *See* EPISTEMOLOGY; KNOWLEDGE; MEMORY.

mindset The theory that an individual's fixed beliefs about their own
existing abilities, skills, or intelligence can prevent them developing to their
full potential in these areas. This is known as a **fixed mindset**—the belief that
it is only a pre-existing talent, rather than hard work, which can bring success
in learning (or other fields). The theory, developed by American psychologist
Carol Dweck (b. 1946), suggests that what learners should aim for is a **growth
mindset**, which is the belief that ability can be developed through hard work.
Its application to education is in encouraging motivation and personal
target-setting.

Further Reading: C. Dweck *Mindset: How You Can Fulfil Your Potential* (Robinson, 2012).

minority **1.** A group of pupils or students identified as different from the
majority by reason of their learning needs, their cultural background, their
religious beliefs, or any other factor which might have an impact on how or

what they learn and their requirements in terms of educational provision and support. *See also* INCLUSION; SOCIAL JUSTICE.

2. A *curriculum subject which is studied by relatively few. For example, ancient Greek is now considered a minority subject.

mission statement A public statement of institutional purpose, aims, and strategy required of schools, colleges, and universities, and usually disseminated through their web site, prospectus, or other promotional literature. *See also* VISION.

mixed ability An approach to teaching in which pupils are not segregated according to their ability, but rather, each class within a year group contains pupils who represent the full ability range. This is in contrast to the use of *selection, *sets, or *streams, and special provision for the *gifted and talented; and was once thought to represent the *comprehensive ideal. On the whole, however, mixed-ability grouping has not met with great success, and its use has declined. As early as 1978, the report by *Her Majesty's Inspectorate *Mixed Ability Work in Comprehensive Schools* claimed that such grouping prevented most pupils from working at a pace and level appropriate to their ability.

mnemonics A strategy used for aiding the *memory, particularly useful when memorizing specific sequences or lists. Widely known mnemonics include *Every Good Boy Deserves Favour*, used by beginners at the piano to recall the sequence of lines in the treble clef: EGBDF; and *one collar, two socks*, as a reminder of the correct spelling of *necessary*. Teachers often find it useful to provide learners with mnemonics of this kind, or to encourage them to devise their own when *rote learning is necessary. *See also* METACOGNITIVE STRATEGY.

mock examination An *examination, usually internally set and marked, which is designed to give candidates experience of the examination process, as well as to identify areas of weakness in their knowledge and understanding which they need to improve before sitting the examination proper. It is commonly used in schools to prepare pupils for public examinations such as the *General Certificate of Secondary Education and *General Certificate of Education *Advanced Level examinations. It can also be used in *higher education, from first degree right up to *doctorate level, where it is not uncommon for a candidate to be given a mock *viva in preparation for the real event. Such examinations are often referred to simply as 'mocks'.

moderate learning difficulties *See* LEARNING DIFFICULTIES.

moderation The process of ensuring that standards of *assessment are consistent between *assessors in the same institution (internal moderation) or between institutions nationally (external moderation). This work is carried out by moderators. It is distinct from *second marking in that it usually involves the scrutiny of samples of assessed work across a range of marks to ensure reliability of assessment, and provides feedback to the assessor(s) rather than to the learner. Neither should it be confused with *verification, which is concerned with monitoring assessment procedures rather than assessment decisions.

Modern Apprenticeship Introduced in 1995 following the *White Paper *Competitiveness—Forging Ahead*, the Modern Apprenticeship was designed to attract the more able school-leavers into *work-based training, where they could gain a *National Vocational Qualification (NVQ) level 3 within three years through a combination of learning on the job and *day release study, often at a *college of further education. For older entrants who might already, at 18 or 19, have gained GCE *Advanced Levels or equivalent, there was an accelerated route to NVQ level 3 in eighteen months. As Modern Apprenticeships evolved, they became more inclusive, expanding to offer a Foundation Modern Apprenticeship for those aiming at an NVQ level 2 qualification, and an Advanced Modern Apprenticeship for those working towards an NVQ level 3 qualification. In 2004 these two routes were renamed 'Apprenticeships' and 'Advanced Apprenticeships' respectively.

Although the term 'Modern Apprenticeship' was originally designed to distinguish this training route from the original *apprenticeships abolished by the New Training Initiative in 1981, the simpler, one-word form has now been adopted in England, although the training route it describes is very different from what was meant by 'apprenticeships' prior to 1981. They have retained the title of 'Modern Apprenticeships' in Scotland, however, where they continue to follow the original format and are run by Scottish Enterprise and Highlands and Islands Enterprise. *See also* YOUNG APPRENTICESHIP.

modular This term describes a course or *programme of study which is made up of a number of *modules, each of which is taught and assessed as a separate *unit of the whole. Normally, students may, if they choose, gain accreditation for one or more module without necessarily going on to complete the full course at that time. An advantage of modular courses is that they can allow students to accumulate modules over time, allowing them, if necessary, to take breaks (intercalate) between modules and to accumulate sufficient credits for the full qualification within a designated time period. *See also* CREDIT; MODULE; MODULE SPECIFICATION.

module A self-contained subdivision of a programme of study which is taught and assessed as a discrete *unit. Courses or programmes which are made up of modules are known as '*modular'. The modules may run sequentially or concurrently. Some may be chosen from a number of options; others may be mandatory, or **core**, modules. In some cases, students may gain accreditation for one or more modules without completing the entire course; or may take breaks (intercalate) between modules, building up to the full qualification over a designated maximum period time. In *higher education, credit for modules may also be transferred between institutions, so that a student who has gained modules at *master's level at one *university, for example, can transfer the credit for those modules towards their master's qualification at another university. Thus, the modular system provides both flexibility in the pattern of attendance and the content covered, and an alternative to the situation where assessment relies solely on one set of examinations at the course's end. *See also* CREDIT; MODULE SPECIFICATION.

module specification The details of a *module, including its aims, learning *objectives, content, mode of study, and *assessment methods. Both the total number of hours of study expected, and the total hours of teacher–student contact, will normally also be specified. The module specification is usually the format in which modules are put forward for *validation and approval, and the basis on which the teacher or lecturer will produce their *lesson plans and *assessment instruments.

monitor A pupil who is given special responsibility for a classroom or playground task, usually as a reward for good or responsible behaviour. For example, a pupil given the job of cleaning the board for the teacher would be known as the 'board monitor'. In the days of school milk, a much-sought-after role among pupils was that of 'milk monitor', which involved the dispensing of milk to the rest of the class. The term is regarded now as somewhat old-fashioned, and has largely fallen out of use in state schools.

monitoring The systematic scrutiny of levels of performance and achievement, not only of pupils and students, but also of teachers, managers, institutions, and *local authorities. The monitoring of *standards nationally is carried out by bodies such as *Ofsted and *Ofqual. The rise in levels and extent of monitoring has been concurrent with the growing emphasis on *accountability and the application of *performance indicators across all sectors of education.

Montessori, Maria (1870–1952) An Italian doctor of medicine who became interested in educational theory as a result of her early work among children with *learning difficulties. Her clinical observations led her to analyse how children learn from what they construct themselves from manipulating materials, and more specifically what they encounter in the environment. She went on to design specialized equipment, and exercises for children to carry out without the assistance of adults. This conflicted with the large-group instruction of set subjects taught in the same way for all children which was the educational norm at the turn of the 20th century. Her hands-on approach to materials in a rich learning environment, and her recognition that children have knowing and willing dispositions to learn, has had a major influence in *early years education and teacher training in the UK, western Europe, Scandinavia, the United States, and Australasia.

Montessori was nominated for the Nobel Peace Prize in 1949, 1950, and 1951, and founded the Montessori Education Association in Washington DC (1913), the Association Montessori International in Amsterdam (1929), the Montessori Training Centre in the Netherlands (1938), and the Montessori Centre in London (1947). These centres continued to engage with and adhere to her educational theories based on a *child-centred curriculum, a structured environment, and imaginative and well-designed teaching materials, with which children can proceed at their own pace and make mistakes. Controversially, Montessori saw adults, including parents, as a threat to the child's freedom to do things without help. *See also* MONTESSORI SCHOOLS.   AW

Montessori schools Schools for young pupils which offer an approach to education developed by Maria *Montessori, based on allowing children to develop at their own pace with plenty of opportunity for practical and imaginative play. Montessori established her first school, the Casa dei Bambini, in Rome in 1907. She designed a series of activities and equipment to encourage the *cognitive development of very young children, including scaled-down furniture (chairs, tables, cookers, dressers, prams), which are now a common feature in most *primary schools, for children to teach themselves through imaginative and practical activity, problem-solving, and trial and error. This self-direction, encouraged by real tasks or apparatus, is not defined as play by Montessori, but rather geared to practical life—perhaps a reflection of her work alongside children with *learning difficulties, whom she encouraged to become independent through the provision of a structured and tranquil environment.

Montessori believed that, through observation, the teacher—or, to use Montessori's term, 'directress'—can provide a range of sequential activities or materials for the child to develop more complex concepts in the progressive development of cognition.

Moser Report (1999) A document which set out the findings of the review of **adult basic education** undertaken by Sir Claus Moser and his consultative group in order to inform a new framework for *lifelong learning. The Report appeared with the recommendation that there should be a **National Adult Basic Skills Strategy**, which would include setting national targets, increasing opportunities for learners, developing a new system of qualifications, and introducing changes to teacher training and *inspection.

The Report had its most noticeable impact on the *further education sector, where, as a result of Moser's recommendations, all teachers of adult basic skills were required to hold a specialist teaching qualification; and teachers of all other subjects in further education were required to demonstrate mastery of a set of skills, including language, *literacy, and *numeracy, and *information communication technology before they could gain their teaching qualification. *See also* ADULT LITERACY.

motivation The will or incentive to learn. Students or pupils who lack motivation will be unable to benefit fully from their education, and therefore they present a problem for the teacher as well as themselves. If their lack of motivation manifests itself in *disruptive *behaviour, unmotivated learners may also present a problem for their peers. The issue of motivation, therefore, is of crucial importance to the teacher, who must endeavour to devise ways to engage the learner's interest. There are broadly two sources of motivation upon which the individual might act. One is **intrinsic motivation**, which arises from within and is typified by the satisfaction to be gained by doing something for its own sake. In this sense, most teachers will ideally strive to develop intrinsic motivation in their learners by helping them to discover the pleasure of gaining understanding or skill. This is sometimes referred to as **learning how to learn**. The other source is **extrinsic motivation**, which is exerted upon the learner from the outside. This involves the use of **rewards** or **sanctions**, and includes such interventions by the teacher as praise, disapproval, or the promise or withholding of enjoyable learning activities. The most common barriers to learners' motivation are fear, boredom, previous negative experiences of education, and lack of hope about future prospects. While the first three may be seen as within the teacher's power and remit to address, the fourth often has its origins in the wider socio-economic context and is therefore unlikely to be open to resolution on an individual, or even institutional, level. *See also* BEHAVIOURIST; FURTHER EDUCATION; MASLOW, ABRAHAM; ROGERS, CARL.

multicultural education Coverage in the school *curriculum of topics which will develop in pupils a clearer understanding of the variety of cultures which go to make up a multicultural society. Its purpose is not only to increase knowledge and understanding but also to encourage tolerance and promote *inclusion and *social justice.

multilingual In an educational context, this is most often used to describe a class, group, or cohort of learners for whom there is not a common first language. In a multicultural, multilingual society many pupils starting school at the age of 5 have greatest fluency not in English but in the language which is spoken in their home. This has implications for the content and style of the teaching needed to meet their individual learning needs. *See also* ENGLISH AS AN ADDITIONAL LANGUAGE.

multimedia The use of a range of teaching resources, particularly *information communication technology, to reinforce or support learning. This might include such resources as data projectors, interactive computer programmes, *interactive whiteboards, and electronic simulations.

multiple choice A form of *assessment or *examination which presents the candidate with a question followed by a series of answers, only one of which is correct. The candidate must identify the correct answer, usually by placing a cross or a tick in a box, electronically or by hand. The incorrect answers are known as 'distractors'. This form of testing was developed in America following the First World War as a means of screening applicants to the army in order to ensure that recruits met at least the minimum level of *intelligence required for their role. It was later adapted to other uses, one of which was the *intelligence test administered by many *local authorities in the United Kingdom as an *Eleven Plus examination. The major advantage of the multiple-choice test, according to its proponents, was that the format of one correct answer enabled the assessment of large numbers of candidates, mechanically in the early days and, later, electronically. It has two major disadvantages, however. It is suitable for the assessment of factual knowledge and understanding, but does not test a candidate's ability to construct a coherent argument, to theorize, or to analyse. It also has a degree of unreliability, in that the candidate may arrive at the correct answer through guesswork. Research suggests that boys score more highly than girls in multiple-choice testing. The reason for this has not been clearly established, but the commonly held hypothesis is that this is related to gender differences in language acquisition and development, as girls have been found to score better in tests requiring essay-style answers.

multiple intelligence A theory, popularized by the American psychologist Howard Gardner (b. 1943), that *intelligence, traditionally seen as an ability or agility which is purely *cognitive, may be more usefully conceived of not as simply limited to mental activity or thinking, but as encompassing a range of functions and abilities. Gardner suggests that intelligence can be divided into seven subcategories. Two of these which have proved useful in thinking about ways in which people learn are *emotional intelligence and kinaesthetic intelligence. An awareness that intelligence may be manifested through ability or agility other than of a cognitive nature enables teachers and others to adapt their teaching style and plan learning activities that will engage and motivate learners who have become reluctant or disenchanted in the face of traditional approaches to teaching and learning as a purely cognitive process. The vocabulary applied to memory reflects the technological age, with the formation and recall of memory described in terms of encoding, storage, and retrieval. In an educational context an over-emphasis on memorizing information, to the detriment of questioning, reflection, and understanding, is associated with surface learning, rather than *deep learning.

Further Reading: H. Gardner *Frames of Mind: The Theory of Multiple Intelligences* (Basic Books, 2011) provides more detail on Gardner's theory.

(∰) SEE WEB LINKS
• Provides an account of Howard Gardner's work.

multi-sensory Lessons which are planned in a way that suits the teacher's own preferred teaching style can leave some pupils unable to understand the point of the lesson. Some believe that using an approach which embraces all three *learning styles (visual, auditory, and kinaesthetic) provides opportunities for all pupils to learn. A lesson which has hands-on activities and promotes discussion is one which suits all preferred learning styles. This is known as using a multi-sensory approach to teaching, which encourages the use of a range of senses. It requires the use of more than one teaching strategy, which provides a balanced opportunity for pupils to learn through their own preferred style and for them to develop their ability to respond to other styles in the process.   TB, LE

Munn Report (1977) Drawn up to present the findings of the Munn Committee, which recommended a restructuring of the curriculum in Scotland to be followed in Standard 3 and Standard 4 to meet the needs of pupils of all abilities; the introduction of teaching and learning methods which reflected pupils' needs and circumstances; and the development of new courses which crossed traditional subject boundaries. Together with the *Dunning Report, this document was the basis of the focus on equality of access to education in the Scottish education system after 1977.   SM

Nasen Formerly known as the National Association for Special Educational Needs, this organization's purpose is to facilitate equal opportunities in education and training for learners who need special or additional support. It was founded in 1992 through the amalgamation of two bodies with a similar purpose: the National Association for Remedial Education and the National Council for Special Education. The Association produces several specialist journals, including the *British Journal of Special Education* and the online publication *Journal of Research in Special Educational Needs*. It is governed by a board of trustees, and its membership consists of both schools and individuals such as parents and students.

National Assessment Bank (NAB) A reserve of National Testing materials which can be used in Scotland by teachers and lecturers. It contains *instruments of assessment, marking guidelines, and other useful information relating to the *internal assessment of national qualifications. Examples from the NAB are often used for the *unit assessment element of the course.   SM

National Association for Gifted Children (NAgC) A charitable organization founded in 1966 and operating in England, Northern Ireland, and Wales (but not in Scotland). Its aim is to secure educational provision for *gifted and talented children which is appropriate to their individual needs and which facilitates and supports the full development of their individual abilities. It provides a source of advice and support to parents and gifted children, as well as to professionals involved in education, including professional development provision for teachers and a web site for older children.

National Association for Special Educational Needs *See* NASEN.

National Association of Head Teachers (NAHT) Founded in Nottingham in 1897, the Association acts on behalf of its members in relation to their terms and conditions of employment, and provides a source of professional development, information, guidance, and support. In 1985 its membership was extended to include deputy head teachers; and, from 2000, assistant head teachers have also been entitled to membership. Members are drawn from both primary and secondary sectors, the current membership standing at in excess of 30 000 school leaders.

((⊕) SEE WEB LINKS)
• Summary of the Association's aims.

National Association of Schoolmasters Union of Women Teachers (NASUWT) One of the largest unions of teachers in the United Kingdom, the Association was formed in 1976 when the two formerly separate unions of its title merged. The NASUWT also represents head teachers, and extends membership to student teachers.

National Certificate One of the successor qualifications which were introduced by some unitary *awarding bodies to replace *General National Vocational Qualifications (GNVQs) when these were phased out between 2005 and 2007. It is also the title of the non-advanced post-school *vocational certificate awarded by the *Scottish Qualifications Authority; and of a number of *Business and Technology Education Council level 3 awards in vocational areas which were available before, and concurrently with, GNVQs.   SM

National Children's Bureau (NCB) A charitable organization whose aim is to improve the lives of children and young people, which includes ensuring their access to a sound education. The Bureau encompasses a multi-agency network of semi-independent organizations concerned with the education, health, and social care of young people. It operates in England and Northern Ireland, and works in partnership with the Scottish and Welsh organizations **Children in Scotland** and **Children in Wales**. Founded in 1963, it now also runs a network for young people themselves, **Young NCB**, which provides a forum for those under 18 to express their views on issues of concern to them, such as drug-taking and *bullying.

National College for Teaching and Leadership (NCTL) An executive government agency responsible for the application of *teachers' standards; the regulation of *initial teacher education, including professional skills tests; and the *continuing professional development for teachers and head teachers, including the *National Professional Qualification for Headship. It was formed in 2013 from a merger of the former Teaching Agency and the National College for School Leadership, and has operational sites in Coventry, London, Manchester, and Nottingham.

(⊕) SEE WEB LINKS
• Provides further information about the role and functions of the NCTL.

National Consortium of Colleges (NCC) An organization whose purpose is to encourage and support employers across all sectors of business and industry in providing *work-based training for their workforce. It works with *colleges of further education to provide a directory of funded work-related provision. Established in 2001, it provides workforce training and development extensively through the modes of *distance learning and *blended learning.

(⊕) SEE WEB LINKS
• Provides links to the range of the NCC's provision for employers.

national curriculum A curriculum for all children aged 5–16 in *maintained schools. Introduced following the *Education Reform Act 1988, revised in 2000,

2002, 2007, 2011, 2013, and subsequently subject to continuing, ongoing changes, its framework sets out what subjects must be taught; the skills, knowledge, and understanding required in each at specified stages or levels, the targets to be achieved in each at each level, and the national testing requirements for assessing and reporting on pupils' achievement.

Within the national curriculum, learning is organized into key stages, which set out the curriculum content for five age groups: *Early Years Foundation Stage for pre-school children; Key Stage 1 for pupils aged 5–7 in *infant schools; Key Stage 2 for pupils aged 7–11 in *junior schools; Key Stage 3 for pupils aged 11–14, and Key Stage 4 for those aged 14–16 in secondary schools. At the end of Year 9, at the age of 14, pupils choose which subjects they will study in Key Stage 4. These will be a combination of compulsory and optional subjects, in which they will be examined for their *General Certificate of Secondary Education at the end of Key Stage 4. An additional language is compulsory for pupils aged 7–14. Sex and relationship education (SRE) is compulsory in secondary schools. The disapplication in 2013 of national programmes of study, attainment targets, and assessments across many subjects at all key stages is symptomatic of a gradual increase in flexibility which has been the pattern of development in the national curriculum since the change of policy on Standard Assessment Tasks (SATs) in 1992. The original intention was that all pupils would sit national tests at the end of each key stage, not only in the core subjects of English, maths, and science, but in their other national curriculum subjects too. Such a project proved impractical and unwieldy, particularly in terms of the paperwork it required from teachers. This led to a boycott of SATs organized by teachers' unions following the Key Stage 3 tests in 1992. In response to this, and in consultation with teachers, the curriculum content and the testing requirements were streamlined. The revised national curriculum specifications which resulted from this became statutory from August 2000, and were amended again following the 2005 *White Paper *Education and Skills*, which set out the policy of lifting national curriculum restrictions for some young learners to allow them to take *vocational qualifications as part of their Key Stage 4 entitlement. Testing is now known as *Standard Tasks, although the original abbreviated term 'SATs' has remained in use.

*Academies are not required to teach the national curriculum, but must offer a 'broad and balanced' curriculum which includes English, mathematics, science, and RE.

((⊕)) SEE WEB LINKS

• Government web site that is the most reliable way of keeping abreast with ongoing changes to the national curriculum. It sets out details both according to key stage and to subject.

national curriculum for Wales A new and distinctive curriculum was introduced in all Welsh schools from September 2000. Revised arrangements have since been developed in the light of recommendations made in a report published by the Qualifications, Curriculum, and Assessment Authority for Wales. Programmes of study offer greater flexibility to teachers and aim to prepare young people for the challenges of adult life, to promote an approach that is more *learner-centred, focusing on skills, building on the **Foundation Phase**, and linking with the **14–19 Learning Pathways Programme**. The development of a single framework for a curriculum, assessment, and qualifications system from 3 to 19 is intended to raise standards and widen opportunities. All pupils in maintained schools study Welsh up to *General Certificate of Secondary Education stage, though the examination itself is not compulsory.   HG

National Education Trust (NET) An independent foundation whose declared aim is to contribute towards improving the quality of education nationally. Founded in 1972 and known originally as the National Council for Educational Standards, the Trust seeks to influence policy and opinion through its bulletins and conferences. To this extent it can be considered a pressure group, with an interest in all sectors of education.

National Extension College (NEC) A provider of *distance learning, *blended learning, and *e-learning, the NEC was founded in 1962 in order to provide educational opportunities for learners who are unable or unwilling to undertake conventional modes of attendance, or who desire a 'second chance' at education. Its *curriculum places it firmly in the tertiary sector, and extends from *General Certificate of Secondary Education courses to professional training and updating in vocational areas such as management and childcare. Operating largely on a basis of *distributed, *asynchronous learning, it is often used by adult learners as a first step towards an *Open University course.

National Foundation for Educational Research (NFER) In existence since 1946, NFER is a registered charity with a wide portfolio of activity in the field of educational research and testing. Its stated aim is to 'improve education and training, nationally and internationally, by undertaking research, development and dissemination activities and by providing information services'. Regarded with respect both nationally and internationally for producing high-quality evidence-based information, NFER has also been instrumental in informing government policy. Although perhaps best known for its national curriculum tests and other school-based tests, the organization has developed ability and attainment tests for wide-ranging application including the driving theory test. NFER's test of *cognitive ability, referred to widely in schools as the *CAT test, assesses numerical, non-verbal, and verbal reasoning, and supplies a forecast of the level of attainment a pupil can expect to achieve in national tests. This information supports the planning of teaching and learning and offers guidance for personalized learning. Commissioned regularly to undertake independent research and evaluation, NFER selects a project methodology that is best suited to the needs of the commissioning client. To facilitate the dissemination of research findings in order that the research can be useful to a wide audience of policy-makers and practitioners, the organization offers services in marketing, media management, and publishing. NFER has a comprehensive and free national and international information service available to members of the public, which sits alongside a dedicated service for local authorities. The organization also produces publications for purchase. *See also* VOLUNTARY ORGANIZATIONS. TB, LE

(⊕) SEE WEB LINKS
• Provides access to NFER research projects and findings.

National Institute of Adult Continuing Education (NIACE) A non-governmental organization, set up in 1949, whose purpose is to support adult continuing education, both through research and through representation of the interests of adult learners. It is a registered charity with a membership made up of both individuals and organizations, and is financed partly through *local authorities, central government, and a number of *universities. One of the Institute's key aims is to promote equality of opportunity for adult learners who have gained least from their years in compulsory education. It operates within England and Wales, with a specialist Welsh committee, NIACE Dysgu Cymru, which is involved in the development of continuing education within the Welsh border.

National Literacy Strategy (NLS) A strategy, which was first announced in 1996 and ran until 2011, for teaching the parts of the *national curriculum for English concerned with the skills of *reading and writing. It enlarged upon, and complemented, the guidance for *Key Stages 1 and 2 and for the *Early Years Foundation Stage, which applied to children aged 0–5. The NLS Framework set out recommended approaches to the teaching of English, as well as suggesting how lessons might best be structured and resourced; and provided objectives for the teaching of English from Year 1 to Year 6, term by term. *See also* LITERACY.

National Literacy Trust (NLT) An independent charitable trust founded in 1993 with the aim of raising standards of *literacy among children and adults nationally, in order to create a 'literate nation'. It draws attention to the wider issues which affect standards of literacy, such as social and economic circumstances, rather than simply focusing on the teaching of literacy in schools. Among its initiatives are the National Reading Campaign and Talk to Your Baby.

(⊕) SEE WEB LINKS
• A list of the Trust's aims and activities.

National Open College Network (NOCN) A credit-based *awarding body whose qualifications are delivered through *further education and *sixth form colleges, *universities and other *higher education institutions, trade unions, employers, *local authorities, private training agencies, and *adult education centres. It is a development of the **Open College Network (OCN)**, which was established in 1975 for the purpose of formally accrediting the education and training undertaken by adults, and its broad purpose is to encourage *wider participation in, and promote access to, *vocationally related *post-compulsory learning and training. It operates as the central body for the eleven OCNs in England, Northern Ireland, and Wales.

(⊕) SEE WEB LINKS
• Provides information about the NOCN's role and provision.

National Professional Qualification for Headship (NPQH) A qualification which became mandatory on 1 April 2004 for all new *head teachers in *local authority schools and is now aimed at aspiring head teachers. It was first introduced by the Department for Education and Employment in 1997. Its focus is on school improvement. Initially, the regulations governing the mandatory status of the qualification allowed for newly appointed head teachers to be 'working towards' their NPQH, but from 1 April 2009 successful completion of the qualification became a requirement of appointment. *See also* HEADSHIP DEVELOPMENT.

National Progression Award (NPA) *See* SCOTTISH PROGRESSION AWARD.

National Qualification Group Award (NQGA) *See* SCOTTISH GROUP AWARD.

National Qualifications (NQs) Qualifications for students studying in Scottish secondary schools or in Scottish *colleges of further education. NQs consist of *Standard Grades, National Courses, and *National Units. National Courses and Units are sometimes called 'new' National Qualifications since they replaced previously existing qualifications in 1999.

(⊕) SEE WEB LINKS
• Details of the format of the NQs.   SM

National Qualifications Framework (NQF) One of four frameworks in England, Wales, and Northern Ireland which set out accredited qualifications, grouping them according to their level from entry level (lowest) to level 8 (highest). The NQF framework is for 'academic' or general qualifications such as the *General Certificate in Secondary Education, *General Certificate of Education *Advanced Level and the *International Baccalaureat. A key purpose of the framework is to clarify for learners, employers, and others equivalence of level as well as appropriate progression routes through the qualifications system. The other three frameworks are: the *Qualifications and Credits Framework for vocational qualifications; the **Framework of Higher Education Qualifications** for higher education; and the qualifications framework for Wales, **CWFW**. In Scotland the *Scottish Credit and Qualifications Framework applies. *See also* EUROPEAN QUALIFICATIONS FRAMEWORK.

(⊕) SEE WEB LINKS
• Provides a chart showing a comparison of qualification levels.

National Record of Achievement (NRA) Originally introduced in the late 1970s, and becoming mandatory from 1993, the NRA was intended to enable pupils to present formally a record of, and gain recognition for, their non-examination and extracurricular achievements as well as their academic ones. In 1996 the *Dearing *Review of Qualifications for 16–19-Year-Olds* recommended a restructuring of the NRA and suggested renaming it the *Progress File. As a result of this review and restructuring, the NRA was phased out in 2009.

National Union of Students (NUS) Originally established in 1922 exclusively for *university students, the NUS currently draws its membership from institutions of both *further and *higher education. Each college or university has its own branch of the union, which sends delegates to the national conferences, which are held twice-yearly. Members elect a national executive committee, which acts to promote the interests of students. *See also* STUDENTS' UNION.

National Union of Teachers (NUT) Founded in 1870 as the National Union of Elementary Teachers, it took its current name in 1889, and is one of the largest of the teachers' unions with a membership which includes both the primary and the secondary sectors of education. Local branches elect delegates to the annual national conference, which debates issues of national educational policy and promotes the interests of teachers.

National Units A unit of *assessment for the Scottish *Highers. Individual National Units may be awarded as qualifications in their own right. Each represents the successful completion of approximately 40 hours of study, assessed by **unit assessments**. Many full-time *National Qualification courses in Scotland's colleges consist of groupings of National Units. SM

National Vocational Qualification (NVQ) Competence-based qualifications in work-related skills areas, designed to reflect the needs of employers and to offer clear progression routes. They were introduced in 1986 as part of the government's declared purpose to rationalize *vocational qualifications within a coherent framework, and are being replaced in some areas by **Qualifications Credit Framework (QCF) awards**, which will involve changes in format. Originally set up under the authority of the National Council for Vocational Qualifications, and now largely falling under the aegis of Ofqual, they were intended to remove barriers to access by, for example, allowing for the *accreditation of prior experience and learning, providing accumulative awards consisting of elements and units which could be gained over time, and providing an **outcomes-based** route to qualifications. In this way, candidates who could demonstrate the relevant competencies to a qualified assessor could be accredited with a qualification or part of a qualification without the necessity of attending a programme of study. This accessibility was part of a government drive to create a more highly qualified workforce. NVQs provide qualifications at all levels from *Qualifications and Credit Framework level 1, involving repetitive tasks carried out under supervision, to the highest levels which denote substantial managerial and executive competence corresponding to a postgraduate level of attainment. All NVQs are based on performance criteria drawn up by lead bodies made up largely of representative employers from the appropriate vocational field. Ofqual endorses the qualifications, while their assessment and administration are the responsibility of a range of *awarding bodies. The introduction of NVQs saw a shift in emphasis in vocational qualifications from input-driven to assessment-driven training. Assessors of NVQs are themselves required to possess units of an NVQ in assessment, originally known as the **Assessor Award**, or the 'D' units, because of their original designation as units D32 and D33 of the Training and Development Lead Body's NVQ in work-based assessment. As well as trainers and assessors in industry and commerce, all teachers in *further education colleges who were involved in the assessment of NVQs were required to gain the assessor qualification. This was usually achieved through the compilation and presentation of a portfolio of evidence.

It was originally intended that NVQs should provide a route both to employment and to *higher education. In the 1991 *White Paper *Education and Training for the 21st Century*, it was suggested that there would be clear equivalence and progression routes between NVQs and general academic qualifications, such as the *General Certificate of Secondary Education. This has not proved to be the case in any generalized sense, and the NVQ remains, on the whole, a route for those seeking specifically to enter employment rather than higher education.

((⊕)) SEE WEB LINKS
• Provides updates on developments relating to NVQs/QCF awards.

National Youth Agency (NYA) Founded in 1991, the NYA supports organizations and agencies which work with young people to promote their personal and social development, which includes their education. The Agency is funded by the Local Government Association and by those departments of central government with whom it works. It provides support for youth work in a number of forms, including resources, the development of innovation in the delivery of services, and the training of leaders and managers involved.

nature or nurture The debate over whether it is a child's genetic inheritance (nature) or their upbringing and environment (nurture) which will have greatest influence on their personality and *intelligence. Work on the human genome project has reignited this debate, with speculation over the possible discovery of genes which govern specific character traits, predispositions, or attributes. One problem raised by attributing much or all of an individual's characteristics to inherited factors is a philosophical one: if we are entirely programmed by our genes, to what extent can we be said to possess free will? Certain advocates of the genetic, or 'nature', argument have brought their point of view into some disrepute in the past with claims that attributes such as intelligence may be classed as an inherited racial characteristic. Those who support the environmental, or 'nurture', argument, on the other hand, maintain that most observable differences between individuals are due not to inherited factors but to their early experiences, the cultural attitudes to which they are exposed, and their learning. Because they share the same genes, identical twins are often used in studies designed to compare their intelligence, health, and behaviour, and these continue to throw new and useful light on the debate. Although it is often claimed in jest that teachers tend to attribute the intelligence of their own children to nature and the intelligence of their pupils to nurture, it seems that most psychologists, sociologists, teachers, and philosophers take the position that elements of both are clearly apparent in a child's development and attitude to learning.

Further Reading: M. Ridley *Nature via Nurture: Genes, experience and what makes us human* (Harper Perennial, 2004) offers an account of the nature versus nurture debate for the lay reader, presenting research which suggests that environment has a greater impact on our behaviour than our genetic inheritance.

((⊕)) SEE WEB LINKS
- Provides a summary of both sides of the nature versus nurture debate.

NEET (not in education, employment, or training) The acronym was coined to describe those young people who are not engaged in any form of education, employment, or training after they have left school. Government statistics in 2003 concluded that approximately 9 per cent of 16–18-year-olds could be classified as falling within the NEET category. Research to discover the factors which might predispose young people to non-involvement and underachievement has been carried out extensively as a result of the *widening participation agenda. Data suggest that within the NEET category there are disproportionate numbers of young people from the following groups: young mothers; those with low achievement at *General Certificate of Secondary Education level; those from a low socio-economic group; and those who were regular truants in Year 11 at school. A more recent acronym coined in 2013 is **NLEET: neither in the labour force nor in education, employment, or training**. This is a term in international use and is distinct from NEET in that it excludes the unemployed (since they are technically part of the 'workforce').

((⊕)) SEE WEB LINKS
- This parliamentary briefing paper on NEETs, 2014, provides figures and sets out policies.

Neill, A. S. (1883–1973) Alexander Sutherland Neill was an exponent of democratic, pupil-centred, or 'free' schooling, and the founder of *Summerhill School. His reaction to his own Calvinist upbringing led him to the conviction that children should not be subjected to the imposition of morals or values by adults in authority over them, and should not be disciplined externally by fear or threat. He argued that the purpose of education was not to control the child or to inculcate a set of values or beliefs, but to 'to find out where a child's interest lies and to help him live it out'. Neill's philosophy and theories of education were not, however, systematic or definitively argued. Rather, it is the application and development of his democratic and *learner-centred approach as manifested in the Summerhill School project, rather than its articulation in a body of philosophical or theoretical writings, for which he is remembered. During his lifetime he was seen as an extremist in terms of educational theory and practice, with his emphasis on children's personal freedom and his insistence on equality of status between teachers and pupils.

One of his early influences was the psychoanalytical work of Sigmund Freud (1856–1939), particularly Freud's work on repression, on which Neill drew when exploring and seeking to resolve pupils' difficulties with life and with learning. Although his emphasis on using the child's interest as a starting point for the planning of learning has much in common with the work of *Montessori, Neill was nevertheless an opponent of her educational methods, viewing them as unnecessarily 'scientific' and moralizing.

He made his first experiment with democratic, pupil-centred schooling in 1921 in Hellerau, a suburb of Dresden in Germany, but shortly relocated it to Sonntagsberg in Austria, claiming that staff at Hellerau were attempting to impose their own values and morals on the children. In Austria he encountered some local hostility to his ideas, and so moved his school again, this time to Lyme Regis in England, where it opened with five pupils. In 1927 Summerhill School moved finally to its current site, near the Suffolk coast. Considered something of an *enfant terrible* in the 1920s world of education, Neill and his unconventional approach to schooling had fallen into relative obscurity by the 1950s, when the number of pupils at Summerhill declined to 25. However, public interest in his work was rekindled by the publication of his book *Summerhill—a Radical Approach to Childhood*, which appeared in America in 1960 and in the UK in 1962. After his death in 1973 his wife, Ena, whom he had married when she was a member of staff at the school, took over as head teacher. On her mother's retirement in 1985, Neill's daughter Zoë took over the leadership of the school. Neill's reaction to his own constrained upbringing led him to place great emphasis on the importance of creating a happy childhood for the pupils in his care. Indeed, he claimed that 'all outside compulsion is wrong, that inner compulsion is the only value'.

Further Reading: Mark Vaughan *Summerhill and A. S. Neill* (Open University Press, 2006).

SEE WEB LINKS
• Provides a biography of Neill, an evaluation of his contribution to educational theory, and an extended bibliography.

newly qualified teacher (NQT) A teacher in schools who has completed their teaching qualification, has gained *qualified teacher status, and is engaged in their first year of teaching. For teachers in *maintained schools and non-maintained *special schools, this has, since 1999, been a mandatory *induction year, during which teachers must demonstrate that they continue to meet the national standards of *qualified teacher status (QTS) as well as the induction standards. The NQT receives individualized support from a designated induction tutor with whom they engage in a professional review of their performance and progress at the end of each of the three *terms. Their teaching is observed, and they themselves are expected to observe the teaching of more experienced colleagues. During this first year of their career, the NQT does not teach more than 90 per cent of a full timetable, and it is the head teacher's responsibility to make sure that this is the case. It is also the head teacher's duty at the end of the NQT year to make a recommendation to the *local authority, or other appropriate body, such as the Independent Schools Council Teacher Induction panel, as to whether the NQT has successfully completed the induction year. On the successful completion of their NQT year, teachers must be registered online through the NQT manager system so that they can be entered on the **teacher register**.

SEE WEB LINKS
• Provides further information relating to NQTs.

norm-referencing Where student performance in an *examination or other assessed work is measured by comparing it with the performance of others, rather than against fixed criteria. Thus, in a group of very high-attaining students a candidate might gain a high score, such as 70 per cent, but still be graded as a low pass if most of the group gained 80 per cent or more. Similarly, where the standard of performance was low overall, a candidate who answered very few questions correctly might gain a high grade if the rest of the cohort performed even more badly. This method of assessing and grading is in direct contrast with *criterion-referenced *assessment. *See also* ASSESSMENT CRITERIA.

Northern Ireland, education in The education system of Northern Ireland is separate and distinct from that of England and has an extremely complex structure, involving nine non-departmental public bodies. These bodies operate independently, collaborate with the *Department of Education (DENI), and are the responsibility of the Minister of Education, including: Belfast Education and Library Board; South Eastern Education and Library Board; Southern Education and Library Board; North Eastern Education and Library Board; Western Education and Library Board; the Council for Catholic Maintained Schools; the Northern Ireland Council for the Curriculum, Examinations, and Assessments; the Staff Commission for the Education and Library Boards; and the Youth Council for Northern Ireland. Other statutory and voluntary groups contribute to the administration of education in Northern Ireland: Comhairle na Gaelscolaíochta (the Council for Irish-Medium Education), the General Teaching Council for Northern Ireland, and the Northern Ireland Council for Integrated Education.

At the time of writing the Minister for Education and head of the DENI is Caitríona Ruane. She is a member of Sinn Féin and has worked as a human rights and community activist, lobbying the United Nations and the European Union on human rights in Northern Ireland. She was an International Observer for the first free and fair elections in South Africa when Nelson Mandela became President. In 2007 the new Minister for Education faced major challenges over the evolution of a single education authority and the end of the *Eleven Plus. In 2006 the *Bain Review (*Schools for the Future*) was published. The report focused on provision for 14–19-year-olds and recommended an end to academic selection and increased collaboration between schools. The current *Transfer Tests are due to end in autumn 2008 and the Assembly has to create new procedures for pupils transferring in 2010 and future years.

Will Haire is the Permanent Education Secretary and principal adviser to the Minister. His presentation to the Members of the Legislative Assembly in April 2007 gave an overview of the challenges facing education in Northern Ireland. Key issues are strikingly similar to those currently being debated in other parts of the UK (14–19 qualifications, development of 'functional skills', inclusion, special education needs, English as an Additional Language, and falling pupil numbers).

The current education system in Northern Ireland reflects the needs of different community groups (Catholic, state, integrated, and Irish-language), while the new legislation proposes to address the needs of geographical areas. Schools will be expected to share lessons and some will become specialists, offering expertise in specific areas of the curriculum.

At the present time the Department of Education in Northern Ireland is responsible for: strategic planning and management of education, curriculum content and delivery, allocating funding to the education and library boards, and covering capital costs for most schools. The five education and library boards oversee the needs of specific areas, fund *controlled schools and satisfy the running costs of *maintained schools. Other responsibilities include: providing milk and meals, and free books and pupil transport; enforcing school attendance; advising on the school curriculum; providing recreational services; employing teachers in controlled schools; and employing non-teaching staff in controlled and maintained schools.

The *Department for Education's Education and Training Inspectorate conducts school inspections and reports to the Department of Education, and publishes reports for parents with recommendations. In 2001 the Department of Education stopped using league tables, following consultation with teachers, schools, parents, and unions.

Compulsory education in Northern Ireland begins at 4 years of age and ends at 16. There are four key stages: Key Stage 1 (4–8 years), Key Stage 2 (8–11 years), Key Stage 3 (11–14 years), and Key Stage 4 (14–16 years).

The curriculum in Northern Ireland is determined by the *Northern Ireland Council for Curriculum, Examinations, and Assessment. Responsibilities of the Council include: assessment of pupils at Key Stages 1, 2, and 3, conducting public examinations, graded objectives in modern languages for students aged 16–19, the regulation of *General National Vocational Qualifications in Northern Ireland, and administering the Transfer Tests. From 2007 a revised curriculum was applied and included annual assessment. The curriculum includes religious education; pupils must have the opportunity to take part in daily collective worship but parents can choose to withdraw children from both.

The state sector incorporates a range of schools. Nursery education in Northern Ireland has received funding from the European Union Special Support Programme for Peace and Reconciliation to increase pre-school education. At the primary stage of education pupils are assessed at Key Stages 1 and 2; children are selected at 11 years for grammar or secondary schools, but this system is now being reviewed. Secondary schools control their own admissions. Controlled schools are owned and funded by the education and library boards and are mainly Protestant, with the Church represented on the board of governors. *Catholic maintained schools are owned by the Catholic Church through a system of trustees. Other maintained schools are owned by the Protestant Church, also through a system of trustees and managed by a board of governors. Voluntary grammar schools are owned by the school trustees and managed by a board of governors. *Grant maintained integrated schools are usually partially owned by trustees and managed by a board of governors. Special needs education is determined by the Education and Libraries (NI) Order 1986;

education and library boards have to provide education for pupils with special needs up to the age of 19. This can take place within either mainstream or separate units.   JH

(⊕) SEE WEB LINKS
- Public Record Office of Northern Ireland providing a history of the DENI.
- Department of Education in Northern Ireland web site, detailing current developments and policies.

Northern Ireland Council for Integrated Education (NICIE) A voluntary organization established in 1987 in order to promote and facilitate integrated education in Northern Ireland.   JH

Northern Ireland Council for the Curriculum, Examinations, and Assessment (CCEA) The CCEA determines the curriculum in Northern Ireland and manages the assessment of pupils at *Key Stages 1, 2, and 3. It also oversees the conduct of public examinations such as the *General Certificate of Education, the regulation of *General National Vocational Qualifications in Northern Ireland, and the administration of the *Transfer Tests (Eleven Plus tests). These tests may be curtailed in 2008. A revised curriculum was introduced during the academic year 2006/7, incorporating annual assessment.   JH

(⊕) SEE WEB LINKS
- Provides more information about the role of the CCEA.

note in lieu A note issued following a statutory assessment of a child or young person's *special educational needs. A statutory assessment usually precedes the issuing of a *statement of special needs. Where it has been decided that the criteria for issuing a statement are not met, a note in lieu is issued. The note in lieu document contains a description of the child's particular needs and sets out clear objectives to be worked towards to enable the child to make progress. It also describes the level of provision which the school is expected to put in place. Progress towards the objectives would be reviewed as part of regular provision in line with the practice of the school for pupils with individual needs.   TB, LE

Notice to Improve Schools in which *Ofsted has judged the quality of education to be inadequate but capable of improvement are served with a Notice to Improve. After a period of six to eight months this is followed by a one-day monitoring visit by inspectors, who evaluate the progress being made towards improvement in the specific issues and areas identified as inadequate. The visit is made at short notice, with only two to five days' notice given, so that an accurate evaluation may be made. In a meeting at the end of the visit verbal feedback is given to the school and, if appropriate, the *local authority, and is later confirmed in writing, both to the school and on the Ofsted web site. The feedback is expected to help the school set the agenda for further improvement, which will be assessed at their next Ofsted *inspection.

Nuffield Foundation Projects and curriculum developments in subjects such as science education are initiated and supported by the Nuffield Foundation, a body dedicated to the funding of curriculum research and development. In the 1960s, 1970s, and 1980s the Foundation developed science and mathematics projects and produced science curriculums for use in schools. These included the *syllabus for *General Certificate of Education *Ordinary Level and *Advanced Level examinations in science subjects. Since the introduction of the *national curriculum and its related programme of study for science, the Foundation has focused instead on the funding of science-related and other educational projects.

numeracy The ability to apply and interpret numbers and numerical information. Identified as one of the essential skills needed in the world of work, numeracy became a core skill on training programmes such as the *Youth Training Scheme and on projects such as the Technical and Vocational Education Initiative in schools. It later became a component of the *key skills which were incorporated into the *General National Vocational Qualification, where it was referred to as *application of number; and later, following the implementation of *Curriculum 2000, it became a key skill applied to all 16–19 qualifications. Teachers themselves, whether in schools or in colleges of further education, must demonstrate an appropriate level of numeracy through the *professional skills test before they achieve qualified status. An individual who is competent in numeracy is termed 'numerate', while one who is not may be referred to as 'innumerate'. One of the earliest references to the term itself was in the Crowther Report (1959), which argued that numeracy, as well as literacy, was an essential skill and central to a sound education.

nursery 1. Until comparatively recently (2000), a nursery was the first classroom setting for 3-year-olds entering school. A nursery is more commonly classified as a *day nursery if it provides full day care for children. Since the establishment of the *Foundation Stage in 2000, and the *Early Years Foundation Stage in 2008, foundation units within schools may incorporate nursery and *reception children aged 3–5 years.
  2. A term used by parents, advertisers, estate agents, and magazines to describe a room in a house decorated and equipped with play, nursing, and sleeping furniture for very young children.   AW

nursery nurse Staff qualified to work with children aged 0–7 in a variety of settings, mainly in *day nurseries and in *nursery, infant, and specialist schools. These duties cover all aspects of physical care and safety, and the nursery nurse is generally responsible for social and educational development. This involves planning for and supervising activities which they will observe. It has become more common to give nursery nurses the title 'teaching assistant' when they work within the maintained school sector.   AW

(⊕) SEE WEB LINKS
• A database of childcare qualifications and the range of training opportunities.

objectives, learning A clear statement of what the student or pupil should have learned by the end of the task, the lesson, the *scheme of work, or the course of study. Learning objectives provide focus and direction, and clarify what must be assessed in order to ascertain whether learning has taken place. They are sometimes referred to as learning **outcomes**. The *programme of study or *syllabus for the course or programme will normally provide a full of list of objectives to be covered, articulated in the form of a list of required learning targets. On the basis of these the teacher will construct a scheme of work, which is then broken down into individual *lesson plans, which, between them, provide coverage of all the learning objectives listed in the syllabus. *See also* BEHAVIOURAL LEARNING OBJECTIVE.

objective test A means of *assessment in which there is no margin for subjectivity, interpretation, or speculation on the part of the assessor or examiner. It involves questions for which there is a clear-cut answer. Simple numerical tests and *multiple choice questions are common examples of objective testing, while assessment requiring a discursive response in the form of an essay, for example, is clearly not. One measure of objectivity is whether the assessment can be carried out by computer.

objectivism The objectivist view of education is that *knowledge is delivered by the teacher to the learner by means of instruction. It assumes that knowledge consists in an accumulation of 'facts' which can be thus passed on unchanged from teacher to learner. Such an approach situates learners as passive recipients of education, and discourages critical analyses and conflicting viewpoints which might arise from individual experience or different contexts. It is a model which necessarily limits learner participation and interaction, emphasizing teacher input rather than teacher–learner dialogue. As a consequence, it encourages learner compliance and places control firmly with the teachers. It is challenged by those with *constructivist views of education on the grounds that it limits the learner by disempowering them and by failing to encourage individuals to test what they are learning against their own experience, and against their own social, political, and economic interactions with others and with the state. Notable critics of the objectivist approach are *Dewey, *Vygotsky, and *Freire.

OCR A unitary *awarding body created by a merger between the Royal Society of Arts (RSA) and the Oxford and Cambridge examination boards. It is normally referred to by this abbreviated form, made up of the initial letters of Oxford,

Cambridge, and RSA. It is one of the three awarding bodies responsible for academic and vocational qualifications for 16–19-year-olds.

Office for Standards in Education, Children's Services, and Skills *See* OFSTED.

Office of the Qualifications and Examinations Regulator (Ofqual) The body responsible for the regulation of national qualifications, including the *General Certificate of Secondary Education (GCSE) and the *General Certificate of Education *Advanced Level (A level), and for monitoring the regime of national curriculum assessments. Ofqual also monitors *Early Years Foundation Stage assessments. It advises government on qualifications and assessment, and schools that have problems or issues with any aspect of national testing are able to raise these with Ofqual directly. It began to operate in shadow form in April 2008, but its definitive role was set out in the **Apprenticeship, Skills, Children, and Learning Act** of 2009. This was later modified by the *Education Act of 2011. It is an independent body with the status of a non-ministerial department, and in England is responsible for reporting to Parliament in the first instance, rather than direct to government. In Northern Ireland it reports directly to the Northern Ireland Assembly. One of its roles is to determine the terms on which organizations which award their own qualifications may gain national recognition for them. Two of the issues which come under its remit are the question of whether A levels and GCSEs in some subjects are more difficult than those in others, and whether judgements about the relative difficulty of different subjects could result in the setting of differentiated examination grade boundaries.

SEE WEB LINKS
• Explains the role and functions of Ofqual.

Ofsted (The Office for Standards in Education, Children's Services and Skills) The body responsible for inspecting schools and other educational and training providers, and monitoring and reporting upon their performance. Created following the Education (Schools) Act 1992, it constituted a new system of schools *inspection which replaced that previously carried out by *Her Majesty's Inspectorate (HMI), a body which had been much reduced in size following reorganization. Ofsted was established as an independent organization which reports its findings directly to Parliament and the Secretary of State for Education. It is headed by Her Majesty's Chief Inspector of Education, Children's Services, and Skills, who leads an inspectorate made up of HMIs and other inspectors, many of whom take part in inspections on a part-time or consultancy basis.

Initially, inspections were carried out under the *Education Act 1992 (section 9) and then later under the School Inspections Act 1996 (section 10). There have been two major changes to the role and functioning of Ofsted since its introduction. One is the introduction of 'lighter-touch' inspections. In 2003 Ofsted produced a strategic plan for the years 2004–7, which included the proposal that it should engage in a fundamental review of its approach to the inspection of schools. Consultation took place between 10 February and 8 April 2004, which resulted in a reformed inspection framework, published in November 2004 and put into effect from September 2005. These changes to the statutory basis of school inspections, including the introduction of small-team, shorter inspections, were enshrined in the Education Act 2005. The second major change was to the scope and remit of Ofsted. In April 2007, following the Education and Inspections Act 2006, four specialist inspectorates, including the Adult Learning Inspectorate, became amalgamated with Ofsted to create an expanded inspection service responsible for monitoring and regulating standards of provision in care for children and young people and inspecting the education and training provision for all age groups as well as in schools. Ofsted is now responsible for inspecting the sufficiency of provision to safeguard and promote the welfare of children and young people. This includes reporting on whether systems are in place to protect them from maltreatment and prevent the impairment of their health or development, and to ensure that their circumstances are consistent with the provision of safe and effective care. These multi-disciplinary inspections of local authorities' provision allow Ofsted to make judgements about the overall quality of provision in the geographical area covered by that local authority. This expansion of its remit is reflected in the revised name, which was originally simply the Office for Standards in Education, although its original abbreviation has been retained.

In 2012, Ofsted made several significant changes to its inspection framework. Most notable was the assertion that the only acceptable standard of education was 'good' or better and this led to the removal of the 'satisfactory' grading which was replaced with the term 'requires improvement'. At this time, short-notice inspections were also introduced, with providers receiving less than 24 hours' notification of their impending inspection. Since 2012 Ofsted inspectors have been required to report on four main categories. These are:

- the achievement of pupils at the school;
- the quality of teaching in the school;
- the behaviour and safety of pupils at the school;
- the quality of leadership in, and management of, the school.

Under the 2014 Framework for School Inspection (Ofsted: The framework for school inspection, April 2014, No. 120100) a school cannot be graded as 'outstanding' overall unless it receives the rating of 'outstanding' in the 'quality of teaching' category. *See also* INSPECTION; LEAD INSPECTOR.   IW

(⊕) SEE WEB LINKS
- Provides access to recent examples of Ofsted inspection reports.

online learning *See* E-LEARNING.

ontology The study and understanding of what exists, or what there is. Ontology addresses the question of the nature of reality. For instance, reality can be taken to be made up only of facts about the material world, as in physics, or of social constructions (or meanings), such as 'family' or 'democracy', which depend on human understanding, as in sociology. In this sense, ontological questions are important in education *research. Answers to questions of reality constrain and underpin theories of knowledge (*epistemology) and theories of how knowledge can be gained (methodology), learned, or taught (*pedagogy). In one sense ontology may be described as the study of what it means to be human. *See also* RESEARCH.   MG

open admission A policy operated by some *universities or other institutions of *higher education allowing students who do not possess the normal entry requirements, such as *General Certificate of Education *Advanced Levels, to gain entry to courses. In the United Kingdom, only the Open University operates an open admissions policy as a norm, although other universities and colleges have admissions regulations for *mature students which are more flexible or open than for applicants who are school-leavers. Sometimes also referred to as **open access**, open admission is more often encountered in American universities. *See also* ACCESS COURSE; NATIONAL OPEN COLLEGE NETWORK.

open-book examination *Examinations where candidates are permitted to take in with them, or are otherwise provided with, copies of the texts on which they are being examined, or of key texts related to the subject in question. In an English literature open-book examination, for example, candidates are able to refer to, and quote from, set texts in order to develop and support the arguments on which their essay-style answers are based. The rationale for allowing books into examinations is based on the belief that the ability of the candidate to memorize, for example, long passages of text or lists of dates is less meaningful educationally than their skills of comprehension and synthesis, and that it is therefore more appropriate to construct and conduct examinations in such a way as to test the latter rather than the former. This concept of higher and lower orders of skills owes much to the categorizations set out in *Bloom's Taxonomy. *See also* ROTE LEARNING.

Open College *See* NATIONAL OPEN COLLEGE NETWORK.

open-ended A form of questioning which requires more than a 'yes' or 'no' answer, and does not restrict the choice of answer to one of a list, as in *multiple choice testing. It requires students to articulate answers in their own words, and thereby it tests their skills of comprehension and synthesis rather than, or as well as, their memory. Open-ended questioning may be used verbally by teachers in class as part of a question-and-answer session to check student progress and understanding; or it may be used in a written form in tests and exams. In some contexts, for example in questionnaires, such questions are known as **open questions**. The *assessment of answers to open-ended questions is usually open to more subjectivity than that of **closed questions** to which there is an agreed objective answer of the factual or true–false kind. Because an open-ended question may have no one definitive or final answer it has a wider range of uses in teaching than simply that of testing students' knowledge. It may be used to encourage learners to draw upon their own *tacit knowledge; to make connections between previous and current learning; to hypothesize or theorize; or to create and invent. *See also* OBJECTIVE TEST.

open enrolment A policy which may be operated by schools of admitting the maximum number of pupils which their capacity allows if there is demand from parents that they should do so, even in the situation where there are *falling rolls, and therefore spare places, in neighbouring schools. The *Education Reform Act 1988 encouraged schools to adopt this practice as a response to the demands of the *market, the assumption being that if excellent schools were fully subscribed to the detriment of others in their area, those less popular schools would be forced to improve their standards of provision in order to compete or even survive. In this way, it was argued, national standards of education could be raised. *See also* CHOICE.

open-plan The design of school accommodation, particularly in *primary schools, which creates open areas for group work and other activities rather than dividing the space into discrete, closed classrooms. The use of open-plan learning environments is associated with *progressive educational methods and a *child-centred approach, and its incorporation into the construction of some new state primary schools in the 1950s signalled a move away from traditional strategies of rank-order seating and *rote learning. One disadvantage reported by teachers is the problem of distraction or disruption by one group of another, particularly when noise levels rise, although the advantages it provides in terms of flexibility are considered by many to outweigh this. About one in ten primary schools in the United Kingdom are of an open-plan design. Some open-plan teaching accommodation exists in other sectors, for example in the art, drama, and textile workshops of further education *colleges.

Open University (OU) A *university which teaches by *distance learning and whose original purpose was to make degree level education accessible to people who have not had the opportunity to attend university in the traditional way. It now, in addition to first degree courses, offers *master's degrees and supervision for *doctorates, as well as short courses in various aspects of professional or personal development. It currently claims to be the largest provider of management education in Europe. In 2007 in total, across all its courses, it had more than 180 000 students enrolled. The students study mainly at home and interact with the university online and through course materials such as books, CDs, videos, and television programmes, as well as local *tutorials and residential or day schools. This style of distance learning is known as **supported open learning**. The support is provided by a tutor and by student services located at regional centres as well as centrally at the university's site in Milton Keynes. Assessment is usually through *examination and tutor-marked *assignments, although some courses use alternative *assessment instruments such as computer-marked assignments, *dissertations, or *project work. The university has thirteen regional centres throughout the United Kingdom.

The concept of the OU has its origins in the 1920s, when the idea of a 'wireless university' was suggested by J. C. Stobard (1878–1933), an educationalist working for the BBC. It was taken up seriously only in the 1960s, when the presence of television in most homes offered interesting possibilities for a 'College' or 'University of the Air'. Harold Wilson (1916–95), elected Prime Minister in 1964, gave the project his support and directed the Minister for the Arts, Jennie Lee (1904–88), after whom the OU's first library was named, to oversee the project's development. The first personnel moved into its site at Milton Keynes in 1969, and the first student applications were taken in 1970. The first OU students began their studies in 1971, and by 1980 enrolment figures had reached 80 000. *See also* ADULT EDUCATION.

SEE WEB LINKS
• Provides links to the OU's courses and fees.

options Components of a course or programme over which the student has some choice. Within the *national curriculum, options are introduced at Key Stage 4 and are chosen by the pupil from the **entitlement** areas of arts, design and technology, humanities, and modern foreign languages. Some courses, particularly those which are made up of *modules, require the student to take a number of mandatory, or **core**, components, and, in addition to these, a specified number of additional components which the student will select from the range offered. This type of structure is known as the **core plus options** model, and is often found in *degree courses, both at first degree and at *master's level. Some confusion was introduced into the meaning of 'option' by the original structure of *General National Vocational Qualifications, where 'option' units were selected not necessarily by the student but by the school or college where the course was taught, and were so called in order to differentiate them from the core units, which were assessed differently.

oracy The skill of communicating clearly by speech, and of comprehending the spoken communications of others. It is used to emphasize the importance of spoken language skills, particularly, but not exclusively, in *primary education, and has been coined relatively recently to stand alongside *literacy and *numeracy as an essential component of a child's education. The importance of oracy was reflected in the *National Literacy Strategy. Comprehension of the spoken word and the ability to speak articulately and fluently are emphasized in the *national curriculum *attainment targets for speaking and listening. Oracy skills are also a component of the Adult Basic Skills Strategy, designed to raise levels of *adult literacy.

oral examination A method of formal *assessment in which the candidate is questioned face to face by the examiner and is assessed on the quality of their response. The examination of candidates in modern foreign languages usually includes an oral component to enable the student's skill in comprehending and conversing in the spoken language to be assessed. Oral examinations may also be conducted as an alternative where the candidate is unable to sit a written examination. *See also* VIVA.

Ordinary Grade (O grade) A Scottish secondary qualification which was replaced by the modern *Standard Grade qualification in the early 1990s, and which could be considered broadly equivalent to the English *General Certificate of Education *Ordinary Level. SM

Ordinary Level (O level) An examination and qualification for pupils of school-leaving age which was in operation from 1951, when it replaced the **School Certificate**, until 1986, when it in turn was replaced by the *General Certificate of Secondary Education. The *General Certificate of Education O level was offered in a range of subjects, pupils usually taking between four and ten, depending on the school's judgement about their level of ability. It was originally intended for the most able pupils as a step on their trajectory towards a *higher education or entry to one of the professions, but became a standard qualification demanded by employers, particularly in English and mathematics. It was partly for this reason that when the Certificate of Secondary Education (CSE) was introduced in 1965 for pupils whose ability to succeed at O level was in doubt, its highest grade—a grade 1—was announced as equivalent to an O level pass at grade A–C, thus allowing CSE candidates the opportunity to gain a qualification which would enable them to choose from a wider range of employment when leaving school. The O level was offered by eight different *examining boards, each with their own syllabus. It was graded A–E, although only grades A–C were considered as a respectable pass grade by universities, other institutions of higher education, and employers. The grade F indicated a fail, and U indicated the result was so poor as to be unclassified. School-leavers applying for *university entrance were usually expected to have eight or more good O level passes; and, for candidates applying to study some degrees at some universities, specific subjects at O level were required, in addition to the stipulated grades at *Advanced Level. These often included English and mathematics, and sometimes O level Latin for those wishing to study for a degree in English. *See also* GENERAL CERTIFICATE OF EDUCATION.

organized games Sporting activities, usually involving teams, which take place within school hours as part of the school *curriculum, and are a component of physical education or sports studies.

originality detection *See* PLAGIARISM.

outcomes *See* OBJECTIVES, LEARNING.

outdoor learning *See* FOREST SCHOOLS; LEARNING THROUGH LANDSCAPES.

out of hours activity A structured activity which takes place after school hours, during school holidays, at lunchtimes, or at break, and is not directly included in *national curriculum requirements. It is usually organized and supervised by teachers, and takes the form of such activities as sports and sporting competitions, drama rehearsals and productions, chess clubs, orchestra and choir practices and performances, and homework clubs. Engagement in these activities is normally voluntary on the part of pupils and teachers alike. *See also* EXTRACURRICULAR.

out of school hours learning *See* STUDY SUPPORT.

outreach Programmes of education or training which are delivered out in the community rather than on the premises of the provider. The purpose of these is to facilitate access to education for groups who might find it difficult or undesirable to attend an educational institution or who otherwise feel themselves excluded from available provision. Such groups include young people who have disengaged from education and training, and ethnic minority groups who may have specific cultural or language needs. Outreach courses are often referred to as 'projects'. They are increasingly forming part of the *curriculum of *colleges and *universities. They are also a characteristic provision of youth services and *adult education. *See also* WIDENING PARTICIPATION.

Oxbridge An abbreviated colloquial term for the *universities of Oxford and Cambridge, often used as an indicator of high status or esteem in such phrases as 'an Oxbridge education'. It is suggestive of a clear distinction between the two earliest universities and the later universities founded in the 19th and 20th centuries, which are often referred to colloquially as 'red-bricks', and 'new universities' or 'ex-polytechnics' respectively.

pace The rate at which a lesson progresses. This is not about the speed with which the teacher can get through the *lesson plan, but rather the sense of engagement and purpose engendered in the learners by the sequencing and length of each activity. The teacher should aim to pace the lesson according to the learners' needs. If it is too hurried, some learners may get left behind; if too leisurely, some may become bored. The pace of the lesson, therefore, calls for a careful balance and, in some cases, *differentiation of activity for individuals or groups.

para-professional Sometimes used to describe staff who assist with teaching in schools, colleges, and universities, such as *teaching assistants, *instructors, and **technicians**.

parental preference Under the *Education Act 1980 parents are permitted to state a preference for which school their child will attend, although under that legislation there was no requirement for schools or *local authorities to comply with parents' declared preferences. At this time the allocation of places fell under the remit of local education authorities, which were responsible for strategic planning of provision in their own geographical area. Following the Education Act 1988, however, schools are now obliged to comply with parental preference, as long as there are places available. Taken together, these two Acts have allowed parents to express a preference over their child's schooling, and to expect a positive response if a place is available, even in cases where the preferred school lies at some distance and in a different local authority from that in which the child lives. If parents are unsuccessful in gaining their first *choice of school for their child, they are entitled to lodge an appeal against the school's decision. Under the School Appeals Code of Practice, 2012, such appeals are heard by independent appeal panels, which exclude from membership any representative of the local authority or member of the *governing body of the school in question. The decision of the appeals panel is final.

Inevitably, the expression of parental preference has led to some schools—usually those which are known to perform best in raising and maintaining pupil attainment—becoming a more popular choice than others. This is reflected in the fact that the number of admissions appeals made in England annually continues to rise. Popular schools may quickly become oversubscribed, and as an inevitable result it becomes the school itself which is in the position of exercising a degree of choice over its intake of pupils. Less popular schools which have not succeeded in gaining as good a reputation have less choice over which pupils they enrol. To some extent, therefore, it could be argued that the introduction of parental preference has led to practices of recruitment and enrolment which bear some echoes of a selective model of school place allocation, since schools which are in a position to exert some choice over their intake will tend to recruit pupils whose potential for attainment will reflect well on the school. *See also* SCHOOL ADMISSIONS.

SEE WEB LINKS
• A parliamentary briefing paper which sets out the key issues relating to parental preference and provides illustrative charts and a full print version of the text.

parent council A form of parent representation and a vehicle for parent decision-making and voice in schools. Such councils were introduced in Scotland by the Scottish Schools Act 2006, and from August 2007 these groups replaced school boards. In England the *Children's Plan, a government initiative launched in December 2007 to enhance provision of education, play facilities, and care for children up to 19 years of age, set out as one of its targets the setting up of parent councils in every secondary school in England.   SM

SEE WEB LINKS
• Provides further information on the role and purpose of parent councils.

parent governor A member of a school's *governing body who represents the parents of pupils at that school. Parent governors make up 25 per cent of the governing body and are nominated by parents and elected by secret ballot. Once elected, they normally serve for four years, and are offered formal training to support their role and responsibilities. The requirement for schools to have a governing body on which parents have strong representation is set out in the *Education Act 1986. A small number of **parent governor representatives** in each area are elected by fellow governors to work with their local authority to provide parents with a voice in locally made policy decisions.

parent partnership service An impartial service provided by all *local authorities to discharge in part their responsibility for making information, advice, and support relating to matters of *special educational needs (SEN) available to the parents of children in their area. Authorities may administrate and manage the service themselves, purchase it from an external provider, or offer a mix of the two. Services must be evaluated regularly and organized in such a way as to engender and maintain parents' confidence that they are being offered neutral, accurate, and unbiased information. Authorities have responsibility for publicizing the service to parents, schools, and relevant agencies and bodies. Additionally, their responsibility extends to informing parents about the service in writing when a proposed statement or amended proposed *statement of SEN is issued or when a decision has been taken not to undertake a statutory assessment of SEN. The core functions of the service are to work with parents to empower them to play an active and informed role in their child's education by offering a wide and flexible range of services; to network and collaborate with schools, local authority officers, and other agencies, including voluntary organizations; and to ensure parents' views are represented in the development of local special educational needs policy and practice.   TB, LA

parents' evening An event at which parents are invited into their child's school to meet the teachers and discuss their child's progress. It is held after school hours and pupils may or may not be encouraged to attend with their parents. It is usual in larger schools, particularly secondary schools, for a schedule of appointments to be drawn up for each teacher so that a parent can 'book' their allotment of time with each of their child's teachers. In secondary schools, separate events are often held for separate year groups. The frequency of parents' evenings will depend upon the school, but parents will normally be provided with such an opportunity to come into school at least once each academic year. It is often said by teachers that those parents who consistently fail to attend parents' evenings are often precisely those whom the school would most wish to engage with about their child's progress or behaviour.

parent–teacher association (PTA) An association organized on an individual school basis, made up of staff and parents, for the purpose of discussing and acting on a number of school-related issues. These may include anything from organizing events to raise funds for the school, to the debating of educational issues such as those raised in an inspection by *Ofsted. It is often run by a committee to which nominated parents are elected by ballot. The extent of its activities and the robustness of its membership will vary from school to school, and will often be dependent to some extent on how far such an association is encouraged by the *head teacher and *governors. Such an association does not exist at all schools. There is, however, a **National Confederation of Parent–Teacher Associations**, which acts as a platform for the views of its constituent members.

p

(((●))) SEE WEB LINKS
• Provides links to further information about the role of PTAs.

parity of esteem Used, particularly in political policy discourse, to refer to an equality in status between routes of study, particularly ones where such equality could demonstrably be argued not to exist. It was a phrase used, for example, to describe the relationship between *grammar school and secondary modern provision as implemented by the Education Act 1944 (*Butler Act), suggesting that the two types of provision were, in some undefined sense, of equal value. More recently, it was used as part of the rhetoric surrounding the introduction of *National Vocational Qualifications and *General National Vocational Qualifications (GNVQs), suggesting that these qualification routes would be held in equal regard, by parents, employers, and *higher education institutions, with the *General Certificate of Secondary Education or *General Certificate of Education *Advanced Levels (A levels). In the *White Paper *Education and Training for the 21st Century* (1991), the government of the day declared its intention to 'promote equal esteem for academic and vocational qualifications'. A clearer sense of what such 'parity' might be taken to mean in practice emerges from a City and Guilds of London Institute newsletter of 1992, which claimed that, 'at Level 3, GNVQ will have parity with A levels and thus provide a viable route to Higher Education'. Claims of parity between the general and the *vocational routes appear to have been made largely on a theoretical basis only. For example, on 13 November 1993, before the first cohort of GNVQ students had even completed their qualification, and therefore before this contention had been put to the test, John Patten, then Secretary of State for Education, announced on Radio 4's *Today* programme that the Advanced GNVQ 'has parity of esteem with A levels'. The urgency to establish credentials for alternative, vocational routes into higher education may be explained by the policy goal of higher participation rates in education and *training after 16, and national targets to create a higher proportion of graduates in the workforce.

Thus, we see that 'parity' in this context tends to be defined in terms of utility. The vocational qualification may be regarded as having 'parity of esteem' in the sense that it will serve the purpose of enabling progression to employment or to higher education just as the general or academic qualification will do. In wider terms of value or status, however, the claims for parity are more difficult to substantiate. It also remains questionable whether parity of esteem is accorded to students on vocational and general education courses within the same institution. One of the initial obstacles to establishing parity for GNVQs was their emphasis on *continuous assessment, which led opponents to argue that, without a rigorous system of *summative and externally assessed *examinations, the new qualification could not realistically be considered as a currency equivalent to a level for progression to higher education. The eventual introduction of more rigorous external assessment did not, however, lead to equality of status. This was not surprising as the lack of parity arose from systemic social, economic, and political causes which rendered it impervious to a simple change of assessment mode.

Evidence suggests that learning providers in the *learning and skills sector, such as *further education colleges, whose *curriculum is largely *vocational, are not considered to have equal status with school sixth forms and *sixth form colleges, partly because they tend to recruit students who have achieved less well in public examinations. Teachers in the learning and skills sector also argue that they themselves do not have parity with their colleagues in schools, basing their argument on the disparity in teachers' pay and conditions of service between the two sectors.

Parity of esteem, therefore, may be used to apply to utility; to value as a currency for progression; to social status; and to pay and conditions. Ironically, it is used most in those contexts where parity is by no means obvious. *See also* TOMLINSON REPORT (1996).

participant research *See* RESEARCH.

part-time education In *further, *adult, and *higher education students may choose, or be obliged for financial or other reasons, to study on a part-time basis, often combining their studies with paid employment. This mode of attendance can apply to a very wide range of provision, ranging from adult education classes in leisure pursuits, to *work-based training, to *postgraduate *research at *doctorate level. Much of teachers', head teachers', and other education professionals' in-service *continuing professional development is undertaken as part-time study in the professionals' own time, usually in the evenings and at weekends while they continue their work during the week. *See also* EVENING CLASS.

pass grade When a candidate's achievement in assessed work is expressed in terms of *grades, a pass grade may refer to any grade above a fail, or, more specifically, just to the category 'pass'. So, for example, where the possible grades are A or distinction (for the highest range of marks), B or credit (for the middle category), C or pass (for a range of marks which are no more than satisfactory), and F or fail, a pass grade may refer to a C or simple pass, or, depending on the context, may be taken to encompass all three of those grades which are indicators that the candidate has passed rather than failed the assessment. *See also* PASS MARK.

passive learning Learning which does not require any activity or active engagement on the part of the learner, other than perhaps taking notes. The learner is not provided with an opportunity to contribute to the lesson in any way, but simply required to take in information from the teacher. In Dickens's *Hard Times* (1854), Mr Gradgrind refers to his pupils as 'pitchers' whom he will fill up with knowledge. This is a useful metaphor for passive learning as it highlights the issue which this style of teaching inevitably raises, of who has control over what constitutes relevant *knowledge. Where learning is passive, the teacher's input is likely to be treated uncritically as 'fact', thus discouraging analysis and other higher-order types of learning. *See also* BLOOM'S TAXONOMY; DEEP LEARNING; FREIRE, PAULO.

passive vocabulary Words which are understood and recognized by the learner, but which cannot necessarily be easily recalled or correctly used. That is, they are not part of the individual's *active vocabulary. In the learning of languages, both spoken and written, including the individual's first language, the passive vocabulary will be acquired more quickly and will be more extensive than the active one.

pass mark The minimum mark which a candidate must achieve in order to be deemed to have successfully passed the *assessment. It is commonly applied in assessments which are expressed in percentages. In such cases the candidate may need to achieve a mark of, for example, 40 or 50 per cent in order to pass. *See also* BORDERLINE; EXAMINATION; PASS GRADE.

pass rate The proportion of candidates who succeed in passing an examination or other assessment. Pass rates can be used as a quality assurance indicator or *performance indicator by an educational institution when evaluating the quality of teaching and learning or some other aspects of their provision. However, although pass rates may be presented as measures of success—for example, when schools publish their pupils' achievements in public examinations such as the *General Certificate of Secondary Education—such bare numerical data do not necessarily indicate accurately how much learning has taken place, nor how much effort has gone into the teaching, since they cannot reflect disparities in the starting points of individuals or groups of learners. *See also* PERFORMANCE TABLES; VALUE ADDED.

pastoral care　Guidance and support which focuses on the learner's welfare and their social and emotional needs, rather than their purely educational ones. Although to some extent all teachers are expected to provide a degree of pastoral care, in secondary schools it is often the *head of year who, among their other responsibilities, has an additional pastoral role in relation to pupils in their year group. In some schools a member of the senior management or senior teaching team, such as a *deputy head teacher, may be designated as having overall pastoral responsibility in the school, the day-to-day operation of which will be delegated as appropriate, to the heads of year or group tutors, for example. Matters of concern are reported by other teachers to those with pastoral responsibility where there is reason to think that the pupil may need additional support. In *colleges and *universities, specialist pastoral care is provided by student support services. *See also* STUDY SUPPORT.

Pavlov, Ivan　*See* BEHAVIOURIST.

pay, teachers'　In England and Wales the basic salary ranges for teachers and head teachers are set out on a progressive scale sometimes referred to as the **salary spine**. However, following the changes set out in the School Teachers' Pay and Conditions document of 2013, schools have the freedom to make decisions about individual teachers' salaries and how quickly the teacher progresses up the pay scale. This allows them to retain and reward the most successful teachers. This model of **performance-related pay** involves the use of annual appraisal and review. Teachers may also be awarded additional points on the salary spine for additional teaching and learning responsibilities, known as **TLR points**; and for responsibilities for supporting *special educational needs (SEN). There is also a differentiation in pay scales between teachers in Inner London, Outer London, the London fringes, and the rest of England and Wales, which is intended to allow for the higher costs of accommodation in London and the surrounding area. This is sometimes referred to as the *London allowance.

　　Pay for teachers in *colleges of further education is calculated on a different scale from that of teachers in schools, and whereas in some cases a further education teacher and a schoolteacher may be teaching classes of comparable size, subject, and age group, the further education teacher is likely to be earning rather less than their opposite number in school. Most colleges in England are members of the *Association of Colleges, which represents the colleges in their capacity as employers when carrying out negotiations on pay and conditions with teachers' unions such as the *University and College Union (UCU) in the National Joint Forum. In Wales there is an additional negotiating forum, *Fforum.

　　Pay for teachers and lecturers in *higher education is negotiated between the Universities and Colleges Employers' Association and unions such as the UCU and the Educational Institute of Scotland. Negotiations take place through an academic subcommittee of the Joint National Committee for Higher Education Staff. The local branches of the unions then negotiate with individual universities, the employers, over the implementation of nationally agreed pay scales. *See also* PERFORMANCE THRESHOLD.

(⊕) SEE WEB LINKS

• Sets out the basic salary ranges for teachers and head teachers in schools in England and Wales and provides a link to the School Teachers' Pay and Conditions document (2013) in PDF.

pedagogy Teaching, as a professional practice and as a field of academic study. It encompasses not only the practical application of teaching, or pedagogic, skills, but also *curriculum issues and the body of theory relating to how and why learning takes place. Because it derives from a Greek expression referring to the education of the young, pedagogy is sometimes taken to be specifically about the education of children and young people, in which case the more recently coined term 'andragogy' is used in relation to the education of adults. 'Pedagogue', once an alternative term for 'teacher', has come to have overtones of pedantry, and is sometimes used now in a pejorative sense. Either 'pedagogic' or 'pedagogical' may be used as an adjective.

performance *See* ACHIEVEMENT.

performance criteria A clear statement of what the candidate must achieve in order to be deemed successful in an assessed task, *assignment, or *examination. The criteria will normally specify what areas of knowledge, skills, and understanding must be demonstrated, and to what level. They are often used as a way of breaking down the learning outcomes or *objectives into more detailed and specific guidance for the student, and may be used by the teacher or *assessor as a checklist when marking or assessing. When assessment feedback is given to the student, either written or spoken, it should be related to the performance criteria in order to convey clearly where these have and have not been met. The use of performance criteria was integral to the original *General National Vocational Qualification, and was seen by some academics and teachers as being very closely related to the use of *statements of competence.

performance indicators (PIs) Levels of performance and achievement of teachers, managers, institutions, and *local authorities are monitored against national *standards and against targets which may be imposed by government policy or by bodies such as *Ofsted or in some cases by the individual educational institutions themselves. Such targets may be referred to as performance indicators, and they reflect a growing emphasis on the notion of *accountability. PIs are usually expressed as numerical data relating to measurable aspects of, for example, recruitment, retention, attainment, and progression.

performance management Also known as appraisal, performance management in maintained schools applies to all staff. The head teacher's performance is appraised by the governing body. Teachers' performance is appraised by the head teacher and involves observation of the teacher's performance in the classroom to assess capability against the New Teachers' Standards (2012) for schools in England. Appraisal also involves the identification of continuing professional development (CPD) needs and the action(s) necessary to address them. Based on the appraisal, recommendations may be made for progression on the salary spine. *See also* PAY, TEACHERS'.

( ) SEE WEB LINKS
• Provides the full text of The Education (School Teachers' Appraisal) (England) Regulations, 2012.

performance-related pay *See* PAY, TEACHERS'; PERFORMANCE THRESHOLD.

performance tables A means of presenting information on individual school performance, often referred to as **league tables**.
   They present data measuring the performance of educational institutions against established criteria, and against other education providers of the same type. Their purpose, according to the UK government, is to allow parents and carers to make informed choices about the most appropriate schools for their children. The first tables comparing secondary schools' *examination results were published in 1992, followed by the publication of tables for *post-compulsory provision in 1993, and subsequently by *primary education in 1997. There was considerable opposition to their introduction from many stakeholders, who felt that the reputation of institutions might be damaged without good reason, particularly because examination results on their own cannot indicate how much progress has been made by students during their time in the institution. To address this, a measurement of the *value added to students' attainment was introduced to the tables in 2003, though the debate over the validity of such published data still continues.
   In Scotland they were abandoned in 2003 by the *Scottish Executive; instead such information is now accessed through the Scottish government's Parentzone Scotland web site, which provides details on individual schools, such as statistics about their examination performance.

performance threshold As a move to introduce some form of performance-related *pay for teachers, a measure was introduced by government in 2000 by which teachers could apply for their performance to be appraised against a set of national standards and, if successful, would cross the performance threshold which would take them onto an upper pay range. To be eligible, teachers had to be on point M6 of the main pay scale, and were required to submit evidence of their performance over the previous two to three years. The decision on whether their application to cross the threshold was successful rested with the *head teacher. Success was dependent on the effectiveness of the applicant's teaching skills alone, and was not influenced by their performance in any additional duties or responsibilities they may have taken on, such as in a pastoral or management role. This measure was not welcomed by teachers' unions, who feared it would prove divisive; nor by many head teachers, who viewed it as administratively burdensome. It was not possible to measure accurately its impact on school performance and quality of learning. However, the introduction of *Teachers' Standards in 2012 meant that from September 2013 any teacher could apply to move from the main pay scale to the upper pay range based on two key criteria:

a high level of competence across all the relevant Teachers' Standards, and sustained and substantial achievement contributing to the success of the school.

(⊕) SEE WEB LINKS
• Provides detailed guidance on threshold progression.

performativity A relatively recent term coined to convey the emphasis which current monitoring of education and training provision by government agencies and other regulatory bodies such as *Ofsted place upon the achievement of set targets or *performance indicators. The measurement of performance against indicators or targets is a largely quantitative approach to the evaluation of a school's, or a college's, or a university's effectiveness in terms of the quality of its provision, and does not easily take account of qualitative data such as pupils' or students' views on their own motivation or their responses to inspired teaching, for example. The term 'performativity' is often used when indicating the limitations of this quantitative, target-based approach to the evaluation of an educational process.

peripatetic teacher A teacher who teaches in several schools within a *local authority area and is employed by that authority, rather than being attached to and employed by one particular school. Such an arrangement is most often made in specialist subjects such as music or a modern foreign language where there is insufficient demand within one school alone to employ a full-time specialist teacher.

personal education plan (PEP) All *looked-after children must have a PEP as part of an overall care plan. The PEP reviews progress in academic and other areas of development. It sets out short- and long-term targets with strategies for enabling the child to reach their full potential. It is the responsibility of the social worker to instigate the plan and seek contributions from the young person, a relevant family member or carer, the designated teacher in school, and any other involved agencies. The PEP is held in school and must move with the child at any stage of transition. It is updated prior to the care plan review, and forms the body of information for the care plan. Ultimately, the PEP folder is the property of the young person.   TB, LA

personal, social, health, and economic education (PSHE) Under the *national curriculum, schools are advised, although not categorically required, to teach a range of topics which will help pupils towards a clearer understanding of society and their role and responsibilities within it, health issues, aspects of personal development, and philosophical and moral questions to do with ethical living. These are classed together as personal, social, and health education. But this is not to say that PSHE is necessarily taught as a discrete subject; aspects of it may be embedded in lessons for other subjects, or covered during tutorial times. There may be areas of overlap between PSHE and two areas of required provision: *citizenship and sex and relationship education, as well as with *religious education.

(⊕) SEE WEB LINKS
• Provides advice on the teaching of PSHE.

personalized curriculum A curriculum in which both the teaching and the content, or programme of study, are tailored to the learning needs of each individual child. It presupposes the facility to monitor closely each child's progress on a day-by-day or week-by-week basis, and to provide 'catch-up' programmes for those pupils whose learning is progressing more slowly. Since 2005 government education policy discourse has emphasized the concept of 'personalization' of the school curriculum; and the introduction for teachers, in September 2005, of 10 per cent of their timetabled time free from teaching for the purpose of planning, preparation, and assessment is viewed as one means by which such an approach might be facilitated, since teachers need time free from classroom teaching in order monitor individual pupil progress, devise individual learning plans, and liaise closely with parents and carers over their child's individual action plan.

The implementation of a personalized curriculum requires the adoption of alternative pedagogical approaches, since it cannot be achieved through conventional whole-class teaching. For example, it requires the teacher to act as a facilitator of learning, rather than instructor or director. It also implies some degree of negotiation between teacher and pupil about what is to be learned and how, a model approaching that sometimes described as 'learner-managed' or 'co-constructed' learning. Moreover, the concept of *personalized learning presupposes an approach to pupil progression which is based on the stage they have reached in their learning, rather than upon their chronological age. How these implications can be squared with the requirements of the externally imposed *national curriculum in its current form, with its age-related key stages and mandatory curriculum content, is as yet unclear.

In practical terms, 'personalization' is likely to take the form in schools of greater use of *setting by ability; strategies to stretch the ability and attainment of those pupils classed as *gifted and talented; additional support for pupils who are falling behind in their learning; more small-group teaching; and more one-to-one tuition. It may also involve an increasing deployment of teaching assistants, working under the supervision of the class teacher, to maintain a constant presence in the classroom while the teacher is engaged with individual pupils or small groups. *See also* STAGE NOT AGE.

personalized learning In personalized learning the curriculum and teaching approaches are adapted to meet the unique needs of every child, enabling them to achieve and participate at the highest level. This will involve a range of pedagogical approaches including the use of learning technologies, and should embrace close links between the school and the family. In recent years there has been a strong emphasis on raising standards in individual schools, and the personalized learning agenda moves this forward to focus on raising standards of achievement for individual pupils. Personalized learning should not be confused with individualized learning or differentiation, although it may contain elements of the two. *See also* INDIVIDUAL LEARNING PLAN; PERSONALIZED CURRICULUM.   TB, LA

Pestalozzi, Johann Heinrich (1746–1827) The founder of what became
known as the 'Pestalozzi Method' for the education of young children, Zurich-
born Pestalozzi believed that children should learn through activity and through
the handling and use of material objects rather than simply through words. He
argued that children should be encouraged to follow their own interests, make
their own discoveries, and draw their own conclusions. In this, he was exploring
and developing the educational ideas of *Rousseau, and particularly Rousseau's
recognition of the potential conflict between the pursuit of individual freedom
and the necessity for civic responsibility. His approach emphasizes the
importance of allowing children room for spontaneity and the freedom to
generate their own ideas and activities, and of allowing them to arrive at their
own answers. In order that they may do this, their ability to reason, judge, and
perceive for themselves must be nurtured and encouraged. In this sense, his
method has much in common with the *Reggio Emilia approach to early
childhood education which was developed in Italy over a century later. A key
underlying principle of the Pestalozzi approach is that it is not enough to provide
children with an education which is purely *cognitive or intellectual; that they
should be given a balanced, whole-child approach to learning based upon
*psychomotor, *affective, and cognitive development, or, in Pestalozzi's
phraseology, 'hands, heart, and head'.

Pestalozzi developed the concept of *Anschauung*, or **object lesson**, which was
the principle that no word should be employed until it was thoroughly
understood by concrete observation or perception, whether it referred to a
material object, an action, or a means of distinguishing one thing from another.
From this his proponents have developed principles which inform much of
modern-day pedagogic practice at all levels, such as the necessity, in effective
teaching, of starting with the concrete before moving to the abstract, and starting
with the simple before moving to the complex.

He also placed great emphasis on the personal dignity of the child as learner,
and the importance of preserving the integrity of each individual personality.
He viewed education as a means of improving conditions for the socially
marginalized, and for society generally. This concern with *social justice and with
kindness, positive regard, and a mutually respectful teacher–learner relationship
also led him to ban flogging in his schools. In seeing each child as the potential,
or 'seed', of the adult they will become, Pestalozzi was concerned that no undue
pressures or influences should warp the development intended by nature and
thereby prevent the child from growing to fulfil their inherent promise. He also
emphasized the potential of everyday life as a source of learning experiences,
claiming that 'There can be no doubt that within the living room of every
household are united the basic elements of all true human education across
its whole range.' Nevertheless, he saw the school as a central part of the
education process, and in this respect his thinking diverged from that of
Rousseau, who was of the view that the one-to-one tutor–pupil relationship
was the optimum means of ensuring a meaningful education.

His initial experiments in establishing a method of schooling at Neuhof were
based on combining education with productive employment, thus enabling the

children to finance their own learning, so that they remained independent of influence or interference by sponsors, stakeholders, employers, or the state. Although this project failed, its basic premise was later taken up by Mahatma Gandhi (1869–1948) as part of his movement to challenge colonialism and achieve independence for India. In 1801 Pestalozzi published a book entitled *How Gertrude Teaches Her Children*. This encapsulated much of the Pestalozzi Method, and is a major source of his subsequent influence on pedagogical theory and the philosophy of education. His ideas were put into practice with great success in his school at Yverdon, which was set up in 1805.

This emphasis on reflection, experimentation, and action in the development of pedagogic practice and ideas makes Pestalozzi one of the earliest examples of what we now refer to as a '*reflective practitioner'. His work has had a major influence on the ideas of later educators such as *Malaguzzi.

Further Reading: A. Brühlmeier and M. Mitchell *Head, Heart and Hand: Education in the Spirit of Pestalozzi* (Open Book Publishers, 2010).

phonics The sounds which make up spoken language. Thus, for example, the letter A has a name (which we pronounce 'ay'), but also represents a number of sounds, depending on its use. The sound it makes in the spoken word 'bad', for example, is different from the sound it makes in 'spade', and different again from its sound in 'scarf', and so on. One of the ways in which children may be taught to read is through recognition of these sounds and the way they link together to build up whole words. This is known as the phonics approach to *reading.

Within the teaching of phonics there are two distinct approaches, **synthetic phonics** and **analytic phonics**, and there is continuing debate over which is the more effective. Synthetic phonics is so called because it 'synthesizes', or puts together, groups of sounds. For example, one phoneme (a word which indicates the smallest unit of sound into which language may be broken down) may be represented in a number of different ways in writing, so that the 'o' sound we hear in 'phoneme' may be represented by other combinations of letters, depending upon the word. Thus, 'ow', 'oa', and 'ough' can sound identical when read aloud, even though they are represented on the page by quite different graphemes (ways we express phonemes in writing). When a child is taught to read English using synthetic phonics, they will learn to recognize up to 44 phonemes and the graphemes used to represent them. From this they can progress to sounding out whole words by blending the phonemes together. Where this approach is used, children begin learning early in their first year of *primary school, and will learn, as a whole class, up to six sounds a week. They are shown the grapheme, listen to the sound, repeat it, and perform a related action, such as drawing the grapheme in the air. This multi-sensory 'drilling' is designed to reinforce the learning. A disadvantage, however, is that phonetically irregular words, for which English is notorious, are not so easily decoded using only this approach.

Analytic phonics is an alternative approach to the teaching of reading which encourages the learner to break down each word into its component sounds and spelling patterns. Thus, the initial vowel sound of the word can be merged with the sound that follows, as in 'c-at', and the inherent rhyme utilized to recognize or form other words which conform to the same spelling pattern (for example, 'h-at', 'r-at', 'b-at', and so on). This approach works well in helping learners to recognize phonetically irregular words, such as 'would', 'should', and 'could' as conforming to a common pattern.

In the current debate over the efficacy of teaching methods for reading skills, government policy encourages the synthetic phonics approach. *See also* PHONICS SCREENING CHECK.

Further Reading: K. Goouch and A. Lambirth (eds) *Understanding Phonics and the Teaching of Reading* (Open University Press, 2008).

phonics screening check A test carried out in Key Stage 1 to measure the pupil's grasp of synthetic *phonics. The pupil is asked to read out a 'word' which is often a combination of letters making a non-word, such as *sheb* or *plun*. They may sound out the 'word' phonetically first, but this is not a requirement. In order to pass the check the sounds must be blended so that the non-word is sounded in the same way as a real word would be, rather than as a collection of constituent sounds. Critics of synthetic phonics point to the likelihood of a child attempting to make a real word from the non-word, so that they may try to make 'ship' of *sheb* or 'plum' of *plun*. However, what could be seen as an intelligent response to the task will in fact be recorded as a failure. Critics also point out that the current emphasis on phonics can delay simple word recognition and may therefore actually delay the acquisition of fluent reading skills. The usefulness of non-words in the teaching of reading remains a matter of debate. *See also* PHONICS.

(⊕) SEE WEB LINKS

• A recording of phonics screening taking place, intended as a guide to best practice for teachers.

Piaget, Jean (1896–1980) A Swiss biologist, Piaget published his first article on the psychology of *intelligence in 1921, and began research into the reasoning processes of very young children in the same year at the Jean-Jacques *Rousseau Institute in Geneva. His made his own children the focus of intense observation, worked as Professor of Psychology at the University of Geneva from 1929 to 1975, and, having produced over 60 books on children and learning, he was regarded by the time of his death in 1980 as one of the most significant psychologists of the 20th century. Piaget was interested in the nature of thought and the development of thinking, and observed that even young children have skills with regard to objects in their environment. Their explorations—first through sensorimotor activity and at a later stage through formal or hypothetical operations—he described as *schemas. He identified a number of specific age-*stage developmental activities: sensorimotor (0–2); pre-operational–symbolic (2–7); concrete–logical operations (7–11); and formal abstract operations (12+). Piaget devised a number of laboratory-based experiments to establish children's *cognitive stage of development, and the similarities between children's actions and responses at certain ages. The experiments included those to test children's ideas of **object permanence** (*Do I look for it? Where has it gone?*); **conservation** (*Is the mass the same if I change its shape?*); **seriation** (*Can I group things in order?*); and **egocentrism** (*Do I know what it is like to be someone else?*). The theory of *constructivism, where an individual constructs knowledge through action from within themselves then discards or modifies ideas when faced with new information which has to be **accommodated** to re-establish the learner's **equilibrium**, has been extremely influential in *pedagogy at all levels of education.

However, subsequent research and replication of these experiments have demonstrated the existence of a much greater variation between children, with the result that Piaget's chronological developmental stages are no longer perceived as rigid norms. It is argued that when the experiments are given contextual meaning in a natural (not laboratory) environment, children are able to demonstrate cognitive understanding at an earlier age than Piaget once claimed.

It is also known that Piaget observed children in isolation from peers and supportive adults. However, **social constructivist** approaches, which are currently influential in pedagogical theory, suggest that children working with others construct knowledge above their own individual abilities, through modelling, negotiation, and language. Nonetheless, Piaget's theories about the stages of development have provided a broad overview of how children think in their *early years, and his influence on education, developmental psychology, and the evolution of human intelligence is still highly regarded by many educationalists.   AW

Further Reading: J. Piaget *The Language and Thought of the Child* (Goldberg Press, 2013).

Piagetian programme A teaching method based on *Piaget's stages of learning and his theory of cognitive development. It involves setting the pupils work which is one stage ahead of their current age-related Piagetian level, thus stretching and challenging them.

Further Reading: J. Hattie *Visible Learning for Teachers: Maximising impact and learning* (Routledge, 2011) draws on a wide range of evidence-based research to identify effective strategies for teachers, including Piagetian programmes.

picture exchange communication system (PECS) A simple communication system involving exchanging pictures for a desired item or activity. It is used extensively with children who have **global developmental delay** and those with *autistic spectrum disorder, who have little or no verbal communication. The system supports the development of functional communication rather than language, starting with single pictures and building up to the use of sentences to make requests. PECS is an aided form of *augmentative and alternative communication.   TB, LA

pilot A trial or experimental period during which a new teaching *method, learning technology, *course, or *programme is run for a restricted number of learners in order to evaluate the effectiveness of its structure or content and make revisions, if necessary, before making it widely available. Notable examples of national pilots, or pilot schemes as they are sometimes known, are the *General National Vocational Qualification pilot of 1992, and the *diploma pilot of 2008, during both of which the newly introduced qualification was subjected to a year's initial evaluation using a limited number of students.

placement Time spent in a place of work, normally unpaid, as part of an educational or training experience. Students or trainees whose course of study requires them to spend some time on *work experience will either have a placement organized for them by their school, college, or university, or be expected to organize their own. This also applies to student teachers, all of whom must spend some time on placement in schools or colleges as part of their *initial teacher training. In departments where large numbers of their students undertake work experience as part of their studies, there may be a designated member of staff responsible for coordinating and monitoring placements, sometimes known as a **placement tutor** or **placement coordinator**. *See also* TEACHING PRACTICE.

plagiarism The act of appropriating someone else's idea or work and passing it off as one's own. The growing problem of plagiarism in the secondary and tertiary sectors of education can be attributed to two major causes. One has been the trend away from end examinations towards *continuous assessment of *coursework. This increased reliance on work produced in unsupervised conditions as a basis for assessing learner achievement, despite its advantages, has also created additional opportunities for unscrupulous students to present work written by others as their own. The other major factor has been the advance in technology and the easy availability of Internet access, which allows a dishonest minority of students to 'cut and paste' text from unacknowledged sources and incorporate it into their own work. More serious still is the international Internet market in essays, assignments, coursework, and dissertations, which allows students to buy bespoke or 'off-the-peg' pieces of written work and present them as their own. The ease with which this may be perpetrated, and the seriousness of the issue, particularly for awarding bodies and for institutions of further and higher education in terms of quality control, has resulted in the development of a range of software designed to identify any instances of plagiarism within a piece of written work. Such software is now widely used in universities and colleges, and students are often required to produce evidence that their work has been scanned and found clear of plagiarism by a designated software program.

'Plagiarism' is also the formal term applied to the practice of copying another pupil's work and submitting it without acknowledging the source. Technically, it would also apply as a consequence of the practice of some parents and carers who make substantial contributions to a pupil's homework or project work but allow the pupil to pass the work off as their own. It is also possible for a student to fall into the error of **self-plagiarism**. This is the practice of using text from previously assessed work and including it verbatim in a subsequent essay or assignment without acknowledging its source. The reason why this is considered unacceptable is because the piece of text being used in this way has already been used to gain the student marks or credit. To resubmit it as though it were an entirely different piece of work amounts in effect to trying to claim two marks or sets of credit for one piece of work. If the piece of text is clearly acknowledged as part of the student's earlier work, however, it is permissible to include it, and such an inclusion is not classed as plagiarism.

Students may also fall into plagiarism through carelessness, simply by forgetting or omitting to cite clear sources for extracts of text which they have quoted, or by failing to make quite clear where their own words stop and the source quoted begins. Experienced teachers in all sectors may find it relatively straightforward to recognize parts of a student's work which are clearly not the student's own. They may notice, for example, an abrupt change in written style, or evidence of a vocabulary which is normally outside the student's experience or expertise. They may even recognize the original source of a passage quoted without acknowledgement. At higher levels, however, and particularly at *postgraduate and *doctorate levels, the recognition of plagiarism may become a more complicated and difficult task. Unwitting plagiarism, where the student unknowingly presents as their own an idea, argument, or theory which has already become the intellectual property of another, through patent or publication, is nevertheless treated as a serious error, and one which postgraduate students are advised to avoid by a very careful scrutiny of existing publications on the topic. *See also* AUTHENTICITY.

(⊕) SEE WEB LINKS
• Provides guidance for the avoidance of plagiarism.

play-based learning An aspect of *early years and *primary schooling *pedagogy in which children learn through play, using these activities to help them to make sense of their world, build social skills and develop the acquisition of specific cognitive skills such as language and numbers. Play-based learning also allows children to experience and learn to cope with challenges and frustrations. It is thought that positive play can improve the child's potential for wider learning.

Further Reading: M. Briggs and A. Hansen *Play-based Learning in the Primary School* (Sage, 2012).

(⊕) SEE WEB LINKS
• Provides further information and examples of play-based learning activities.

playground An outdoor area on the school premises where pupils play, under supervision, at break times and during the lunchtime break. The area may also be used during lesson times for *organized games, physical education, and other activities such as measuring, drawing, or nature observation. Unlike the *playing field, it will usually have a hard surface so as to be usable in all weathers. During outdoor break times the supervision of pupils by teaching staff is known as **playground duty**, and is usually organized on a rota system. In primary schools these breaks are commonly known as **playtime**.

playgroup, pre-school A registered childcare facility that offers sessional care—usually between two and three hours per session—for children between the ages of 2½ and 5. Pre-school playgroups are commonly organized by a committee of parents and staffed by a qualified and experienced supervisor with a team of staff who are additionally supported by parents helping on a voluntary rota basis. Playgroups are required to register with *Ofsted to meet national standards, which specify the suitability of carers, premises, and record-keeping. There is an annual inspection. Playgroups can be in community centres, schools, church halls, leisure centres, or youth and sport facilities, often sharing a building with a range of community groups. The maximum number of children in a group is normally 26, but this will depend on the size of the room and the building facilities. The staff ratio is one adult to four children aged 2 and one adult to eight children aged 3-5. Playgroups provide children with pre-school experiences such as art, craft, and construction activities, music and movement, large physical play, books, and stories. Pre-school playgroups are required to provide teaching and care which complies with the *Early Years Foundation Stage framework for all children aged 1-5.   AW

playing field A grassed area which is usually, but not always, adjoining the school, and is used for activities such as *organized games and competitive sports. The number of schools with extensive playing fields has fallen for two reasons: successful and popular schools wishing to expand their teaching accommodation may use playing field land for this purpose, while those in need of additional finance may apply through their local authority to sell some or part of their playing fields to raise funds. Such applications for approval are made to the *Department for Children, Schools, and Families. This trend has, however, recently reversed, and some schools are seeking additional space for use as playing fields. *See also* PLAYGROUND.

P scales Performance scales, the use of which is required by law when schools are reporting *Key Stages 1, 2, and 3 on the attainment of pupils with *special educational needs (SEN) who are working below *national curriculum level 1.

Plowden Report (1967) An advisory report into primary education and progression to the secondary phase, carried out by the Central Advisory Council, chaired by Lady Plowden (1910-2000). Among its recommendations was to replace *infant and *junior schools with a system of *first schools and *middle schools, thus raising the age at which the pupil began their secondary education to at least 12. This was not, however, widely implemented. The Report also advocated more parental involvement with schools, the setting up of educational priority areas where social disadvantage could be specifically addressed, and more flexibility in the age at which children start school. It is perhaps most famous for having advocated putting the child at the centre of the educational process, a recommendation which does not on the face of it appear contentious, but which subsequently led to criticisms from right-wing educators that the Plowden Report had endorsed and encouraged a *progressive approach to education which was ultimately to prove counterproductive. This negative view is challenged, however, by the majority of educationalists, who view the Report as ground-breaking for its time. *See also* BLACK PAPERS.

points *See* UNIVERSITIES AND COLLEGES ADMISSIONS SERVICE.

polytechnic Institutions of *higher education which existed under that name between 1969 and 1992, after which they were redesignated *universities. The first of these were established following the 1966 *White Paper *A Plan for the Polytechnics and Other Colleges* and were intended as a means of providing specialist higher education for those students intending to go on to work in industry and commerce. They operated under the control of their *local authority, which was also responsible for funding them. Their degrees and other awards were validated through the **Council for National Academic Awards (CNAA)**. The *Education Reform Act 1988 removed the polytechnics from local authority control and set up the Polytechnics and Colleges Funding Council, through which they were henceforth to be funded. This was soon afterwards merged with the University Funding Council as a result of policy presented in the 1991 White Paper *Higher Education: A New Framework*, which set out the argument for abolishing the distinction between polytechnics and universities. Finally, the *Further and Higher Education Act 1992 awarded polytechnics the power to confer their own degrees, and granted them the right to call themselves universities.

portfolio Candidates for *competence-based qualifications may be required to compile and present evidence of their achievement in the form of a portfolio for the purposes of assessment. This is particularly the case where the candidate is claiming *accreditation for prior experience or learning. The portfolio might contain evidence such as witness statements of the candidate's competence, photographs of completed work or artefacts, and certification of qualifications already gained. In art and design courses a student's portfolio will contain examples of their work.

positivist *See* RESEARCH.

post-compulsory All education undertaken after the age of compulsory schooling. Although it was until recently also referred to as **post-16 education**, the raising of the age at which learners are legally allowed to leave education or training has meant that definitions of 'post-compulsory' have changed. In a literal sense it applies to all education and training provision available after the formal school leaving age, including *higher education and *adult education. However, it is more usually taken to indicate *further education and training, and that sector in general, as in the expression **post-compulsory education and training (PCET)**. *See also* RAISING OF THE SCHOOL-LEAVING AGE.

postgraduate The levels of qualification and study above the first or *bachelor's degree, and designated level 7 and above in the *National Qualifications Framework. Such study includes *master's degrees and *doctorates, which are known as *higher degrees; and also postgraduate diplomas. The term may also be used to refer to the students themselves, so that a *graduate who undertakes further study is known as a postgraduate.

Postgraduate Certificate of Education (PGCE) The teaching qualification taken by some graduate entrants to the profession. Since this qualification was originally awarded at *higher education undergraduate level, its title was deemed to be misleading, making it appear that the term 'postgraduate' applied to the level of the qualification itself, rather than to the entry qualification of the student teachers. As a consequence, higher education institutions who validated the PGCE agreed to introduce instead a differentiated award which would allow student teachers to take the qualification at its original level and gain a Professional Graduate Certificate of Education (PGCE), or, with the agreement of their tutors, to undertake a proportion of the work at master's level in order to gain a Postgraduate Certificate of Education (PGCE). Thus, the postgraduate certificate is now postgraduate in the real sense that it denotes achievement at master's level. The identical initials, while a possible source of confusion, are designed to be non-divisive. *See also* QUALIFIED TEACHER STATUS.

((⊕)) SEE WEB LINKS
• Provides links to detailed information about both qualifications: the professional and the postgraduate certificates.

prefect A pupil in their final year of secondary school who is granted special status and given responsibilities such as monitoring the behaviour of younger pupils. It is a system which originated in *independent schools in the 19th century, where prefects were often given the power to discipline younger pupils. A prefect system still operates in many independent schools and some *maintained schools. Prefects are usually selected by the head teacher and senior staff, and a **head boy** and/or **head girl** is often appointed from among the prefects chosen.

preparatory school An *independent school for day pupils or boarders aged up to 13 years. Its name derives from its role in preparing its pupils for selective examinations: the *Eleven Plus or the *Common Entrance Examination for independent secondary schools. Such schools do not necessarily follow the *national curriculum. For example, they will offer Latin and French for pupils preparing for the Common Entrance Examination. They are often referred to by the abbreviated form '**prep school**'.

pre-school **1.** The years of a child's life before compulsory schooling begins, as in 'the pre-school years'.
  2. May be used to describe a child who is too young for, but approaching, school age, as in 'a pre-school child'.
  3. May be used as a synonym for *playgroup.
  4. In Scotland all 3- and 4-year-olds are offered free part-time education, which equates to five sessions of 2½ hours per week. *See also* PRE-SCHOOL LEARNING ALLIANCE.

Pre-School Learning Alliance A registered charity, previously known as the Pre-School Playgroup Association, which was established in the 1960s as a response to the growth of community and parent-run groups for children under statutory school age. Parents and employed staff began to establish local committees, known as branches, who then became part of a county, regional, and national structure. National staff and training officers supplied information, support, and training for all volunteers and staff, as well as accreditation of courses, which were delivered at *further education colleges or on site in the *playgroups themselves. There now exists a national centre which supports regional offices and 400 local branches of volunteers who shape the direction of the charity. Through the Alliance, parents and staff in *pre-schools can access a range of training opportunities including *National Vocational Qualifications in childcare, training, and support.   AW

(⊕) SEE WEB LINKS
• Provides details of the organization, training, and support of pre-school staff.

pre-vocational education A course designed to prepare pupils and students aged 14–19 for eventual entry to a programme of specific *vocational training which will lead to a skills qualification. Such pre-vocational provision—of which the short-lived *Certificate of Pre-Vocational Education, developed in response to an initiative from the Department of Education and Science, and introduced in 1983 for 16–18-year-olds who had left the schooling system with few qualifications, is an instructive example—usually provided the student with some limited experience in a chosen vocational area, together with a curriculum which emphasized the acquisition of the *key skills: communication, *numeracy, and *information communication technology. The term is little used now, since the curriculum model and format underpinning it was incorporated first into *General National Vocational Qualifications (1993) and then again into parts of the *14–19 Diploma (2007). As originally conceived, pre-vocational education was targeted at those students who were not expected to progress to *Advanced Level study or to *higher education, but who were expected to leave school at 16 and seek employment. It was intended not only to help them to gain the key transferable skills they would require, but also to make an informed vocational choice. To some extent the role of such courses has become redundant as fewer and fewer school-leavers expect to enter the workforce without first gaining higher qualifications of some kind.

primary education In England and Wales this refers to provision for children aged 5–11. It is usually divided into two phases: the *infant school for 5–7-year-olds, which delivers *Key Stage 1 of the *national curriculum, and the *junior school for 7–11-year-olds, which delivers Key Stage 2. This system operates in all areas except those where first and *middle schools have been introduced. It has been formally in existence since the *Education Act 1944 (*Butler Act), having replaced the system of *elementary schools, which, up until the mid-1920s, took pupils aged 5–14 (constituting, for many, the only schooling they would receive), and later aged 5–11. During the primary phase of their education, pupils take two national tests in the form of *Standard Tasks, one at age 7 and the next at age 11. In Scotland primary education is between the ages of 5 and 12, and follows a national curriculum, although there is no synchronous national testing.

primer A textbook, particularly an introductory text which sets out the basics of a subject. For example, a Latin primer would contain tables of conjugations for verbs and declensions for nouns, as well as other details of grammar and lists of vocabulary. It is a term less widely used now than previously, perhaps because of the accessibility of key subject information on the Internet. It derives from Latin *primus*, 'first'.

principal The title given to the chief executive of a *college of further education. It is also used at some *universities instead of the title vice-chancellor. In a small minority of English secondary schools it is a title given to the *head teacher, although this use is the norm in American schools, as many English pupils will be aware through watching the confrontations between Principal Skinner and his nemesis, Bart Simpson, on the television show *The Simpsons*.

principal teacher In Scotland the head of a subject area is referred to as a principal teacher; for example, a principal teacher of mathematics.   SM

prison education Now more usually referred to as **offender learning**. The policy for the education and training of offenders falls under the remit of the *Department for Business, Innovation, and Skills. The policy relating to younger offenders, the School Age Offender Policy, is under the aegis of the *Department for Education. For both groups of offenders the teaching of *literacy and *numeracy are of primary concern, although education and training at all levels is made available as appropriate to offenders serving custodial sentences. All are entitled to a minimum of 30 hours' education and training, with an emphasis on the acquisition of skills for employment. The curriculum is managed and coordinated by a director of learning and skills within the institution, who is responsible directly to the governor. Some teaching in prisons is done on a voluntary basis, particularly in the area of basic literacy skills. Research suggests that prison education makes inmates less likely to re-offend.

(⊕) SEE WEB LINKS

• Provides links to news reports on prison education and re-offending statistics, and relevant scholarly articles.

private education *See* INDEPENDENT SCHOOLS.

probationary year *See* QUALIFIED TEACHER STATUS.

problem-solving *See* KEY SKILLS.

professional body A body which sets the professional and academic standards for those who wish to practise within the profession concerned. The endorsement of such bodies may be required for awards in *further and *higher education which constitute or incorporate professional qualifications; and in some cases the body itself may be responsible for shaping the *syllabus of courses leading to such awards. The nearest equivalent for the teaching profession is the *General Teaching Council. The standards for the profession, however, are set by government agencies such as the *Training and Development Agency for Schools and *Lifelong Learning UK, and differ according to the sector of education concerned.

professional development *See* CONTINUING PROFESSIONAL DEVELOPMENT.

Professional Graduate Certificate of Education (PGCE) A teaching qualification awarded to non-postgraduate entrants to the profession. Originally, there was a unitary qualification for graduate entrants, known as the *Postgraduate Certificate of Education (PGCE), which was usually awarded at *higher education level 3, which is the equivalent of a first degree. The ambiguous title of the award, which could be taken to suggest that the term 'postgraduate' applied to the level of the qualification itself, rather than to the entry qualification of the student teachers, was eventually judged to be misleading. As a consequence, higher education institutions who validated the postgraduate certificate agreed to introduce instead a differentiated award which would allow student teachers to take the qualification at its original level 3 and gain a Professional Graduate Certificate of Education, or, with the agreement of their tutors, to undertake a proportion of the work at master's level in order to gain a Postgraduate Certificate of Education. Since this may be achieved through a process of differentiation by outcome and assessment, it can allow both groups of student teachers to follow the same programme. The potential divisiveness of this restructuring and renaming is further minimized by the fact that the two qualifications retain the identical abbreviation.

Professional Graduate Diploma in Education (PGDE) A one-year postgraduate qualification required for teaching in Scotland. As with the *Postgraduate Certificate of Education and the *Professional Graduate Certificate of Education, student teachers will have already achieved a degree qualification before embarking on this course. PGDE courses are offered at six universities: Aberdeen, Dundee, Edinburgh, Glasgow, Paisley, and Strathclyde.   SM

professionalism A level of behaviour and performance expected of teachers as professionals. This encompasses not only the standard of their teaching, but also the application of an appropriate set of values, and conformity to an accepted code of practice. One factor which sets teachers apart as a profession is their daily close contact with children and young people, and the consequent necessity to act as positive role models. Another is that, unlike other professions, such as medicine and the law, teachers have their standards of practice imposed externally by one of a range of government bodies, depending on the sector, as well as by the *General Teaching Council, which, among its other functions, sets standards of professional conduct. Nevertheless, because of these two factors, an understanding of what we mean by 'professionalism' is of key concern to teachers and their unions. *See also* PROFESSIONAL BODY.

professional skills test Mandatory tests in *literacy and *numeracy, undertaken by all trainee teachers intending to teach in the *primary or secondary sectors of education. They are designed to ensure that all teachers gaining *qualified teacher status (QTS) possess an appropriate level of skill in these key curriculum areas. The introduction of the tests was proposed in the 2000 *Green Paper *Teachers: Meeting the Challenge of Change*, and the tests were first implemented during the academic year 2001/2. The tests are taken and assessed electronically, and all trainee teachers must successfully complete both before they can be awarded QTS or QTLS. There is currently no national key skills assessment required of teachers entering the *higher education sector.

(⊕) SEE WEB LINKS
• Provides a link to the tests.

professor The title given in institutions of *higher education to the most highly ranked teaching posts, where the teachers in question are an acknowledged authority in their field. It may also, as is the practice in some post-1992 universities, be attached to management posts such as head of department or faculty, where it is often an honorific rather than an indication of the post-holder's academic standing. Where the professorship is a permanent part of the academic structure and requires the post-holder to give academic leadership in a particular subject area or faculty, it is known as a 'chair' in that field or subject concerned. A professorship can also be awarded by an institution as a personal title in acknowledgement of an individual's academic standing in their field, nationally or internationally.

profound and multiple learning difficulties (PMLD) *See* LEARNING DIFFICULTIES.

programmed learning *See* COMPUTER-ASSISTED LEARNING.

programme of study (PoS) The subject knowledge, skills, and understanding which are required to be taught in each subject during each *key stage of the *national curriculum. Each national curriculum subject has its own PoSs for each stage. It is upon these that the teacher will base their *schemes of work and *lesson plans. *Further education and *higher education institutions also have PoSs, outside the national curriculum.

Progress File Their Progress File enables students, both adults and those aged 13–19, to present a record of their achievements formally and to set their goals in relation to work as well as learning. It is used for action planning and the recording and reviewing of achievement. The introduction of Progress Files was first recommended in the 1996 *Dearing *Review of Qualifications for 16–19-Year-Olds*, which suggested restructuring the *National Record of Achievement (NRA) which was then in current use, and renaming it the Progress File. The File is in use in all sectors of education and training, and replaced the NRA fully by 2009.

progression The transition from one stage of education or training, or one level of qualification, to the next. Thus, a pupil is said to progress from *primary to secondary education, or from one *key stage to another of the *national curriculum. At some points in the student's academic career there will be more than one possible **progression route**. For example, at the end of Key Stage 4 a pupil might be advised to take a *vocational direction rather than an *academic one. One measure of a qualification's worth or currency is how it serves the student in terms of progression. A useful example here is the *General Certificate of Education *Advanced Level, which offers a progression route into *higher education, but is also valued by employers when considering applications for jobs.

progressive A contentious term when applied to education, and taken to mean anything from a principled opposition to corporal punishment to allowing pupils complete freedom to learn as and when they please. It is often employed to indicate the opposite of 'traditional', as in the debate over the relative merits of *comprehensive and selective education, where proponents of *selection refer to comprehensive education, in pejorative terms, as 'progressive'. In this sense it implies a slipping of standards of achievement and a tolerance of inappropriate behaviour. On the other hand, it has been used in a very positive sense by those advocating educational reform, such as the abandoning of *rote learning in favour of discovery and understanding, which was seen as progress against the draconian methods of 19th- and early 20th-century educators. Under the Conservative governments of the 1970s and 1980s, 'progressive education' became a regular target of criticism in *White Papers, where it was blamed for a number of social ills, including youth crime and high levels of unemployment. Because of the extent to which the term has become politicized, it is perhaps now better treated as an example of rhetoric rather than as an educational term with a precise and agreed meaning. *See also* BLACK PAPERS; PLOWDEN REPORT.

project 1. A programme of *research into some aspect of education, undertaken by an individual or team of researchers.
2. A piece of assessed work undertaken by a pupil or group of pupils, which explores or develops a topic, often of their own choice. *See also* ASSIGNMENT.

prospectus A brochure produced by a *school, *college, or *university, whose contents are often replicated on their web site, which sets out information about the institution and the provision it offers. All maintained schools are required by law to produce a prospectus for the benefit of parents and others, and to include in it information on the school's admissions policy and the policy relating to pupils with *special educational needs. The document may also contain the governors' annual report in part or in full, and details of the school's *national curriculum, *General Certificate of Secondary Education, and *General Certificate of Education *Advanced Level results. Universities and other institutions of *higher education may produce separate prospectuses for undergraduate and for postgraduate provision. It is normal practice for larger institutions such as colleges and universities to provide an online prospectus as well as a hard-copy edition.

provision mapping A part of the school self-evaluation process. Provision mapping looks at the levels and types of *special educational needs (SEN) and plans the most effective ways of using resources to make provision for those who need support which is 'different from and in addition to' that which is given to all students. Provision mapping enables the SEN coordinator to keep an overview of support interventions. It clearly identifies individual students and the type of support they receive on a weekly basis and the staff who support them. Provision mapping enables comparisons to be made between methods of intervention in terms of progress and achievement, and cost-effectiveness. Most schools begin by identifying a particular group of students who might be vulnerable or have additional educational needs. Provision mapping is closely linked to schools' *graduated approach to supporting SEN. Head teachers find provision maps useful as a detailed record against which they can plan SEN funding. It is a good indication for outside agencies and local authority officers to gain an overview of SEN provision for individual students.   TB, LE

psychomotor One of the three domains of learning identified in 1956 by Benjamin *Bloom (1913–99) and his team of educational psychologists, and used to describe learning which requires the development of some level of physical coordination or practical skill. This could involve learning, at one extreme, a relatively simple, lower-order skill, such as placing a smaller box inside a larger one, to, at the other extreme, a complex procedure requiring skills of the highest order, such as brain surgery or ballet. The teaching and learning of psychomotor skills is usually achieved through a process of **demonstration and practice**, and can normally be assessed through an observation of the learner's performance. Derived from the terms 'psyche' (mind) and 'motor' (movement), the concept of the psychomotor domain is best understood in terms of the learner's development of the ability to coordinate thought and activity in order to perform a task at a required level of skill. In terms of educational values, achievements in the psychomotor domain sometimes appear to be accorded less status than those in the *cognitive domain; a pupil who is skilled at mechanical tasks, for example, may be regarded differently from one who is skilled at mathematics. This distinction can also be seen in prevailing assumptions about the difference in status between *National Vocational Qualifications, which are largely associated with the psychomotor domain, and *General Certificate of Education *Advanced Levels, which are generally regarded as addressing the cognitive domain. Many educationalists would argue, however, that such clear-cut distinctions are misleading, and that the learning of most practical tasks, and particularly those of a higher order, also inevitably involves cognitive learning in terms of the required underpinning *knowledge and understanding.

(⊕) SEE WEB LINKS
• Provides details of the levels of learning in the psychomotor domain, with examples of level-related key words.

public school *See* INDEPENDENT SCHOOLS.

pupil A child or young person who is enrolled at a school, or a learner of any age who is being given expert tuition in a creative skill; for example, an artist's pupil or a piano pupil. *See also* STUDENT.

pupil-centred *See* LEARNER-CENTRED.

pupil-led learning A pedagogical approach which uses the pupils' interests or enthusiasms as a starting point and supports them in developing projects which then act as a vehicle for the acquisition of knowledge, understanding, and skills relevant to their *curriculum. It encourages pupils to accept responsibility for their learning, to work collaboratively on group projects, and to become actively engaged rather than *passive learners. Pupil-led learning can also include the practice of involving learners in the setting of ground rules and deadlines. *See also* LEARNER-CENTRED; TALK-LESS TEACHING.

pupil premium Additional government funding for schools to support the learning of disadvantaged pupils and pupils whose parent or parents are serving in the armed forces. The funding is calculated on the number of pupils in the school who have been in care for a period of six months or longer, and on the number who have been entitled to free school meals during the previous six years.

SEE WEB LINKS
• Provides links to further information on the pupil premium.

pupil referral unit (PRU) A type of school maintained by the *local authority for children of compulsory school age who require *education otherwise than at school. A high percentage of children attending PRUs have been permanently excluded from mainstream schools, but other groups of learners—such as those at risk of permanent exclusion, pregnant and teenage mothers, pupils with medical needs, pupils in hospital, and those who would benefit from a work-related curriculum—may also access this provision. PRUs are established to meet the specific needs of the relevant local authority's area and policy. Some units will be on a single site while others may have many locations but be under a single management structure. Units may set up to offer education to discrete types of learner, e.g. hospital schools. There is no requirement to follow the *national curriculum, but the curriculum offered must be appropriate to the needs and ability of each individual child (including any *special educational need) placed in the provision, while ensuring that public resources are used efficiently. Pupils permanently excluded from school must receive full-time education amounting to 25 hours per week, whereas pupils with medical needs have a minimum requirement of five hours or more if their condition allows. PRUs are subject to *Ofsted inspections and should have regard to the need to plan for the reintegration of pupils into mainstream education where possible. No child may be placed in a unit without the agreement of the child's parents.   TB, LE

pupil–teacher ratio The number of pupils in a class or school divided by the number of teachers. In a *maintained *primary school the number of teachers employed will be based largely on the number of pupils on the school roll, so that if the number of enrolments falls, teaching posts may be lost rather than *class sizes reduced. In secondary schools the situation is rather more complicated, as specialist teachers must be employed to cover each curriculum subject. A pupil–teacher ratio which creates class sizes of more than 30 pupils will normally raise concerns from parents and teachers, as it is widely believed that pupils will benefit more from being part of a smaller group in which the teacher is able to give more attention to each individual. For example, in *independent schools the pupil–teacher ratio is normally significantly lower than in the maintained sector. However, the relationship between pupil–teacher ratios and the effectiveness of teaching must also take into account the nature of the learning activities. The effectiveness of a teacher-centred *method such as exposition or *lecture may be very little affected by class size, while *learner-centred activities such as discussion or *discovery learning may work much better in group sizes which allow the teacher to give individual attention where it is needed. By the same principle, the pupil–teacher ratio will have an impact on the range of learning activities which the teacher is able to facilitate effectively.

p

Qualifications and Credit Framework (QCF) A credit transfer system for England, Wales, and Northern Ireland which sets out a taxonomy of nationally recognized vocational qualifications, grouping them according to level, from entry level (lowest) to level 8 (highest). Each qualification is made up of units and each unit has a credit value. One credit equates roughly to 10 hours of study. The framework encompasses three types of qualification: awards, certificates, and diplomas. It is referenced to the *European Qualifications Framework, so that it is possible to understand the equivalence or relative level of qualifications across much of Europe. The QCF is regulated by the *Office of the Qualifications and Examinations Regulator (Ofqual) in England, by the **Department for Children, Education, Lifelong Learning, and Skills (DCELLS)** in Wales and by the **Council for Curriculum, Examinations, and Assessment (CCEA)** in Northern Ireland. Scotland has its own framework: the **Scottish Qualification and Credit Framework (SQCF)**.

(((⊕))) SEE WEB LINKS

• Provides a comparison between the QCF and the SQCF.

qualified teacher learning and skills (QTLS) Introduced in 2008 to denote a teacher's qualified status to teach in the further education sector and, from April 2012, finally recognized as a qualification for teaching in schools, on condition that the teacher is a member of the *Institute for Learning. From September 2001, and following a recommendation in the 1998 *Green Paper *The Learning Age*, all teachers in *further education and the skills training sector were required to hold, or to be working towards, a nationally recognized teaching qualification for that sector of education, known variously as the *lifelong learning sector, *further education and training, or (except in Scotland) the *learning and skills sector. Initially, the standards for these qualifications were drawn up by the Further Education National Training Organization (FENTO), which endorsed a range of teaching qualifications awarded by higher education institutions and other *awarding bodies, such as the *City and Guilds of London Institute. These standards were known as the **FENTO standards**. They were replaced in 2007 by a revised set of national standards drawn up, following consultation with the sector, by a body known as Lifelong Learning UK (LLUK) and its standards and verification arm, Standards and Verification UK (SVUK), which replaced and took over some of the functions of FENTO. The revised standards were known as the **QTLS standards**, and it became a requirement that all newly appointed teachers to the sector must hold a qualification which met these standards, such as an SVUK-endorsed *Certificate of Education or *Postgraduate or Professional Certificate of Education, or a teaching qualification at an appropriate level from one of the commercial awarding bodies. Following a change of government, much of the detail of these requirements was overturned, beginning with the dissolution of LLUK and SVUK in 2011. Following a period of uncertainty between this dissolution and the publication of the findings of the Lingfield Review (2012), it is now apparent that teachers for the sector will still be expected to gain a sector-specific teaching qualification and to demonstrate proficiency in communication, numeracy, and IT skills. An additional category of qualification has also been introduced: that of Associate Teacher Learning and Skills (ATLS) suitable for part-time teachers or those on fractional contracts, who are not required to gain a higher level teaching qualification.

Prior to 2001 the further education sector employed large numbers of teachers with no formal teaching qualification. This was due largely to the focus of the sector on specialized vocational training, which meant that it was the quality of the vocational skills which the teacher would be expected to pass on, for example in catering, mechanical engineering, hairdressing, or electronics, which were seen as of paramount importance, rather than the quality of their teaching. It therefore tended to be skilled craftspeople, specialist instructors, or experts with professional qualifications in their specialist vocational area who were recruited as 'teachers'. This model, of the experts passing on their skills and knowledge, was closely related to the traditional concept of *apprenticeship. Teacher training, if it took place, was usually voluntary, and was normally undertaken on a part-time, in-service basis, either within the college itself, or at a neighbouring higher education institution. When the requirement for a teaching qualification was introduced, all remaining unqualified teachers within the sector were required to undertake in-service training in order to gain their qualification, regardless of the length of their teaching experience.

The introduction of QTLS was presented at government policy level as a means of securing for further education teachers an equal status with teachers in schools.

Further Reading: Department for Education and Employment *The Learning Age: A Renaissance for a New Britain* (HMSO, 1998) sets out the original government argument for requiring all further education teachers to have a teaching qualification.

SEE WEB LINKS
• Provides further information on routes to ATLS and QTLS.

qualified teacher status (QTS) All teachers who enter the profession to teach in state *maintained schools in England and Wales are required to have achieved, or be working towards, a teaching qualification which satisfies the national *teachers' standards for qualified teacher status. There are several available routes to QTS. The most usual are full-time teacher education programmes offered by *universities and other *higher education institutions, which lead to the awards of *Bachelor of Education for non-graduate candidates, or *Postgraduate Certificate of Education or *Professional Graduate Certificate of Education for those already possessing a degree. There are also employment-based routes, which allow the teaching qualification to be gained while the candidate is teaching in a school. The standards consist of two components: Teaching, and Personal and Professional Conduct. To gain QTS, all candidates must also achieve a satisfactory score in a compulsory test of their literacy, numeracy, and *information technology skills, which is undertaken online and administrated by the *National College for Teaching and Leadership (NCTL). The current standards, introduced in 2012, replaced the QTS standards previously published by the former Teaching and Development Agency. They apply specifically to teachers in England and also in Wales with the addition of specific reference to issues in Welsh schools. *Academies, however, may employ teachers who do not hold QTS, providing such teachers can demonstrate professional competence. Teachers who hold teaching qualifications awarded outside the United Kingdom, but who wish to teach within the UK, may be required to undertake the **overseas trained teacher** route in order to gain QTS, although there is a growing movement towards establishing a system of recognition and equivalence between teaching qualifications awarded within the European Union. *See also* INITIAL TEACHER TRAINING.

( ) SEE WEB LINKS

• Provides links to detailed information about the professional skills test.
• Provides a link to the full text of the 2012 Teachers' Standards.

qualitative *See* RESEARCH.

Quality Assurance Agency for Higher Education (QAA) An independent body established in 1997 to oversee standards of provision in *higher education. It carries out audits in individual universities and other higher education institutions, examining the internal systems of quality management, as well as carrying out a review of the standards of teaching and learning in individual subject areas. Thus, the quality of both management and teaching come under scrutiny in a QAA review. This will include, but will not be restricted to, institutional and departmental systems for quality control, including the monitoring and provision of professional development for staff, the processes for ensuring the rigour and accuracy of assessment decisions, the lines of communication and control in relation to quality management, and the effectiveness of teaching provision. Thus, the QAA's overall purpose is to ensure, in the public interest, that internal quality controls are effective and fully operational in higher education. Higher education institutions undertake **internal audits** or **subject reviews** in which the QAA criteria framework is applied in order to arrive at a judgement about the quality of their own provision. The Agency is funded by higher education institutions themselves, through subscriptions, and also by contract to major funding bodies of higher education. An early application of the concept of **quality assurance** to an educational context can be found in the 1991 *White Paper *Higher Education: A New Framework*. It provides an example of the trend for importing the vocabulary of the business world into the vocabulary of education.

(⊕) SEE WEB LINKS

• Provides further details of the role of the QAA.

quantitative *See* RESEARCH.

radical educators From a historical perspective this is a 19th-century movement which arose from concerns that the education being offered to the artisan classes was little more than a process of indoctrination designed to stifle enquiry and discourage questions about the worker's place and meagre rewards. This was a debate over what constituted 'useful knowledge'; and also about what it meant to be educated, and who was empowered to define which knowledge was 'useful' and which was not. The response of the radical educators was to set up an alternative to the existing educational provision for working people. This would offer 'really useful knowledge', which provided a more *liberal education in the sense of being wide and not exclusively instrumental or work-related. Its three main thrusts, as identified by Johnson (1981), were political knowledge aimed at bringing about democratic change; social science, informed by social cooperation, secularism, and feminism; and an exploration of the questions of poverty and exploitation. Such a curriculum might even today be described as radical.

Also sometimes classed as radical educators are those teachers and theorists who take a *progressive, *learner-centred, or unconventional approach to the education of children. This category includes educationalists such as Loris *Malaguzzi, Maria *Montessori, A. S. *Neill, Johann *Pestalozzi, and Rudolph *Steiner. *See also* MECHANICS' INSTITUTES.

Further Reading: R. Johnson 'Really Useful Knowledge: Radical Education and Working Class Culture 1790–1848' in J. Clarke et al. (eds) *Working Class Culture: Studies in History and Theory* (Hutchinson, 1981).

raising of the school-leaving age (Rosla) The statutory minimum school-leaving age was raised from 15 to 16 in 1972, and the first cohort of pupils to be affected were those who reached the age of 15 in the academic year 1972/3. This change had a dramatic impact on secondary schools, and particularly those without sixth forms, who were obliged to provide pupils with a suitable curriculum for the additional year of their schooling. For some years subsequently pupils who would by choice have left school at 15 were widely referred to as 'Rosla pupils'. The idea of raising the minimum leaving age had been discussed as early as 1944 in the Education Act (*Butler Act), and had been recommended in the **Newsom Report** in 1963. Some commentators have seen more recent developments such as the *Youth Training Schemes of the 1980s and the introduction of *General National Vocational Qualifications in the 1990s as government strategies indirectly to raise the leaving age still further with the goal of keeping all young people in full-time education or training until the age of

18. Historically, the minimum school-leaving age has risen steadily, from 10 in 1880, to 11 in 1893, and to 12 in 1899. In 1918 it was raised to 14, and again to 15 in 1947. By 2013 all young people were required to stay in school, training, or workplace training until the age of 17, rising, from 2015, to 18. This does not mean that they have to remain in school or continue with an academic curriculum, but that they are required to be receiving education or training of some kind. This most recent change was not technically, therefore, a raising of the *school*-leaving age, but rather an extending of the period of education and training necessary before young people become eligible to join the workforce.

(⊕) SEE WEB LINKS

• Provides answers to questions about the school-leaving age and post-16 options for young people.

Raising Skills, Improving Life Chances A landmark *White Paper published in 2006 as part of the government's response to the *Foster Report of 2005 into *further education (FE). It confirmed the judgement, expressed in that Report, that the role and purpose of the further education sector was one of skills training. Among its proposals were four national targets for education and training, and six key areas of reform, which included, in addition to the clarification of FE's role:

• developments to meet the needs of employers and learners;
• the introduction of mandatory *continuing professional development for all teachers in the sector;
• extending the 'market' in skills training to more providers outside FE colleges;
• reforms to the funding for 14–19-year-olds' education to facilitate dual provision in school and college;
• more autonomy for colleges in relation to their funding bodies.

range The extent and depth of knowledge, skills, or understanding, and the contexts in which the learner must be able to apply these. In this specific sense, it is part of the terminology originally used in the assessment of *General National Vocational Qualifications, where elements of achievement were required to be demonstrated across a range. A **range statement** was a list of contexts in which the elements should or could be demonstrated. Reference to a range, therefore, was a means of refining and clarifying the *objectives or outcomes of the learning in order to aid the *assessor in their task.

reader 1. A title conferred in *universities and some other institutions of *higher education to acknowledge a lecturer's academic standing. In terms of seniority and status it sits between the grade of senior lecturer and the position of *professor. The bearer's full title identifies their specialist field; for example, reader in education.
  2. A textbook containing extracts of the work of one author, or of several authors on a common subject or theme. The purpose of such a volume is to provide an overview of a subject or of an author's works as an introduction for students or for a general readership.

readiness The point at which a learner is receptive to what is to be learned. This will differ from learner to learner and be dependent on a number of factors, including level of maturity, prior learning, and motivation. It is most commonly used in relation to teaching *reading, in the phrase **reading readiness**. The concept of readiness includes the notion that it may be counterproductive to coerce a child into learning before they are ready. Teachers and educationalists are by no means unanimous on this point, many arguing that readiness can be achieved through the teaching and learning process and is not a point arrived at passively simply by waiting. The idea that children go through a series of *stages which correspond with their state of readiness for certain types of learning has been underpinned in the past by reference to *Piaget's work on stages. More recently, however, this concept of development in fixed stages has been widely questioned.

reading Reading ability is tested throughout school years and was commonly recorded in terms of reading age, although it is more usual now to express competence in reading in terms of readability levels. The *Rose Report (2006) identifies five competencies in a beginner reader's 'toolkit' which they will need if they are to be able to read:

- recognition of letters (and groups of letters such as digraphs) (*st*);
- the ability to sound out phonemes (*s*);
- the ability to hear and blend phonemes (*str*);
- the reading of phonically regular words (*sat*);
- the reading of some irregular words (*she*).

These competencies, however, are part of the subject of a continuing debate about the teaching of reading and its central importance to successful schooling. Two polarized approaches to the teaching of reading are the **look–say** method, which uses a whole-word approach to recognizing and remembering words when encountered in new text, and the *phonics approach, whereby children are taught to sound out and blend specific phonemes (sounds).

Schools in England have traditionally used a variety of approaches and reading schemes (these included among others Dick and Jane, Janet and John, Initial Teaching Alphabet (ITA), Pirates, and the Oxford Reading Tree) to reinforce word recognition in familiar and sequential texts. More recently this has been succeeded by a 'real books' approach, where children could choose their own books from classified sets, and vocabulary would vary from simple to complex and small number to greater range. The disadvantage of this approach was that children had to learn new vocabulary with each chosen book and this could place some children at a distinct disadvantage if book-reading was not a common activity at home.

With the onset of the *National Literacy Strategy in 1997, a more systematic *literacy hour was adopted in *primary schools, introducing a phonics approach to the learning of reading, together with individual and shared reading, the use of a Big Book for all children to look at, and diverse activities to reinforce phoneme and word recognition.

The Rose Report suggests that 'there is much convincing evidence to show from the practice observed that, as generally understood, *"synthetic" phonics is the form of systematic phonic work that offers the vast majority of beginners the best route to becoming skilled readers' (para. 47). Under current government policy, the use of *synthetic phonics is the preferred approach to the teaching of reading in *Key Stage 1. AW

reading age *See* AGE, READING.

received pronunciation (RP) Sometimes called colloquially a 'BBC accent', RP is a standard form of pronunciation rather than a local accent, although it is generally associated with the south-east of England. At one time it was considered the most socially acceptable accent, and was encouraged in schools at the expense of regional pronunciation and dialects. It was usual, and even expected, as late as the 1970s, that television and radio announcers and newsreaders would use RP, theoretically in order to be widely understood. This hegemony is now giving way, with the result that regional accents and dialects are becoming valued for the richness they bring to the language. Now, however, rather than local accents, it is the argot and jargon of youth culture, with its 'innits' and glottal stops, for which RP is seen by some as a corrective.

reception The class into which pupils enter when first starting *primary school at the age of 5. Depending on the size of the intake and the internal organization of the school, there may be more than one reception class. The teachers responsible for these classes are known as **reception teachers**, and the first year of the pupil's schooling is sometimes referred to as their **reception year**. *See also* INFANT SCHOOL.

record of achievement *See* NATIONAL RECORD OF ACHIEVEMENT; PROGRESS FILE.

rector 1. The title given to the *head teacher of a Scottish school.
2. The rector is the third ranked official of *university governance (behind the chancellor and the principal and vice-chancellor) in the four ancient Scottish universities: Aberdeen, St Andrews, Edinburgh, and Glasgow. The post-holder is elected at regular intervals (usually every three years to enable every undergraduate completing a degree to vote at least once), and their role includes the chairing of meetings of the University Court, the governing body of the university. The election of the rector is considered by many students to be integral to their ability to shape the university's agenda and it is one of the main functions of the rector to represent the interests of the students. To some extent the office has evolved into that of a figurehead, with a trend towards celebrities being elected to the role; but there has been a resurgence of interest in recent years in the idea of electing more experienced figures in order to avoid the possibility that the status of the rector as chair of the Court might be discontinued. SM

red-brick A descriptor used to differentiate the *universities built in major cities in the 19th and early 20th centuries from the ancient universities of Oxford and Cambridge. The term came into use following the publication of a work entitled *Redbrick University* by Bruce Truscott in 1943, and is thought to have been coined by the author. The reference to 'red bricks' is intended to contrast with the historical stonework of many *Oxbridge colleges.

refereed journal *See* JOURNAL, ACADEMIC.

reflective practice Teachers can learn from their own teaching experience in order to develop their pedagogic skills by reviewing specific incidents in their professional practice and reflecting upon them in order to draw conclusions about how they might improve their own performance as teachers. This is the process known as reflective practice. Although it is closely related, in principle and purpose, to *action research, and employs the same cycle of reflection–action–reflection–planning, it is for teachers a continuing, often daily, process of self-appraisal and action planning. The reflective process might be formulated in a series of questions such as the following:

- What incident or issue in my teaching am I most concerned about?
- What might I wish to change about it, and why?
- How might this be achieved? What theories might I draw on to inform my decision?
- Did it work? If so, why? If not, why not? How does this accord with current theories?
- If it worked, is there a general principle here that I could use again?
- If it did not work, what might I try next, and why?

The ability of the teacher to reflect upon their practice in order to adapt and develop it is described by Gregorc (1973) as the 'fully functioning' phase of their professional development in which they have developed skills of self-evaluation based on self-referenced norms, and are taking responsibility for their own continuing professional development. *See also* JOURNAL, REFLECTIVE.

Further Reading: A. F. Gregorc 'Developing Plans for Professional Growth' *NASSP Bulletin* 57/377 (1973); A. Pollard *Teaching: Evidence-Informed Professional Practice* (Continuum, 2005) examines the reflective practice of teachers in schools.

Reggio Emilia An approach to the education of young children in the *pre-school and *primary phase which is based on the belief that children's learning should be unconstrained by formal *curriculum planning, but rather should allow children themselves a voice in the direction and content of their learning, in order to ensure that they find their learning meaningful. It operates on the principle that learning should involve children using all their senses; that intellectual curiosity should always be rewarded; and that they should be presented with the freedom to express themselves in as many ways as possible. At the heart of the Reggio Emilia philosophy is the belief that the relationships which are built between the child and the *educator, between the child and the world, and between the child and other children are essential to the process of learning. The relationship between the child and the teacher should not be one based on unequal power or status, but rather one in which the child is carefully listened to and respected. The approach itself takes its name from the Reggio

Emilia district of Italy, where parents rebuilding village schools in the 1940s after the ravages of the Second World War wished to establish a democratic and child-centred education for their young children which reflected the value which society should place upon its young. The first schools were built by parents and children using bricks and other materials salvaged from bombed buildings.

What began as an experimental approach soon gained momentum as the 1950s brought a migration of workers and their families from the comparative poverty of southern Italy to the more prosperous industrial north, including the district of Reggio Emilia. The care and education of children whose parents were both working outside the home was of major parental concern, and so provided added impetus to the establishment of pre-schools which were run as cooperative ventures with heavy parental involvement. Indeed, the importance of parental involvement is a central element of the Reggio Emilia approach. Parents are accorded respect as the child's initial teacher, and are involved in every aspect of the schools' provision, some acting as volunteer teachers within the school, and many maintaining the same philosophy of education in the child's home activities and general upbringing. This strong sense of continuity between the child's home life and school is a key aspect of the Reggio Emilia approach; and its emphasis on community support for young children and their families reflects the belief, embedded in Italian culture, that the welfare and well-being of its children is a primary responsibility of the state.

The Reggio Emilia approach encourages a high level of teacher autonomy. Although they are provided with extensive opportunities for professional development, teachers' professional practice is not constrained or regimented by *targets, *national curriculum standards, or *attainment tests for pupils. Instead, teachers are encouraged to set their own targets and to base their planning and teaching on the close observation of children's day-to-day individual and group needs. To this end, two teachers routinely work together with the children, one observing and noting—through photographs, video recording, and handwritten notes—children's conversation and play in order that these can be used as the starting point for developing further learning activities. This development and exploration is shared with a specialist teacher known as the *atelierista* (literally, one who works in an 'attic' or studio), who encourages the children to express themselves symbolically through artistic work, which may include drawing, painting, music, puppetry, or some other form of creative expression. Co-teaching is an essential part of Reggio teacher training. There are no professional hierarchies, however, within the school, and no differentiated salary scale. Teachers are given six non-contact hours each week in order to facilitate their tasks of documentation, project development, and liaison with parents. Parents, too, are involved in the planning and evaluation of activities. A *pedagogista* has responsibility for educational leadership of several schools, a role which involves mentoring staff, developing awareness of the theories which support their practice, and leading the collective discussions of teachers and parents from those schools as they explore ways of building upon children's enthusiasms and activities. This reflective, responsive approach, which puts the child at the centre of the educational process, is directly at odds with the concept of an externally imposed national curriculum and the implementation of mandatory and standardized attainment tests.

Since children are considered to be born with the innate ability to explore and discover the world, a typical Reggio Emilia school is designed with the purpose of facilitating the child's exploration of the environment. Indeed, the environment itself is referred to as the child's 'third teacher', the first being the parent and the second the teacher. It includes an *atelier*, or art studio, and usually further small *ateliers*, or art corners, attached to each classroom. The layout of the school is designed to echo that of a town or civic community, with an indoor *piazza*, or town square, for communal activity and socializing, off which the classrooms and eating area are situated, with no long corridors or hallways, hallmarks of an institution, for the child to negotiate. Children, therefore, can become involved with all the activities of the school, including helping with the preparation of meals and keeping the communal spaces clean. Every classroom has access to an outdoor area for exploration and play. There is also a 'welcome area', which marks the intersection between school and the wider world, and where parents and carers are encouraged to linger and to interact with teachers and each other.

A major exponent of the Reggio Emilia approach was Loris *Malaguzzi, who became involved in the building of the first schools, and was instrumental in bringing the Reggio Emilia approach to the notice of the rest of the world. Elements of the approach are applied in Scotland's early years education, and there is a movement to explore how these principles might be used more extensively.

Further Reading: L. Thornton and P. Brunton *Understanding the Reggio Approach* (David Fulton, 2005) gives a full explanation of the philosophy underpinning the Reggio Emilia approach to early years education, and how it is applied in practice;
M. Valentine *The Reggio Emilia Approach to Early Years Education* (rev. edn, Learning and Teaching Scotland, 2006) gives a clear explanation of the Reggio Emilia approach to education and explores how elements of this approach might be applied in Scotland's schools.

register 1. A record of *attendance. Teachers in schools are required to keep accurate registers, which include a record of lateness as well as of attendance and absences. These are used as a basis for identifying persistent cases of *truancy or school refusal. In *further and *higher education the keeping of an attendance register is also a requirement. Where this is done by electronic means it is known as a computerized register. This facilitates the processing of attendance, retention, and completion data in colleges, universities, and larger schools where greater numbers of registered enrolments are involved.

2. The use of language appropriate to a specific context or social situation. The uses or contexts may be broad categories, such as formal and informal; or more narrowly defined, such as undergoing an interview or dining with friends. The ability to identify or adopt a vocabulary and style of communication appropriate to the situation and context was one of the requirements implicit within the *National Literacy Strategy. The *minimum core language and literacy skills which teachers preparing for the status of *qualified teacher learning and skills are required to demonstrate include an understanding of the concept of register and its implications for student learning.

Further Reading: R. Hoggart *The Uses of Literacy* (Penguin, 1992).

registrar A senior administrative post in a college or university whose holder is responsible for student enrolment and the administration of records, including those of student completion and achievement, awards and examinations, and the business of institutional committees.

regius professor *Professorships (or **chairs**) at the *universities of Oxford and Cambridge and some Scottish universities, which were funded, or **endowed**, by the Crown and for which the Crown retains the right to nominate appointees. In practice, candidates are chosen on the advice of senior government ministers. The first such chair to be founded was that of Regius Professor of Divinity at Oxford University in the 15th century.

reliability *See* ASSESSMENT.

religious education (RE) This is a non-statutory part of the *national curriculum at all stages, which means that parents can withdraw their child from part or all of the RE offered by their school. Each school's curriculum for RE is drawn up locally, either by the individual school or by a representative body of parents, teachers, and faith groups from a number of local schools. The purpose of this is to ensure that the RE curriculum should reflect the cultural and religious background of the population from which the school draws its pupils. It is usual for RE to provide pupils with the opportunity to investigate a range of faiths and beliefs, and to explore philosophical and practical questions of values and ethics. *See also* DENOMINATION.

remedial Previously used to describe education or special classes provided as a remedy for those whose achievement was significantly below the level expected of their year group. Because it presents a *deficit model of the learner it is now considered by many to be an unacceptable term, and has been largely superseded by the concept of special education. *See also* SPECIAL EDUCATIONAL NEEDS.

remission A reduction in a teacher's hours of class contact made to allow them to undertake some other, non-teaching role. For example, a university teacher responsible for managing the recruitment of large numbers of students to a particular programme of study may have a number of teaching hours remitted from their timetable to allow them to do this.

report Schools are required to send parents or carers at least one report each academic year detailing their child's progress in *national curriculum *core subjects and, at Key Stage 2, the results of their *Standard Tasks (SATs). The report must also make clear how the pupil's SAT score compares with those of others in their age group. Parents are also informed of their child's attendance record, their attitude to learning, and their general progress. Schools may include other information, such as the results of internal examinations, or progress in subjects and activities outside the core subjects. The report forms part of the essential communication between school and home, and often suggests ways in which parents and carers can support the child in improving their performance.

research The systematic search for answers to certain questions, often using empirical evidence but also using logical arguments and reflection on social understandings. The search may aim at discovering facts, putting forward theories, increasing understanding, and/or changing practice. Both the systematic search and the conclusions drawn are then made public and are subject to critical scrutiny. The primary purpose of education research varies from **project** to project and from researcher to researcher. The different purposes are indicated in terminology: 'research on education', 'educational research', and 'educative research'. Research on education includes research carried out for academic purposes, regardless of its impact on the world of education—so-called 'blue skies' research. It may be carried out by researchers who work in *higher education departments of education but also in departments of cultural studies, history, philosophy, psychology, and sociology. Educational research is intended to improve educational practices, though sometimes over the long term. Educative research is intended to enact educative relations—for those engaged in the project and those beyond. These three kinds of research may overlap, especially the second and third. All three may be called education research.

Education research has continuities with research in other disciplines, notably the social sciences and the arts and humanities. It may also take the form of *action research and/or *reflective practice which is also found in other professions such as nursing or town planning. Within all these areas there are controversies about *epistemology and *ontology: about what there is to be known, what can be known and, therefore, what counts as data, evidence, systematic inquiry, and argument—and what kinds of conclusion can properly be drawn from them. Therefore, researchers have to be able to give a rationale for the conduct of their enquiries. This rationale is termed 'methodology'. A distinction is often made between methodology, *methods, and techniques in research. Methodology refers to the overall rationale, and depends on the view taken of ontology and epistemology. Method is the strategy undertaken to fulfil the rationale; and the term 'technique' refers to the specific research tools used, such as large-scale questionnaires, structured interviews, or video tapes.

Methodologies mirror the deep divisions found between different ontological and epistemological positions. These divisions are complex, multiple, and overlapping. They include positivist versus interpretivist, qualitative versus quantitative, and objective versus committed (feminist, social justice, anti-racist, Marxian, etc.). Further distinctions can be made between methodologies aiming at practical wisdom and those seeking theoretical understanding, or between those methodologies seeking an illumination of practice against those which want to evaluate it against criteria. Any of the interpretivist, qualitative, and/or committed methodologies may be postmodern in outlook. In this context, 'postmodernism' is an umbrella term for a number of reflexive, ironic approaches to knowledge which see it as always already imbricated with power and which are sceptical towards any universal 'grand narratives' as accounts of reason, truth, and knowledge.

A positivist approach depends on an epistemology which takes the world as made up of facts and theories which can be falsified or verified through the testing of hypotheses. The interpretivist approach takes the world as made up of social meanings constructed by human beings. These can be interpreted and understood but measurement is relatively insignificant in doing so. Not surprisingly, then, quantitative research is often assumed to be positivist because it depends on measurement and may use statistical techniques. Similarly, qualitative research which uses data such as words and pictures is often assumed to be interpretivist. But this is too simplistic. Hypotheses need not be tested using statistics; meanings can be surveyed and counted. Complicating the picture even further, with the dimension of objective versus committed, research which is feminist, Marxian, or otherwise committed, etc. may also be quantitative or qualitative, positivist or interpretivist. Similarly for research which is aiming at objectivity. Moreover, some of these techniques and methods can be carried using a postmodern approach. Postmodern methodologies are particularly relaxed about combining different methods and techniques, viewing each one as giving only partial and provisional knowledge. The result of such combinations is sometimes called **bricolage**.

Educational research is carried out at all levels of the education system and it serves a number of practical purposes, ranging from investigations of practice in a single classroom, as, for instance, in some action research, to projects intended to inform national policy. At every level, the research may be driven by the educational commitments of individual researchers. They may be self-funded, or funded through their own institution or through **grants** from national research councils, especially the *Economic and Social Research Council. Alternatively, the research may be commissioned or facilitated by institutions including national and local government, charities, unions, and quangos who want to make use of the answers for their own purposes.

The roles of the researchers vary. They may be teachers or academics. They may be independent consultants or employed by local or central government. They may be students working for first degrees, diplomas, masters', or doctorates. Quite often they may be more than one of these at the same time since educational research is typically carried out by people with knowledge and experience of practice and policy, often some time after their initial period of full-time education is over.

Research is made public in different ways depending on its purpose and on its intended audience. Research reports can be found in learned journals aiming at a primarily academic audience. Professional magazines and newspapers publish reports aimed at practitioners, policy-makers, and the general public. Research reports are also presented to commissioning bodies, which sometimes make them available to a wider public. All of these forms of reporting are increasingly found on the World Wide Web. Research is also reported orally at seminars, conferences, in-service days, and public meetings. Occasionally, research is published in creative ways, for instance, using drama or an installation.

Issues of ethics are key in all education research. There are two aspects to this: moral virtue and intellectual virtue. Firstly, education is inescapably concerned with human beings, so researchers are necessarily involved in social relationships in which moral virtues are relevant. An example is found in the ethical requirement to obtain informed consent from participants. However, cases exist where the requirement should be disregarded. Either way, the judgement is an ethical one. Equally, the judgement about what counts as 'informed consent' is an ethical one. Secondly, education is bound up with strongly held opinions, and is used by interested parties to influence policy and practice. So intellectual virtues such as honesty, careful attention to evidence and argument, and open-mindedness are crucial in high-quality education research.   MG

( ) SEE WEB LINKS
• Full text of the Revised Ethical Guidelines for Educational Research (2011) (British Educational Research Association).

Research Excellence Framework (REF) An evaluation of the *research and publications carried out in institutions of *higher education, which is undertaken every four years in order to determine the level of funding which will be awarded. It is conducted jointly by the *Higher Education Funding Council for England, the *Scottish Funding Council, the *Higher Education Funding Council for Wales, and the Department for Employment and Learning, Northern Ireland. The assessment for each academic field is made by a specialist sub-panel. The research and publications of each department or faculty within the institution are scrutinized and evaluated against criteria set by the funding body. These include such factors as impact and scope. Each department, therefore, must decide which of its staff to enter for the exercise in order to gain as high a score as possible. Those departments or faculties whose score falls below a predetermined level will receive no government funding for research for the following four years. The quest for a high REF rating will often influence decisions about academic appointments, as applicants with a lengthy and prestigious list of publications to their name will be much sought after. Some academics have suggested that the REF is flawed in that it perpetuates inequalities of status between pre- and post-1992 universities. Since the emphasis in many of the latter has been on teaching rather than on research, some, it is claimed, are hampered in building up a sound research base as the most able researchers are drawn to posts where funding for research is assured. *See also* JOURNAL, ACADEMIC.

( ) SEE WEB LINKS
• Provides information about the process of the exercise and the criteria used.

research fellow A post in a *university or other *higher education institution which is held on a short-term rather than permanent contract and is created specifically to enable the holder to carry out *research into a named field or topic. Such a post is often sponsored or funded by external bodies, and widely advertised.

research grant *See* RESEARCH.

research project *See* RESEARCH.

revenue support grant (RSG) The money devolved from central
government to *local authorities each year to subsidize the services which the
authority is responsible for providing. These include primary and secondary
education. At the end of each calendar year the government issues a standard
spending assessment (SSA) to all local authorities for the distribution of the RSG,
which encapsulates the government's view of what the authority needs to expend
to deliver a standard level of service. This includes an SSA specifically for
expenditure on education within the authority. The revenue support grant was
formerly known as the rate support grant.

review An inspection by the *Quality Assurance Agency of *higher education
provision is euphemistically termed a 'review'.

reward *See* MOTIVATION.

rising fives Children who start school before the statutory age for doing so,
either a term or more before they reach their fifth birthday, or at the beginning of
the term in which their fifth birthday will fall. A policy of admitting rising fives to a
*reception class is therefore often one involving admissions each term (rather
than only once a year) to *primary school. This practice has been widespread in
England for many years, but has been recently under review. *Local authorities
are currently required to ensure that all children receive schooling from the start
of the term *following* their fifth birthday.

Robbins Report (1963) The Report of the Committee on Higher Education,
chaired by Lord Robbins (1898–1984) between 1961 and 1964. The Report
recommended an expansion in *university provision to allow all suitably
qualified candidates an opportunity for *higher education should they wish it.
It proposed this be initiated by the founding of six new universities and by raising
a number of existing colleges to university status. It also suggested raising the
status of teacher training colleges by encouraging partnerships with universities
and introducing a teaching qualification with degree status. Such colleges were
to be renamed *colleges of education. Within 24 hours of the Report's
publication, the government issued a *White Paper supporting many of its
recommendations. Some recommendations, however, such as the suggestion
that undergraduate degree courses be extended from three to four years and
broadened in scope, did not find wide support. The success of the
recommendations was reflected in the rapid expansion of university provision
in the decade between 1965 and 1975. The Robbins Report has played a major
role in shaping higher education provision as it exists today.

Rogers, Carl (1902–87) An American psychologist who wrote extensively
about the psychology of learning. He discarded the term 'teacher' and used
instead 'facilitator' in order both to stress the centrality of the learner in the
learning process, and to argue against the formation of the traditional power

relationship which assumes a higher status for the teacher in relation to the learner. Instead, he presented the learning process as one which is to the mutual benefit of both the learner and the facilitator of learning, arguing that 'the facilitation of significant learning rests upon certain attitudinal qualities which exist in the personal relationship between the facilitator and the learner' (Rogers 1983: 121). In claiming that a relationship of trust and respect is essential to successful learning, Rogers also argued that the facilitator–teacher should demonstrate an 'unconditional positive regard' for the learner. In other words, the teacher's attitude should be non-judgemental and accepting; and the learner should be made to feel valued and cared for. This is often cited as epitomizing the extreme application of *humanist learning theory. It was Rogers's belief that all organisms have a tendency towards 'actualization', the development of its full potential. In educational terms this suggests that the teacher's role is to facilitate the learner's progress towards this goal, rather than to deliver an externally imposed standard curriculum.

Further Reading: C. Rogers *Freedom to Learn for the 80s* (Merrill, 1983).

Rose Report (2006) The Rose Report on the teaching of reading skills in *primary schools identified five competencies which children should be able to demonstrate before they can progress to the successful acquisition of reading skills. These are:

- recognition of letters (and groups of letters such as digraphs) (*st*);
- the ability to sound out phonemes (*s*);
- the ability to hear and blend phonemes (*str*);
- the reading of phonically regular words (*sat*);
- the reading of some irregular words (*she*).

As well as stressing the importance of 'pre-reading skills' acquisition, the Report, whose full title was *An Independent Review of the Teaching of Early Reading*, was instrumental in encouraging the use of *synthetic phonics as the most effective approach to the teaching of reading to young pupils, suggesting that '"synthetic" phonics is the form of systematic phonic work that offers the vast majority of beginners the best route to becoming skilled readers' (para. 47).

(⊕) SEE WEB LINKS
- The full text of the Rose Report on reading.

rote learning Learning which does not necessitate understanding, but is undertaken systematically and mechanistically, usually through repetition. Examples might be the chanting of multiplication tables, or the reciting of passages learned 'by heart' but with no accurate comprehension of content. Such activities were an integral part of education in the 19th and early 20th centuries, but find little acceptance today. To learn something by rote implies an *intention* to learn which is not present when, for example, the lyrics of a song or the sequence of numbers for a telephone call become committed to memory through repeated exposure or frequent use. *See also* DEEP LEARNING; MEMORY.

Rousseau, Jean-Jacques (1712–78) A Swiss philosopher who became known as an educational theorist, setting out his ideas in a semi-fictional work, *Émile; or, On Education* (1762). Rousseau was interested in the idea of humans being able to live and learn more fully in a natural environment. The three *cognitive stages he identified were pre-12 years (survival), 12–16 years (reasoning and development of complex thought), and post-16 (adulthood); and he argued that each of these could be reached and more fully realized away from the artificial constraints of 'civilized' society. He claimed that virtue could be nourished through simple activity and gradual participation in society at the child's own pace; and argued that society and human nature were incompatible. His emphasis on protecting the 'innocence' of children reflects the Romantic notions of the philosopher John Locke (1632–1704) which were also to be found later in the work of the poet and mystic William Blake (1757–1827). He saw the *teacher as a facilitator, supporting an education appropriate to each stage of a child's development. In this sense he was an early exponent of individualized or *personalized learning. His approach was *child-centred, in the sense that he claimed a *curriculum should follow a child's own path of enquiry which might be very much like that of his eponymous character Émile, wandering through the countryside, becoming interested in the smells, sights, sounds, and textures of encountered objects and the simple responses a child makes. Rousseau recommended that a child's emotions should be educated before their reason, placing an emphasis on experience.

John Darling, in his book *Child-Centred Education and its Critics* (1994), argues that the history of modern educational theory can be traced back to Rousseau's theories. In practice, Rousseau's ideas to some extent resonate with current *early years *pedagogy. His notion that children could not calculate or demonstrate complex thinking before the age of 12 may reflect his own childhood education of solitude and self-learning, having been abandoned by his father when he was 10, after his mother died shortly after childbirth. Rousseau's ideas about education and child-rearing appear to conflict with his own practice as a parent, as he was not confident of his own fatherhood skills and gave up his five children to a foundling hospital, where he felt they would lead a more beneficial life. AW

Royal Society of Arts (RSA) *See* OCR.

rubric The written instructions provided for candidates as part of an *examination or test. It is now more colloquially referred to as **exam terminology**, and the ability to read it carefully and understand it accurately is an aspect of examination technique which teachers may formally cover with pupils prior to examinations.

Ruskin speech *See* GREAT DEBATE.

sabbatical A period of leave, with full pay, for the purpose of undertaking research or a course of study, or to write for publication. This arrangement is rarely available now outside *higher education; and even within that sector it is less common in some institutions than others. The original meaning conveyed by the word is of something which occurs every seven years, although current practice is much more variable. In the 1960s and 1970s it was not unusual for teachers in schools to be granted year-long sabbaticals, funded by their *local authority, to undertake professional development activity such as, for non-graduates, the gaining of a degree. More recently, secondments for teachers in any sector in the UK have become comparatively rare. However, in some Australian universities secondments from teaching duties are routinely available for academic staff with a proven track record of publications, to allow them to pursue their research projects. *See also* CONTINUING PROFESSIONAL DEVELOPMENT.

sanction Used in preference to the term 'punishment' to refer to measures taken by an institution or individual teacher in response to non-compliant or unacceptable *behaviour by learners. This includes the withholding of rewards or privileges, or more direct measures such as *detention. The imposition of sanctions and the giving of rewards are part of the behaviour management approach to classroom control.

sandwich course A course of study which involves a period of time, often a year, spent gaining practical experience in applying, and observing the practice of, the subject being learned. The practical experience constitutes the filling in the metaphorical sandwich, being preceded and followed by a period of study at the learner's college or university. Thus, an undergraduate degree which is taught as a sandwich course will normally take four years rather than the usual three, as the second or third year will be spent working outside the institution. An example of this might be a degree course in a modern language, where a year is spent abroad in the relevant country, improving the learner's language skills. Another would be a degree course in engineering which included a year spent working within the industry. Such an arrangement is distinct from a course involving *work experience, such as *initial teacher training, which normally runs concurrently with, or for limited periods between, studies in the institution.

schema As understood in current early childhood *pedagogy, a schema is 'a pattern of repeatable behaviour into which experiences are assimilated and that are generally co-ordinated' (Athey 1990). *Piaget first identified repeated behaviours as skills, which, once assimilated, are transferred to other activities and adapted, if necessary, to satisfy a child's drive to learn and succeed. An example of this might be the action of a push-button mechanism which activates sound or pictures. Once the child has learned this behaviour, this will be repeated when the child is offered the opportunity to interact with more sophisticated mechanisms. AW

Further Reading: C. Athey *Extending Thought in Young Children: A Parent–Teacher Partnership* (PCP, 1990) identifies commonly observed schema characteristics.

scheme of work A plan setting out how the *programme of study (PoS), *syllabus, or *curriculum will be translated into teaching and learning activities, including the sequencing of content, the amount of time spent on each topic, and how the specified learning *objectives will be assessed. Some schemes of work are drawn up centrally, such as those which provide teachers with a template for translating *national curriculum programmes of study into a series of *lesson plans. Others may be drawn up by teachers themselves, as is the case in many courses of *further and *higher education, where the creation of the scheme of work forms part of the planning process for the department, team, or the individual teacher.

scholarly activity In some *universities and *higher education institutions, teachers' conditions of service require that they be allowed a proportion of their working hours for scholarly activity, which may include research, reading, or writing.

scholarship 1. A high level of academic learning and skill in a recognized academic *discipline or field.

2. An award which may be offered to chosen students of exceptional ability who are seeking entry to a selective school or an institution of *higher education, and who have successfully passed an examination or interview conducted for the purpose of identifying worthy candidates.

3. A colloquial term at one time used for the *Eleven Plus examination.

school 1. Institution in which pupils are taught. These may be identified according to the age of the pupils: *pre-schools or *nursery schools, *infant schools, and *junior schools (collectively termed *primary schools), and secondary schools; or, in some local authorities, pre-schools or nursery schools, *first, *middle, and secondary schools. They may also be identified according to whether they are *maintained (state) schools, *academies, or *public (private, fee-charging) schools; and whether they are selective (operate a process of *selection over pupil enrolment) or non-selective. Secondary schools may be designated *grammar schools or *comprehensive schools. Schools which are supported by recognized religious organizations are known as *faith or *denominational schools; and those with sponsorship from industry and commerce are called trust schools. Further categories are those of *special schools for pupils with *special educational needs, and *specialist schools, where there is an emphasis on a specific aspect of the *national curriculum, such as *information communication technology.

2. A subdivision of a college or university, roughly equivalent to a department, as in 'the School of Education'.

3. At Oxford University it can refer to a course leading to a *first degree, and to all those who work within that subject.

school adjudicator Under section 25 of the School Standards and Framework Act 1998, the admissions procedures of *maintained schools are subject to the scrutiny and ruling of adjudicators appointed by the *Secretary of State. Since 2007 the adjudicators may also direct schools to admit a pupil who has been excluded from, or refused admission by, every suitable school locally; and to direct the admission of *looked-after children. They do not, however, act on complaints from individual parents about allocation of school places or parental choice of schools.

(((⊕))) SEE WEB LINKS
• Provides details of adjudicators' main functions.

school admissions Despite the growing emphasis over the last quarter of the 20th century on the element of parental *choice in their child's schooling, admission to the first school of choice is not always possible if the school chosen is oversubscribed. Schools are required to have an admission policy which is both public and transparent, making clear the criteria which will be applied when selecting pupils for admission. Parental appeals against schools' admission decisions have risen sharply since the policy of parental choice replaced the previous system operated by *local authorities of allotting a catchment area to each school so that the choice of schools, in non-selective systems, was limited and determined by where pupils lived. *Admissions appeals can be made by parents against a school's decision not to admit their child.

school boards Set up in Scotland through the School Boards (Scotland) Act 1998, these provided a forum for parental representation in Scottish schools. In August 2007 they were replaced by *parent councils.   SM

School Certificate From 1917 the School Certificate was the national school-leaving qualification, taken at the age of 16 and requiring passes in five subjects. It was replaced by the *General Certificate of Education *Ordinary Level in 1951.

school development plan *See* SCHOOL IMPROVEMENT PLAN.

School Direct A training programme providing a school-based training route for graduates to *qualified teacher status, set up in 2013 to replace the *Graduate Teacher Programme. It is a one-year programme of teaching experience in an approved primary or secondary school which may also include a *Postgraduate Certificate of Education Qualification. It offers two routes: one in which the trainee must pay fees but may be eligible for financial support in the form of a bursary or scholarship; or alternatively a salaried route aimed at high-quality graduates who have at least three years of relevant work experience.

(⊕) SEE WEB LINKS
• Provides links to detailed information about both routes.

school improvement plan Most schools produce this annual plan, sometimes called the **school development plan**, although it is no longer obligatory. They do so drawing upon and linking to their most recent *inspection findings and recommendations and their own self-evaluation. It sets out strategies to improve key aspects of the school's performance such as teaching and learning, school management, attendance, safety, and provision for pupils with *special educational needs. The plan is subject to a formal review annually by the school's governing body.

school-leaving age *See* RAISING OF THE SCHOOL-LEAVING AGE.

school meals The *Education Act 1944 (*Butler Act) required all *local authorities to operate a school meals service to provide a midday meal in all schools, for which parents of pupils were charged a nominal weekly sum. This requirement was withdrawn by the Education Act 1980, as was the requirement that school meals meet a minimum nutritional standard, although meals for pupils whose families were on low incomes and in receipt of benefits continued to be provided free of charge. In line with the policy of introducing market competition into all aspects of public life, school meals services were put out by local authorities to tender. This led to what was widely recognized as a decline in nutritional standards. This was addressed in the School Standards and Framework Act 1998, which empowered the *Secretary of State to regulate minimum nutritional standards. These standards were put in place in 2002. Nevertheless, the continuing poor nutritional quality of some school meals was subsequently brought to public attention by a campaign conducted by the celebrity chef Jamie Oliver (b. 1975), who has been credited in some quarters with securing thereby an increase in government funding to ensure that minimum standards of nutrition can be met. It was proposed, subsequently, that local authorities should arrange for all children in infant schools (age 5 to 7) to be offered a free cooked lunch at school from September 2014.

(⊕) SEE WEB LINKS
• Discusses the policy announcement of free school lunches for infant pupils.

school profile Prior to the 2011 Education Act, one of the responsibilities of the governing body of a school was to publish online a school profile, which was designed to communicate with parents about the school's progress, priorities, and performance as measured against its *targets. This means of communicating progress against targets replaced the previous requirement on *governing bodies to produce an annual report to parents following the *Education Act 2005.

school record *Maintained schools are required to keep records of pupils' academic achievements and progress, including results of *national curriculum attainment levels at the end of *Key Stages 1, 2, and 3. The record for each pupil accompanies them through their compulsory schooling, passing from teacher

to teacher in the *primary phase, and from school to school as they progress
through the system or move to a different area. Under the provisions of the Data
Protection Act 1998, pupils and parents are entitled to see what is recorded in the
pupil's record. Most school records are now kept in electronic form.

school refuser *See* TRUANCY.

school report *See* REPORT.

Scotland, education in To an external observer, there would be nothing
particularly distinctive about the structure of Scottish education, at least by
comparison with that in other developed countries. Distinctiveness lies in
interpretation.

The period of compulsory education lasts from 5 to 16. The primary stage
occupies the first seven years of this, after which pupils transfer to secondary,
which lasts four to six years. Most of this takes place in public institutions
(nineteen out of twenty pupils), entry to which is not based on any formal
measures of intelligence: the remainder attend private schools which charge fees
and, at the secondary stage, are nearly all *selective. This structure of primary
schooling was laid down in the last few decades of the 19th century; the pattern of
secondaries emerged between the 1930s and the 1960s.

At each end of the period of schooling, Scotland has been participating
recently in the international movement towards extending the period of
attendance. The proportion of 4-year-olds in *nursery school rose from under
10 per cent in the early 1970s to over 95 per cent by the late 1990s. From ages 16
to 18, a growing proportion of pupils have chosen to remain in full-time
education—an increase from around one-third in the early 1970s to
three-quarters in 2008. Nearly all of that is at school: only about one in twenty
of the age group spends this period in college.

Upon leaving school, around one in three enters full-time *higher education,
and about one in four a full-time course of *vocational education. By age 21, the
rate of participation in higher education has risen to around one-half, because
many of those who take the vocational route use it to enter advanced courses.
Fewer than one in ten of the higher education students leave Scotland for this
study. The remainder attend institutions in two formally differentiated sectors.
One is based in the same colleges as provide vocational non-advanced courses,
and accounts for about 24 per cent of undergraduate students in higher
education, attending one-year and two-year mainly vocational courses. The
remainder mostly take four years to obtain a *degree, attending 21 higher
education institutions. These institutions are formally equal, but in
practice—through reputation based on historical legacies—divide into three
sub-sectors: universities created in the early 1990s from former technological
colleges (about 27 per cent of all undergraduate higher education students);
four *universities founded in the 1960s, three of them also based on older
technological colleges (18 per cent), and four universities which date from the
15th and 16th centuries (30 per cent). These types of higher education institution
differ in prestige, in entry requirements, in the balance of their courses between

*academic and vocational and between arts (or social science) and science (or technology), and in the amount of research which their staff carry out: broadly, the older the institution, the less dominated by applied science, the higher the entry requirements, and the more *research.

Since the 1960s there has been a massive rise in the proportion of the age group taking externally assessed *examinations in the last three years of secondary school, from one in four to almost all. Attainment in these examinations has been steadily rising, and this has encouraged school-leavers to stay on beyond the compulsory stage and to enter post-school courses. Part of the explanation of rising *attainment has been the rising aspirations of girls: by the late 1970s they had overtaken boys in attainment at the end of secondary schooling, and by the 1990s also in their rate of entry to higher education. Something the same has been true of people of various immigrant origins—Ireland and central Europe in the 19th and early 20th centuries, Asia and others parts of the former British empire in the second half of the 20th: their attainment and participation has risen and overtaken, as a proportion, that of the majority. There has also, since the 1990s, been some narrowing of *social class inequalities in attainment and participation. But all this equalization provides only part of the explanation of rising participation: all social groups have taken part to unprecedented extents in this educational revolution.

Nevertheless, if this structural account might seem familiar to an observer, the meanings attached indigenously are distinctive, as they are in any country, and they derive from history. The key feature of current interpretations of education in Scotland is uniformity. The secondary and primary sectors have standardized *curriculums, and the strength of the consensus around them is one reason why this is not imposed by law. The curriculum is broad, requiring pupils up to age 14 to study English, mathematics, science, social science, art, music, and religion, and to engage in physical exercise. Most of this breadth is maintained to age 16. There is uniformity also in the dominance of the public schools, non-selective and less socially segregated than most systems in developed societies (despite open enrolment since 1981); the association of about one in six of them with religious denominations (mainly the Roman Catholic Church) relates only to their general ethos, not, except in a few topics such as religious and moral education, to details of the curriculum or *assessment, and so represents a less strongly religious sector than in many other countries. And there is uniformity from the teachers themselves, over nine out of ten of whom have been educated in the quite small and homogeneous Scottish system of higher education.

The preference for uniformity is extending now to higher education. When the new Scottish Parliament took responsibility for Scottish education in 1999, one of its most prominent early acts was to abolish fees charged to undergraduates at the outset of a course. (They were replaced by, in effect, a graduate tax, the proceeds from which are used to subsidize *bursaries.) The state agency which funds higher and *further education has resisted pressure to concentrate research funding in only a few international centres, preferring research networks. Higher education remains predominantly public, in its governance (through legal regulation) and in its funding (more than 60 per cent from public funds).

These current predilections for a largely uniform, mainly public system were consolidated in the middle of the 20th century, when the consensus was established that the Scottish way of reconciling merit selection and equity was to favour individual selection within common institutions. Thus, there would be mostly common schooling—to avoid the exacerbation of invidious social distinctions by institutional boundaries—but increasing amounts of formal *certification within them. In practice, then, social distinctions that remain are those created in society rather than those created by structures of educational provision: *gender or social class distinctions operate much more within schools than between them.

That mid-century settlement built upon the previous main wave of reform in the first few decades of the century. It responded to the international movement for universal secondary schooling by creating a single dominant concept of Scottish secondary education. That idea was firmly academic. It was the characteristic preparation required by the new professional classes, centred on literary studies and mathematics, including science and foreign languages, but only for a minority Latin. It became, in the 1920s, the curriculum not only of the older secondary schools inherited from the 19th century, but also of the much larger number of new secondaries created by public authorities before the First World War to cater mainly for the lower-middle class and the skilled working class. The curriculum was shaped by the *Scottish Leaving Certificate, which is the direct ancestor of today's school examinations; its credibility was strengthened by the even greater homogeneity of teacher culture then than today. Even in the 1930s, this senior secondary course catered for fewer than one-third of pupils, and only about one in twenty passed the full Certificate; but, over the next two decades, its dominant prestige came to subsume all attempts by policy-makers to create diverse tracks for the remainder. The merit-selective democracy of this process was aided by the absence in Scotland of anything like the dominant elite institutions found elsewhere.

These structures in turn drew upon a much older tradition of highly competitive but systematically public provision, dating ultimately to the Reformation, consolidated for universal elementary schooling in a key 1696 Act of the old Scottish Parliament, and renovated for it in 1872 and for the universities in Acts of 1858 and 1889. This tradition was not democratic in any 21st-century sense of the term; but it left three key legacies: it was public, it believed that open competition was the only way of reconciling excellence with equal human worth, and it venerated the academic.

Scottish debates about structures of education today cannot help being shaped by these predecessors. The Scottish Parliament has inaugurated unprecedented inquiry into the role of curricular breadth and standardization, academic learning, examinations, and public accountability. Reform of some sort is inevitable. But the attachment to uniformity, to public control, and to a singularly academic interpretation of worthwhile learning is not likely to wither readily.   LP

History

During the medieval period, education in Scotland followed the pattern of European schooling, with the Roman Catholic Church organizing schooling.

Church schools and grammar schools were founded in major towns, and in 1496 an Education Act introduced compulsory schooling for the eldest sons of nobles. The foundation of the universities of St Andrews in 1413, Glasgow in 1451, and Aberdeen in 1495 led an era of Enlightenment in education. The Protestant Reformation made literacy important as the means through which true believers could achieve spiritual enlightenment, and in 1616 the Privy Council commanded that every parish in Scotland should have a school (by the end of the 18th century this had been achieved in the majority of parishes). By the end of the 17th century a considerable proportion of the population was literate and the education system was more advanced than that in England and other European countries. The 18th century was a 'golden age' for Scottish education, contributing to advancement in intellectual enlightenment and the industrial revolution. Scottish universities attracted students from other parts of the country who were unable to study certain subject areas in Oxford and Cambridge universities owing to the more traditional nature of the courses available: this could be seen particularly in the field of medicine, where Scottish universities gained a better reputation. In 1872 education in Scotland became compulsory for all children between the ages of 5 and 13, and by 1888 the Leaving Certificate had been introduced and the leaving age raised to 14. The Leaving Certificate was replaced in 1962 by the Scottish Certificate of Education, and by the introduction of *Ordinary Grades (later replaced by *Standard Grades in the early 1990s) and *Highers. Corporal punishment was abolished in 1986. In 1999 the new Scottish Executive set up an Education Department and an Enterprise, Transport, and Lifelong Learning Department, which together took over the work of the Scottish Education Department. Currently, the Scottish curriculum is undergoing review and reform under the *Curriculum for Excellence initiative begun in 2004 which aims to create a single, coherent curriculum for children aged 3–18. In addition, the *McCrone Report of 2000 has had wide-ranging implications for and effect upon the conditions of teachers within the education system.

Structure

Scotland offers all 3- and 4-year-olds free nursery education. Primary education, for children aged 5–12, follows a national curriculum. The curriculum studied between the ages of 5 and 16 is broad, requiring study of English, mathematics, science, social science, art, music, and religion, as well as engagement in some form of physical activity. In addition, students may have access to qualifications in Scottish Gaelic. Indeed, more than 60 primary schools now teach Gaelic, the majority of these being located in the highlands or islands of Scotland. The curriculum is not set by law but has flexibility based upon the guidelines set by *Learning and Teaching Scotland under the aegis of the Scottish Parliament. There is no external testing for pupils in primary education; instead pupil attainment between the ages of 5 and 14 is assessed by teachers through the process of national assessment. Secondary education in Scotland begins for pupils at the age of 11 or 12 and runs for a compulsory four years, with two final years being optional. Pupils sit Standard Grade exams at the end of the fourth year of study. They will usually study between seven and nine subjects, and may choose to remain for another one or two years to study for **Access**, **Intermediate**, or Higher Grade exams in Year 5, after which they may go on to

study for *Advanced Highers in Year 6, the qualifications necessary for access to a
Scottish university.

The traditional four-year undergraduate courses allow for a broad first year
curriculum with an in-depth focus from the second year, and lead to a *master's
degree, although recently some Scottish universities have begun to offer alternative
three-year courses leading to a *bachelor's degree. In 1999 the Scottish Executive
abolished tuition fees for Scottish students. Instead students pay a one-off
Graduate Endowment at the end of their course. Scottish students who wish to
attend a university elsewhere in the UK will usually remain at school for a sixth
year, completing the Advanced Higher—equivalent to the original sixth year study
or an English *Advanced Level. Further education is provided at colleges or
schools. Students may accumulate *National Units, which can be combined to
build a *National Qualification. Many full-time National Qualification college
courses are made up of groupings of National Units. Currently, under the direction
of the Scottish Parliament, Scottish education is undergoing extensive reform,
with the focus on the development of the Curriculum for Excellence initiative,
with the goal of providing a more coherent and inclusive education for all
which is linked with an emphasis on *lifelong learning.   SM

Scottish Certificate of Education This replaced the *Scottish Leaving
Certificate in 1962.   SM

Scottish Credit Accumulation and Transfer (SCOTCAT) A framework
designed to make it easier for students to transfer educational *credit between
Scottish institutions of higher education by setting out equivalence and
comparisons between qualifications as measured by SCOTCAT points. This
function is now part of the role of the *Scottish Credit and Qualifications
Framework.   SM

Scottish Credit and Qualifications Framework (SCQF) A framework
which aims to help learners, employers, and providers of learning to see clearly
how Scottish learning programmes and qualifications relate to each other in
terms of level. In the SCQF there are twelve levels, ranging from level 1 (Access 1)
to level 12, which is associated with postgraduate doctoral studies. *See also*
NATIONAL QUALIFICATIONS FRAMEWORK.   SM

(⊕) SEE WEB LINKS
• Provides an interactive diagram showing where qualifications sit within the SCQF.

Scottish Enterprise, Highlands and Islands Enterprise Scottish
Enterprise is Scotland's main economic development agency, funded by the
Scottish government. This agency aims to develop Scotland's economic potential
through supporting business development. The agency works with companies and
individuals, as well as with *universities, *colleges, *local authorities, and other
public sector bodies to achieve these goals. The Highlands and Islands Enterprise
fulfils the same purpose in the highlands and islands of Scotland.   SM

(⊕) SEE WEB LINKS
• Provides details of the aims and activities of Scottish Enterprise.
• Provides details of the aims and activities of the Highlands and Islands Enterprise.

Scottish Funding Council (SFC) The SFC allocates resources for teaching and learning, as well as for research and other activities in Scotland's colleges and universities, in support of the Scottish government's priorities for education. *See also* HIGHER EDUCATION FUNDING COUNCIL FOR ENGLAND.　SM

Scottish Group Award (SGA) The SGA consists of a number of courses and units which fit together to make a coherent *programme of study for older pupils and students. Group Awards are available at all five levels of study within *Higher Still (from Access level 2 to *Advanced Higher). A Group Award can be gained in one year of full-time study or built up over a longer period of time. Awards are made up of courses, *units, and external assessments combined to form a group which is recognized by employers, colleges, universities, and other providers of education and training. There are two types of SGA: **General Awards**, which do not specify mandatory subject content but do have set requirements in terms of the number of courses, units, and core skills which must be included; and **Named Awards**, which do specify certain subject requirements as well as a set number of courses, units, and core skills.　SM

(⊕)) SEE WEB LINKS
• Provides further details about the Scottish Group Awards.

Scottish Leaving Certificate Established in 1886, the Leaving Certificate was awarded to students leaving secondary school in Scotland who achieved a minimum standard of proficiency in education. This was replaced by the Scottish Certificate of Education in 1962.　SM

Scottish Negotiating Committee for Teachers (SNCT) Introduced in 2001, SNCT is a tripartite body comprising members from teaching organizations, *local authorities, and the Scottish government, which oversees the implementation of the new conditions of service and pay laid down in the 2001 document *A Teaching Profession for the 21st Century*.　SM

(⊕)) SEE WEB LINKS
• Provides details of the SNCT's role.

Scottish Progression Award (SPA) A vocational qualification which recognizes and accredits the skills and knowledge used in the workplace. SPAs are designed to provide basic skills which will be attractive to employers and which candidates can build upon when working towards achieving a full Scottish Vocational Qualification (SVQ). However, unlike SVQs, there is no requirement to produce evidence from the workplace. Students can receive accreditation through college, school, or training.　SM

(⊕)) SEE WEB LINKS
• Provides an outline of this qualification and details of the subject areas in which it is currently available.

Scottish Qualification for Headship (SQH) First piloted in 1998, the SQH is the qualification required of those wishing to achieve headship of schools in

Scotland. It is equivalent to the English *National Professional Qualification for Headship. *See also* HEADSHIP DEVELOPMENT.   SM

Scottish Qualifications Authority (SQA) Established in 1997, the SQA is an executive non-departmental public body sponsored by the Scottish government Education Department. It is the national body in Scotland responsible for the development, *accreditation, *assessment, and *certification of qualifications other than degrees, including *vocational qualifications. As well as its accreditation role in relation to qualifications, it is also responsible for approving the bodies which award them.

SEE WEB LINKS
• Provides further details about the organization and the function of SQA.

Scottish Qualifications Certificate (SQC) Awarded to all students in Scotland on successful completion of courses, providing details of all *units gained and the marks awarded.   SM

Scottish Vocational Qualification (SVQ) Vocational qualifications awarded in Scotland. They are equivalent to *National Vocational Qualifications in England and Wales.   SM

Secondary Heads Association (SHA) An association for *head teachers of both *maintained and *independent schools, formed in 1976 from an amalgamation of the Headmasters' Association and the Association of Headmistresses. *See also* TEACHERS' UNIONS.

secondary modern school *See* TRIPARTITE SYSTEM.

second marking The *assessment of a piece of student work by two teachers in order to ensure that the mark or grade awarded is accurate and reliable. It is a process which is most valuable when the assessment method is vulnerable to some degree of subjectivity on the part of the marker; for example, in the assessment of essay-style answers or longer pieces of student work such as written *assignments and *dissertations. The second marking may be carried out as 'blind' marking, which means that neither teacher sees the comments or assessment decision of the other prior to arriving at their own decision. Alternatively, the second marker may have access to the first marker's comments and the grade or mark awarded. Second marking, or double marking, is an important feature of assessment in courses where the student outcome depends wholly or heavily on *continuous assessment. *See also* MODERATION.

secondment The release of a teacher from their normal post for a limited period in order to allow them to take up a temporary post elsewhere, often to advise on good practice; or to undertake a relevant course of study or professional development. *See also* SABBATICAL.

Secretary of State for Education The member or members of the Cabinet responsible for the development and implementation of national education policy take their title from the government department to which they are appointed head. In 1964, when the Department of Education and Science (DES) was created, it was headed by the Secretary of State for Education and Science. The reorganization of the department in 1993 led to a change in title, with the DES becoming the Department for Education and the minister responsible known as the Secretary of State for Education. The merging of the DES and the Employment Department in 1995 necessitated a further change of title to Secretary of State for Education and Employment, heading the Department for Education and Employment. In 2001 the government department underwent a further change of name, becoming the Department for Education and Skills (DfES) and headed by the Secretary of State for Education and Skills. In 2007 the DfES was replaced by two new government departments, each headed by their own secretary of state: the Department for Children, Schools, and Families, and the Department for Innovation, Universities, and Skills. The latter became part of the new Department for Business, Innovation, and Skills in 2009, while the former was replaced by the Department for Education in 2010.

The repeated changes in title, both of department and of minister responsible, have to some extent reflected governments' priorities and policies in education over the decades. In summary, then, the titles of secretaries of state responsible for education over the past half-century have been as follows:

1964–93	Secretary of State for Education and Science
1993–5	Secretary of State for Education
1995–2001	Secretary of State for Education and Employment
2001–7	Secretary of State for Education and Skills
2007–2010	Secretary of State for Children, Schools, and Families
2007–2009	Secretary of State for Innovation, Universities, and Skills
2010–	Secretary of State for Education
2009–	Secretary of State for Business, Innovation, and Skills

Cabinet responsibility for education in schools has, therefore, since 2007, been separated from that for *post-compulsory education and training in the *higher education and the *lifelong learning sectors, and these policy responsibilities are now divided accordingly between the two secretaries of state. Working with each are junior ministers with delegated responsibility for specific areas of provision. As well as these elected colleagues, the secretaries of state have the support of a team of unelected civil servants to advise and support them on policy and other issues. *See also* WHITE PAPER.

selection The practice by *maintained secondary schools of selecting their intake of pupils, or (previously) of that selection being carried out by the *local authority through a process of testing pupils at *Eleven Plus. Following the *Education Act 1944 (*Butler Act), pupils were selected according to ability to go to the type of school considered best suited to them. In most local authorities this system of selection was replaced in the 1970s by a system of non-selective, *comprehensive secondary education, following the Education Act 1976.

However, the policy of selection for secondary schooling was enabled to continue in some areas because the 1976 Act was superseded by the Education Act 1979, which made the abolition of selection optional rather than mandatory. It has been argued that the practice of selection at the age of 11 continues, not only in those areas where *grammar schools remain, but also as an inevitable result of *market competition within the schooling system, which has caused successful schools to become oversubscribed and therefore enabled them to operate some degree of selection over their intake. Specialist schools, introduced briefly in the 1990s, were permitted to select up to 10 per cent of their pupil intake, based on testing of *aptitude for the specialist subjects, rather than on *ability, and thereby echoing the aims of the earlier *tripartite system. In a small minority of local authorities in England, schools still select pupils, using Eleven-plus testing. This is in contrast to Australia, for example, where selection for entry to secondary schools is common practice.

self-assessment The compilation of a self-assessment or self-evaluation document by schools is no longer obligatory; but many schools still find this a useful practice, in that it presents their progress and their quality assurance processes for scrutiny in preparation for inspections. Previously, under Ofsted's **New Inspection Framework**, which came into operation in September 2005, it was a requirement that schools carry out this process of self-evaluation, which was then documented in a self-evaluation form (SEF). *Ofsted teams used the school's SEF as a basis for planning their *inspection of the school, together with the school's previous Ofsted report and the school's performance documentation. Inspectors were then able to evaluate the school's presentation of itself in the SEF, and examine how far this was compatible with the available evidence. Issues for inspection arose from any apparent inconsistencies between the SEF's conclusions and the existing evidence, and from any significant weaknesses highlighted by the SEF, or from any obvious omissions. School self-assessment meant that inspections could proceed with what has been termed 'a lighter touch', with visits from inspectors lasting a shorter time and involving a smaller team than previously. Inspections could now focus on seeking clarification, if any was needed, of information contained in the SEF. Self-assessment allows schools to evaluate their own progress against the appropriate inspection schedule, and to present the evidence, statistical or otherwise, on which they have made their evaluative judgements. It also allows schools to identify their own strengths and areas requiring development, and to explain how the former are being developed and the latter addressed. Most schools update their self-evaluations at least annually, and may include feedback from pupils and parents about the school provision. Although no longer a mandatory document, a school's self-assessment report is still commonly referred to in the original terminology as the 'SEF'.

semester An alternative method of dividing up the academic year into periods of student activity, used by some institutions in preference to the three-*term model. It has been imported from the North American *higher education system, where the academic year consists of two semesters, each about fifteen weeks long, with lengthy breaks between them.

seminar A meeting between a *tutor and a small group of students for the purposes of teaching and learning. It can take a number of forms. For example, students may be asked to present their work or ideas to the rest of the group; or the tutor may encourage discussion of a relevant text or recent *lecture. *See also* TUTORIAL.

semiotics The study of signs and symbols, both individually and grouped together in sign systems. Sometimes referred to as **semiology**, it is an area of study which investigates the importance of language in the construction of meaning. Semiotics has become an important concept in the educational study of linguistics, sociology, media, film, and cultural studies, largely as the result of the work of C. S. Peirce (1839–1914) and Ferdinand de Saussure (1857–1913). Peirce, who preferred the term 'semiosis', proposed a triadic model which had within it the operation of three subjects in a chain of meaning. Thus, signs can be either **iconic** in that they resemble what they stand for, or **indexical** in that they have some causal connection with what they stand for, or **symbolic** in that they have no causal link with and do not resemble what they stand for, but work only through conventional association.

In his *Course in General Linguistics* (1916), Saussure proposed a dualistic model of meaning production, going against classical thought, which assumed a natural relationship between the object world and the linguistic sign, and proposing instead that this relationship was arbitrary. Two key terms used in semiotics are *parole*, the actual utterances of a language community, and *langue*, the underlying structure of language from which utterances are chosen.

This science of signs and meaning production as an academic study of language later informed the work of a range of theorists associated with **structuralism** such as Roland Barthes (1915–80) and Claude Lévi-Strauss (1908–2009). The study of semiotics suggests that the ideas (or *ideologies) we consider common sense and universal are in fact a matter of convention; the rules and conventions of language inform how we learn to perceive the world. Semiotics has been influential in shaping the approaches to teaching and educational research, particularly in *higher education.   CH

senior curriculum team (SCT) The title sometimes given to the team of teachers in a secondary school who have combined responsibility for curriculum matters. This might consist, for example, of the *deputy head responsible for curriculum, the department or subject heads, the whole-school literacy coordinator, and any other teachers with a whole-school curriculum responsibility.

senior leadership team (SLT) The title usually given to the team of teachers and managers who have responsibility for the leadership of a school or college. This would include *principals, *head teachers, their *deputies and/or *assistants; department or *faculty heads; and others with institution-wide leadership responsibilities, such as *mentors and staff with professional development responsibilities. Sometimes the title 'senior leadership team' is used in preference to 'senior management team' (SMT), primarily in order to emphasize the idea of the institution as a team rather than as a group or organization which has to be 'managed' or controlled. This can mean that the role and purpose of an SLT may be indistinguishable from that implied by the term SMT. Although practical and academic distinctions have been clearly and often drawn between the functions of leadership and management, in the context of choosing the title for the senior team of a school or other educational institution, the distinction may be a semantic one whose choice is indicative of the approach or style determined by the governing body or the team concerned.

senior management team (SMT) *See* SENIOR LEADERSHIP TEAM.

senior teacher A role of increased responsibility for a subject area within a Scottish secondary school. The use of this term is now largely in decline.   SM

Service Children's Education (SCE) SCE provides schooling, in English, from the pre-school stage to sixth form for the dependent children living with Ministry of Defence personnel who are serving overseas. SCE schools follow the *national curriculum; and teachers, who are recruited mainly from the United Kingdom, have *qualified teacher status.

((⊕)) SEE WEB LINKS
• Provides further details of SCE.

sets Sub-groups of pupils from a larger mixed-ability class or cohort who have been grouped together according to their ability level in a particular subject. In *comprehensive secondary schools, where classes contain pupils from a wide ability range, sets may be used as a means of *differentiating by activity, task, or outcome, according to pupils' abilities and needs in specific subjects. It can be an alternative to the practice of segregating pupils into ability 'streams' or classes across the curriculum, and has the advantage of still allowing some subjects to be taught to the mixed-ability class.

severe learning difficulties (SLD) *See* LEARNING DIFFICULTIES.

single-level tests As part of the *personalized learning initiative, *Standard Tasks (SATs) were replaced by single-level, teacher-assessed tests for 7-14-year-olds, applied, within limited parameters, according to pupil readiness rather than at a specified age. This development was presented as a response to concerns expressed by parents and teachers at the pressure imposed on children by the continued application of SATs. The revised approach, piloted under the title Making Good Progress, required pupils in *Key Stages 2 and 3 to take tests of 50 minutes' duration in reading, writing, and mathematics. The tests operate twice a year so that teachers had a degree of flexibility to enter pupils when they believed they were able to attain a specified level. Unlike the original *national curriculum tests, in which the pupil had only to reach the grade's threshold in order to be awarded the grade, the revised tests required pupils to demonstrate that they had securely reached each level before the grade could be awarded.

Under this single-level testing system, pupils making slow progress in English or mathematics could be identified and then receive one-to-one tutoring in those subjects. Schools received funding bonuses for successful results, and worked to targets aimed at increasing the number of pupils who progressed through two levels in one key stage. The findings of the review and evaluation of the pilot in 2010 was used to inform current policy on testing.

(⊕) SEE WEB LINKS
• 2010 evaluation of single-level tests.

situated learning A model of learning first proposed by Jean Lave and Étienne Wenger, which suggests that learning is a social activity which arises from our engagement with our daily lives. They describe this process as one of participating in a **community of practice**, and argue that such communities are found everywhere, whether we are engaging with work, school, home, our civic or social involvements, or our leisure pursuits. In some communities of practice we are central players, while in others our role may be more peripheral. As we engage in these activities, we interact with others and with the wider world in terms of our socio-historical and economic context; and in so doing we necessarily adjust and tune the ways we relate. We can call this process 'learning'. It is a collective enterprise, and results in practices and behaviours which reflect our collective pursuits and are 'owned' by the 'community' which has been created by this shared endeavour. This is what Lave and Wenger term a 'community of practice'. Thus, situated learning is neither a form of education nor a set of *pedagogical practices, but is rather a way of framing the process of learning firmly within a context of lived experience, as something which takes place through participation in group involvement with daily life. It is a joint enterprise, engagement in which binds individuals into a social unit or 'community', one which develops, as do the individuals within it, over time. In practice, there is an argument for linking certain pedagogical practices or environments with situated learning. These might include, for example, learning undertaken in 'real' environments appropriate to the subject, such as horticulture taught in a garden or greenhouse, or *field trips organized to engage learning with practice in the 'real world'. However, as a model it calls into question several widely held assumptions about education and the learning process. For example, it challenges the idea that learning is an individual activity—something undertaken by individuals. It also challenges the idea that learning or education is a process which is separate from our everyday lives, and that it has a start and end point. Perhaps most of all, this approach calls into question the assumption that learning is always a result of teaching.

Further Reading: J. Lave and E. Wenger *Situated Learning* (Cambridge University Press, 2013).

sixth form college A *tertiary institution providing education for 16–19-year-olds, and covering broadly the same curriculum as that provided by a school sixth form. This includes a range of *General Certificate of Education *Advanced Levels (A levels) and *Vocational A levels. Sixth form colleges do not provide a skills-based vocational curriculum such as that found in *colleges of further education. Teachers in a sixth form college may have *qualified teacher status or *qualified teacher learning and skills status.

skills **1.** An area of education and training concerned with *vocational qualifications and usually *assessed and *accredited through *National Vocational Qualifications. The term is reflected in current terminology for further education (FE) and work-based training, which is often referred to collectively as the 'learning and skills sector'. The *Foster Report (2005) defined the role of FE colleges as that of skills training. This understanding of the term derives from the classification of learning into three domains, based on *Bloom's Taxonomy: the cognitive, the affective, and the psychomotor, of which the latter is concerned with the acquisition of physical or practical skills.

2. Skills need not be defined so narrowly, however. For example, one may apply skill to thinking (the cognitive domain) and to the sensitive handling of another's feelings (affective domain). *See also* KNOWLEDGE.

skills agenda The focus on the improvement of the basic *vocational skills of the United Kingdom workforce in the first decade of the 21st century. The term was first coined in this context in 2003 in the *White Paper *21st Century Skills: Realising Our Potential*, which identified the need to raise skills levels to those of the more economically prosperous countries of the European Union. This theme was developed in two more White Papers: *14–19 Education and Skills* (2005) and *Getting on in Business, Getting on in Work* (2005). Sector skills councils and **Regional Skills Partnerships** have a central remit to work to this agenda through employer-led developments in unitized qualifications for the workplace; 14–19 vocational programmes; and the provision of funding to encourage employers to release staff for training. *See also* EMPLOYER ENGAGEMENT; 14–19 AGENDA; SKILLS; WORK-BASED LEARNING.   VC, KA

Skills Funding Agency The government body responsible for funding skills training in England's *further education colleges and training organizations. Its other responsibilities include the funding and coordination of apprenticeships in England and the maintenance of individual learner records.

(⊕) SEE WEB LINKS
• Provides further details of the Agency's role.

Skills in the UK *See* LEITCH REPORT.

Skinner, B. F. *See* BEHAVIOURIST.

social and emotional aspects of learning (SEAL) A resource for primary schools aimed to support them in the development of pupils' social and emotional skills. The framework and materials were designed to facilitate pupils' progression in these skills as they advanced year by year through the school, and to involve parents and carers in their progress. This initiative encouraged a whole-school approach as well as classroom activities, and incorporated a range of continuing professional development activities for

teachers. Part of the *Primary National Strategy, SEAL was implemented
with the support of Children's Service departments within all
*local authorities.

social class A term which refers to societal hierarchies, expressed as the
positioning of people within that society in relation to one another and
determined largely by level of education and occupation and also to a great
extent by the individual's economic value relative to other members of society.
Social class is closely associated with culture and the cultural beliefs and
practices of communities and, as such, forms an important part of personal
identity. Because it is hierarchical, those individuals and communities who are at
the bottom of the hierarchy are at increased risk of marginalization and social
exclusion. Other characteristics which may lead to marginalization and social
exclusion such as gender, race, sexuality, or disability, and which also form
important aspects of personal identity, are heavily mediated by the social class of
the individual. Social class is also closely related to power in society, since
economic and political power is principally located with the middle
classes—those who have been able to access high levels of education, exploit its
advantages, and secure the economic rewards that this has offered.

Concerns around social class in an educational context are related to the
significant class-based inequalities within the education system. These
inequalities relate to a situation where young people have widely differing
educational experiences—and achieve widely differing outcomes—based on the
cultural values, beliefs, and practices associated with education within their
community and their physical access (largely determined by catchment area) to
higher or lower achieving schools which often offer different types of curriculum.
The English education system has historically been complicit in the reproduction
of class structures and ensures that young people reach the age of 16 with the
credentials and education appropriate to class-specific occupations. These
occupations and levels of credential reflect those that their parents achieved
before them, an illustration of the notion of educational inheritance where those
parents with limited educational and material resources are unable to generate
academic profits for their children in the same way as those with more significant
educational and material resources. Concerns related to access to education and
educational outcomes within a class context exist in many education systems,
particularly those of economically powerful countries with well-established
universal access to education.

Although government defines social class according to a wide range of
categories and sub-groups, it is unrealistic to discuss educational issues within
the context of eight or more separate groupings, and in many texts a much
broader differential is used and the terms 'working class' and 'middle class'
(and occasionally 'underclass') are found. These relate to the social class of the
parents of the young person, and are often used to illustrate inequalities in the
education system. Hence, the term 'working class' has become synonymous with
disadvantage and is used in the context of limited parental education and
credentials, with occupations which might be defined as mundane, low-pay,

and low-skill. However, this fails to differentiate the working class from the so-called underclass, which constitutes the children of parents who either have never worked or are, in the long term, economically inactive. The term 'underclass' is synonymous with poverty, social exclusion, and marginalization. In contrast, the term 'middle class' is often used to imply advantage and is related to higher levels of educational achievement and professional, technical, or managerial occupations which provide security of tenure, opportunities for advancement and career progression, and high economic returns. In addition to parental social class, a commonly used measure of disadvantage in educational research is the number of children within a school who are eligible for free school meals.

There are strong social class correlations in the outcomes of national examinations and assessments and in government school *league tables, in which schools in more affluent areas drawing from middle-class *catchments invariably dominate the top of the league, with the bottom dominated by schools in disadvantaged areas drawing from more socially excluded catchments. Some areas of education are more transparently class-specific than others. For example, *independent schools have a largely middle-class intake, while the English *further education colleges provide a predominantly skills-based curriculum to young people from lower social classes. It has been suggested that the present post-16 system in England offers tripartite 'pathways' which reflect the hierarchy of ancient Greek society described in Plato's *Republic* as well as contemporary social class structures. Within these pathways the academic 'gold standard' *General Certificate of Education *Advanced Levels, the full-time vocationally orientated level 3 programmes (e.g. BTEC National Diploma), and the occupationally based *National Vocational Qualification are the routes into higher education, training, and employment. However, the employment, salary, and thus the life opportunities which result from following the different routes are widely different, particularly for those who do not hold the necessary credentials to enter level 3 post-16, and who have to undertake lower-level vocational programmes. Historically, vocational programmes have tended to be regarded as of lower status than academic programmes. They are significant in the replication of classed (and gendered) inequalities and have been widely criticized for socializing young people into particular job roles.

Such class-based differentials also extend to *higher education, where, despite numerous policy initiatives intended to create more opportunities for less advantaged young people, proportionately more middle-class young people enter university. Of those working-class young people who do enter higher education, proportionately fewer attend high-status institutions and proportionately more undertake their higher education programme within a further education setting. They are statistically more likely to withdraw before completing their programme and statistically less likely to achieve higher grades.

Because social class is a characteristic deeply intertwined with personal identity and associated with embedded societal structures, values, and practices it often leads to discrimination. This is multifaceted and takes place at all levels from the use of playground insults such as 'snob' or 'chav' to the direction of (mainly working-class) low-achieving 16-year-olds to vocational programmes which are held in lower esteem and provide fewer opportunities in terms of future income and education than the academic programmes to which the higher-achieving (mainly middle-class) young people are directed. Because of the complex relationships between social class, inequality, and discrimination, it is a fundamental issue in debates around *social justice, equality, and inequality in education. LA

(⊕) SEE WEB LINKS
• Presents a BBC report of alternative categorization of social class.

social interactionism As an approach to education this theory emphasizes the importance of the location of learning within a particular sociocultural environment, as well as the belief that learners are instrumental in constructing their own knowledge and understanding. Social interactionists adhere to the wider *constructivist theory of learning, and place an emphasis on the role which language plays as a medium of learner interaction, pointing out that it is through language that cultural and philosophical ideas are shared and developed. The contextualized and situational nature of learning is, according to the interactionists, a key element in driving cognitive development. This view takes account of the diversity of individuals within any learning group, particularly in the way they interpret or make sense of the world, and suggests that interaction between learners and between learner and teacher provide an important stimulus to learning, which would be missing in an *objectivist learning environment, where learners are passive and compliant recipients of learning. Pupils' self-concept—the view each of them has of herself or himself as an individual—is formed largely through interaction with others, and will change and develop according to the way they see themselves reflected in those interactions. This can affect pupil motivation and confidence, for example, if the view that is reflected back to them is a negative one in terms of their ability or attainment. This is one example of how the individual constructs their own meanings from their own interpretation of their social interactions. Learning based on an interactionist approach, therefore, presupposes a collaborative relationship between teacher and learner, rather than a relationship of learner dependency; and is likely to involve built-in opportunities for learners to discuss, collaborate, and become actively involved with the learning process. This model is above all predicated on the belief that meaning is created by the learner, rather than simply received unquestioningly from the teacher. *See also* VYGOTSKY, LEV.

social justice A term which refers to the good of the whole community, where that is taken to include both the good of each and the good of all, in an acknowledgement that one depends on the other. In Western thought the roots of the concept go back to both Plato and Aristotle. In *The Republic*, Plato drew attention to the connection between the virtuous individual and the socially harmonious state. Aristotle took these ideas further in his *Nicomachean Ethics* and *Politics*, where he introduced the idea of social justice as dependent on a fair distribution of goods in society.

Current ideas of social justice draw on these ideas and expand on them. Social justice is closely associated with fairness. It is also closely associated with individuals as members of the community in relation to respect: self-respect and mutual respect. (It should be noted that in discussions of social justice, the terms 'self-esteem' and 'recognition' are more common than the terms 'self-respect' and 'mutual respect'.) Thus, social justice depends both on respect and also on a right distribution of benefits and responsibilities. It includes paying attention to individual perspectives at the same time as dealing with issues of discrimination, exclusion, and respect, especially on the grounds of (any or all of) race, *gender, sexuality, special needs, and *social class.

Since social justice could never be achieved once and for all, it is best understood as always in process. Working towards social justice means resolving possible tensions about the well-being of individuals, of whole societies, and of diverse social political groups. Inevitably, any resolution will be provisional. Human beings are creative and need room for individual expression and action. They have a diversity of cultures. So human societies are never static. As they change, so too do the tensions and balances between different interest groups and social sectors. Social justice is more a journey than a destination.

Equality is central to all ideas of social justice as fairness. At its simplest, equality means sameness: however, in relation to human beings and their societies, sameness is more a matter for judgement than measurement, simply because each person is a unique individual. Moreover, there is the question, Equality in or of what? For example, any judgement about what counts as equal resources has to take need into account. For instance, if disabled students are to enjoy equal education with the rest, they may sometimes require more resources than able-bodied ones, depending on the nature of the disability and the environment.

Key terms are **equal opportunity** and **equality of outcome**. A socially just society would ensure that no individual or social group had less opportunity to benefit from educational provision. It would also expect that no social group would, on average, achieve better or worse than other social groups. (Equality of outcome refers to social political groups. Of course, some individuals will—and should—achieve much more than others.) Thus, the different educational achievements of girls and boys is one example of a social justice issue. Another is the relatively high proportion of black boys who are excluded from school in the UK.

Self-identity is also a key concern for social justice. Respect for self and others affects but is also an effect of prejudice and discrimination experienced by a range of social groups. These include racism, sexism, homophobia, disability, class prejudice, and prejudice against outsiders to mainstream society such as travellers, refugees, and asylum seekers. Reasons for unfair discrimination also include religion, ethnic heritage, language, dialect, and coming from rural or inner-city areas. Most of these raise issues of a fair distribution of resources. However, they are also all issues of respect and therefore of self-identity.

Educators wishing to tackle social justice issues, whether as policy-makers, teachers, or researchers, need to pay attention to ways of working for social justice in context, focusing especially on self-esteem, empowerment, voice, partnership, consultation, and collaboration. They also need to focus on finding approaches to specific areas of disadvantage, including multicultural, intercultural, or anti-racist education, for instance, in the area of race. Similarly for gender, sexuality, special educational needs, and social class. These are all useful headings under which to make a social justice audit of teaching methods and strategies and also the processes of policy-making. Similarly, considerations of social justice are relevant in every curriculum area from mathematics to social studies. The curriculum areas where it may be easiest to address justice issues directly are citizenship and personal and social education. Another useful mechanism is through the equal opportunities policies in schools, colleges, and universities. *See also* INCLUSION. MG

Further Reading: S. Ball *The Education Debate* (Policy Press, 2008) explores the impact of education policy and ideas on social class divisions.

social skills Sometimes called 'social and life skills', these are concerned with the ability to interact and communicate appropriately with others in a variety of settings. Originally included as one of the 'core' skills (forerunners of *key skills) which formed part of the curriculum for young people on the *youth training programmes of the 1980s, it was considered to be one of the skills employers required to see in young job applicants. This range of skills is similar to that now embedded in the *national curriculum as part of *personal and social education.

Socratic questioning A form of questioning which aims not to test or assess, but to draw out the learner's *tacit knowledge. It takes its name from the Athenian philosopher Socrates (469–399 BC), who was said to use this approach in teaching his pupils. *See also* DIALOGIC TEACHING.

SOLO taxonomy (The Structure of Observed Learning Outcomes Taxonomy) A way of classifying the increasing complexity of a learner's understanding as they explore a given topic. The concept was originally proposed by John B. Biggs and Kevin Collis in *Evaluating the Quality of Learning: The SOLO Taxonomy* (New York: Academic Press, 1982). The taxonomy describes five tiered levels of understanding:

- Pre-structural: The learner has no understanding or is under misconceptions.
- Uni-structural: The learner is aware of one relevant aspect.
- Multi-structural: The learner is aware of several aspects, but these are viewed independently and the learner does not perceive or understand connections between them.
- Relational: The learner can draw links between the aspects to see them as a coherent whole. Understanding of the topic is significantly enhanced by this ability to see the relationships between various aspects of the learning.
- Extended abstract: The learner is able to make links beyond the original subject area and transfer the principles and ideas to other areas of their learning.

The model has grown in popularity and is sometimes used by teachers to assist differentiation for a class of learners who are all working at various levels of understanding. *See also* BLOOM'S TAXONOMY; DIFFERENTIATION; LEARNING OUTCOMES.   IW

🌐 **SEE WEB LINKS**
• Provides a number of links to sources of further information about SOLO taxonomy.

spaced learning A strategy for learning which involves alternating concentrated learning activity with distraction breaks. The material or content to be learnt may be complex and condensed. It is repeated three times, the first and second times being followed by breaks of ten minutes during which learners engage in activity such as physical exercise which has no relevance to the learning content. Spaced learning in an educational context is based on research into long-term memory creation and recall. *See also* MEMORY.

🌐 **SEE WEB LINKS**
• Links to full text document explaining the process of spaced learning.

special educational needs and disabilities (SEND or **SEN)** The term 'special educational needs' became commonly used after the report published in 1978 by the Committee of Inquiry into the Education of Handicapped Children and Young People (the *Warnock Report). Prior to this, the terms 'handicapped' and 'retarded' were in common usage when describing young people with SEN. The main cause for seeking new terminology was to remove the negative focus of those words and the medical labelling of children used before the Report. It was also felt that the labels 'handicapped' and 'retarded' had a negative effect on the way people felt about themselves. The Code of Practice for SEN (revised 2001) sets out clear criteria and guidance for the assessment of SEN, but differing systems for interpretation of assessment data mean that one school's reasons for describing a student as having SEN may be quite different from another's. The term 'SEN' is generally applied where medical or cognitive disorders exist which create *barriers to learning and which require support for the learner on a long-term or ongoing basis. There are those who will require support on a temporary or indefinite basis owing to personal and family circumstances such as bereavement or a parent who is in prison: there is still much debate around whether or not it is appropriate to link students who require additional learning support owing to life circumstances with those who have cognitive disabilities under the banner of SEN. Not all children who are disabled as defined by the Disability Discrimination Act 2005 will have special educational needs. This debate widens with the introduction of *personalized learning which embraces methods of working with students with SEN and applies them to others. Some *local authorities are combining the term 'additional educational needs' with SEN when referring to provision for students who are experiencing barriers to their learning. Children with SEN will require in school interventions which are

additional to or different from those provided as part of the school's usual
approaches and strategy.   TB, LE

((⊕)) SEE WEB LINKS
• The full text of the SEN code of practice and related regulations.

special educational needs coordinator (SENCO) The person in a
school responsible for implementing the Code of Practice for Special Educational
Needs (SEN). The SENCO supports the head teacher in the strategic direction
and development of *special educational needs provision and coordinates the
development and implementation of policy. They must contribute to the
in-service training of staff in matters relating to SEN. Other responsibilities held
are to provide guidance and support for teachers in the school so that they are
able to identify and assess students with *learning difficulties and set effective
targets for individual students. The SENCO, in consultation with other key staff,
usually writes *individual education plans containing relevant targets and
strategies which act as guidance for those who implement the plans. It is the duty
of the SENCO to ensure staff have all the information they need to plan for
effective teaching to meet the needs of all pupils. They deploy staff and resources
used to support pupils with SEN. A key role of the SENCO is to coordinate and
chair annual *statutory review meetings for pupils who have *statements of
special educational needs. This includes requesting advice from all involved
adults, including parents and professionals from outside the education sector,
preparing a detailed school advice document, and writing the report following
the review meeting. These tasks must be carried out in accordance with the
guidance and timescales set out in the Code of Practice for SEN. The SENCO
is the key link person with external agencies who support the school in the
identification and assessment of any special needs in children. The SENCO is
usually the school's contact for all multi-agency work with regard to SEN.
The role of SENCO is complex and has in recent years been regarded as a
senior management post. There are national standards for the role which
were developed from the Code of Practice for SEN.   TB, LE

((⊕)) SEE WEB LINKS
• The full text of the SEN code of practice and related regulations.
• Provides details of the SENCO's role and relevant professional qualifications.

Special Educational Needs and Disability Act 2001 (SENDA) An Act
which repealed the exemption of education from the Disability Discrimination
Act 1995 and made it unlawful for educational institutions in both the pre- and
post-16 education sectors to discriminate against disabled pupils and students.
Examples of discrimination would be refusing a place to a student with motor
impairment simply because the school or college had no lift to the upper floor
and providing learning materials in written format only for students with a
learning difficulty affecting the ability to decode written language. The Act is
all-embracing, covering admissions, education, and associated services
(for example, school trips, student residential accommodation, and access to
leisure facilities), but excludes requirements for the removal or alteration of

physical features and the provision of auxiliary aids or services. The Act places a duty on the responsible body (normally governors) of all institutions to be anticipatory in making reasonable adjustments to existing provision. *See also* ACCESSIBILITY PLANS.   TB, LE

Special Educational Needs and Disability Tribunal (SENDIST)
Established by the *Education Act 1993, the Special Educational Needs Tribunal had its remit extended by the *Special Educational Needs and Disability Act 2001 to allow it to consider claims of discrimination. The Tribunal is independent of influence from the government and has no connection with any local authority. It sits in private except in prescribed circumstances, to consider parents' appeals against the decision of local authorities about children's *special educational needs or to hear cases presented as discriminatory. The Tribunal can order local authorities to assess a child, issue a *statement of special educational needs, or make amendments to parts 2 (needs), 3 (provision), and 4 (placement) of an existing statement of special educational need. In claims of discrimination the Tribunal can order any action it thinks reasonable, although it cannot order the payment of financial compensation.   TB, LE

specialist school A secondary school which specializes in the teaching of a particular area of the curriculum. From 1994 *maintained schools were able to apply for specialist status in design and technology, mathematics, and modern languages. This range was gradually expanded, until schools were able to apply for specialist status in arts, business and enterprise, engineering, humanities, languages, mathematics and computing, music, science, sports, and technology. The purpose of specialist schools was to boost pupil achievement in the specific curriculum area. They were permitted to select up to 10 per cent of their pupil intake, based not on pupils' *ability, but on their *aptitude for the specialist subject. By 2010 there were almost 3 000 such schools in England, when the programme was ended by the Coalition government and the special funding became absorbed into general budgets for schools. Today the term 'specialist school' does not relate to any specific policy initiative nor have any formal definition beyond that which the school itself applies, for example if laying claim to consistently excellent results in any one curriculum area.

special measures Schools on special measures are those which have been identified by *Ofsted or *Estyn in England or Wales as giving cause for concern and being at risk of *failing. They become subject to regular short-notice inspections designed to monitor improvement. If no improvement is apparent senior managers or members of teaching staff may be dismissed and the governing body replaced by an appointed executive committee to oversee progress. Schools which are judged unable to improve may be closed down.

(((()))) SEE WEB LINKS
- Provides a link to advice for teachers and others working in a school under special measures.

special school A school that provides education for children and young people with complex or specific needs which generally cannot be fully met in the mainstream setting. Some special schools are generic in nature and cater for a wide spectrum of need while others offer education to discrete groups of learners such as those with a hearing impairment. Staff–student ratios are high and the setting will have enhanced resources. Funded by local authorities or private organizations, some schools offer residential placements or a 24-hour curriculum. Pupils on roll will usually have a *statement of special educational needs. Historically many pupils attended the same special school for the duration of their compulsory schooling, but more frequently now schools are organized into primary and secondary schools in line with mainstream education. TB, LE

specific learning difficulty (SLD) *See* SPECIAL EDUCATIONAL NEEDS.

spelling The spelling of English is notoriously difficult, and the ability to spell accurately is usually only acquired by pupils over a number a years, rather than being a goal at some early stage of the education process. A major debate over the teaching of spelling has been whether a pupil's ability to write creatively will be stifled by an insistence on correct spelling. Some who lament inadequate *literacy levels among school-leavers believe that an emphasis on creativity over accuracy may be to blame. Others, such as George Bernard Shaw (1856–1950), have taken a more radical view, and suggested that all English spelling should be approached phonetically. Some pupils who have persistent and severe problems with spelling may be diagnosed as suffering from *dyslexia, while for others the difficulty may lie in their underexposure to the written word. *See also* READING.

spiral curriculum *See* CURRICULUM, SPIRAL.

spiritual, moral, social, and cultural education (SMSCE) An aspect of the school curriculum in England aimed at developing a set of core values, embedded across all *national curriculum subjects in *maintained schools, and included as part of the curriculum in *academies and free schools. Its components are broadly defined in the following ways: **spiritual** refers to the pupil's developing sense of self and 'non-material wellbeing'; **moral** refers to the pupil's understanding of right and wrong; **social** is concerned with the understanding of individual rights and responsibilities; and cultural includes both the development of aesthetic sensibility and an understanding of traditions and values. Schools are also expected to encourage respect for British values; avoid the promotion of extremist or partisan political views; and ensure a balanced presentation of any political issue.

sports day An annual event held by some schools in which pupils (and sometimes parents) compete in races and other competitive sporting events. In secondary schools where a house system exists, the competition may be between the houses. However, for many schools, and particularly those in the *primary sector, sports day has come to be less about competition and sporting excellence and more about inclusion and celebration.

staff development *See* CONTINUING PROFESSIONAL DEVELOPMENT; IN-SERVICE EDUCATION OF TEACHERS.

staff–student ratio (SSR) *See* CLASS SIZE; PUPIL–TEACHER RATIO.

stage not age A phrase used to summarize the approach implicit in the concept of a *personalized curriculum, and often used as a 'shorthand' for this approach by those professionals in schools and local authorities who are responsible for encouraging the implementation of personalization. It encapsulates the idea that a pupil should be provided with the learning experiences and curriculum content which are appropriate to the *stage of development which she or he has reached, rather than that all pupils be given an education which is standardized to 'fit' their chronological age.

stages A number of educationalists and psychologists have described human *cognitive development and the capacity for learning in terms of the individual's progress through a series of consecutive stages. *Piaget, for example, suggested that the human being goes through four main stages of cognitive development, each of which corresponds with a chronological stage in terms of the individual's age. His theory locates the first three of these stages in childhood and early adolescence, and has had a great influence on educational thinking and practice, particularly in the *primary phase of education. The stages which Piaget identified are as follows:

- Stage 1: Sensorimotor stage. This corresponds with infancy and has six sub-stages. Intelligence is manifested through motor activities, and knowledge of the world is based upon these physical experiences and interactions. Memory (or 'object permanence') is acquired at about 7 months; and as the infant's physical skills and mobility develop, so do their intellectual activity, including some language (or 'symbolic') ability.
- Stage 2: Pre-operational stage. This corresponds with the 'toddler' and early childhood period, and has two sub-stages. Intelligence is demonstrated through language use (or 'symbols'); and both memory and imagination develop. The child's thinking at this stage is egocentric and non-logical.
- Stage 3: Concrete operational stage. This corresponds with the years of primary schooling and early adolescence. Intelligence is demonstrated through the ability to manipulate symbols (language) in relation to objects. The tendency to think egocentrically diminishes as operational thinking develops.
- Stage 4: Formal operational stage. This corresponds with adolescence and adulthood, when intelligence is demonstrated through the ability to use symbols (language) logically in relation to abstract concepts. Early in this stage, during adolescence, there is often a temporary return to egocentric thinking. The formal operational stage is not reached by everyone; and some would argue that it is only attained by the minority of adults.

This idea of stages constitutes an important aspect of the *constructivist theory of learning. One of the implications this theory has for teaching is that children should not be expected to attempt learning which demands skills or abilities which are in advance of the stage at which they are currently functioning. Thus, in early childhood, for example, children should not be confronted with tasks which demand operational thinking. This is not to say, however, that teachers and parents should not challenge or stretch the child, but rather that such challenge should remain within the parameters appropriate to the child's developmental stage. More recent research has suggested that the link between developmental stage and chronological age may be less clearly defined than Piaget's original research suggested.

Where Piaget's theory focuses on cognitive development through infancy, childhood, and adolescence, *Erikson's description of personality growth as a series of stages is often used to inform the theoretical underpinning of the education of adults. Known as 'psychosocial stages', and complementing in some ways the psychosexual stages described by Freud, Erikson's stages are presented as a response to the demands of society, which, as the individual's development proceeds, trigger a series of personal conflicts or crises. Erikson identifies eight stages. The first three relate closely to Freud's psychosexual stages, as is evident from the terminology used, and are the oral, anal, and genital stages. The fourth stage, 'latency', covers the period when children are expected to acquire the skills which will equip them for adult life, and in Western society is coterminous with the period of primary schooling. The fifth stage, 'puberty and adolescence', confronts young people with the task of defining themselves and adapting to the roles imposed upon them by society. The three subsequent stages mark further adult rites of passage; and it is these which are sometimes used to inform *adult education theory. They are (6) young adulthood, when the individual must discover whether they are able to form intimate relationships; (7) adulthood, which presents the individual with the challenge of contributing to society ('generativity') or failing to contribute and instead 'stagnating'; and (8) maturity, the eighth and final stage, which presents the individual with the challenge of achieving 'integrity' and acceptance of self and one's place in the world, or failing to do so and falling into 'despair'. Erikson argues that it is not only the external demands of society which drive these crises or stages, but that there is also an inbuilt human developmental 'timetable' which determines the sequence and direction of individual personal development. His concept of a healthy or integrated personality is one which is in harmony with the society within which it is situated. On these grounds, his theory of stages has been criticized as conformist and as tending to reinforce, rather than interrogate in educational terms, the social status quo. *See also* STAGE NOT AGE.

Standard Assessment Tasks (SATs) *See* STANDARD TASKS.

Standard Grades Scotland's educational qualifications for students aged around 14–16 years. Standard Grade courses are taken over the third and fourth years of a student's secondary schooling. Students will typically study seven to nine subjects at Standard Grade. The Standard Grade replaced the

Scottish *Ordinary Grade in the early 1990s. It is broadly equivalent to the
*General Certificate of Secondary Education qualification taken in other parts
of the UK.   SM

standardization The practice of ensuring that work is being assessed to the
same *standard and against the same criteria by teachers, examiners, and
*assessors in every institution. This is usually done through a process of
*verification, by an external verifier or an external examiner.

standards A means of defining the quality—of work or of performance—which
must be attained. In education there are two main levels at which standards
are set and monitored: the national and the institutional. National standards
are used to regulate both the quality of the educational and training process,
and the levels of *attainment required in nationally recognized testing or
qualifications. Thus, for example, the *national curriculum and its associated
testing or assessment regime sets national, *key stage-specific standards for pupil
achievement; and there are professional standards in place which define the
training and performance requirements for teachers in schools, and which
are applied nationally. On an institutional level there are standards set by
individual schools and colleges in relation to, for example, student behaviour or
attainment targets. The monitoring of standards may also be carried out at an
institutional level through a process of *verification, which is designed to
ensure standardization across centres of delivery and assessment. 'Ensuring
standards' and 'raising standards' have become key phrases in educational
policy since the 1980s. *See also* TEACHERS' STANDARDS.

Standard Tasks (SATs) Originally called **Standards Assessment Tasks**, but
officially renamed **Standard Tasks** in 1990, SATs have informally retained their
original abbreviated name, and have been an integral part of the *national
curriculum assessment process. Originally administered at the end of *Key Stages
1, 2, and 3, they are now externally applied in England only towards the end of
Key Stage (KS) 2 (year 6) at age 11 in English and mathematics. The tests are then
marked externally and by the school; and used as a basis for teachers to make an
assessment of the *attainment *level at which the pupil is working. The KS2 SATs
test pupils at levels 3 to 5, with an expected average outcome of level 4. However,
pupils identified as particularly able can be entered for level 6. SATs have been
criticized by teachers and parents for imposing an unproductive level of pressure
and stress on pupils. Partly as a result of this, the system which has largely
replaced them, *single-level testing, is intended to be more consistent with a
*personalized learning, '*stage not age' approach to pupil assessment.
    In Scotland there are no synchronous national assessments at *primary level.
In the 5–14 curriculum each curricular area is divided into six levels, A–F.
Assessment to attain these target levels can be taken when the teacher considers
pupils ready. This is often completed as individuals or small groups; whole years

do not sit tests. The levels are used as a confirmation of the student's current standard.

(⊕) SEE WEB LINKS

• Examples of KS2 SATs papers may be downloaded from this site.

statemented *See* STATEMENT OF SPECIAL EDUCATIONAL NEEDS.

statementing officer An officer of the *local authority who collated the multi-professional advice from the **statutory assessment** process to establish the provision required to meet a student's *special educational needs and monitor their progress through the annual *statutory review. If the statementing officer agreed with recommendations for changes to the statement, following a statutory review, they amended the statement to include the changes. The term, still in use, does not yet reflect the introduction of the **Education, Health, and Care Plan (EHCP)** in 2014. *See* STATEMENT OF SPECIAL EDUCATIONAL NEEDS.   TB, LE

statement of competence *See* COMPETENCE.

statement of special educational needs A legal document which was issued by the *local authority (LA) following a **statutory assessment**. Written advice was sought from parents, educational professionals, medical agencies, the psychology service, and social services. Contributors were required to respond within six weeks. The views of the student were also sought. A statement recorded personal details, including name and address, date of birth, and home language. A detailed description of the student's special needs followed. This was set out according to the areas of need identified during the assessment process. The LA decided what special educational provision was required to meet the student's *special educational needs (SEN). Objectives were then written which related to all areas of special needs described in the earlier part. Arrangements for monitoring progress towards the objectives were clearly set out. The main vehicle for review was the *statutory review, which was required to occur at least annually. The next section named the school where the special educational provision would be made. Parents were able to state a preference that their child not be educated in a mainstream school. If no preference was made, the LA had to endeavour to place students in a mainstream school. An exception to this would be if this was not compatible with the education of other children. Other needs which could be identified by social services, health services, or other agencies were set out in the next part of the statement. Non-educational needs and provision were also recorded. Parents would be informed quickly of all decisions relating to the process as it affected their child. Regulations for the time limits were set out in detail in the Code of Practice for Special Educational Needs. The process for issuing a statement would usually be no more than 26 weeks.

The terms 'statement' and 'statemented' have long been an integral part of the vocabulary of teachers, and especially of those teaching pupils with special educational needs. The sweeping reforms put in place from September 2014, therefore, have initiated changes not only to the processes but also to the vocabulary of SEN. Following the *Green Paper *Support and Aspiration: A New Approach to Special Educational Needs and Disability* (2012), statements for children and young people are replaced by an **Education, Health and Care Plan (EHCP)**, which is designed to take a co-ordinated approach to education, care, and support. The age range covered is extended to include young people in education or training up to the age of 25. All parents, not only those whose child has an SEN, have a right to express a preference for a named school. However, the school is not necessarily obliged to take the child, as was usually the case under the statementing system. On the other hand, the EHCP approach does not place so much emphasis on inclusion into mainstream education, thus giving parents more flexibility to request special schooling where this is felt to be of benefit to the child. The EHCP system is also designed to reduce the time taken to document the child's needs. It works in tandem with increased screening for SEN which included progress checks for all 2-year-olds.

(⊕) SEE WEB LINKS
• The full text of the SEN code of practice and related regulations.

state school *See* MAINTAINED SCHOOL.

statutory assessment *See* STATEMENTING OFFICER; STATEMENT OF SPECIAL EDUCATIONAL NEEDS.

statutory review A meeting held to monitor progress towards the objective set out in a *statement of special educational needs. It is appropriate to decide if any amendments to the description of needs or the provision described in the statement should be made. Statements must be reviewed at least annually, though it is possible to call interim meetings if necessary. All involved professionals and parents must be invited to the review. The views of the student must also be sought and recorded in the report from the meeting. Guidance for the timescales for the review can be found in the Code of Practice Special Educational Needs. Copies of the report are sent to all involved in the review and to the *local authority.   TB, LE

Steiner, Rudolf (1861–1925) An Austrian philosopher and head of the German Theosophical Society. Rudolf Steiner's most lasting and significant influence has been in the field of education. Having given a series of lectures on a range of theological and philosophical ideas to the workers of the Waldorf-Astoria cigarette factory in Stuttgart, he was asked to establish and lead a school for the children of the factory employees in 1919. There are now currently more than 600 independent Steiner Waldorf Schools in over 32 countries. In the UK they are most commonly referred to as 'Steiner schools'.

  Steiner designed the school curriculum based on his notion of the three stages of a child's spirituality and the development of the body, spirit, and soul. He claimed that children learn through physical activity, imitation, and the development of temperament by watching adults who model required behaviours. For Steiner, there is no question of childhood being a preparation for life, but rather a spiritual and rhythmic journey when the natural fusion of the spirit (existing pre-birth) and body takes place. The Steiner Waldorf Schools, therefore, emphasize a carefully planned environment with activity, in the *early years, based on play with natural materials, oral storytelling of traditional fairy tales and role play, with a gentle introduction to reading and writing from the age of 7. Children sing, speak, model, paint, and perform household duties, absorbing the environment without transforming it, and developing an inner moral sense projected by family and school values.

One of the more unusual parts of the curriculum involves eurhythmy, which engages children in spiritual gestures to chanting and music. Steiner believed that eurhythmy enhanced coordination and strengthened the ability to listen. (Some of this may have informed current exercises included as part of *Brain Gym activity). He also claimed that such gestures developed the imagination and nourished the spirit. Steiner claimed that an education built on cooperation, love, and inner peace would be more beneficial to children's intellectual, moral, and creative well-being than one based on regimentation or coercion. Current practice in Steiner schools reflects this educational philosophy, with the same teacher educating children from 4 to 7, then 7 to 11. After the age of 11, in the UK, children in Steiner schools are able to follow the statutory *national curriculum.

Proponents of the Steiner approach to the education of young children have been vocal in their opposition to the *Early Years Foundation Stage curriculum, which sets learning targets for children aged 0–5, arguing that the imposition of this framework is incompatible with the Steiner approach to early years learning.   AW

Stevenson Report (1977) The report of a review into the use of technology in UK primary and secondary schools published in 1997 and entitled *Information and Communications Technology in UK Schools*. Widely regarded as an important milestone in the development of ICT for education, it warned that, at the date of its publication, "the state of ICT in schools [was] primitive and not improving". In its recommendations it urged the UK government to make the improvement and development of ICT provision a priority, suggesting that this was best done not through the provision of large amounts of hardware but by developing the ICT skills of teachers both in *initial teacher training and in their *continuing professional development. The data on which its conclusions were based can be found in the **McKinsey Report**.

(((⊕))) SEE WEB LINKS
• Provides a full text version of the report and a link to the McKinsey Report data.

streaming Allocating pupils to different classes according to their ability, rather than teaching them in mixed-ability classes. This was a common practice in *grammar schools and secondary schools during the era of *selection between the 1940s and early 1970s, and was continued in some *comprehensive schools, despite the comprehensive principle of non-selection, since teaching pupils across the entire ability range in one class, it was claimed, was found in some cases to disadvantage both the more able pupils and those who needed additional support. Streaming is used more in secondary than in primary schools, although some primary schools do employ it. More usual in the primary sector is the organization of pupils by ability into *sets, particularly for English and mathematics.

student One who studies, usually in the *tertiary sector at college or university, although it is not unusual to refer to older pupils in schools as 'students', too.

Student Awards Agency for Scotland (SAAS) The Scottish government agency responsible for funding students who continue in education after 16. The remit of SAAS is to provide financial support for eligible Scottish-domiciled students on courses of higher education throughout the United Kingdom.   SM

(⊕) SEE WEB LINKS
• Explains the SAAS remit and describes support available to Scottish students.

student loan *See* LOAN, STUDENT.

students' union 1. A society of students at a college or university which organizes social events and other activities and is represented on key institutional committees which deal with academic matters.
   2. The building or bar on campus where students gather for social purposes. *See also* NATIONAL UNION OF STUDENTS.

study leave A period of paid leave granted to teachers in schools and in further and higher education for the purpose of undertaking a course of study related to their professional development. It is shorter than a *sabbatical, and may take the form of a release from duties for a few hours a week for a limited time in order for the teacher to attend a course. Study leave is not a right, and a strong case usually has to be made by the individual seeking it. *See also* SECONDMENT.

study skills The skills which learners need to possess in order to be able to study effectively. These include such disparate skills as time management, the ability to take relevant notes, listening skills, research skills, the ability to use information technology productively, and, of course, the ability to read and to write at the appropriate level. There has been a growing realization that students may need structured support in the development of study skills, and, to this end, guidance is now provided in most colleges and universities, as well as in schools, often in the form of workshops and tutorials.

study support Opportunities for supporting learning which are organized outside school hours and in which pupil participation is voluntary. Such activities and opportunities may be scheduled before or after the school day, during school holidays or at weekends, or during break times or lunchtime. They may typically include a breakfast club, which provides pupils with their breakfast as well as organized activities or time for study; a *homework club where pupils have space and relative quiet in which to work; learning about learning, a service offering support and advice to pupils about the skills needed for thinking, studying, and revising; and subject-focused activities, such as clubs for those with an interest in science, literature, languages, or drama.

subject leader A teacher with school-wide responsibility for a particular curriculum area. It is a title most often used in *primary schools. An alternative form also in use is **subject coordinator**.

Success for All (2002) A strategy document published by the *Department for Education and Skills, which sets out proposals for reforms designed to enable *further education colleges and other training providers in the *lifelong learning sector to be more responsive to local and national training needs. This included the need for them to work more closely with employers, and to ensure that provision supported and encouraged principles of equality and diversity. It also stressed the need to develop systems of *e-learning in order to provide wider access to education and training. *See also* WHITE PAPER.

(⊕) SEE WEB LINKS
• Provides the full text of this document.

sufficiency A term applied in the assessment of students' work or performance when the question arises of whether there is enough evidence of successful achievement to allow the *assessor to make an informed *assessment decision. It is commonly used in assessment for *vocational qualifications, where the question might be one of how many successful performances of a specific task constitute a sufficiency of evidence for the candidate to be judged competent to a national standard. Similar questions of sufficiency of evidence can arise over the assessment of written work, where it may be important to ascertain whether the learner can perform consistently at the required *standard.

summative assessment *Assessment which takes place at the end of a course of study and provides the final judgement on, or 'sums up', the candidate's performance. The most common form of summative assessment is the end *examination.

Summerhill School A private school, founded by A. S. *Neill, an early proponent of pupil-centred democratic schooling in which children are acknowledged to have the right to make decisions about what and when they will learn. Founded in 1921 near Dresden, Germany, and now currently occupying a large Victorian house and grounds near the east coast in Suffolk, the school is run as a democratic community consisting of about 95 children aged between 5 and 18, with about one member of staff to every 20 children. All—staff and pupils alike—have equal status as members of that community. Although run mainly as a *co-educational *boarding school, drawing children from a diverse range of racial and cultural backgrounds, it also takes day pupils and provides a curriculum which includes *General Certificate of Secondary Education subjects. One of the ways in which it differs from a conventional school is that children are under no compulsion to attend lessons, and are provided with free access to communal areas where they can play, socialize, or engage in creative activities.

The school timetable is created in response to the subject choices made by older pupils, and makes their preferred subjects available, although not mandatory. This democratic approach is based on Neill's philosophy that children learn self-confidence, tolerance, and consideration not from any externally imposed discipline, but from being given the freedom to think and choose for themselves. For the child, the most important right is considered to be the right to play. According to this approach, the decision to engage in formal learning should be a choice made freely, and therefore attendance at lessons should be optional.

The professional role and practice of the teachers within this community are also different in some respects from those required of teachers in conventional schooling environments. For example, they will offer one-to-one teaching for pupils who prefer this to a classroom approach; and they meet every day in order to discuss individual pupil progress and to plan the best response and provision for each child. As the philosophy on which the school is based rejects any imposition of hierarchy, teachers cannot use their authority as adults in order to impose values, nor their adult power to intervene in problem-solving. Instead of teacher-imposed *sanctions, issues of *discipline, *bullying, and negative or *disruptive *behaviour are solved by community meetings or by 'ombudsmen' elected from within the community. The rejection of hierarchy also applies between pupils themselves, the older children having no more rights or authority than the very youngest.

The original Summerhill provision was part of an international school in Hellerau, outside Dresden, but was relocated by Neill in the first instance to Sonntagsberg in Austria, and then, in the early 1920s, to Lyme Regis in England, where it opened with five pupils. In 1927 it moved to its current site, still retaining the original name. During the Second World War the school was evacuated to Wales, while the premises in Suffolk were used by the army. Pupil figures fell in the 1950s; but interest in the school and in the philosophy of democratic, pupil-centred schooling was kindled by the UK publication in 1962 of Neill's book *Summerhill—a Radical Approach to Childhood*. The school continues to attract controversy, often depicted in the press as being excessively liberal in its attitude to learning and behaviour management. Its emphasis on individual fulfilment and goal-setting sets it at odds with two dominant current trends in state education: the *instrumentalist emphasis on education for employment or the good of the economy, and the growth of statutory testing and assessment. In 2006–7 the school was engaged in a much-publicized conflict of ideas with *Ofsted, which was finally resolved in the courts in Summerhill's favour.

The philosophy of Summerhill School is reflected in Neill's claim that 'The function of the child is to live his own life—not the life that his anxious parents think he should live, nor a life according to the purpose of the educator who thinks he knows best.'

Further Reading: A. S. Neill *Summerhill—a Radical Approach to Childhood* (Gollancz, 1962).

summer school 1. Informal, non-examined courses held in schools during the summer holidays, usually to help pupils improve their attainment in literacy or numeracy, or to undertake a range of creative or sporting activities. Attendance is not obligatory.

2. Residential summer schools are also held, usually on a suitable university *campus, by the *Open University in order to provide its students with an opportunity to interact and to engage in traditional modes of learning.

super-head A *head teacher who, because of their proven outstanding ability as leader and manager of their own school, is given responsibility for raising standards of achievement in other schools besides their own, or in a group or cluster of schools. The introduction of the 'super-head' (1997) or 'superhead' (2005) has been twice presented as an innovative measure by *secretaries of state responsible for education. In December 1997, during David Blunkett's term as Secretary of State for Education and Employment, it was announced that 'super-heads' would be introduced as part of the *Education Action Zone (EAZ) initiative, their role being to raise school standards at the group of schools within an EAZ area. These super-heads are chosen from among those head teachers who have a proven ability to raise standards in schools which were *failing or which were previously showing poor results, and they receive enhanced salaries, funded from the capital sums invested by the government in the EAZ.

The term 'super-head' was presented again as a policy initiative in 2002 under the Secretary of State, Estelle Morris, in the context of school partnerships and clusters. Heads with 'strategic vision', it was announced, would take control of a group of schools in an initiative to spread their expertise. Clusters of schools would operate under one governing body and one super-head, who would take responsibility for strategic planning, while each school would retain a head teacher with primary responsibility for teaching and learning.

The response from head teachers in general to the concept and creation of super-heads has always been cautious, some welcoming the creation of an enhanced leadership role, equivalent to that of chief executive, while others have argued that effective leadership requires the head teacher to be a constant presence in their own school, and that in practical terms turning around the performance of a failing school or group of low-achieving schools is not a task which could readily be accomplished on a part-time basis.

supply teacher A teacher employed by the school on a temporary basis to cover the teaching of a member of staff who is absent. They may register with *local authorities, or with private supply agencies, and their services are called upon as needed.

support staff This can be used to describe a wide range of non-qualified teacher status staff, from *teaching assistants to technicians and administrators.

surface learning *See* DEEP LEARNING.

syllabus A specification of the content of a course of study. The term itself is closely associated with courses of general or academic study, such as the *General Certificate of Secondary Education. For the *vocationally focused *General National Vocational Qualification, on the other hand, the term used was not 'syllabus' but 'specification'. A single *curriculum may encompass several syllabuses, just as the *national curriculum encompasses the syllabus or *programme of study for each subject area. In drawing up a *scheme of work and individual *lesson plans, the teacher translates the contents of the syllabus into an appropriately sequenced series of lessons designed to enable learners to achieve the learning outcomes which the syllabus sets out.

synthetic phonics   *See* PHONICS; PHONICS SCREENING CHECK.

tabula rasa The mind in its original, uninformed state, before any learning begins. This concept is found in the philosophy of John Locke (1632–1704) and Jean-Jacques *Rousseau; but it is one which many educators do not accept, since it assumes that the mind is shaped solely by what is learned, and discounts the idea of individual predispositions or inherited characteristics. In this sense, it reflects the argument that nurture, not *nature, is of predominant importance in shaping an individual's cognitive skills. The literal meaning of this Latin phrase is a (writing) tablet scraped clean (of writing), suggesting that a young pupil's mind is open to be shaped as the teacher wishes.

tacit knowledge *Knowledge or understanding which the learner possesses, but which they are not aware they possess until the teacher helps them to articulate it by drawing it out, often with the technique of *Socratic questioning. This model of learning stands in direct contrast to approaches such as *rote learning, which begin with the assumption that all knowledge resides in the teacher and is transmitted to the learner, who must then memorize it. The recognition of tacit knowledge is also a recognition that the learner, not the teacher, plays the central role in the learning process. *See also* LEARNER-CENTRED.

Talk-Less Teaching A mode of teaching which maximizes opportunities for learners to contribute to classroom dialogue as well as participate actively in lessons. This approach aims to reduce poor-quality teacher talk which can lead to inattention and restlessness in learners. While the methodology does not characterize lecture-based learning as ineffective, it recognizes that too much teacher talk can prevent the teacher from ascertaining essential information during a lesson about the extent of learners' understanding and progress. Talk-Less Teaching focuses on the importance of gathering feedback from learners about their progress during lessons so that teachers can assess the impact of their teaching as the lesson proceeds. This emphasis on noting visible progress means a teacher is encouraged to adapt to the emerging needs of the learners as the lesson unfolds. The pedagogy also places importance on requiring active participation from all learners with its 'no passengers' approach to classroom instruction. Learners are encouraged to be self-reliant, self-reflective, and proactive, rather than over-relying on the teacher or being habitual passive recipients of learning. The celebration of learners' own questions, peer teaching, and collaborative activities are often key features of Talk-Less Teaching. *See also*

ACTIVE LEARNING; COLLABORATIVE LEARNING; DIALOGIC TEACHING; LECTURE; VISIBLE LEARNING.

Further Reading: I. Wallace and L. Kirkman *Talk-Less Teaching: Practice, Participation and Progress* (Crown House Publishing, 2014).

targets Part of the vocabulary associated with improvement and raising standards. Successive governments have drawn up national or 'floor' targets (sometimes referred to as 'floor standards') for education and training, such as those announced by the *Department for Education (DfE) in 2013 for primary and secondary schools. In 2011, the Department for Education announced its intention to end the requirement for schools to set their own targets, and 2012 saw the final round of statutory target-setting in schools. After this time, schools were no longer obliged to report these targets to the *local authority (LA), and LAs were no longer required to report them to central government. While schools are no longer required to set these statutory whole-school targets, many school leaders do continue to set internal targets for their own schools. Schools are, however, expected to set appropriately challenging targets for individual learners and groups of learners through the analysis of pupil performance data. These targets are used to monitor and track learners' progress. IW

⊕ SEE WEB LINKS
• Sets out the 2013 targets for primary and secondary schools.

task An activity or piece of written work which is undertaken by the student in order that their achievement or progress may be assessed. An *assignment may be divided into a number of tasks, each carrying a stated number of marks and each of which the student is required to complete in order that their overall performance or *competence may be measured.

The word is also used in the term *Standard Task (originally Standard Assessment Task), which is used to describe *national curriculum *assessments of pupil attainment.

taught time In the context of schools, taught time represents the number of hours which pupils spend in lessons. A report produced by *Ofsted in 1994, with the eponymous title *Taught Time*, suggested that there was insufficient evidence of a correlation between levels of pupil achievement and length of teaching time to support arguments for an increase in the recommended minimum taught time in schools. It may be taken, however, to support the argument that the quality of learning is not solely dependent on the quantity of teaching. In *further and *higher education, taught time refers to the number of hours of active teacher contact, as opposed to hours of structured or supervised independent study, such as that undertaken in project work or for research. Thus, a *module at *master's level, for example, might be designated as involving the student in 120 hours of study, 30 of which are taught time.

Taunton Report (1868) Although distant in terms of time, the Taunton Report remains significant today in that it throws light on the origins of a peculiarly English educational characteristic, which some would claim persists in various guises: the ranking of educational needs according to *social class. The Report, produced as a result of the Taunton Commission into education, claimed that there were three grades of parents. In the 'first' grade were those who wished their children to receive schooling up to and beyond the age of 18, and who had 'no wish to displace the classics from their present position in the forefront of English education'. Significantly, such parents were considered unwilling for their children to receive an education aimed at preparing them for work. The 'second grade' of parents, who wished their children to be educated to the age of 16, were thought to approve of a curriculum which included not only Latin, but also 'a thorough knowledge of those subjects which can be turned to practical use in business'. This would include little that we would now term *vocational, but rather English, mathematics, natural science, and perhaps a modern language. The 'third grade' of parents, whose children might be educated to the age of 14, were considered to belong to 'a class distinctly lower in the scale', and to desire an education for their children which included no classics but only reading, writing, and arithmetic. This uncritical grading of educational provision according to social status seems shocking to us today; but two of its underlying assumptions—that curriculum subjects acquire increasing status the further removed they are from the world of work, and that prestige is attached to, and conclusions about social status drawn from, a school education to the age of 18—can still be seen as integral to common-sense assumptions about education and training a century and a half later. *See also* PARITY OF ESTEEM.

taxonomy The practice of classification, particularly in biology, where organisms are grouped according to similarities of structure or genes. In more general educational terms it most commonly refers to the classification of different orders of learning *objectives created in the 1950s by Benjamin Bloom (1913–99). *See also* BLOOM'S TAXONOMY.

Taylor Report (1977) Published as a result of the Taylor Inquiry set up in 1975, the Report recommended a greater involvement by *governors in curriculum issues within English and Welsh primary and secondary schools. It further suggested that members of governing bodies should be drawn in equal numbers from parents, representatives of both the *local authority and the local community, and *teachers. These recommendations can be seen as a step towards establishing the composition and active involvement of governing bodies as they exist today.

teacher Although most usually referring to one who teaches in a school, the title of 'teacher' also applies in a wider context to include professionals in other educational institutions, as well as those working outside such institutions who nevertheless have a *pedagogical role, such as giving instruction in the playing of a musical instrument. 'Teacher', therefore, may be used in both a specific (referring to a profession) and a more general (referring to an activity) sense. There is a growing tendency to refer to professionals teaching in *further education, too, as 'teachers'—for example, in *White Papers and in the professional standards for the sector—rather than as 'lecturers', by which title they were previously known; and the same trend is noticeable, although to a lesser extent, in the context of *higher education. This development may reflect a growing recognition both that effective teaching may involve more than the ability to deliver a lecture, and that educational professionals in universities and colleges are usually required to demonstrate a wider range of teaching skills than the term 'lecturer', when taken literally, would suggest. Thus, 'teacher' may be taken to cover a range of more specific terms which, as well as 'lecturer', include 'trainer', 'instructor', and 'tutor'.

Although, like most other professions, teaching requires a lengthy period of training and adherence to a professional code of conduct, many would argue that teachers are not normally accorded parity of status with other professions, such as the law and medicine. During the 1980s they were for a time subjected to what Stephen Ball (1990) refers to as a 'discourse of derision' when they appeared to be held culpable both by the popular press and in White Paper rhetoric for a number of national ills, including the high proportion of unskilled and unqualified school-leavers, an under-skilled workforce, and high levels of national unemployment. Nevertheless, well-qualified and highly motivated individuals continue to enter the profession in large numbers, most acknowledging that it provides them with an opportunity to bring about positive change in learners' lives. *See also* NEWLY QUALIFIED TEACHER; QUALIFIED TEACHER STATUS.

Further Reading: S. Ball *Politics and Policy Making in Education* (Routledge, 1990).

teacher assessment levels The formal *assessment of a pupil's performance in English and maths made by the *teacher at the end of *key stage 2 is expressed in terms of the level at which the pupil is currently working. Assessment is made against the levels of attainment expected at this stage, which are between levels 3 and 5. This assessment is no longer a formal requirement but is still used by many schools. *See also* STANDARD TASKS.

teacher competency framework A descriptive taxonomy of teachers' roles, functions, and required knowledge and skills. Such a framework is applied in a number of countries under a variety of names. In Australia, for example, it is known as the Competency Framework for Teachers. In Scotland it is known as the Framework on Teacher Competence (FTC) and falls under the aegis of the General Teaching Council for Scotland. In England the *teachers' standards serves the equivalent purpose.

teachers' conditions of service Conditions of service for schoolteachers are set out in an annual document by the *Secretary of State responsible for schools. This is known as the *School Teachers' Pay and Conditions Document*, and specifies the annual number of working hours (including teaching and other duties) for the individual teacher. In response to the rising number of administrative tasks which teachers were expected to undertake, a number of amendments to their conditions of service were introduced in 2004 in order to reallocate some non-teaching administrative duties to clerical or support staff within the school, and to allow guaranteed preparation and planning time to *primary school teachers.

teachers' pay *See* PAY, TEACHERS'.

teachers' standards Effective from September 2012, these standards set out
the minimum professional requirements for teachers in terms of both their
practice and their conduct. They are used to assess trainee teachers working
towards *qualified teacher status (QTS), as well as *newly qualified teachers
(NQTs) completing their statutory induction period. The standards are also used
as a point of reference in conducting *teacher appraisals. They consist of two
sections. The first relates to standards of professional practice in teaching and
supporting learning. The second, which is concerned with standards of conduct,
is used as a basis for decision-making by the *National College of Teaching and
Leadership when deciding on cases of alleged misconduct.

(⊕) SEE WEB LINKS
• Provides the full text of the teachers' standards.

teachers.tv A free digital television channel, launched in 2005, to provide
teachers and other education professionals with relevant programmes which
support their *continuing professional development. In 2010 it was reduced to an
online provision only; and was discontinued altogether in 2011 as result of
government money saving measures. Much of its material, however, is archived
and can still be accessed as a teacher development resource either recorded to
disk or as streamed videos.

(⊕) SEE WEB LINKS
• Links to streamed videos for use in schools.

teachers' unions Organized national bodies formed to promote and protect
teachers' interests and to negotiate the pay and working conditions of members.
Most teachers' unions are sector-specific, the *National Union of Teachers and
the *National Association of Schoolmasters Union of Women Teachers being two
of the largest unions for schoolteachers in England and Wales, and the
*University and College Union the largest for teachers in *colleges and
*universities. Other major unions include the *Professional Association of
Teachers, and, in Scotland, the *Educational Institute of Scotland. Separate
unions exist for educational professionals who work in a management role.
These include the *National Association of Head Teachers and the *Secondary
Heads Association.

teacher training *See* QUALIFIED TEACHER STATUS.

teaching and learning responsibility (TLR) Responsibility which schools
can allocate to individual teachers for specific issues relating to teaching and
learning, which carry additional salary, calculated as **TLR points**. They were
introduced in January 2006, and are available in two bandings. TLR1, the higher
band, carries a higher maximum and minimum salary than TLR2. There can be
different levels of TLR payment within one band, and the value of payments
within the set minimum and maximum for each band is a matter for individual
schools' discretion, so long as there is a £1 500 differential between each level of

payment within the two. The governing body, in consultation with staff, make the decision about how many TLRs will be offered within the school, which bands they will be, and their value in terms of additional salary. TLR points are only awarded to teachers who have significant levels of responsibilities which are not part of every teacher's workload. For example, a teacher who has taken on the role of whole-school *literacy coordinator would fall into this category. One of the key criteria for awarding TLR points is that the teacher's additional duties must be focused on teaching and learning (rather than, for example, administration or management), and must involve the leadership or development of a curriculum area, or of pupil development across the curriculum. To be awarded TLR points in the higher band, a teacher must also have line management responsibility for a significant number of other staff. The TLR replaced the previous system of Management Allowances used in schools. *See also* PAY, TEACHERS'.

teaching assistant (TA) Sometimes, and increasingly, referred to as a learning support assistant or LSA, this is an adult employed to assist a qualified teacher in the classroom. They may have a general role in the classroom or may be assigned to assist a particular student who needs additional support in literacy, numeracy, or the acquisition of English as a second language; or has a *statement of special needs. The responsibilities of a teaching assistant can vary greatly and depend to a large extent on whether they are working in primary or secondary education. Typical activities might include preparing resources for lessons, putting up displays, administrative tasks such as photocopying or *marking, and working with individual children or small groups. The qualifications and experience required are decided at a local level, by the school or *local authority. Where specific requirements or qualifications are required, training towards these may often be provided on the job.

teaching practice (TP) Trainee teachers receiving their initial teacher education for the *primary, secondary, or *further education sectors are required to undertake a period of practical experience in a *school (which is known as **school based training**) or *college appropriate to the sector in which they plan to teach. During this they are expected to observe the teaching and other professional practices of qualified and experienced teachers, and to carry out teaching themselves, under supervision, for gradually increased periods of time. This allows them to apply and reflect upon the theoretical knowledge and understanding which they have gained during their training in college or *university. Their performance in their teaching practice *placement is assessed by their college or university tutor and by a designated member of staff in the placement school or college, who may also be the trainee teacher's *mentor. In order to be considered for *qualified teacher status, the trainee teacher must reach the required standard of attainment in their teaching practice as well as in their theoretical work.

teaching style Just as pupils and students can be said to have differing *learning styles, so teachers will vary in the style of teaching with which they are most comfortable. For example, where one teacher possesses the skills best suited to deliver a lecture to a large group of learners, another may feel that their strength lies in working at an individual level with small groups of learners, using such techniques as question and answer. Whatever the individual teacher's preferred teaching style, however, they are expected, as professionals, to develop and use a wide range of approaches and styles which are appropriate both to the needs of their learners and to the nature and level of their subject. Nevertheless, most teachers will admit to having a preferred style of teaching with which they feel at their most confident. *See also* METHOD.

teaching to the test Both teachers and parents have expressed concerns that the pressures exerted by national regimes of testing and examinations are leading teachers to focus too narrowly on the knowledge necessary to enable learners to pass the test or end examination, rather than developing in them an understanding of the subject and its context within the wider field of knowledge. Teaching in this way has become known as 'teaching to the test'. Many educationalists and teachers claim that such an instrumental approach stifles enquiry and is detrimental to the education process.

TeachMeet An informal, pre-arranged meeting of teachers for the purpose of sharing best practice. Originating in Scotland in 2006, and now held regularly in many countries, including England, Northern Ireland, Republic of Ireland, Canada, Australia, Eastern Europe, and Scandinavia, a TeachMeet takes the form of short presentations and round table discussions. Teachers volunteer beforehand, through the TeachMeet web site, to present or demonstrate an innovative and successful strategy, idea, or resource. There is open entry and no attendance fee is charged.

(((⊕))) SEE WEB LINKS
• The TeachMeet web site, which provides details of recent events.

team teaching A strategy which involves two or more teachers working simultaneously with the same group of learners. This might be employed for practical reasons in particularly large classes when the *pupil–teacher ratio justifies the deployment of more than one teacher; or on educational grounds where the subject expertise of more than one teacher is necessary for the students' learning of a specific topic. Team teaching is also useful for conducting peer evaluations, since it allows teachers an opportunity to provide reciprocal feedback on one another's performance.

Tech levels *See* VOCATIONAL A LEVELS.

Technical and Vocational Education Initiative (TVEI) An initiative set up in 1983 and aimed at supporting school and college provision of technical and *pre-vocational courses for 14–18-year-old pupils. Funded by the Department of Employment (DoE), and operating through locally organized advisory teams, TVEI also promoted **core skills**, including those in communication, numeracy, and information technology, which were the forerunners to today's *key skills. Although the TVEI was formally linked to the Manpower Services Commission

and later the Training and Enterprise Council through their common connection
with the DoE, local TVEI teams often worked very closely with their *local
authority advisory service for schools. In many areas they extended their remit to
provide training and policy advice on equal opportunities issues. Their funding
began to be withdrawn from 1991, which brought the initiative to a gradual end.
It is seen as a landmark intervention of the late 20th century in terms of core
skills, *inclusion, and *information communication technology.

Technological Baccalaureate *See* BACCALAURÉAT.

technology **1.** Educational technology encompasses the strategies and
techniques relating to the learning process, as well as the equipment and
resources used to support it.
   2. A *national curriculum subject introduced in 1989 and combining the
subject areas of craft, design, and technology, art, business studies, home
economics, and information communication technology. It has now become
known as **Design and Technology**.

term Traditionally there are three terms in the academic year, during which
pupils or students are expected to attend for classes. These are usually referred to
as Autumn, Winter, and Summer terms, although some universities use
alternative, traditional names, such as *Michaelmas Term for the Autumn Term.
The academic year begins at the commencement of the Autumn Term and
ends at the close of the Summer Term, with breaks at Christmas, Easter, and
July–August. School terms are usually longer than college or university terms,
and are punctuated by *half-term breaks, usually of a week's duration round
about the term's mid-point. In 2001 the Independent Commission on the
Organization of the School Year recommended that schools should adopt a
six-term year, incorporating a shorter summer break. This was to be in place
by 2005, but is proving contentious and difficult to implement in many *local
authority areas. Those who support the idea of reorganizing school terms in this
way suggest that it would have advantages for the timing and assessment of
public examinations such as the *General Certificate of Secondary Education and
*General Certificate of Education *Advanced Level.

terminal examination Also known colloquially as an **end exam**, the
terminal examination is one which takes place on completion of the course of
study. Examples include *examinations for the award of a *degree at the end of
the period of *undergraduate studies; and the examinations in *General
Certificate of Secondary Education subjects which take place at the end of *Key
Stage 4. A terminal examination is a means of carrying out a *summative
assessment, rather than an ongoing *formative evaluation which aims to help
learners to improve their performance.

terminate To end formally a student's enrolment on a course at college or
university, either because they have not completed the required work, or because
they have failed to reach the required standard. At many colleges of further or
higher education, student work which fails to meet the necessary criteria will be

'referred' back to the student for a second attempt, although in such cases it is normal to award no more than the minimum pass mark if the student's resubmission is successful. The student may be 'failed and terminated' if their work still fails to meet the grade. Despite its associations, termination in this context is not so quite so sinister a matter as the word might suggest.

tertiary college An institution which provides both a general sixth form *curriculum and *vocational *further education for students aged 16–19. The name derives from the fact that such colleges provide the third stage of education, after *primary and secondary. They are distinct from general further education *colleges in that they cater for a specific age group and offer a less extensive and varied curriculum.

testing The process of assessing and measuring a learner's attainment in a task, a lesson, a subject, or a *programme of study. In schools it is a term most commonly associated with the national testing which takes place at the end of each *key stage. The trend towards extensive national testing, while applauded by some educators as contributing to a raising of achievement, is viewed less favourably by others who consider it imposes a pressure on pupils and teachers alike, which is detrimental to the learning process and the purposes of education. *See also* STANDARD TASKS.

Te Whaariki The New Zealand Ministry of Education early childhood curriculum policy statement, published in 1996. It is a framework for providing children's early learning and development within a sociocultural context. It emphasizes the learning partnership between teachers, parents, families, and children, and is the bicultural, incorporating Maori as well as Western cultural values. It represents a national curriculum for the early childhood sector in New Zealand, and is intended to encourage the aspirations of children as competent, confident learners and communicators who know that they can make a valued contribution to society. Its philosophy closely reflects that which underpins the development of *Reggio Emilia schooling, and it has been influential in the design of the UK *Birth to Three Matters framework.

Its four broad principles of empowerment, holistic development, family and community, and relationships are interwoven; hence Te Whaariki: a Maori word meaning a woven mat for all to stand on. Within those principles there are five strands: well-being, belonging, contribution, communication, and exploration. The principles and strands are assessed through narrative observations, or learning stories, of children's activities and dispositions, with additional evidence of photographic records to highlight learning processes.

This curriculum framework is closely aligned to the experiential and philosophical ideas of *Rousseau, *Dewey, *Isaacs, *Vygotsky, and *Malaguzzi, and has therefore attracted international interest among *early years practitioners. AW

Further Reading: Ministry of Education *Te Whaariki: He Whaariki Matauranga mo nga Moi Aoteroa. Early Childhood Education* (Learning Media, 1996).

(((●))) SEE WEB LINKS

• Presents the theoretical origins of the Te Whaariki curriculum in New Zealand.

thesis 1. A lengthy piece of academic writing presenting an argument based on research, and presented for *assessment towards an academic award at *postgraduate level, such as a *master's degree or a *doctorate. A thesis at this level is usually expected to contribute something new to existing knowledge within its field.

2. An original idea or contribution to knowledge, for which a carefully argued case is presented, usually, but not always, in the form of sense 1 above.

Thus, the term may refer to the written document or to the argument contained within the text. *See also* DISSERTATION.

thinking skills Incorporated into the teaching of *national curriculum subjects, particularly in *primary schools (*Key Stages 1 and 2), the development of thinking skills in young pupils is thought to improve the quality of their learning and raise their standard of attainment in school-based tests. The term itself covers a range of different approaches, exercises, and activities, the common elements of which usually include problem-solving and classroom discussion. Most approaches stress the importance of language and articulation, and some use specific teaching strategies to develop pupils' *cognitive skills. In the UK in the 1980s and 1990s the **Cognitive Acceleration** through Science Education project provided evidence to suggest that the development of thinking skills improved Key Stage 3 pupils' attainment in science; and this project has now been extended into other national curriculum subject areas.

Of all the names associated with the development of thinking skills, it is perhaps that of Edward de Bono (b. 1933)—and his concept of *lateral thinking as a tool for problem-solving—which is most familiar in the UK. Other approaches include that of the American philosopher Matthew Lipman (1922–2010), who founded the Institute for the Advancement of Philosophy for Children in New Jersey. His belief that young pupils were generally encouraged to accept facts and opinions from teachers without questioning these for themselves led him to develop an approach to the teaching of thinking skills which involves classes of pupils and their teachers reading specially constructed stories, or 'novels', together and exploring the questions or anomalies which these give rise to through guided discussions. The questions addressed arise from the children's curiosity rather than from any pre-planned agenda from the teacher. This approach to thinking skills involves children in exploratory thinking as well as discussion with their teacher and their peers. It is known as **philosophy for children**.

Another key name in the development of thinking skills is that of Reuven Feuerstein (1921–2014), who worked on the cognitive assessment of young immigrants entering Israel at the end of the Second World War. His project was to improve young learners' performance in cognitive tests. This led to the development of a programme of activities which could be used to improve children's learning process, providing appropriate activities to address each different area of difficulty and to enrich learning. These activities were known as 'instruments'; and thus Feuerstein's approach became known as the **instrumental enrichment** programme.

Lateral thinking, cognitive acceleration, philosophy for children, and instrumental enrichment are only some of the approaches which may inform the teaching of thinking skills in schools.

Further Reading: P. J. M. Costello *Thinking Skills and Early Childhood Education* (Routledge, 2013).

threshold *See* PERFORMANCE-RELATED PAY.

timetable The formal organization of teachers' and learners' time, and the allocation and coordination of timings, accommodation, and other resources within an educational institution. The timetable provides information about who should be where, and at what time. Individual learners and teachers each have their own timetable showing how their formal teaching or learning time will be spent. These may cover a day, a week, a *term, a year, or a programme covering several years. The institutional timetable is a collation and summary of all this information. In some organizations or departments a specific member of staff has responsibility for drawing up and coordinating timetables, although the process is more usually carried out now electronically through the use of specialized software. This task is known as 'timetabling'.

Tomlinson Report (1996) The Tomlinson Report *Inclusive Learning* played a key role in the *post-compulsory sector's *widening participation agenda. Where the *Kennedy Report of 1997 examined ways of improving learning opportunities for all, the Tomlinson Report explored widening participation specifically for learners with *learning difficulties or disabilities. Tomlinson found that students with *special educational needs were underachieving in the post-compulsory sector; were unable to access the wider curriculum; and were, for the most part, lacking in confidence, possibly because of their previous school experience of education and learning. The Report found that historically learners with learning difficulties or disabilities were excluded from mainstream opportunities in the post-compulsory sector. It also found that this form of exclusion affected the culture of learning providers such as *further education colleges.

Tomlinson recommended that the responsibility should be on the educational institution to empathize and respond to the individual, and to address the needs of that individual learner. Among the Report's recommendations was a requirement that institutions should publish their own disability statements, with information regarding entry and openness of access, which should operate regardless of age, gender, ethnicity, or disability. The Report envisaged that such a focus on inclusive learning would improve the quality of learner experience for students with difficulties or disabilities, and, indeed, change the culture of educational establishments by focusing on planning with and supporting the needs of individuals. VC, KA

Tomlinson Report (2004) Entitled *14–19 Curriculum and Qualification Reform: Final Report of the Working Group on 14–19 Reform* (Department for Education and Skills, 2004), the Report of the group led by Sir Mike Tomlinson was instrumental in the introduction of the *14–19 Diploma. It suggested that such a diploma should be introduced over a ten-year period from 2005 and should eventually replace all existing public examinations at *National Qualifications Framework levels 2 and 3, including the *General Certificate of Secondary Education, *General Certificate of Education *Advanced Levels, and equivalent vocational qualifications. Other radical reforms recommended in the Report included the replacement of all coursework by one extended **project** undertaken by each pupil in *Key Stage 4, and a substantial reduction in the number of examinations which pupils are required to take. It was also influential in the introduction of the *personalized curriculum, suggesting that pupils should be encouraged to progress at their own rate rather than be constrained to progress in cohorts organized according to age group.

topic An integrated, thematic approach to learning, implemented mainly in *primary schools, which uses a particular focus such as 'water' or 'Romans' through which to develop pupils' knowledge and understanding of required *national curriculum subjects such as mathematics and English, as well as to encourage their creative and imaginative skills.

trainee Someone undergoing *training. It has come to be used in preference to 'student' for learners on *vocational programmes, and is part of the vocabulary of *National Vocational Qualifications. It is also applied by government agencies such as the *College of Leadership and Teaching, to student teachers. Its use raises the questions of how we define the difference between a student and a trainee and of whether there is a value judgement—for example, about status—implicit within the distinction between provision which is described as 'education' and that which is described as 'training'.

training Usually applied to *vocational learning or learning of a practical rather than a theoretical nature. There are, however, anomalies in this regard, since it is usual to refer to 'trainee teachers' and 'trainee doctors', contexts in which a substantial body of theoretical learning is involved as well as practical skills. Perhaps the broadest distinction to be made between education and training is that the latter is instrumental in preparing the learner for a specific task, job, or profession, while education has a more general, developmental purpose as envisaged in the concept of *liberal education. *See also* TRAINEE.

training college *See* COLLEGE OF EDUCATION.

Training for Work (TfW) Run by *Scottish Enterprise, TfW provides training support for people in Scotland who are unemployed or are actively looking for work. The programme is targeted at adults aged 25 and over.   SM

training school A secondary school which, in partnership with a local *university or other *higher education institution involved in teacher training, develops strategies for *initial teacher training and trains their staff to develop *mentoring skills with which to support trainee teachers who undertake training within the school. In return for taking on this role, schools are offered additional funding. The scheme was recommended in the 1998 *Green Paper *Teachers: Meeting the Challenge of Change*, and was introduced in 2000. *See also* TEACHING PRACTICE.

Transfer Test A term referring to the *Eleven Plus tests in Northern Ireland which have survived as part of the system of academic selection. These tests continued in practice until autumn 2008. The **Burns Report** of 2001 stated, 'we have been left in no doubt that the eleven-plus transfer tests are socially divisive, damage self-esteem, place unreasonable pressures on pupils, primary teachers, and parents, disrupt teaching and learning at an important stage in the primary curriculum and reinforce inequality of opportunity'. It is interesting to note, however, that results at *General Certificate of Secondary Education and *Advanced Level are significantly better in Northern Ireland than England and Wales, although it has not been proven that these statistics have any causal relationship with the continued practice of *selection.   JH

(⊕) SEE WEB LINKS
• Provides further information about the Transfer Test.

transition The progression of pupils from one stage or school to another; most notably, from *primary to secondary school. It is recognized that the challenges this presents can prove stressful for many pupils, as it usually involves exchanging their position as an older child in a smaller school for that of a younger child in a much larger one. Moreover, pupils at this stage must often exchange the security of one teacher and one classroom for a system in which they will be taught by several different teachers every day, and expected to move from classroom to classroom in the process. To acknowledge and ease this difficult transition, schools may adopt a number of strategies, such as the provision by secondary schools of 'taster' visits for primary pupils so that they may familiarize themselves with the school they will soon be attending; and visits by secondary teachers to primary schools to introduce themselves to pupils who will shortly be making the transition. One of the arguments used in the *Plowden Report in support of introducing *middle schools was that they would ease the transition by introducing gradual change in the 'middle years' rather than the abrupt transplanting of pupils at 11. Transition applies to any stage of progression, including that from secondary school to *further or *higher education.

tripartite system The division of the secondary sector into three types of school: *grammar schools, technical schools, and modern schools, as suggested in the **Spens Report** (1938). Following the *Education Act 1944 (*Butler Act), *local authorities were permitted to provide a range of secondary schooling. Some opted for the tripartite system, while others established a dual system of grammar and secondary modern schools. Both involved the selection of pupils by ability at 11, which aimed to provide each child with the secondary education best suited to their *abilities and *aptitudes. Within authorities operating a tripartite system these abilities were classified as academic (grammar schools), technical (technical schools), and practical (secondary modern schools). The system was replaced by non-selective, *comprehensive secondary education in most local authority areas during the 1970s following the Education Act 1976. *See also* BIPARTITE SYSTEM.

tripos A course of study leading to an *honours degree at Cambridge University, where the student is required to pass two tripos examinations in order to be awarded their *Bachelor of Arts. The name refers to the three-legged stool on which, in medieval times, graduates sat to deliver a satirical speech at their degree ceremony.

truancy The persistent failure to attend compulsory schooling. Many secondary schools report this as a growing problem, with pupils who truant now being referred to as **school refusers**. Schools are required by law to report on truancy numbers, and to work with local education welfare officers to address problems of attendance with individual pupils and their parents or carers. In *White Paper rhetoric, truancy has been associated with subsequent unemployment and even criminality. On the whole, school refusers are often among the lowest of achievers, particularly in the *key skills of *numeracy and communication; although the causal relationship between truancy and low achievement is not clear-cut, in the sense of whether pupils play truant because they are low achievers or are low achievers because they truant. Parents of persistent truants can be prosecuted and fined or sentenced to a term of imprisonment.

tuition fees *See* FEES.

tutor In schools, *teachers responsible for supporting the work or welfare of a group of pupils may be designated a tutor, as in 'form tutor' and 'year tutor'. In *further and *higher education a tutor is responsible for overseeing the workload of a student or group of students, and for providing support in matters relating to their studies. Trainee teachers on *teaching practice, for example, have a tutor to advise them and to monitor their progress in their *placement. A tutor may also be a subject specialist who guides or advises the student in a specific aspect of their academic discipline, such as supporting students through their *master's degree or *doctoral studies. Like the term 'teacher', 'tutor' cannot be defined by one specific role. Broadly, it could be said that tutoring involves providing support for learning, often for individuals or relatively small groups of learners, while teaching suggests a more actively didactic role. *See also* TUTORIAL.

tutorial A meeting between a *tutor and one or more students (sometimes referred to as tutees) which focuses on some aspect of the students' learning or *assessment. They are an integral part of *higher education provision, but are also used in *further education and in some schools. In terms of time and resources, tutorials are considered costly because they normally involve tutors working with relatively small numbers of students. Perhaps for this reason, the inclusion of extensive tutorial support in students' *timetables is becoming increasingly problematic in some higher education departments.

underachiever Someone whose *academic performance falls measurably below what might be expected from what is known of their *ability, learning potential, or *intelligence. Reasons for underachievement can include language or cultural difficulties, where the learner's ability to express themselves is hampered by their lack of language skills or lack of familiarity with culturally specific concepts and ideas. Emotional problems or difficulties in the home environment can also be the cause of underachievement, as can lack of motivation or a curriculum which does not challenge or engage.

undergraduate A student on a *higher education course which leads to the award of a *first *degree or *bachelor's degree. On achieving their degree—in other words, going through the process of **graduating**—they are referred to as *graduates. Undergraduate can also be used as an adjective to describe the level of study for a first degree, as in the phrase, 'an undergraduate programme'.

unit A component or subdivision of a course or *programme of study, which may be taught or assessed as a discrete section of the whole. The term was also used in a very specific sense from 1993 to describe the component parts of a *General National Vocational Qualification (GNVQ), which were separately assessed and could be accumulated over time in order to gain the full GNVQ award. In the process of tailoring the design of the GNVQ and the *modular *Advanced Level (A level) to become more compatible for the implementation of *Curriculum 2000, the term 'unit' was gradually dropped in favour of 'module', so that the *Vocational A level, which succeeded the GNVQ, was subdivided into modules rather than units. The term is still in use in the wider context of educational and training programmes, however, as in the phrases 'unit of study' and 'unit of assessment'.

Universities and Colleges Admissions Service (UCAS) The organization which processes candidates' applications for a place at a *university or other *higher education institution to study for a *first *degree, a university *diploma, a *Higher National Diploma or for *teacher training. It was formed in 1992 as a consequence of the merger between the Universities Central Council on Admissions (UCCA) and the Polytechnics Central Admissions Systems (PCAS), which followed as a result of the *Further and Higher Education Act 1992, which granted polytechnics university status. Applicants to higher education who have yet to sit their *Advanced Levels (A levels) will normally be offered a place which is conditional on their achieving the required number of

A level points. Those whose results fail to gain them their conditional place, or those who have waited until after their results to make their application, may go through the UCAS **clearing** process, which aims to match suitable applicants to places which remain unfilled.

(⊕) SEE WEB LINKS

• An explanation of the role and functions of UCAS.

university An institution of *higher education with the authority to confer degrees and which has been granted university status. Since the *Further and Higher Education Act 1992, which gave university status to polytechnics, most major towns and cities can boast a university, and sometimes more than one. The proliferation of universities has catered for the steep rise in the percentage of young people going on to higher education, for which the current government target is 50 per cent. Until relatively recently, however, a university education was accessible to the very few. The first universities to be established in England were Oxford and Cambridge, which were both founded in the 13th century. In Scotland, St Andrews, Aberdeen, and Glasgow were the earliest, dating back to the 15th century; Edinburgh was established in 1582. It was not until the 19th century that university provision began to be extended, largely funded by private benefactors, in some of the major cities. Following the Second World War, there was a very rapid expansion, including the founding of the universities of York, Warwick, and Lancaster in the 1960s. These universities were known as 'new universities' to distinguish them from the older institutions such as Oxford, Cambridge, Glasgow, and Durham, and the *red-brick universities founded at the turn of the century. With the abolition of the *binary system in 1992, the total number of universities again rose considerably. In England the nominal head of a university is known as the chancellor, and is normally a public figure. The executive head is usually known as the vice-chancellor, who, together with the board of governors, is ultimately responsible for the operation of the university as a corporate business.

There has been a growing debate in the 21st century about what the role of universities should be. On one side there is the argument that they are an essential factor in economic growth and that this should be their primary purpose, whether through the development of cutting-edge research or by producing graduates who are equipped above all to enter the world of work and become a useful component in the workforce. Those who oppose this view argue that the value of universities lies in their ability to nurture intellectual inquiry, a project which is impeded by the imposition of economic imperatives. In some ways this dialectic can be seen as embodied in the growing divide between universities where the emphasis is on teaching for vocational preparation and those where the emphasis is on inquiry and research; a divide which is perpetuated to some extent by funding mechanisms such as the *Research Excellence Framework (REF).

Further Reading: S. Collini *What are Universities For?* (Penguin Books, 2012).

University and College Union (UCU) The union for professionals in the
*post-compulsory education sectors of *further and *higher education, including
managers, administrators, researchers, and librarians as well as teaching staff.
Established in 2006 by the amalgamation of the National Association of Teachers
in Further and Higher Education (NATFHE) and the Association of University
Teachers (AUT), it is currently the largest union of its kind worldwide.

((⊕)) SEE WEB LINKS
• Provides information about the role of UCU.

university college A college which provides *higher education but which
does not have a charter to confer *degrees. Such colleges operate in partnership
with a university or other college of higher education, and it is from the partner
institution that the university college's *graduates gain their degree.

university entrance Still the most usual route for progression to
*undergraduate studies at *university are *General Certificate of Education
*Advanced Levels (A levels). The minimum requirement is normally two A level
passes, but most universities, through their faculties or departments, stipulate a
specific minimum number of points which must be gained to secure a place,
which are calculated on the basis of the A level grades achieved. The number of
points required will differ from subject to subject, depending upon the demand
for places. Places for which there is a high level of competition, such as medicine,
will normally require a higher point score than those which consistently
under-recruit. As well as the A level route, most universities accept alternative
entry qualifications for adult students, such as the *Access to Higher Education
qualification. The *Open University, as its name suggests, accepts students with
no formal entry qualifications. *See also* ACCESS COURSE.

((⊕)) SEE WEB LINKS
• Provides tariff tables with point scores for a range of national qualifications, including
A levels.

University of the Third Age (U3A) In the UK, U3A is a self-help *adult
education organization consisting of local groups nationwide, each called a U3A,
which operate as learning cooperatives. Aimed at and organized by those who
have reached 'the third age'—in other words, who have retired from paid
employment—U3As draw upon their own membership as a learning resource in
order to learn in fields of their choice. The role of learner is more important than
the role of 'teacher', which often revolves or is shared among the group to take
account of individuals' experience, expertise, and gathered wisdom. There is no
externally set syllabus. Currently, over 300 areas of interest are available and
members attend interest groups in fields as disparate as computing, philosophy,
and walking. Fine distinctions are not made between educational and recreation
activities; it is social learning and companionship which are emphasized. There
are no admission requirements and no assessments are involved nor awards
conferred. U3A has been in existence in the UK since 1982. Each local group is an
operationally independent charity run on a voluntary basis with a committee

functioning as trustees. U3As have representation on the National Executive Committee via their regional representative. The national umbrella organization, the **Third Age Trust (TAT)**, provides not only services such as a learning resource centre, other learning support including a handbook for interest group leaders, and indemnity insurance, but also enriching activities such as summer schools and online courses. U3A is an international movement founded in Toulouse, where, in 1972, the city's university provided a successful summer school for retired people which prefaced the first Université du Troisième Âge. The French model of the U3A is quite different from that operated in the UK. There, courses are provided by learned institutions for students. Internationally five models of U3A have been identified, all of which are dedicated to the ideal of providing non-award-bearing learning opportunities for those in the third age of life. The international body linking U3As, the International Association of Universities of the Third Age, is based in Paris and promotes understanding and the maintenance and development of third age learning. *See also* LATER LIFE LEARNING.

upper school This term usually refers to Years 12 and 13 in a secondary school, to distinguish older pupils from those in compulsory education in *Key Stages 3 and 4, which may be referred to as 'lower school'. This meaning probably originates from a similar usage in traditional public, fee-paying schools.

u

vacation Also referred to as school holidays, these are the periods of time between *terms when a school, college, or university does not hold full-time classes. Traditionally the three main vacations are at Christmas, Easter, and Summer. Colleges and universities do not 'close' during periods of vacation (except for statutory bank holidays), and teaching staff are not automatically entitled to take leave during these breaks in teaching although they constitute a vacation for full-time students. In schools, teachers may be required to attend during vacations for meetings and *continuing professional development events. *See also* TERM.

validation The process by which degrees and other awards are approved by *universities or other *awarding bodies, both for programmes of study within the awarding institution itself, where this is appropriate, and for those taught in partner institutions, such as *colleges of further education, where the qualification awarded is in the university's or the awarding body's name. In order to be validated, such programmes and awards must go through a formal validation procedure, the purpose of which is to ensure that all aspects of quality assurance are in place with regard to the content, teaching, administration, resourcing, and assessment of the programme. To this end, a **validation document** is usually prepared, explaining how all these aspects will be covered. In the case of university-validated awards, this is submitted to a **validation panel** made up of relevant university staff and including one or more external members from other universities or academic bodies. The decision-making process which ensues is known as the **validation event**. If the programme being considered for validation is to be delivered by an institution other than the awarding body, for example in a local college, an inspection of the site and its facilities may form part of the validation process.

validity *See* ASSESSMENT.

value added The difference a *school, *college, or *university has made in the education of its learners compared to the provision of an equivalent institution. Recognition of value added is an alternative—and some would argue fairer—method of making comparisons between the performance of institutions in the same sector than comparing data such as *examination results or the scores for *national curriculum tests, since it takes into account the starting point of learners and the actual progress made, or, as it is sometimes expressed, 'the distance travelled', rather than simply the level of achievement attained. Thus, for example, schools which recruit less able or less advantaged pupils can be recognized for their achievement, if value added is taken into consideration, in a way which they would not be in a simple quantitative comparison of scores with a *selective school recruiting only pupils of high ability.

verification The process carried out by an *awarding body in order to ensure that the processes of *assessment are being carried out in accordance with the body's regulations and requirements. This normally includes scrutinizing the procedures for assessment, *moderation, *second marking, and the recording of assessment decisions. It is involved not with checking the assessment decisions, but rather the procedures by which they are arrived at. Those appointed to carry out this role on behalf of the awarding body are known as **external verifiers**. In some cases there may be a process of internal verification prior to the external verifier's visit. This will be carried out by a member of the teaching team, who, for the purpose of this role, is known as the **internal verifier**. The role of the verifier is distinct from that of examiner or moderator, since it focuses on processes rather than outcomes.

verifier *See* VERIFICATION.

vertical grouping The grouping of children of various ages, usually in primary education, for the purposes of, for example, project work. This is also known as 'family grouping'. Where vertical grouping is a standard arrangement, the pupil will remain with the same teacher throughout their time at the school, rather than moving 'up' a class at the beginning of each year.

vice-chancellor *See* UNIVERSITY.

virtual learning environment (VLE) Computer software which enables teachers to permit controlled access to the materials, processes, and administrative systems that support their programmes, to track students' progress on them, and to develop communications networks with (and among) students, fellow teachers, and support specialists for feedback and guidance. It is a means by which *e-learning may be delivered and supported. Institutions may build their own platforms for virtual courses, or engage commercial companies to develop appropriate systems. All learners' details would then be entered onto a central database, from which tutors would enrol chosen students onto specific courses. One of the chief benefits of a VLE is that students can study using any computer with Internet access, allowing provision of an online or *blended learning model. A virtual learning environment can also be a subsystem of a *managed learning environment. *See also* INFORMATION AND LEARNING TECHNOLOGY.   VC, KA

visible learning *See* EVIDENCE-BASED TEACHING (EBT).

vision Closely linked to, or embodied in, the *mission statement, particularly of *colleges and universities, and embodying a summary of the institution's purpose and direction, 'vision' is one of many examples of business language usage which have become part of the vocabulary of education. Senge (1990) describes vision as an articulation of the envisioned future which the institution wishes to create, while Barrett (1998) suggests it is a statement of how the institution will achieve fulfilment of purpose. Both of these theorists are writing in the context of the management of large business organizations. In colleges and universities the organizational vision is decided by those with executive power.

Further Reading: R. Barrett *Liberating the Corporate Soul* (Butterworth Heinemann, 1998) and P. Senge *The Fifth Discipline* (Random House, 1990) both provide further discussion of corporate vision relevant in the context of educational institutions.

visual impairment A general descriptor to denote all levels of difficulty with seeing, from minor impairment to blindness. Some children and young people with seriously impaired vision may be educated in specialist schools, but many learners with visual impairment attend mainstream education where they are entitled to additional support in schools, colleges, and universities. This may take a variety of forms including, for example, the provision of specialized technology, such as laptops with speech feedback. *See also* SPECIAL EDUCATIONAL NEEDS.

((⨁)) SEE WEB LINKS

• Provides guidance on teaching and learning in relation to learners with visual impairment.

viva The abbreviated and more popularly used form of **viva voce**, an *oral examination used as a matter of course in the assessment process for higher degrees, notably the Doctor of Philosophy (Ph.D. or D.Phil.) and Master of Philosophy (M.Phil.), but also for other examinations, particularly where the candidate's result is *borderline. A panel for the Ph.D. viva will consist of a minimum of two examiners who are recognized experts in the candidate's field. At least one of them will be appointed from outside the university or higher education institution where the candidate is registered. He or she is known as the **external examiner**. In addition, at least one will be appointed from inside the institution, and is known as the **internal examiner**. The candidate is required to defend his or her thesis in the face of questions from the examiners. Some institutions now also appoint an internal member of staff as chair in order to ensure that the viva is conducted in accordance with institutional regulations. *See also* DOCTORATE.

vocational Directly related to employment, usually in a specified sector or trade. Education is referred to as vocational if it involves skills training or if it prepares the learner to enter directly into skilled or semi-skilled employment. This is to distinguish it from *academic or general education, such as *Advanced Level and *General Certificate of Secondary Education; and from **general vocational education**, of the type offered by the *General National Vocational Qualification in the 1990s, which is designed to equip learners with a transferable set of skills necessary for entering the world of work across a broad sector of employment. Therefore, we can broadly map two kinds of education: education for the development of the individual, which is known as general, *liberal, or academic, and education for work, now termed vocational or skills training. Research suggests that vocational qualifications are, on the whole, still accorded rather less esteem than general, academic ones, despite the introduction of equivalence levels, as set out in the *National Qualifications Framework. The distinction between vocational and academic education is sometimes referred to as the **vocational–academic divide**, to denote the difference in status between the two. The reasons for this lack of parity are largely historical.

In the 18th and early 19th centuries, education beyond a very basic level was accessed by an elite which was mostly male, and its purpose was to produce the cultured gentleman. With the growth of industries there came the recognition that a range of knowledge beyond the gentleman's education in Latin and Greek would be essential to the country's industrial progress, but it was considered that an education of this sort was only suitable for those who must take paid employment. As a consequence, what was referred to as 'useful' knowledge became associated with trade and the artisan class. Thus, a classical education, also referred to as a liberal education in the sense of broad and life-enhancing, remained associated with an elite; while, in contrast, a scientific or vocational education was considered to be narrower in purpose, equipping the learner only with the skills to earn their living. Despite successive governments' policy statements from the 1980s to the present day stressing the need for *parity of esteem between the two, the vocational–academic divide is still apparent, for example in the disparity of pay and status between teachers in the further education sector and those in schools. A further distinction related to the divide is that between 'training' and 'education', with 'training' more usually associated with the vocational curriculum. Definitions of the two, as well as the contexts in which they are used, tend to reinforce the view that training is concerned with a lower order of skills and knowledge. An extreme example would be that we speak of 'animal training' rather than 'animal education'. However, an education and training which leads to professional qualifications in medicine, law, and the Church, while still spoken of as 'vocational' (in the sense that those entering these professions are said to have a vocation for them), is accorded high, rather than low, status. No doubt the operational word here is 'professional', but it is also significant that all three of these 'vocational' training routes have traditionally involved a substantial degree of classical learning—a knowledge of Latin, for example—originally associated with a high-status education.

It is interesting to note that although historically an academic education was considered to be liberal and 'broad', while education for the purposes of work was thought of as focused and 'narrow', the application of these two terms is today quite the reverse, the academic route being described as narrow and the introduction of vocational elements into the curriculum for 14–19-year-olds, for example through the 14–19 Diplomas, being presented as a broadening of that curriculum. *See also* MECHANICS' INSTITUTES; NATIONAL VOCATIONAL QUALIFICATION.

Vocational A levels Two new level 3 (A level equivalent) vocational qualifications for 16–19-year-olds were introduced in 2014. These are the **Tech Level**, which can be counted towards a Technological Baccalaureat and is available in a range of specific occupational areas such as patisserie and motor

vehicle engineering; and the **Applied General Qualification (AGQ)**, which
covers wider, more general occupational areas such as business or health. Both
are recognized by relevant trade or occupational groups, and are also intended
as an alternative route, for some into *higher education (HE). However, the
extent to which they will be accepted as part of university entry requirements
remains to be seen. In many ways the introduction of the two new qualifications
echoes that of NVQs and *General National Vocational Qualifications
(GNVQs) towards the end of the 20th century. In both cases a claim was made of
*parity of esteem with traditional A levels.

(⊕) SEE WEB LINKS
• Provides access to performance tables for vocational qualifications for 14–19-year-olds.

vocational awarding bodies *See* AWARDING BODY.

vocational education and training (VET) An alternative title for the
*further education sector. Others are *learning and skills sector (except in
Scotland), continuing education, and the *lifelong learning sector. *See also*
VOCATIONAL.

voice output communication aid (VOCA) A device holding electronically
stored speech specifically designed to enable individuals without natural speech
to communicate. Speech is stored either digitally or via a speech synthesizer.
These can be used by learners who would not otherwise be able to communicate.
There is a range of VOCAs available; some are dedicated communication
devices while others are laptop computers with specialist software installed.
Frequently computer-based devices are programmed to include additional
features such as an environmental control system. How the device is accessed is
dependent on the needs of the user and can be via direct touch, specialist
switches, light pointers, or infrared sensors. *See also* AUGMENTATIVE AND
ALTERNATIVE COMMUNICATION.   TB, LE

voluntary organizations Groups of like-minded people who work towards
a common cause. Organizations may have charitable status, operate without
profit, be staffed by unpaid volunteers, or have a governing body which does not
receive payment. The number of such organizations in the United Kingdom
totals over 250 000 with many whose work is allied to the education sector. These
allied voluntary organizations are used extensively by schools as sources of
ideas, providers of teaching and learning resources, and givers of advice and
guidance. Some organizations offer direct support to pupils and parents on
issues relating to the safety of children.   TB, LE

Voluntary Service Overseas (VSO) An organization whose purpose is to
bring aid and support to developing countries, often in the form of education and
training projects. It recruits volunteer teachers and trainers in the United
Kingdom on fixed-term contracts and pays them a minimum salary, usually at
the going rate for teachers in the country where they are working.

(⊕) SEE WEB LINKS
• Provides a list of subjects and skills in which teachers or trainers are needed.

Vygotsky, Lev (1896–1934) A Russian psychologist who defined one of the most important concepts of educational theory currently embedded in contemporary approaches to teaching and learning: the **zone of proximal development (ZPD)**. The majority of *teachers now recognize that if students, young and old, are given tasks to accomplish that are just beyond their actual *competence, but are able to secure the support of others, it is likely that they will be able to manage the task better than if they are left alone to struggle with it. The teacher's skill is to observe carefully and monitor a student's progress in order to provide a task within the proximal reach of that learner and to suggest who their learning partner might be to provide a **scaffold**, or support, to enable this achievement. This social strategy development theory of learning focuses on the connections between people and the cultural context in which they act, and requires learning to become a reciprocal experience for the students and teacher, thus creating a community of learners. This approach represents a contrast to previously established principles of the individual construction of knowledge, as proposed by *Piaget. Vygotsky's ideas took some time to be translated into English, and therefore his controversial influence continues to challenge established psychological and educational theory of age–stage development.

In recent years, Vygotsky's educational theories have been applied in the *pre-schools of *Reggio Emilia, where *dialogic teaching and thinking between children and peers, children and adults, and teachers and parents is fundamental to the project-based *curriculum. Deep *reflection on this continuous narrative of learning requires teachers to be researchers into children's understanding, and is similar to *Dewey's belief that teachers must use their greater knowledge of the world to help make sense of it for the children, and thus stretch their active and emerging competencies.   AW

Further Reading: L. Vygotsky *Mind in Society* (Harvard University Press, 1978).

V

Wales, education in The third term of the National Assembly for Wales began in May 2007, following the elections. Education is a significant area of responsibility devolved to the Assembly, covering *early years and *schools, family policy, further education (FE) and higher education (HE), *adult and *community education, qualifications, and the careers service. Notably, teachers' *pay and conditions of service and pensions remain the responsibility of Westminster, as does the maintenance of the database of teachers' records, though teacher training and support are devolved to the Assembly. Education in particular is an area where the Assembly has been very proactive in developing distinctive policies, and there have been several changes in the administrative process to support that development. During 2006 the Welsh Assembly department responsible for education and training was expanded to assume responsibility for all education and training with the exception of HE in higher education institutions (HEIs) and in certain instances in *colleges of further education. Funding for these is the responsibility of the *Higher Education Funding Council for Wales.

The *Education Act 2002 provided Wales with the opportunity to develop its educational policy along lines which differ in a number of ways from that elsewhere in the UK. That development has been seen clearly as part of the aim to break down barriers between departments, as exemplified in the Assembly document *A Winning Wales* (2002), which covers education and economic development, giving a sense of the potential for cohesive policies across boundaries in a small country. *A Winning Wales* is one of a number of ambitious documents setting the strategy for the devolved Assembly; those relating to education in particular are *The Learning Country* (2001) and *The Learning Country: Vision into Action* (2006). The first sets out a ten-year strategy for education in Wales, covering all ages, with the emphasis on a continuum of learning from *pre-school through to *lifelong learning and *skills updates. The second reinforces the original document, giving an overview of progress so far and updating the strategy.

Certain key issues, such as *widening participation in *post-compulsory education, are central drivers across all the jurisdictions, though the strategies for implementation are often distinctive. In the *widening access agenda, for example, geographical and demographic features in Wales are reflected in the Reaching Wider initiative (2002), whereby the Funding Council supports broad groupings of HEIs in delivering initiatives which respond appropriately to local and regional factors. Other policies which are common throughout the UK include enhanced early years provision, improvements in buildings and environment, and the aspiration to reconnect with disaffected children and young people. In a number of instances, however, Wales has either adopted different methods of achieving those goals or has developed distinctive initiatives such as the *Welsh Baccalaureate.

Over recent years the Minister for Education has commissioned a series of in-depth reports in a number of areas. The emphasis in the guidance for all of these has been on evidence-based recommendations, and resource has been invested to enable a significant level of research and analysis to support the process. Studies and pilots have been carried out in relation to the initiatives at pre-school and school stages, with the implementation of programmes such as Flying Start (2007) for early years education.

A report on full-time HE provision made recommendations for student support, funding, and fees, proposing a variable fees structure and a clear, enabling support system. This resulted in an Assembly vote which introduced a Wales-specific fee remission grant for all Welsh-domiciled students choosing to study at a Welsh HEI, thus effectively reducing their fee commitment. The fee remission grant was non-means-tested. Part-time students constitute 41 per cent of all student enrolments in Welsh HEIs. The balance between full- and part-time varies enormously between institutions, but the overall percentage is significant. In 2006 a report on part-time HE study was published, and subsequently ratified by the Assembly, recommending increased student support for part-time students and advising that additional funding should be given to institutions, allocated in proportion to their numbers of part-time students, to enable them to respond to local and regional factors in the provision of courses. The new regimes for both part- and full-time HE were implemented in the same academic year, beginning September–October 2007.

Some important issues to be addressed by the education sector in Wales include falling rolls in schools, which is a particular challenge in some of the more rural areas; challenges around the Welsh-medium policy; the *transition phase between primary and secondary; and funding levels, especially for post-16 education.

Support for the teaching profession is a priority in Wales, with the *Newly Qualified Teachers programme and certificate, and the ongoing support offered to teachers in Years 2 and 3 of their professional life. There is also provision for additional training for teaching through the medium of Welsh, particularly at the school stage. Indeed, the Welsh language is important to the education strategy of the Welsh Assembly, with the number of Welsh-medium schools increasing. There are, however, problems around some ambitious targets in relation to the Welsh language, particularly at HE level.

Considerable effort has been invested in the early years and foundation stage, with the Flying Start programme providing part-time places for 3-year-olds whose parents want them to enrol and pilot schemes in structured activity learning for the 3–7-year age groups. All *infant class sizes now conform to the statutory limit. The appointment of a Children's Commissioner has been an important step forward and again indicates the aspiration for joined-up, pan-Wales thinking. The dispersed population in some parts of Wales creates particular challenges such as in the support for children with *special educational needs, where maintaining a full range of services can be difficult for some of the smaller rural local authorities. To meet that challenge, the National Steering Group for SEN in Wales was established with an all-Wales remit, allowing for collaboration between authorities, but also for *peripatetic services.

At secondary stage there have been some interesting initiatives, notably the Learning Pathways for 14–19-year-olds. The approach here is to develop a variety of learning routes geared to the individual with support from learning coaches for advice and guidance. The development of the Welsh Baccalaureate has been an important and successful Welsh initiative, and has established a qualification which is now accepted by the *Universities and Colleges Admissions Service as part of the qualification calculations for entry to university.

The development of the Credit and Qualifications Framework for Wales (CQFW) is a further example of the aspirations towards cohesion of provision and support of the learner. From 2005 all accredited learning, including mainstream qualifications offered in Wales, has gradually been brought into the single unifying structure of the CQFW. The Framework is designed to create flexibility for the learner and to offer a guide to comparable and equivalent levels of achievement and qualifications whether these are gained through learning in the workplace, the community, at school, at college, or at university.

For both the FE and the HE sectors, a major factor has been the clear policy of significant movement towards collaboration and reconfiguration. There have been some notable developments in sustainable collaboration, such as the merger between the University College of Medicine and Cardiff University, and the move by the Royal College of Music and Drama to become an Associate of the University of Glamorgan. HG

Warnock Report (1978) The report of the Committee of Inquiry into the Education of Handicapped Children and Young People, chaired by Mary Warnock, and viewed as revolutionary at the time of its publication. The Report was to change radically the educational picture for children with disabilities as most of the recommendations became enshrined in law in the *Education Act 1981. The Report introduced the term '*special educational need' to identify any child needing extra or different support, and argued that 20 per cent of children have special needs at least for some part of their educational career. It further introduced new terms to identify groups of children with the intention of moving away from the previous medical labelling of children: these were 'speech and language disorders', 'visual disability and hearing disability', 'emotional and behavioural disorders', and 'learning difficulties: specific, mild, moderate and severe'. The Report recommended that segregated 'special' schools should be for those with the most complex and multiple disabilities which were long-term, and that mainstream schools should develop to meet the needs of all other children. It put forward three models for the *integration of children with disabilities—**locational**, **social**, and **functional integration**. This recommendation for mainstreaming children had criteria attached: parents should be in agreement with the placement; the child's educational needs were capable of being met in a mainstream school; the local education authority was using its resources efficiently; and the education of other children was not affected. To help facilitate the integration of children the Report recommended an expansion in special needs advisory and support services. With the aim of protecting the educational needs of the most severely disabled and ensuring they received appropriate resources to make progress, the Report recommended *statements of special needs. These statements were to be issued by local authorities to individual children only after a five-stage assessment process had been followed. Once issued the local authority had a statutory duty to make the provision listed on the statement.											TB, LE

web-based learning *See* E-LEARNING.

webinar A type of *distributed online learning commonly used for the purpose of *continuing professional development. As its name suggests, the webinar takes the form of a seminar accessed through the World Wide Web. These have the advantage that participants do not have to travel to a central venue for professional development, thus saving their institution both time and money. As well as being used by teachers, webinars are an increasingly popular *e-learning resource for professional development in other professions, such as the law. They may be pre-recorded or live and interactive.

(((●))) SEE WEB LINKS
• Provides links to examples of webinars.

weighting When the overall *assessment of a candidate's *coursework or *examination performance is based on a series of tasks which have each been awarded a mark or grade, it must be clear whether each of those contributory marks or grades counts equally towards the final one awarded, or whether some tasks carry more 'weight' than others. So, for example, in an examination which consists of four tasks, each of equal difficulty and therefore weighted equally, they will each count as 25 per cent of the overall mark or grade. However, if, of the four tasks, one is more challenging or requires a longer answer than the others, the percentage marks it carries should be weighted accordingly.

Welsh Baccalaureate A new, broader post-16 qualification piloted since 2003 and offered at Advanced and Intermediate levels from September 2007 in 76 approved centres. The *Universities and Colleges Admissions Service allocates 120 tariff points to the core qualification. Students who successfully complete the Welsh Baccalaureate at Advanced Level will therefore have the equivalent of an A grade *General Certificate of Education *Advanced Level in addition to the points they earn from their optional studies.											HG

Welsh-medium education A policy priority for the Welsh Assembly working through a number of public bodies, including *Estyn, the education services provider **WJEC**, and in particular the **Welsh Language Board**, which has responsibility for the promotion and development of Welsh-medium education. The Board's Education and Training Department reviews *local authority policies, approves and monitors the implementation of their Welsh Language Schemes, and maintains a strategic overview of Welsh-medium education and training. The Board allocates grants to local authorities on an annual basis to support the teaching of Welsh. In the post-16 sector the Assembly Bilingual Learning Unit aims to promote bilingualism and Welsh-medium education and training in *colleges of further education and workplace training providers, and there is an ambitious target for Welsh-medium delivery in higher education institutions. HG

Wenger, Etienne *See* COMMUNITY OF PRACTICE.

White Paper A government discussion document which sets out government policy on a specific issue. It is usually the precursor of legislation, and as a type of command paper it is often the subject of statements or debates in the House of Commons. It is issued by a government department and contains detailed proposals for legislation. It represents the final stage in the process of creating legislation before the government introduces its proposals to Parliament in the form of a bill. For example, the 1991 White Paper *Education and Training for the 21st Century* set out the government's argument that *colleges of further education would operate more effectively if they were given freedom from *local authority control, and was followed in 1992 by the *Further and Higher Education Act, which legislated to bring this about. White Papers are often prefaced by a statement in the House from the *secretary of state of the government department sponsoring the proposals. In the case of education White Papers, this will be either the Secretary of State for Schools, Children, and Families, or the Secretary of State for Innovation, Universities, and Skills. A White Paper is sometimes produced following the consultation process which is undertaken when the government issues a *Green Paper.

Over the past three decades there has been frequent publication of White Papers on all aspects of education, reflecting the frequent policy developments and the rapid rate of change in every sector of the education system. Examples of landmark White Papers are:

1981   *A New Training Initiative: A Programme for Action*, which set out the argument for a year's work-related training scheme for all school-leavers, a policy which eventually led to the *Youth Training Scheme

1992   *Choice and Diversity: A Framework for Schools* argues for new arrangements for the inspection of schools, which resulted in the setting up of *Ofsted

2001   *Schools: Achieving Success*

2003   *The Future of Higher Education*
         21st Century Skills: Realising Our Potential

2005   *Skills: Getting On in Business, Getting On at Work*
         14–19 Education and Skills sets out the argument for allowing some 14–16-year-olds to undertake part of their learning in colleges of further education, which resulted in this becoming a widespread practice
         Higher Standards, Better Schools for All

2006   *FE Reform: Raising Skills, Improving Life Chances*
2007   *Care Matters: Time for Change*
        The Children's Plan: Building Brighter Futures
2010   *The Importance of Teaching* proposes wide-reaching reforms to
        compulsory education and teacher training.

See also EDUCATION ACT.

 SEE WEB LINKS

• Provides a link to the full text of the most recent White Paper on education, and an
  evaluation of its impact.

widening access Part of the *widening participation agenda, the drive to
widen access to education focuses particularly on those potential learners who
find themselves excluded from educational or training opportunities by
difficulties to do with their access to it, rather than out of choice. Such difficulties
might include access in the literal sense, for those who live some distance
away from provision or who have a disability which affects their mobility or
ability to gain entry to the *campus or buildings where learning is offered. They
might also include cultural or language issues which make it difficult for the
potential learner to access information about provision or to attend classes at the
institution concerned. Adults in full-time work may also have difficulty in
attending courses which are taught during their working hours. Awareness of
issues over access has led to an expansion in outreach classes and community
education, and in the development of *distance learning, *blended learning, and
*e-learning models. *See also* INCLUSION; INCLUSIVITY; KENNEDY REPORT;
WARNOCK REPORT.

widening participation Encouraging people to enter *further and *higher
education who have previously been under-represented in these sectors. This
includes people from a wider range of educational, social, ethnic, and cultural
backgrounds, and from a wider range of abilities and skills. A drive to widen
participation in *post-compulsory education and training is presented as part
of the government's policy to create a more highly skilled workforce. To this end,
specific targets were set in the 2006 *White Paper *Further Education: *Raising
Skills, Improving Life Chances*, which include:

• participation rates by 16–19-year-olds to increase by 15 per cent by 2015;
• the number of adults gaining a *National Qualifications Framework level 2
  qualification to reach at least 3.6 million by 2010;
• 50 per cent of all 18–30-year-olds to be participating in *higher education
  by 2010.

Concerns have been raised by some educationalists over the apparent
contradiction at the heart of a policy which aims both to widen participation and
at the same time to raise standards of achievement.

Widening participation and access is a focus for Scottish universities. In 2001
every higher education institution signed a seven-point commitment to
improving social inclusion in higher education (*Commitment to Inclusion*, March

w

2001). This issue has been addressed in the 2005 *Learning for All* document by the Scottish Funding Council. *See also* INCLUSION; KENNEDY REPORT.

(⊕) SEE WEB LINKS
• Explains the role of HEFCE in widening participation in HE.

work-based learning (WBL) The development and assessment of skills within and directly related to the workplace. Many learners have been able to gain work-related qualifications in the form of *National Vocational Qualifications, which recognize the competencies gained in the workplace. Traditionally, *further education colleges have provided employers with the support and underpinning knowledge and assessment for WBL, but it can be facilitated through part-time study at non-workplace locations, such as schools, further education colleges, and training providers, or through full-time learning within the work setting.

Modes of WBL are numerous: Increased Flexibility, which funds partnerships between further education colleges, schools, and providers of work-based learning, and apprenticeship programmes both offer a taste of WBL within the school curriculum at *Key Stage 4 *Foundation degrees were launched by the UK government in 2000 to meet the needs of employers, especially in developing the higher levels of technical skill required to enable the workforce to satisfy regional, national, and global demands. The foundation degree programme also allows for progression to an honours degree, linking work-based with more traditional higher education. These degrees are designed to be delivered in a flexible manner using learning in the workplace supported by a further education college or university, and with the use of *e-learning. Increasingly, teacher training is taking the form of work-based learning, with routes to *Qualified Teacher Status now available through full-time work in the classroom.   VC, KA

Workers' Educational Association (WEA) Part of the *adult education sector with its roots in the self-improvement movement of the 19th century, a movement whose aim was to raise the level of intellectual achievement of the working classes. In the 1960s, 1970s, and 1980s, however, it became for a time more closely associated with the middle classes and the concept of education for leisure. It is a registered charity operating through 650 local branches which run classes in a variety of subjects, from English literature to reflexology, mainly taught by teachers, lecturers, and other experts who are contracted on an hourly basis. Founded in 1903 and organized through *universities, the Cooperative Society, and trade unions, it became widely regarded as part of the labour movement between the First and Second World Wars. As it gained its 'middle-class' image, however, it also gained financial support from central government, some direct and some through *local authorities. This enabled local branches to subsidize their courses and thereby keep the cost of fees down. In 1993 the WEA came under the aegis of the *Further Education Funding Council in terms of its funding, and from this point it was required to bid for financial support against providers such as further education *colleges and private vocational training agencies. As the criteria for funding became increasingly concentrated on provision which led to *National Qualifications Framework qualifications, and as local authorities' role in funding was eroded, the WEA was no longer able to subsidize fees at the same level. This had repercussions on levels of recruitment and the range of courses it was able to offer. In 2007 it ran over 10 000 courses, providing for over 110 000 adults.

(⊕) SEE WEB LINKS

• Sets out the WEA's mission, aims, and values.

work experience The placement of a pupil, student, or trainee in a work environment where they will gain supervised experience of working within that business, company, or organization. It was an integral part of early youth training programmes such as the *Youth Opportunities Programme and the *Youth Training Scheme, where the trainee was placed with an employer to receive on-the-job training—that is, training of a practical, experiential kind—and attended a further education *college or other training provider for part of the week in order to receive off-the-job training, which often included the underpinning theoretical component of the work skills they were acquiring. This pattern of attendance was similar to the *day release arrangements which operated for trainees in employment. Work experience was extended into some full-time *programmes of study in *further education in the 1980s, notably *Business and Technology Education Council courses in vocational areas such as business education. In schools it is now common practice to encourage pupils to undertake one or two weeks of closely supervised work experience at the end of Year 10. In *higher education, some four-year degree courses include a year of work experience, and are often referred to as *sandwich courses, the year in work representing the filling in the middle. For some qualifications the experience of work is an integral and essential component, as, for example, for a degree in medicine. Students studying for language degrees are normally encouraged or required to spend a year overseas as part of their programme, practising the language they are studying while at the same time gaining work experience, often as an English language assistant in a school.

w

Year 11 Information System (Yellis) This system provides tests which are used nationally by secondary schools to gauge the potential of their *Key Stage 4 pupils. Schools choose whether or not to participate in this type of standardized assessment. Test results can be used by secondary schools as a baseline for *value added measures. They are also used to predict *General Certificate of Secondary Education grades for core GCSE subjects. Yellis tests provide an alternative baseline to Key Stage 3 *Standard Task results, which are the outcome of specific learning and instruction, rather than innate potential. Yellis produces baseline tests for Years 10 and 11. These tests are assessed externally by Yellis and results are returned to the school shortly afterwards. *See also* COGNITIVE ABILITIES TEST; MIDDLE YEARS INFORMATION SYSTEM. IW

Yellis *See* YEAR 11 INFORMATION SYSTEM.

Yellow Book The informal title given to a report compiled by advisers in the Department of Education and Science in 1975 on national standards in education. It was broadly critical of standards in both primary and secondary schools. Elements of this report informed the **Ruskin College speech** given by James Callaghan (Prime Minister 1976–9) in 1976 which is credited with opening the continuing *Great Debate on education and training.

Young Apprenticeship The Young *Apprenticeship programme originated as part of the 14–19 and Skills agenda whose framework shaped *vocational education and training in the first decade of the 21st century. The programme offers an opportunity for able 14–16-year-olds to combine the practical application of skills and knowledge in a *vocational context, with the chance to gain qualifications that relate to specific occupational areas. It is seen as an addition to the range of vocational options at *Key Stage 4, where pupils can follow specific vocational programmes outside school, in partnerships with employers and involving long-term work placements.

The first cohort of 1 000 learners started their two-year programme in September 2004 in art and design, business administration, engineering, health and social care, and the motor industry. For the second cohort, the programmes expanded to include sports management, leadership, and coaching; performing arts; hospitality; and textiles. *See also* MODERN APPRENTICESHIP. VC, KA

Youth Council for Northern Ireland The Youth Council for Northern Ireland was established under the Youth Service (NI) Order 1989, and the

legislation defines its functions as follows: to advise the Department of
Education, education and library boards, and other bodies on the development
of the Youth Service; to encourage cross-community activity by the Youth
Service; to encourage the provision of facilities for the Youth Service and facilities
which are especially beneficial to young persons; to encourage and assist the
coordination and efficient use of the resources of the Youth Service; and to
grant aid to regional voluntary youth organizations towards their
administration.   JH

youth offending team (YOT) Youth offending teams are multi-agency
teams set up in each *local authority area. They comprise representatives from
education, health, the police, the probation service, social services, housing
officers, and the drugs and alcohol misuse team; each team is led by a youth
offending team manager. This multi-agency approach ensures thorough
assessment, planning, and delivery of appropriate support to young offenders.
The main role of a youth offending team is to work with young people aged 10–18
who are subject to court orders either in the community or in custodial
situations. There is currently a new initiative for teams to work with children
aged 8–13 who are identified as at 'risk of offending'; this is called the Youth
Inclusion Support Programme.   TB, LE

Youth Opportunities Programme (YOP) A forerunner of the *Youth
Training Scheme (YTS) and the first national training programme for
16–18-year-olds not in education or work. Established in 1981 as part of the
training agenda for school-leavers and adults set out in the 1981 *White Paper
A New Training Initiative, YOP provided a programme of individual *work
experience combined with attendance at further education classes with a
generalized *vocational focus. The programme was short-lived and was
succeeded within two years by YTS.

Youth Training Scheme (YTS) YTS replaced the *Youth Opportunities
Scheme (YOP) in 1983 and became the mainstay of the national training
agenda set in 1981 by the *White Paper *A New Training Initiative*. Like YOP, it
involved substantial (in terms of time) *work experience which was intended to
provide **on-the-job training**, as well as requiring the trainee to complete a
programme of *vocationally related skills delivered in *colleges of further
education, private training agencies, or—in organizations with the facility to
accommodate this—in the workplace. The **off-the-job** *curriculum also
included such transferable core skills as communication, numeracy, and a set of
skills known as 'social and life skills'. Trainees were paid a nominal 'wage' for
which employers were subsidized by government funds paid through the local
Manpower Services Commission, and later through the local **Training and
Enterprise Council**. By 1988 there were over 500 000 contracted placements on
the scheme. Criticisms of the programme included the allegation that many
trainees were gaining little valuable experience in the workplace, were being
given menial or meaningless tasks, and were failing to gain real employment
on completing the scheme, and the suggestion that the scheme was intended as

a means of omitting the numbers of unemployed school-leavers from the national unemployment figures. On the other hand, many of those involved, both organizations and trainees, claimed that it provided valuable experience and a genuine route into employment for young people. It was replaced by Youth Training in 1989. *See also* KEY SKILLS.

zero tolerance A refusal to permit or tolerate *behaviour which is inappropriate, illegal, or unethical. In schools and other educational institutions this will include behaviours such as *bullying, and racial or sexual harassment, and may also include, for example, the use of offensive language, the use of mobile phones in class, and the wearing of certain types of dress or jewellery. The term itself is part of the rhetoric of recent policy debates about law and order. It is also closely linked to the **Respect** agenda. Thus, governments, too, will express their zero tolerance of certain behaviours, such as street violence. Some schools and colleges operate what is referred to as a 'zero tolerance policy' in order to enforce acceptable behaviour and adherence to the law and rules of the institution. Such a policy sets out clearly the behaviours which are specifically prohibited and their consequences—usually *exclusion or suspension. *See also* SANCTION.

zone of proximal development (ZPD) *See* VYGOTSKY.

Appendix 1

Time Line

1833   The Factory Act introduces a mandatory two hours of schooling each day for children

1840   The Grammar Schools Act permits grammar schools to introduce subjects other than the classical languages into their curriculum

1856   A government Education Department is created

1868   The *Taunton Report recommends three grades of provision in grammar schools according to pupils' social class

1870   The Elementary Education Act establishes school boards empowered to create new schools and fund schooling for children of the poor

1880   The Education Act makes school compulsory for children up to the age of 10

1902   The *Education Act abolishes school boards and replaces them with local educational authorities whose role is to manage school funding, employ teachers, and allocate school places

1917   *School Certificate is introduced

1918   The Education Act makes school compulsory for children up to the age of 14

1944   The Education Act introduces the tripartite system; secondary education becomes free in maintained schools and the school-leaving age rises to 15

1951   The *General Certificate of Education at Ordinary and Advanced Level replaces *School Certificate and Higher School Certificate

1964   The Department of Education and Science is established

1965   Comprehensive schooling is recommended in government Circular 10/65. The Certificate of Secondary Education is introduced

1967   The *Plowden Report on children and primary schools

1973   The *school-leaving age is raised to 16

1976   The Education Act requires local authorities to submit plans for comprehensive education

1979   The Education Act repeals the 1976 Act

1981   The *White Paper *A New Training Initiative: A Programme for Action* sets out the argument for a year's work-related training scheme for all school-leavers, a policy which eventually leads to the *Youth Training Scheme

1986   The Education Act requires maintained schools to increase parental representation on their governing body

1988   The Education Reform Act introduces the national curriculum; the *General Certificate of Secondary Education replaces GCE Ordinary Levels and the Certificate of Secondary Education

1992   The White Paper *Choice and Diversity: A Framework for Schools* argues for new arrangements for the inspection of schools, which results in the setting up of Ofsted

1993   The Department for Education replaces the Department of Education and Science

1994   The Education Act introduces the Teacher Training Agency

1995   The Department for Education and the Employment Department merge to become the Department for Education and Employment

1996   *Dearing Review of Qualifications for 16–19 Year Olds

1997   The *National Literacy Strategy is introduced

        The *Kennedy Report, *Learning Works*

1998   The *General Teaching Council is established

1999   *Moser Report, *A Fresh Start: Improving Literacy and Numeracy*

2000   The Learning and Skills Council replaces the Further Education Funding Council and the Training and Enterprise Councils

        Curriculum 2000 is introduced

2001   The Department for Education and Skills replaces the Department for Education and Employment

2002   City *academies are introduced

2003   The *Green Paper *Every Child Matters stresses the need for accountability and integration between services and organizations in support of young people

2005   The White Paper *14–19 Education and Skills* sets out the argument for allowing some 14–16-year-olds to undertake part of their learning in colleges of further education, which becomes widespread practice

        The White Paper *Higher Standards, Better Schools for All: More Choice for Parents and Pupils* argues for the need to create a system of independent non-fee-paying state schools in which schools can decide whether they wish to acquire a self-governing trust or become a self-governing foundation school; for parents to receive regular meaningful reports during the school year; for more grouping and setting by subject ability; for clarification of the legal right of teachers to discipline pupils

2006   The Education and Inspections Act enables all schools to become trust schools by forming links with external partners; enables local authorities to take on a new strategic role including appointing school improvement partners for maintained schools; introduces a tighter admissions framework; requires local authorities to provide free transport for the most disadvantaged families; introduces new specialized diplomas for young people; provides new nutritional standards for food and drink served in maintained schools; merges several existing inspectorates into a single inspectorate to cover the full range of services for children and young people, as well as lifelong learning

        The White Paper *Further Education: Raising Skills, Improving Life Chances* confirms further education's role as one of skills training; sets national qualification targets; introduces regulatory continuing professional development for teachers in further education; reforms funding for 14–19 learning

2007   The Department for Education and Skills is replaced by two new departments: the Department for Children, Schools, and Families and the Department for Innovation, Universities, and Skills

The Further Education and Training Act implements the proposals set out in the *Foster Report (2005) and the White Paper *Further Education: Raising Skills, Improving Life Chances* (2006); sets in motion the restructuring of the Learning and Skills Council; grants English colleges of further education the right to award foundation degrees

2008 The White Paper *Innovation Nation* emphasizes higher education's role in supporting the national economy

2010 The Academies Act enables all maintained schools to apply for academy status

2011 The *Education Act introduces a raft of reforms, which include greater regulatory powers to *Ofqual; greater powers of intervention to the *Secretary of State for Education; the abolition of the GTC; and the authority for *Ofsted to grant some schools exemption from regular inspections. It further expands the *academies programme and gives free *early years provision for disadvantaged 2-year-olds. Its key emphasis is on *discipline in schools and protection for teachers from false allegations. *Exclusion appeal panels are replaced by **review panels** which are not empowered to force schools to reinstate excluded pupils

2012 The Green Paper *Support and Aspiration* on SEN introduces the idea for Education, Health, and Care Plans (EHCP) to replace *statements of need; and for parents of children with SEN to be given a greater choice over whether their child should receive special or mainstream schooling

2014 EHCPs are put into operation for children and young people from birth to age 25 with SEN

2014 Free school lunches introduced for all infant school pupils

Educational Provision in Some Other English-Speaking Countries

Regulation and administration

Australia
: The Department of Education provides national leadership in developing and implementing policies. Each state and territory has its own Department of Education which collaborates with the central government and is responsible for the regulation of educational provision

(⊕) SEE WEB LINKS

Canada
: There is no national or federal ministry of education, although there is federal involvement in some aspects of provision such as vocational training which can be subsidized by the federal Department of Labour. Each province and territory has its own ministry or department responsible for elementary, secondary, and post-secondary provision and policy

(⊕) SEE WEB LINKS

New Zealand
: The Ministry of Education is responsible for education policy, administration, and regulation across all sectors

(⊕) SEE WEB LINKS

South Africa
: A national framework for school policy is provided by the national Department of Education, which is responsible for national education and training as a whole, including higher education. Each of the nine provinces has its own Department of Education, which has direct administrative responsibility for schools

(⊕) SEE WEB LINKS

United States
: There is no national or federal ministry of education. Control and funding comes from three levels: federal, state, and local. The state and national governments have a power-sharing arrangement, with the states exercising most of the control. At the primary and secondary school levels, curriculums, allocation of funding, teaching, and other policies are set through locally elected school boards with jurisdiction over school districts

(⊕) SEE WEB LINKS

Compulsory provision and early years

Australia
: Pre-school provision varies according to the state or territory, and is often in kindergartens attached to primary schools. Education is compulsory for ages 6–16 (15 in Tasmania), and is delivered through:

• primary school: Years 1–6/7 (ages 6–12/13) (depending on state)
• secondary school, high school: Years 7/8–12 (ages 12/ 13–18) (open and selective)

Sixty-six per cent of provision is in government-funded schools; the rest is in fee-paying independent schools. Both government and independent schools adhere to the same curriculum framework

Canada (outside Quebec)

Pre-school provision (Grade K) is in kindergarten (or equivalent) and varies according to province. Education is compulsory for ages 6–16 (18 in Ontario, 15 in Alberta):

• elementary school: Grades 1–6/7/8 (ages 6–11/12/13) (depending on province)
• junior high school/middle school/intermediate school: Grades 7–9 (ages 12–15)
• high school: Grades 10–12+ (ages 15/16–21 and under)
Eight per cent of pupils attend private schools

New Zealand

Pre-school provision consists of kindergartens (ages 3–5), kohanga reo, and early childhood centres (ages 0–5). Education is compulsory for ages 6–16 (15 with parental permission), and is delivered through:

• primary school: Years 1–6 (ages 5–13)
• intermediate school: Years 7–8 (ages 11–13)
• secondary school: Years 9–13 (ages 13–18)

Some schools cater for pupils across two or all of these groups. Most pupils start school at 5 and remain until 18. Students with special educational needs can stay in school until 21. Eighty-six per cent of provision is in state schools; the rest is in integrated or private schools

South Africa

Grade 0 (or Grade R) is reception year for 6-year-olds, provided in nurseries or primary schools. Education is compulsory for ages 7–15 (or completion of Grade 9) and is delivered through:

• primary school: Grades 0–6 (ages 6–12)
• high school: Grades 7–12 (ages 12–18)

Ninety-five per cent of provision is in government-funded schools; the rest is in fee-paying independent schools. Government and independent schools adhere to the same curriculum framework

United States

There are no mandatory public pre-school or crèche programmes. Education is compulsory for ages 6–16 or 18, depending on the state. Compulsory provision is divided into three levels: elementary school, middle school, and high school. Grade levels in each vary from state to state:

• elementary school: Kindergarten–5th/6th Grade (ages 5/6–11)
• middle school: 6th–8th Grade (ages 11–14)
• high school: 9th–12th Grade (ages 15–18)

Students may attend public, private, or home schools. Approximately 85 per cent of students attend the public schools

Post-compulsory education

Australia	Higher education takes place in universities. Bachelor's degrees take three to four years. Associate degrees (roughly equivalent to the UK's foundation degree) take two years. Both are assessed through coursework. Technical and further education (TAFE) is provided in institutes of technical and further education (which may also offer higher education courses) and registered training organizations (RTOs). TAFE institutions and RTOs must comply with the Australian Quality Training Framework (AQTF)
Canada	Higher education takes place mainly in universities. Bachelor's degrees normally take three years, or four years with honours. Vocational education is provided in community colleges and technical colleges, some of which may also offer higher education courses leading to a degree
New Zealand	Higher education takes place in universities, colleges of education, polytechnics, and wananga. A bachelor's degree normally takes three years, with an additional year for honours. Vocational education takes place in polytechnics and technical colleges
South Africa	Higher education takes place in universities and at private institutions, registered with the Department of Education, offering specific degrees and diplomas. Further education and training (FET) is provided both in Grades 10–12 of secondary school and in further education and training institutions and colleges
United States	Post-secondary education in the United States is known as college or university and commonly consists of four years of study leading to a bachelor's degree. Vocational education is provided by community colleges, which may also offer higher awards such as the associate's degree

Qualifications framework and key awards

Australia	Qualifications are classified in a national Australian Qualifications Framework (AQF). The major school-leaving qualification is the Senior Secondary Certificate of Education (SSCE), which requires two years' additional study following Year 10, and prepares students to enter higher education or technical and further education. There is testing of literacy and numeracy in primary and secondary schools, which varies from state to state. Although universities regulate much of their own provision, vocational education and training (VET) is regulated by AQF
Canada	There is no federal framework for qualifications or testing because of the distributed nature of jurisdiction for education. The main school-leaving qualification is the High School Diploma, which is the minimum qualification required for entry to governmental jobs and to higher education
New Zealand	The New Zealand Qualifications Authority co-ordinates qualifications in the secondary and tertiary sectors through the National Qualifications Framework (NQF). The National Certificate of Educational Achievement (NCEA) is New Zealand's main national

qualification for secondary school students and is part of the NQF. Entry to universities is open, requiring only the minimum NCEA. However, many universities operate a selective admissions procedure

South Africa   There is a National Qualifications Framework (NQF) which encompasses three bands of education and training: general education and training (including adult basic education), further education and training (FET), and higher education and training (HET). The main school-leaving qualifications are the Matriculation endorsement (matric), in which three subjects must be passed at the higher level for entry to higher education; and Standard Senior Certificate, necessary for progression to technical qualifications

United States   There is no federal framework for qualifications. At the primary and secondary school levels, curriculums are set through the locally elected school boards. There is standardized testing under the No Child Left Behind Act, which requires that all American states must test students in public (i.e. state) schools to ensure that they are achieving the desired level of minimum education. The main school-leaving qualifications are the High School Diploma or the General Educational Development (GED) test certificate

Appendix 3

International Comparisons of Qualifications

1. UCAS publishes an extensive list of international qualifications which may be considered to be the equivalent of National Qualification Framework (NQF) level 3 (the level of GCE A levels) or above, and may therefore be offered as meeting the entry requirement for higher education. The publication includes information on the currency and equivalency of each qualification in terms of progression. This document can be accessed at:
http://www.ucas.com/how-it-all-works/explore-your-options/entry-requirements/tariff-tables#

2. The European Qualifications Framework (EQF) enables comparison of qualifications across Europe. The web site provides an interactive table which gives up to five examples of qualification for each NQF level. This can be accessed at:
http://ec.europa.eu/eqf/compare_en.htm

Oxford Quick Reference

A Dictionary of Chemistry

Over 4,700 entries covering all aspects of chemistry, including physical chemistry and biochemistry.

'It should be in every classroom and library ... the reader is drawn inevitably from one entry to the next merely to satisfy curiosity.'

School Science Review

A Dictionary of Physics

Ranging from crystal defects to the solar system, 4,000 clear and concise entries cover all commonly encountered terms and concepts of physics.

A Dictionary of Biology

The perfect guide for those studying biology — with over 5,500 entries on key terms from biology, biochemistry, medicine, and palaeontology.

'lives up to its expectations; the entries are concise, but explanatory'

Biologist

'ideally suited to students of biology, at either secondary or university level, or as a general reference source for anyone with an interest in the life sciences'

Journal of Anatomy

Oxford Quick Reference

A Dictionary of Psychology
Andrew M. Colman

Over 9,000 authoritative entries make up the most wide-ranging
dictionary of psychology available.

'impressive ... certainly to be recommended'
Times Higher Education Supplement

'probably the best single-volume dictionary of its kind.'
Library Journal

A Dictionary of Economics
John Black, Nigar Hashimzade, and Gareth Myles

Fully up-to-date and jargon-free coverage of economics. Over 3,400
terms on all aspects of economic theory and practice.

'strongly recommended as a handy work of reference.'
Times Higher Education Supplement

A Dictionary of Law

An ideal source of legal terminology for systems based on English law.
Over 4,200 clear and concise entries.

'The entries are clearly drafted and succinctly written ... Precision for the
professional is combined with a layman's enlightenment.'
Times Literary Supplement

A Dictionary of Education
Susan Wallace

In over 1,250 clear and concise entries, this authoritative dictionary
covers all aspects of education, including organizations, qualifications,
key figures, major legislation, theory, and curriculum and assessment
terminology.

Oxford Quick Reference

The Concise Oxford Dictionary of English Etymology
T. F. Hoad

A wealth of information about our language and its history, this reference source provides over 17,000 entries on word origins.

'A model of its kind'

Daily Telegraph

New Oxford Rhyming Dictionary

From writing poems to writing birthday cards, and from composing advertising slogans to music lyrics, this dictionary has what every writer (or budding writer) needs. It contains rhymes for over 45,000 words, including proper names, place names, and foreign terms used in English.

'All wordsmiths are bound to enjoy feeling indebted (fetid, minareted, rosetted . . .)'

Julia Donaldson (author of *The Gruffalo*)

The Oxford Dictionary of Slang
John Ayto

Containing over 10,000 words and phrases, this is the ideal reference for those interested in the more quirky and unofficial words used in the English language.

'hours of happy browsing for language lovers'

Observer

Oxford Quick Reference

The Concise Oxford Companion to English Literature
Dinah Birch and Katy Hooper

Based on the best-selling *Oxford Companion to English Literature*, this is an indispensable guide to all aspects of English literature.

Review of the parent volume:
'the foremost work of reference in its field'

Literary Review

A Dictionary of Shakespeare
Stanley Wells

Compiled by one of the best-known international authorities on the playwright's works, this dictionary offers up-to-date information on all aspects of Shakespeare, both in his own time and in later ages.

The Oxford Dictionary of Literary Terms
Chris Baldick

A best-selling dictionary, covering all aspects of literature, this is an essential reference work for students of literature in any language.

A Dictionary of Critical Theory
Ian Buchanan

The invaluable multidisciplinary guide to theory, covering movements, theories, and events.

'an excellent gateway into critical theory'

Literature and Theology

Oxford Quick Reference

A Dictionary of Marketing
Charles Doyle

Covers traditional marketing techniques and theories alongside the latest concepts in over 2,000 clear and authoritative entries.

'Flick to any page [for] a lecture's worth of well thought through information'

Dan Germain, Head of Creative, innocent ltd

A Dictionary of Media and Communication
Daniel Chandler and Rod Munday

Provides over 2,200 authoritative entries on terms used in media and communication, from concepts and theories to technical terms, across subject areas that include advertising, digital culture, journalism, new media, radio studies, and telecommunications.

'a wonderful volume that is much more than a simple dictionary'
Professor Joshua Meyrowitz, University of New Hampshire

A Dictionary of Film Studies
Annette Kuhn and Guy Westwell

Features terms covering all aspects of film studies in 500 detailed entries, from theory and history to technical terms and practices.

A Dictionary of Journalism
Tony Harcup

Covers terminology relating to the practice, business, and technology of journalism, as well as its concepts and theories, organizations and institutions, publications, and key events.

Oxford Quick Reference

A Dictionary of the Bible
W. R. F. Browning

In over 2,000 entries, this authoritative dictionary provides clear and concise information about the important people, places, themes, and doctrines of the Bible.

The Oxford Dictionary of Saints
David Farmer

From the famous to the obscure, over 1,400 saints are covered in this acclaimed dictionary.

'an essential reference work'   *Daily Telegraph*

The Concise Oxford Dictionary of the Christian Church
E. A. Livingstone

This indispensable guide contains over 5,000 entries and provides full coverage of theology, denominations, the church calendar, and the Bible.

'opens up the whole of Christian history, now with a wider vision than ever'   Robert Runcie, former Archbishop of Canterbury

The Oxford Dictionary of Popes
J. N. D. Kelly and M. J. Walsh

Spans almost 2,000 years of papal history: from St Peter to Pope Benedict XVI.

'well-researched, extremely well written, and a delightful exercise in its own right'   *Church Times*